The Regime Change Consensus

Why did the United States invade Iraq, setting off a chain of events that profoundly changed the Middle East and modern U.S. history. *The Regime Change Consensus* offers a compelling look at how the United States pivoted from a policy of containment to regime change in Iraq after September 11, 2001. Starting with the Persian Gulf War, the book traces how a coalition of political actors argued with increasing success that the totalitarian nature of Saddam Hussein's regime and the untrustworthy behavior of the international coalition behind sanctions meant that containment was a doomed policy. By the end of the 1990s, a consensus emerged that only regime change and democratization could fully address the Iraqi threat. Through careful examination, Joseph Stieb expands our understanding of the origins of the Iraq War while also explaining why so many politicians and policymakers rejected containment after 9/11 and embraced regime change.

Joseph Stieb is a post-doctoral researcher at the Ohio State University's Mershon Center for International Security Studies. His articles and essays can be found in *The International History Review*, *The Washington Post*, *War on the Rocks*, *Arc Digital*, and *The Raleigh News-Observer*.

Military, War, and Society in Modern American History

Series Editors
Beth Bailey, University of Kansas
Andrew Preston, University of Cambridge

Military, War, and Society in Modern American History is a new series that showcases original scholarship on the military, war, and society in modern US history. The series builds on recent innovations in the fields of military and diplomatic history and includes historical works on a broad range of topics, including civil-military relations and the militarization of culture and society; the military's influence on policy, power, politics, and political economy; the military as a key institution in managing and shaping social change, both within the military and in broader American society; the effect the military has had on American political and economic development, whether in wartime or peacetime; and the military as a leading edge of American engagement with the wider world, including forms of soft power as well as the use of force.

The Regime Change Consensus

Iraq in American Politics, 1990–2003

Joseph Stieb

Ohio State University

CAMBRIDGE
UNIVERSITY PRESS

CAMBRIDGE
UNIVERSITY PRESS

Shaftesbury Road, Cambridge CB2 8EA, United Kingdom

One Liberty Plaza, 20th Floor, New York, NY 10006, USA

477 Williamstown Road, Port Melbourne, VIC 3207, Australia

314–321, 3rd Floor, Plot 3, Splendor Forum, Jasola District Centre, New Delhi – 110025, India

103 Penang Road, #05–06/07, Visioncrest Commercial, Singapore 238467

Cambridge University Press is part of Cambridge University Press & Assessment, a department of the University of Cambridge.

We share the University's mission to contribute to society through the pursuit of education, learning and research at the highest international levels of excellence.

www.cambridge.org
Information on this title: www.cambridge.org/9781108978385

DOI: 10.1017/9781108974219

First published 2021
First paperback edition 2022

A catalogue record for this publication is available from the British Library

Library of Congress Cataloging-in-Publication data
Names: Stieb, Joseph, author.
Title: The regime change consensus : Iraq in American politics, 1990–2003 / Joseph Stieb, Ohio, State University.
Other titles: Iraq in American politics, 1990–2003
Description: Cambridge, United Kingdom ; New York, NY : Cambridge University Press, 2021. | Series: Military, war, and society in modern American history | Includes bibliographical references and index.
Identifiers: LCCN 2020057741 (print) | LCCN 2020057742 (ebook) | ISBN 9781108838245 (hardback) | ISBN 9781108974219 (ebook)
Subjects: LCSH: United States – Foreign relations – Iraq. | Iraq – Foreign relations – United States. | Iran-Iraq War, 1980–1988. | United States – Politics and government – 1989– | Iraq – Politics and government – 1991–2003. | Iraq War, 2003–2011 – Causes.
Classification: LCC E183.8.I57 S75 2021 (print) | LCC E183.8.I57 (ebook) | DDC 327.73055–dc23
LC record available at https://lccn.loc.gov/2020057741
LC ebook record available at https://lccn.loc.gov/2020057742

ISBN   978-1-108-83824-5   Hardback
ISBN   978-1-108-97838-5   Paperback

To my parents, Lisa and Jeff

Contents

Acknowledgments   *page* viii
List of Abbreviations   xi

Introduction   1

1 A Hope, Not a Policy: Containment and Regime Change
   during the Gulf Crisis, 1990–1991   14

2 The Fallout from Victory: Containment and Its Critics,
   1991–1992   54

3 The Long Watch: The High Years of Containment,
   1993–1996   98

4 Saddam Must Go: Entrenching the Regime Change
   Consensus, 1997–2000   140

5 Not Whether, but How and When: The Iraq Debate from
   9/11 to the Invasion   189

   Conclusion: Containment, Liberalism, and the Regime   248

Bibliography   260
Index   265

Acknowledgments

Many people played important roles in the making of this book, and I'm deeply grateful to all of them. My teachers at St. Francis Xavier School, especially Claire Davis and Jeanne Tully, stoked in me a foundation and passion for learning and an appreciation of kindness and humility. My teachers at Xaverian Brothers High School taught me discipline and made me the thinker I am today. Thanks in particular to Chris Heaton, Ed Pirozzi, Dan Tucker, and Dan Scanlan. My professors at Trinity University and Oxford University, especially David Lesch, Linda Salvucci, Peter O'Brien, Simon Head, and Carey Latimore, developed my abilities in history and prepared me for graduate work. Thanks to Mark Bradley and Richard Weyhing at the University of Chicago for advising my masters' thesis and supporting my applications to doctoral programs.

My time as a PhD student at the University of North Carolina at Chapel Hill was incredible, and I need to thank my outstanding professors and advisers. Thank you to Matt Andrews, Navin Bapat, Mark Crescenzi, Harry Watson, Kathleen DuVal, Klaus Larres, and Donald Reid. My dissertation committee found the perfect balance of sharpening and supporting my work, and I enjoyed getting to know each of them. Thanks to Ben Waterhouse for his detailed readings of my chapters and for long and productive dialogues. Thanks to Michael Morgan for challenging me to expand the relevance of my arguments and to look at history from a broad lens. Thanks to Daniel Bolger for his comments and support, particularly on the military aspects of this book, and his good humor throughout the project. Thanks to Hal Brands for his incisive reading of the project, which was incredibly helpful in transforming this into a book.

My dissertation adviser, Wayne Lee, has pushed my scholarship further than anyone in this process, which is exactly what I signed up for. He, however, did not sign up to advise a dissertation on the origins of the Iraq War, but he supported me nonetheless. Thanks to him, this book is sharper, stronger, and, of course, much shorter. Getting a "good" comment out of Wayne on a chapter was cause for celebration, and even though he is a Duke fan, I'm honored to be his student.

I had a wonderful set of friends and colleagues at UNC who helped me complete this book and grow as a person. Thank you to everyone in Ben Waterhouse's writing group for their time and effort in challenging and improving my work. They include Maikel Borrego, Jessica Auer, Robert Richard, Evan Faulkenbury, Ashton Merck, Melanie Sheehan, Sam Finesurry, Brian Fennessey, and Joshua Akers. Joshua Tait and Robert Colby, as well as their brilliant wives Kate and Erin, offered extensive feedback on my work as well as invaluable friendship. Thanks in particular to Eric Burke, who read my work even when he did not have to, for his friendship, support, and about two million texts during and after graduate school. I am a better person for knowing all of these people.

My archival work was supported by thoughtful and friendly archivists in a number of places: the George H. W. Bush Library, the William J. Clinton Library, the George W. Bush Library, the National Archives, the Library of Congress, and the Seeley G. Mudd Library.

This book was revised and published during my first year as a postdoctoral researcher at the Mershon Center for International Security Studies at the Ohio State University. I am enormously grateful to Chris Gelpi and Teri Murphy for this opportunity and for their emotional and intellectual support during my transition to Ohio State. Thanks to Kyle McCray and Kelly Whitaker for their assistance as well. I also need to thank my research team here at Mershon: Peter Mansoor, Jennifer Siegel, and Richard Hermann. Thanks especially to Peter for reading the entire manuscript and for offering his insights. This book could not have been completed on schedule without the support of the Mershon Center, and I am grateful to be part of such a vibrant intellectual community.

It has been a pleasure to work with Cambridge University Press on this project. Debbie Gershenowitz took the initial interest in the book, and Cecelia Cancellaro has guided me toward publication with patience, clarity, and positivity. Thanks to Rachel Blaifeder, Ruth Boyes, Gayathri Tamilselvan, and Ekta Niwrutti for help with different stages of publication. I am overjoyed to be part of the Military, War, and Society in Modern American History series and to be working with the brilliant editors of this project, Beth Bailey and Andrew Preston. Thanks especially to Andrew, whose input and guidance were crucial for turning this project from a dissertation into a book.

I have also worked with wonderful high school teachers who have helped me develop my ideas and become a better teacher. The brilliant faculty of Lenox High School helped me start my career as a teacher and encouraged me to pursue graduate work. Thanks especially to Peter Starenko, Robin Getzen, David Fisher, and Bill Irvin. I also need to thank superb faculty of East Chapel Hill High School's history department for their support and intellectual engagement, especially Maureen Galvin, Hans Hiemstra, Sam Atwood, and Lauren Stapleton.

I want to thank my family for their love and support. My parents, Lisa and Jeff, instilled in me a great love of learning and the resilience to do difficult things. They gave me opportunities to grow as a scholar and, more importantly, as a person. They made me proofread everything I have written since second grade, and it has paid off. This book, as with all good things in my life, would have been impossible without them. Thanks to my father for reading every draft chapter along the way and for offering invaluable edits and suggestions. Thanks to my aunt Linda Hodge, a history teacher herself, who gave me my first real history book when I was a kid. Thanks also to my aunt and uncle Lani and Alan Dill, who generously supported me during graduate school.

Thanks especially to Barbara Scannell, my beloved maternal grandmother, who passed away while I was in graduate school. My handwriting has never reached her standards, but I hope this book does.

Finally, a million thanks to my amazing wife, Lisa Ibarra. She is my partner in all aspects of life, and my best friend. She moved to Chapel Hill and Columbus to help me pursue my dream, she supported me and grounded me throughout the writing of this book, and she helped me put work aside when I needed to. She picked me up from campus when I missed the bus, talked with me about history and politics, and endured during the ups and downs of life with me. I owe her, and love her, an incalculable amount. Thanks also to Harriet, who was present for the writing of every sentence in this book.

Abbreviations

AEI	American Enterprise Institute
BNL	Banca Nazionale del Lavoro
CCC	Commodity Credit Corporation
CENTCOM	United States Central Command
CIA	Central Intelligence Agency
CPSG	Committee for Peace and Security in the Gulf
DIA	Defense Intelligence Agency
IAEA	International Atomic Energy Agency
ILA	Iraq Liberation Act
INA	Iraqi National Accord
INC	Iraqi National Congress
JCS	Joint Chiefs of Staff
KDP	Kurdish Democratic Party
KTO	Kuwaiti Theater of Operations
MEPP	Middle East Peace Process
MOU	Memorandum of Understanding
NEA	Near Eastern Affairs Office, State Department
NDZ	no-drive zone
NFZ	no-fly zone
NIC	National Intelligence Council
NIE	National Intelligence Estimate
NSA	National Security Agency
NSD	National Security Directive
OSP	Office of Special Plans
PCTEG	Policy Counter-Terrorism Evaluation Group
PNAC	Project for a New American Century
PUK	Patriotic Union of Kurdistan
R2P	Responsibility to Protect
SAM	Surface-to-Air Missiles
SCIRI	Supreme Council for the Islamic Revolution in Iran
UNMOVIC	United Nations Monitoring, Verification and Inspection Commission
UNSCOM	United Nations Special Commission
WMD	weapons of mass destruction

Introduction

The US invasion of Iraq in 2003 was the worst US foreign policy blunder since the Vietnam War. Between 2003 and the departure of US combat forces in 2011, a total of 4,410 American military personnel died in Iraq and 31,957 were wounded, according to the Department of Defense.[1] In the aftermath, Iraq descended into a civil war that cost the lives of hundreds of thousands of Iraqi civilians.[2] Although the "surge" of US troops in Iraq from 2007 to 2008 helped tamp down this violence, the Iraqi state continued to be dominated by corrupt Shia parties that rigged elections, hoarded resources, and abused the Sunni minority.

The persistence of these political tensions and the civil war in Syria set the stage for the rise of the Islamic State, which seized several major cities in Iraq in 2014 and perpetrated horrible atrocities. The United States and its allies were forced to reengage in fighting in Iraq and Syria and to counter a global resurgence of Islamic State-inspired terrorism.[3] The US Army's official history of the Iraq War, published in 2019, concluded that "an emboldened and expansionist Iran appears to be the only victor" of the war in Iraq, as the war destroyed one of Iran's main geopolitical rivals and installed in its place a weak, corrupt, and

---

[1] US Department of Defense, "Operation Iraqi Freedom U.S. Casualty Status," February 5, 2019, dod.defense.gov, accessed February 5, 2019, https://dod.defense.gov/News/Casualty-Status/.

[2] "Iraqi Deaths from Violence 2003–2011," January 2, 2012, iraqbodycount.org, accessed February 5, 2019, www.iraqbodycount.org/analysis/numbers/2011/; Amy Hagopian et al., "Mortality in Iraq Associated with the 2003–2011 War and Occupation," *PLoS Medicine* 10, no. 10 (2013), https://journals.plos.org/plosmedicine/article?id=10.1371/journal.pmed.1001533#abstract1.

[3] On the rise of the Islamic State and its global reach and appeal, see Daniel Byman, "ISIS Goes Global," *Foreign Affairs* 95, no. 2 (March/April, 2016): 76–85; Joby Warrick, *Black Flags: The Rise of ISIS* (New York: Doubleday, 2015); Graeme Wood, *The Way of the Strangers: Encounters with the Islamic State* (New York: Random House, 2017); Martin Smith, "Confronting ISIS," October 11, 2016, pbs.frontline.org, accessed November 5, 2016, www.pbs.org/wgbh/frontline/film/confronting-isis/.

compliant regime.[4] Meanwhile, in US domestic politics, the failure to find significant weapons of mass destruction (WMD) programs and the poorly handled occupation undermined public faith in basic governmental competence. The cost, length, and brutality of the war, moreover, created what one political scientist called an "Iraq Syndrome": a weakening of Americans' willingness to assume global leadership that has empowered anti-interventionist wings of both major parties.[5]

With this dismal outcome in mind, it becomes essential to understand how alternatives to war were discredited. The primary alternative to regime change was the policy of containment, which the United States imposed on Iraq following the Persian Gulf War in 1991. Under this policy, the United States and an international coalition applied economic sanctions, weapons inspections, no-fly zones, and occasional military strikes on Iraq. Containment sought to keep Iraq militarily weak, prevent it from threatening its neighbors and vulnerable internal minorities, destroy its WMD, and, if possible, create the conditions for Saddam Hussein's downfall. Many commentators who predicted these outcomes have declared that the United States should have stuck with containment, which they claim managed the Iraqi threat at reasonable cost. Nonetheless, most of these scholars have not asked tough questions about why an ostensibly effective policy became so unpopular in US politics by the late 1990s.[6]

Over the course of the 1990s, a consensus formed in US political and intellectual circles that the United States and its allies could not contain the Iraqi threat and had to remove the Baathist regime and establish democracy in Iraq. Critics of containment believed this policy was unsustainable because Saddam's personality and the totalitarian nature of his regime made Iraq immune to "management" strategies like containment. Saddam would never cease his pursuit of WMD and regional domination, and as the pillars of containment inevitably weakened, he would break out of this "box," rebuild his WMD, and again threaten regional stability. Before 9/11, few supporters of this consensus called for invasion, but they did see containment as a failure and regime change as the only realistic solution.

---

[4] Joel Rayburn and Frank Sobchak, eds., *The U.S. Army in the Iraq War, Volume 2: Surge and Withdrawal, 2007–2011* (Carlisle Barracks, PA: United States Army War College Press, 2017), 639–640.

[5] John Mueller, "The Iraq Syndrome," *Foreign Affairs* 84, no. 6 (November, 2005): 44–54.

[6] See David Cortright and George A. Lopez, "Containing Iraq: Sanctions Worked," *Foreign Affairs* 83, no. 4 (July, 2004): 90–103; James Bamford, *A Pretext for War: 9/11, Iraq, and the Abuse of America's Intelligence Agencies* (New York: Doubleday, 2004), 382; Hans Blix, *Disarming Iraq* (New York: Pantheon Books, 2004), 269; Richard Haass, *War of Necessity, War of Choice: A Memoir of Two Iraq Wars* (New York: Simon & Schuster, 2009), 269.

The concept of Iraq as a totalitarian state played a crucial role in the arguments against containment. Containment's critics claimed that Saddam's absolute control over Iraq meant that there were few social or political points of leverage that containment could exploit to compel his moderation or removal. They even viewed a coup against Saddam as an inadequate solution. Real regime change, especially for neoconservative and liberal advocates, required uprooting the entire Baathist system and ideology. Only democratization could ensure that Iraq would no longer seek WMD, threaten its neighbors, or mistreat its people. By the late 1990s, most regime change advocates had come to believe that containment had deteriorated and that the United States should not waste time and resources trying to restore a strategy that was bound to fail.

I call the interpretation of the Iraqi threat outlined in the preceding paragraphs the "regime change consensus." This book documents how a political and intellectual coalition formed after the Gulf War around this set of ideas. This coalition had neoconservatives at the helm, but it also drew significant support from Republicans and Democrats, liberal intellectuals, and left-wing and religious anti-sanctions activists. At times of intense focus on Iraq, these actors functioned as a united political coalition against containment, while at other times they formed a general base of common thinking about the Iraqi problem. This broad coalition made the regime change consensus the dominant viewpoint on Iraq in US politics by the end of the 1990s. Their signal achievement was the 1998 Iraq Liberation Act, which declared regime change in Iraq as an official US foreign policy goal. President Bill Clinton pursued containment to the end of his term, but the decisive shift toward the regime change consensus had occurred before he left office in 2001, leaving containment with few public defenders.

The Regime Change Consensus focuses not just on official policy-makers but also on a broader political and foreign policy establishment that, in political scientist Stephen Walt's words, "actively engage[s] on a regular basis with issues of international affairs."[7] These actors include legislators, intellectuals, academics, activists, experts, members of the media, and other public figures. They tried to create consensus on Iraq by writing books, reports, and articles, testifying before Congress, appearing in the

---

[7] Stephen Walt, *The Hell of Good Intentions: America's Foreign Policy Elite and the Decline of U.S. Primacy* (New York: Farrar, Straus, and Giroux, 2018), 95. See also Christopher Layne, "The U.S. Foreign Policy Establishment and Grand Strategy: How American Elites Obstruct Strategic Adjustment," *International Politics* 54, no. 3 (May, 2017): 260–275; Patrick Porter, "Why America's Grand Strategy Has Not Changed: Power, Habit, and the U.S. Foreign Policy Establishment," *International Security* 42, no. 4 (Spring, 2018): 9–46.

media; and creating lobbying networks; among other methods. Elite members of this establishment also act as gatekeepers by shaping what people and ideas will find broad audiences, who will be legitimized as mainstream or expert, and who will be marginalized.[8] While there were dissenters, these foreign policy and political elites discredited containment and established the regime change consensus as the dominant interpretation of the Iraqi threat.

Containment and the Causes of the Iraq War

The existing body of research on the causes of US decision to invade Iraq in 2003 focuses on two major explanatory pillars: neoconservatives and the September 11 terrorist attacks. While these factors were crucial, this framework does not explain how a wide swathe of Americans, including many legislators, media figures, intellectuals, and much of the public, came to support the war. Had President George W. Bush's push for war met a political brick wall from this broader establishment on the grounds that his administration had generated little new evidence of Saddam's WMD or that containment was an adequate policy, it is conceivable that Bush would have backed down. The political establishment's support for the war was neither immediate nor unqualified, but it was crucial for paving the road to war.

Bush and the neoconservatives may have put Iraq on the table after 9/11, but why did so many Americans seem primed to buy his argument for war? Why, moreover, did so few Americans argue that the United States should use the urgency and international sympathy of the post-9/11 moment to reinvigorate containment rather than invade Iraq? Why did so few members of this establishment, including many with deep reservations about the war, not promote containment as a viable alternative?

Answering those questions requires us to map the spectrum of debate about Iraq in this time period, particularly the discrediting of containment and the rise of the regime change consensus within the broader establishment. As Bush and other Iraq hawks pressed for invasion in 2002, a number of skeptics raised doubts about the push for war. These included Secretary of State Colin Powell, British Prime Minister Tony Blair, Congressional leaders like Senators Chuck Hagel and Joe Biden, and influential former policy-makers like James Baker and Sandy Berger. Following what I call the "Powell–Blair approach," they contended that the evidence of Iraq's WMD and links to al-Qaeda were weak, that the

---

[8] Walt, *Hell of Good Intentions*, 91–93.

administration had not prepared adequately for occupying Iraq, and that Bush should build a coalition before going to war.

However, the fact that members of this Powell–Blair approach had abandoned containment to varying degrees prior to 9/11 illuminates why they focused on shaping how the United States pursued regime change as opposed to whether it should do so. The arguments of Powell, Blair, and others were largely tactical; they convinced Bush to give inspections and diplomacy more time and to build a coalition. However, they conceded the point that the United States should pursue regime change if these measures failed because they too saw no end point for Iraq other than Saddam's overthrow. Because the dominant perceived lesson of the 1990s within the US political and policy establishment was that Saddam would never accept complete inspections nor abandon the pursuit of WMD, members of the Powell–Blair approach held little faith in inspections when they were renewed in late 2002. Thus, when Bush prematurely declared that diplomacy and inspections had failed in early 2003, the majority of the political establishment either supported the war or offered no alternative. This book shows how the terms of debate on Iraq since 1990 developed in such a narrow way that it gave Bush a fundamental advantage in building a wide base of domestic support for invasion, especially after it made a cursory effort to address the problem peacefully.

Understanding the actions and perspectives of this group of leaders requires a stronger grasp of why containment became so broadly disfavored in the 1990s. If figures like Blair, Powell, or key Democratic leaders had rallied around a new containment strategy, they could have, for example, blocked Bush's efforts to attain Congressional approval for military action against Iraq. Indeed, there were influential policy-makers, intellectuals, and politicians who still believed that a reinvigorated containment strategy could prevent Saddam from building WMD, keep his military weak, and stymie his regional ambitions. Figures such as former National Security Advisor Brent Scowcroft, national security expert Richard Haass, and political scientist John Mearsheimer consistently held that Saddam did not directly threaten the United States, that containment had kept Iraq weak, and that with some adjustment containment could manage his threat to US interests in the region.[9]

This book's explanation for the discrediting of containment from 1990 to 2003 improves upon the other main explanations for the Iraq War,

---

[9] Brent Scowcroft, "Don't Attack Saddam," *Wall Street Journal*, August 15, 2002, A12; Haass, *War of Necessity*; John Mearsheimer and Stephen M. Walt, "An Unnecessary War," *Foreign Policy* 134 (January–February, 2003): 52–53.

neoconservatives and 9/11, and offers a more complete grasp of the roots of the US decision to invade by showing how alternatives to regime change were discredited across the political spectrum. Numerous scholars have traced how neoconservatives and other Iraq hawks fixated on overthrowing the Baathist regime after the Gulf War. By the 1990s, neoconservatives like Paul Wolfowitz and the writers William Kristol and Robert Kagan had come to define themselves as "conservative internationalists, with a strong commitment to vigorous American global leadership, to American power, and to the advancement of American democratic and free-market principles."[10] Policy scholars Ivo Daalder and James Lindsay usefully define neoconservatives as "democratic imperialists."[11] They believed that the United States has a unique right and responsibility to use its overwhelming military power to create a "benevolent global hegemony," in Kristol and Kagan's terms.[12] This meant that the United States would maintain strategic primacy in key areas of the world and use that power to spread democracy and capitalism.[13] Neoconservatives exercised tremendous influence on the Republican foreign policy establishment and the broader foreign affairs discourse in magazines such as *Commentary* and *The Weekly Standard*, think tanks like the American Enterprise Institute, and political action networks such as the Project for a New American Century.

Nonetheless, not all Iraq hawks were neoconservatives. Daalder and Lindsey distinguish between neoconservatives and "assertive nationalists" like Defense Secretary Donald Rumsfeld and Vice President Dick Cheney. Assertive nationalists share the neoconservative belief that the United States should use its military supremacy to eradicate threats and maintain its status as the world's undisputed superpower. Both groups are unilateralist in their skepticism of international laws and institutions that might restrain US power.[14] Assertive nationalists, however, prefer to

---

[10] Robert Kagan and William Kristol, "Introduction: National Interest and Global Responsibility," in *Present Dangers: Crisis and Opportunity in American Foreign and Defense Policy*, ed. Robert Kagan and William Kristol (San Francisco: Encounter Books, 2000), viii.

[11] Ivo Daalder and James Lindsay, *America Unbound: The Bush Revolution in Foreign Policy* (Hoboken, NJ: Wiley, 2005), 46–47.

[12] Robert Kagan and William Kristol, "Toward a Neo-Reaganite Foreign Policy," *Foreign Affairs* 75 (July/August, 1997): 20.

[13] Daalder and Lindsay, *America Unbound*, 15, 45–48; Gary Dorrien, *Imperial Designs: Neoconservatism and the New Pax Americana* (New York: Routledge, 2004), 26, 126–128; Jacob Heilbrunn, *They Knew They Were Right: The Rise of the Neocons* (New York: Doubleday, 2008), 161–227.

[14] Daalder and Lindsay, *America Unbound*, 15; Stefan Halper and Jonathan Clarke, *America Alone: The Neoconservatives and the Global Order* (New York: Cambridge University Press, 2004), 11.

pursue more narrowly defined national interests and are skeptical of democratization, human rights, and nation-building. Bush himself haphazardly blended neoconservatism and assertive nationalism. He entered office committed to a more unilateralist foreign policy but later embraced both democratization abroad and the preventive use of force.[15]

During the 1990s, neoconservatives and assertive nationalists combined with other groups to lead the campaign against containment. Many of these committed Iraq hawks then assumed key positions inside the George W. Bush administration, including Cheney, Rumsfeld, Wolfowitz, and numerous others in the Defense Department and on the vice president's staff.[16] Although they had different motives, this group intervened with Bush immediately and persistently after 9/11 to promote the idea that Iraq should be the focus of the US response. They based this argument on the idea that rogue states like Iraq might hand WMD to terrorists to use against the United States.[17] This "nexus" between WMD, rogue states, and terrorists negated containment and deterrence and necessitated a "preventive" response. Bush became convinced of this argument at some point in late 2001 or early 2002.[18] His administration then took this argument public in 2002, using selective and exaggerated

---

[15] Michael Mazarr explores the contradictions between Bush's hope for democratization and his disdain for nation-building. See Michael Mazarr, *Leap of Faith: Hubris, Negligence, and America's Greatest Foreign Policy Tragedy* (New York: Public Affairs, 2019), 191–193, 222, 245–246. For more on how Bush's foreign policy views fit aspects of neoconservatism and assertive nationalism, see James Mann, *Rise of the Vulcans: The History of Bush's War Cabinet* (New York: Viking, 2004), xii–xiii, 255–257; Daalder and Lindsay, *America Unbound*, 36–40, 123; Halper and Clarke, *America Alone*, 134–135; Frederick Kaplan, *Daydream Believers: How a Few Grand Ideas Wrecked American Power* (Hoboken, NJ: Wiley, 2005), 115–117, 137–142.

[16] Gary Dorrien identifies twenty neoconservatives who served in top positions in Rumsfeld's Defense Department or Cheney's staff, including Wolfowitz, Elliott Abrams, Kenneth Adelman, John Bolton, Douglas Feith, Zalmay Khalilzad, Scooter Libby, William Luti, Peter Rodman, Paula Dobriansky, Stephen Cambone, and David Wurmser. Of the twenty-four signatories of PNAC's original statement of principles, eight served in high-ranking positions in the Bush administration. See Dorrien, *Imperial Designs*, 2.

[17] After the war, Wolfowitz said in an interview that "the one issue that everyone could agree on" was "weapons of mass destruction as the core reason," suggesting that neoconservatives and assertive nationalists in the Bush administration had different motives for supporting the Iraq invasion but coalesced around the WMD rationale. See Paul Wolfowitz, interview by Sam Tannenhaus, *Vanity Fair*, May 9, 2003, accessed April 15, 2020, https://archive.defense.gov/Transcripts/Transcript.aspx? TranscriptID=2594.

[18] Michael Mazarr contends that while there was no single meeting in which President Bush made the decision to invade, between September 11, 2001, and the start of 2002, the administration had "irrevocably committed itself to the downfall of Saddam Hussein, whatever that would require." Mazarr, *Leap of Faith*, 12, 140.

intelligence, fear-mongering, and the post-9/11 psychological need for action to build political momentum for the war.[19]

Some scholars have dismissed the importance of neoconservatives in bringing about the war, often because of the broader political establishment's hard line on Iraq. The long-standing hawkishness of Al Gore, for instance, and his top advisors on Iraq ostensibly renders the neoconservatives unnecessary for explaining the Iraq War.[20] Consider, however, that after 9/11 there was no sudden outcry from Congress, the public, or key US allies for war with Iraq. As this book explains, many within those groups had been primed to support a regime change argument by their pre-9/11 abandonment of containment. However, the crucial initial impetus for invading Iraq came from mostly neoconservative Iraq hawks within the administration, including Wolfowitz, Rumsfeld, and Douglas Feith, all with a long-standing desire to topple Saddam. The role of neoconservatives thus remains essential if insufficient to the overall task of explaining why the United States invaded Iraq.

The second pillar stressed in current scholarship on the causes of invasion is the effect of the September 11 terrorist attacks on US foreign policy. 9/11 drastically altered the strategic risk calculus of the administration's top policy-makers, who felt a deep sense of shock and responsibility for stopping future attacks. The attacks significantly expanded Americans' willingness to support a massive military campaign against both the perpetrators and a larger set of actors, including rogue states with possible WMD programs. 9/11 also created political and intellectual space for the neoconservatives to argue, both within the government and in public, that seeking regime change in Iraq and democratization in the Middle East would destroy the root causes of terrorism. Absent 9/11, the war almost certainly would not have happened given that virtually

---

[19] Prominent examples of neoconservative-focused interpretations include Paul Pillar, *Intelligence and U.S. Foreign Policy: Iraq, 9/11, and Misguided Reform* (New York: Columbia University Press, 2011), 15–20, 55; John Mearsheimer and Stephen Walt, *The Israel Lobby and U.S. Foreign Policy* (New York: Farrar, Straus, and Giroux, 2007), 229–262; Stephen Kinzer, *Overthrow: America's Century of Regime Change from Hawaii to Iraq* (New York: Times Books, 2006), 288; Heilbrunn, *They Knew They Were Right*, 6; Todd Purdum, *A Time of Our Choosing: America's War in Iraq* (New York: Times Books, 2003); Mann, *Rise of the Vulcans*; Dorrien, *Imperial Designs*; Halper and Clarke, *America Alone*, 201–210; William Kristol and Robert Kagan, "The Right War for the Right Reasons," *The Weekly Standard*, February 23, 2004, 20–28.

[20] Frank Harvey, *Explaining the Iraq War: Counterfactual Theory, Logic and Evidence* (New York: Cambridge University Press, 2011), 1–22; Mazarr, *Leap of Faith*, 9–10, 85–86; Steven Hurst, *The United States and Iraq since 1979: Hegemony, Oil, and War* (Edinburgh: University of Edinburgh Press, 2009), 1; Sheila Carapico and Chris Toensing, "The Strategic Logic of the Iraq Blunder," *Middle East Report* 36, no. 239 (Summer, 2006): 6–11; Max Boot, "It's Time to Retire the 'Neocon' Label," *Washington Post*, March 13, 2019.

no one in the political establishment was calling for a ground invasion of Iraq beforehand despite the broad consensus on the need for Saddam's eventual overthrow.

9/11 and the rise of neoconservatives are vital but insufficient factors for understanding the causal road to the Iraq War. The hitherto overlooked story of the delegitimization of containment must also be incorporated as an essential factor. These three elements worked in tandem: the fear and anger generated by 9/11 functioned as a massive Overton Window for the spectrum of acceptable foreign policy initiatives.[21] In turn, well-placed neoconservatives with a fixation on Iraq seized this opportunity, literally before the dust of the Twin Towers had settled, to reorient the response to 9/11 toward Iraq. The fact that containment, the main alternative to regime change, had been so discredited across the wider political and intellectual spectrum meant that Bush was pushing on an open door when he made the public case for war. He faced an establishment that basically agreed with the necessity and morality of regime change and mostly limited its critiques to the means of achieving this end in large part because its members had already dismissed containment.

Most scholarship and memoirs on Iraq pass the 1990s by with little commentary on containment, while other works contend that containment became delegitimized simply because it failed as a policy.[22] This claim of failure played a central role in the regime change consensus. Architects of the war like Rumsfeld have claimed since 2003 that "[w]hen the second Bush administration came into office in January 2001, the Iraq 'containment' policy was in tatters."[23] Too many scholars of the Iraq War have echoed this viewpoint, which renders the history of containment into

---

[21] An Overton Window refers to a sudden, rapid widening of the range of acceptable ideas, policies, or actions, often because of a shocking event. See Maggie Astor, "How the Politically Unthinkable Can Become Mainstream," *New York Times*, February 26, 2019.

[22] For studies that ignore containment, see Kinzer, *Overthrow*, 288; Christian Alfonsi, *Circle in the Sand: Why We Went Back to Iraq* (New York: Doubleday, 2006); Peter Galbraith, *The End of Iraq: How American Incompetence Created a War without End* (New York: Simon & Schuster, 2006), 67–69; Lawrence Freedman, "Iraq, Liberal Wars, and Illiberal Containment," *Survival* 48, no. 4 (Winter, 2006): 51–41. For studies that seek to explain the origins of the Iraq War but offer little explanation for the decline of the containment policy, see Lloyd Gardner, *The Long Road to Baghdad: A History of U.S. Foreign Policy from the 1970s to the Present* (New York: New Press, 2008); Michael MacDonald, *Overreach: Delusions of Regime Change in Iraq* (Cambridge, MA: Harvard University Press, 2014); Purdum, *A Time of Our Choosing*; Hal Brands and Peter Feaver, "The Case for Bush Revisionism? Reevaluating the Legacy of America's 43rd President," *Journal of Strategic Studies* 41, no. 1–2 (2018): 1–41. The most thorough, nonideological case that containment failed was Kenneth Pollack, *The Threatening Storm: The Case for Invading Iraq* (New York: Random House, 2002), 211–243.

[23] Donald Rumsfeld, *Known and Unknown: A Memoir* (New York: Sentinel, 2011), 416–418; Douglas Feith, *War and Decision: Inside the Pentagon at the Dawn of the War on Terrorism* (New York: Harper Collins, 2008), 194–200.

a nonquestion. Moreover, for intellectuals and public figures who now regret their support of a disastrous war, there is little incentive to challenge the assumption of containment's failure.

This assumption of the manifest failure of containment is overdue for challenging. Certainly, key planks of the policy weakened over the course of the 1990s. The coalition's willingness to enforce sanctions and support punitive military strikes on Iraq faded over time, allowing Saddam's regime to access more resources and brazenly challenge inspections. In addition, Saddam expelled the inspectors in December 1998, undermining the coalition's ability to control his WMD production. Finally, by the mid-1990s Saddam had survived a series of internal challenges and reestablished his control over Iraq, thus presenting the possibility that containment might have to stay in place for decades.

However, despite these problems, containment succeeded in many ways, at least in terms of the limited goals originally established by George H. W. Bush. The Iraqi military and economy remained weak. Iraq made few threats to its neighbors after the Gulf War, and when it did, it quickly backed down in the face of US threats of retaliation. UN weapons inspectors destroyed the vast majority of Iraq's WMD programs, and after 2003 it became clear that Saddam had neither large WMD stockpiles nor active programs.[24] In addition, no-fly zones in the north and south meant that Saddam's control was limited or nonexistent in about 40 percent of Iraq's territory. While Saddam remained in power until the end of the decade, containment's strictures forced him to focus on internal control over external expansion.[25]

Given its underappreciated successes, the claim that containment became discredited in US politics because it "failed" as a policy is neither self-evident nor sufficient. The idea that containment simply collapsed over time is particularly unhelpful in explaining why numerous politicians, intellectuals, and policy-makers opposed containment virtually from its inception, well before the crises of the late 1990s. In reality, the view that containment had failed was an interpretation of an ambiguous policy with numerous successes as well as some shortcomings. The ideas that critics of containment advanced combined with events to push more Americans to believe that containment had failed and that regime change was the sole alternative.

[24] See section on "Regime Strategic Intent" in Volume 1 of Department of Central Intelligence, Iraq Survey Group, *Key Findings,* September 30, 2004, cia.gov, accessed July 15, 2018, www.cia.gov/library/reports/general-reports-1/iraq_wmd_2004/.
[25] Joshua Rovner, "Delusions of Defeat: The United States and Iraq, 1990–1998," *Journal of Strategic Studies* 37, no. 4 (June, 2014): 482–507.

This book concludes that the terms of debate between 9/11 and the March 2003 invasion of Iraq should not be understood as pitting regime change against containment. This question had largely been settled by the late 1990s with the ascent of the regime change consensus. Rather, the prewar conversation centered on how to pursue regime change, not whether it should be pursued. The public figures who argued against invasion and for the renewal of containment became a decided minority compared to those who enthusiastically backed regime change and those who, however reluctantly, saw no other alternative. Thus, along with 9/11 and the neoconservatives, the discrediting of containment is an essential precondition for the US decision to invade Iraq.[26]

Between Triumph and Tragedy: The Bigger Historical Picture

This project places Iraq policy in a broader context, showing how trends and ideas in the 1990s shaped the debate about Iraq. The political legitimacy of containment suffered because this policy stood between two massive triumphs for the United States – the Cold War and the Persian Gulf War – and one horrible tragedy – 9/11.

The first triumph was victory in the Cold War as the Eastern Bloc and the Soviet Union collapsed between 1989 and 1991. These developments undermined the containment of Iraq by fueling the sense that the world was moving inexorably toward liberal democracy and capitalism, making containment appear intolerably status quo-oriented or even cynical.[27] Universalistic thinking about human rights and democracy saturated US thought about the world in this moment of great confidence. Liberals, neoconservatives, and humanitarian activists all intensified their assaults on the concept of state sovereignty, treating it as a right to be earned rather than inherent characteristic of statehood, thus paving the way for armed intervention.[28] Containment's defenders argued that the United States should be careful about destabilizing Iraq because of its fractious ethno-sectarian divisions and inexperience with liberal democracy. However, even though the containment of the Soviet Union was

---

[26] Perez Zagorin, "Theories of Revolution in Contemporary Historiography," *Political Science Quarterly* 88, no. 1 (March, 1973): 44–45.

[27] For examples, see Francis Fukuyama, *The End of History and the Last Man* (New York: Avon Books, 1992); Samuel P. Huntington, *The Third Wave: Democratization in the Late Twentieth Century* (Norman: University of Oklahoma Press, 1991).

[28] G. John Ikenberry, *Liberal Leviathan: The Origins, Crisis, and Transformation of the American World Order* (Princeton, NJ: Princeton University Press, 2011), 238–240, 245; Robert Jackson, *Sovereignty: The Evolution of an Idea* (Malden, MA: Polity Press, 2007), 114–135.

seen as a success, the ideological mood that emerged from the Soviet defeat ironically put the defenders of Iraqi containment at a disadvantage. The temper of the times made it easy to portray them as racially and culturally insensitive or stuck in a Cold War mentality.

The second triumph was the 1991 Gulf War, in which the United States led a coalition to eject Saddam's forces from Kuwait in an unexpectedly easy fight. This overwhelming military victory fed the belief that the United States was now a benevolent hegemon that should use the "unipolar moment" to remove rogue regimes and construct a liberal democratic world order.[29] Why tolerate the existence of an odious dictator like Saddam when the United States had the power to remove him and no superpower rival could stand in its way? Why not remove the Baathist regime when a democracy could be expected to grow in its place, just as autocracies were collapsing and democracies rising in Eastern Europe, East Asia, and Latin America?[30] Containment was a poor fit for the national mentality that emerged from these dual triumphs and shaped political culture in the 1990s and early 2000s. This mentality was one of universalistic political thinking, optimism about overwhelming US power, and frustration with holdouts to this wave of world-historical progress like Baathist Iraq.[31]

The tragedy came with the al-Qaeda terrorist attacks on 9/11. Before 9/11, politicians and intellectuals, including Clinton, had defined the post–Cold War world as globalized and interdependent. They recognized that these factors meant greater vulnerability to events in other states, but they generally saw these trends as net positives. The free movement of ideas, goods, and people would universalize values and cultures, foster prosperity and democracy, and discredit retrograde ideologies.[32] 9/11 instantly reversed this optimistic script by highlighting the negative aspects of interdependence and the ability of small groups to cause asymmetrical destruction. US awareness of global terrorism and weapons proliferation had increased throughout the 1990s, but 9/11 drove home

---

[29] Charles Krauthammer, "The Unipolar Moment," *Foreign Affairs* 70, no. 1 (Winter, 1990/1991): 23–33.

[30] MacDonald, *Overreach*, 1–7.

[31] John Mearsheimer, *The Great Delusion: Liberal Dreams and International Realities* (New Haven, CT: Yale University Press, 2018); Nuno P. Monteiro, *Theory of Unipolar Politics* (New York: Cambridge University Press, 2014); Walt, *Hell of Good Intentions*, 22–23, 53.

[32] Anthony Lake, "From Containment to Enlargement" (speech, Washington, DC, September 21, 1993), accessed April 15, 2017, www.mtholyoke.edu/acad/intrel/lakedoc .html; Derek Chollet, *America Between the Wars: From 11/9 to 9/11: The Misunderstood Years between the Fall of the Berlin Wall and the Start of the War on Terror* (New York: Public Affairs, 2008), 312–314; Michael Hunt, *The American Ascendancy: How the United States Gained and Wielded Global Dominance* (Chapel Hill, NC: University of North Carolina Press, 2007), 266–276.

the true potential of these menaces. Terrorists plotting in the mountains of Afghanistan and unstable dictators tinkering with biological weapons in Iraq now appeared as imminent threats in a shrunken world.

Growing numbers of Americans, including top Bush policy-makers, felt that the United States could no longer tolerate the political dysfunction, religious extremism, and authoritarianism of the Middle East and the terrorism that these pathologies had spawned. The mostly neoconservative vision of the United States using its massive power to accelerate worldwide democratization took on greater urgency and appeal. Defeating the active terrorist threat and transforming Middle Eastern politics emerged as national security imperatives as domestic constraints on armed intervention waned.

In this historical moment, bookended by two victories and one tragedy, containment, a strategy of management and restraint, satisfied neither the optimistic mood created by the Gulf War and Cold War victories nor the fear and vulnerability fostered by the tragedy of 9/11. Before 9/11, containment did not do enough to create the better world that many Americans envisioned, nor did it promise to eliminate a threat to vital US interests. After 9/11, relying on containment to hamstring Iraq's WMD programs appeared unrealistic and risky to many, even if the policy could be restored to full strength. After 9/11, Bush and other US leaders wanted to eliminate problems like Saddam, not manage them. The triumphs and tragedy noted here set the historical stage for the Iraq War by creating a conducive environment for the ascendency of the regime change consensus. Nonetheless, to explain the Iraq War fully, we must understand how, in between these turning points, a set of organized political actors delegitimized containment and made regime change the only accepted means to both create a better world and prevent a second 9/11.

1 A Hope, Not a Policy
Containment and Regime Change during the Gulf Crisis, 1990–1991

Introduction

Saddam Hussein's invasion of Kuwait on August 2, 1990, sounded the death knell for the US policy of constructive engagement toward Iraq. This policy had continued US support for Iraq during the Iran–Iraq War in an attempt to moderate Iraqi behavior. In the long run, the failure of engagement ingrained the "lesson" in US thinking about Iraq that any attempt to incentivize Saddam to change his behavior was pointless. George H. W. Bush responded to the invasion by mobilizing US forces to deter an invasion of Saudi Arabia in Operation Desert Shield, forming an international coalition to impose sanctions on Iraq, and demanding that Saddam leave Kuwait. The United Nations Security Council resolutions passed in the fall of 1990 defined the coalition's main goals as ejecting Iraqi forces from Kuwait and restoring full Kuwaiti sovereignty. Resolution 678 in November 1990 authorized the use of "all necessary means," including the use of force, if Iraq did not withdraw by January 15, 1991.[1]

In the United States, President Bush received widespread support for rallying the international community behind this strategy. Americans across the political spectrum agreed that Saddam threatened the US ability to maintain the free flow of oil from the Middle East, and they were shocked by Iraq's brutalization of Kuwait. The fact that this invasion came in the waning days of the Cold War made this crisis especially important in terms of setting a precedent for how the United States, its allies, and the United Nations would deal with aggression in the post–Cold War world. Secretary of State James Baker aptly summarized the case for intervention: "A very dangerous dictator, armed to the teeth, is threatening a critical region at a defining moment in history."[2]

---

[1] United Nations Security Council Resolution 678 (November 29, 1990), in *The Gulf War Reader: History, Documents, Opinions*, ed. Christopher Cerf and Micah Sifry (New York: Times Books, 1991), 156.

[2] Senate Committee on Foreign Relations, *U.S. Policy in the Persian Gulf*, 101st Cong., 2nd sess., December 5, 1990, 110.

This domestic consensus began to falter after November 8, 1990, when Bush announced that the United States would double its conventional forces in Saudi Arabia to create a "viable offensive option" to force Iraq out of Kuwait.[3] At this point, Americans divided along more partisan lines over how to achieve the UN's goals. Most Congressional Democrats argued that the use of force against Iraq was unnecessary and risky, preferring to stick with sanctions. In contrast, the Bush administration, Republicans, and some Democrats supported the shift to an offensive option as the only guaranteed way to force Saddam out. They contended the coalition might fray and Saddam might consolidate control of Kuwait before the sanctions compelled Iraq's withdrawal.

Alongside these debates about how to liberate Kuwait was the difficult problem of Saddam as a long-term threat to US interests in the region. Most policy-makers and commentators agreed that it was not enough for the United States to allow a return to the status quo ante after the crisis. Even if Saddam Hussein agreed to all the Security Council's demands, he would retain a massive military machine, advanced weapons of mass destruction (WMD) programs, and possibly vengeful intentions.

This problem led the United States to consider a host of goals beyond the Security Council mandate. A minority of commentators, mostly outside the government, argued that the United States should directly seek to overthrow Saddam and his regime. The Bush administration unanimously rejected this idea. Nevertheless, the White House believed that the United States needed to severely weaken Saddam during this crisis and contain him afterward to ensure the destruction of his WMD programs, among other goals. One question that generally went unanswered in this debate was whether the United States could stabilize the region and prevent Iraq from threatening its neighbors if Saddam survived the war.

Historians Lawrence Freedman and Efraim Karsh call this question about how to deal with Saddam in the long run the "Saddam problem." They distinguish it from the Kuwait problem: the short-term question of how to eject Iraq from Kuwait.[4] Some solutions to the Kuwait problem, such as compelling Saddam to freely withdraw his forces, would do little to address the Saddam problem. The United States would still need a policy after the Kuwait crisis to prevent future Iraqi aggression. The fear was that if the United States permitted the world's relationship to Iraq to

[3] George H. W. Bush, "The President's News Conference in Orlando, Florida," September 11, 1990, George Bush Presidential Library and Museum Public Papers, accessed November 12, 2016, https://bush41library.tamu.edu/archives/public-papers/2381.

[4] Lawrence Freedman and Efraim Karsh, *The Gulf Conflict, 1990–1991: Diplomacy and War in the New World Order* (Princeton, NJ: Princeton University Press, 1993), xxxii.

return to pre-August 1990 normalcy, Saddam would rise again as a nuclear-armed power, rebuild his military, and try to dominate the Gulf. At that later point, he might be unstoppable. The United States would have to contain Saddam Hussein at the minimum and engineer his overthrow at the maximum to preclude this nightmare scenario.

During the Gulf Crisis, the debate between the minimalist and the maximalist approaches to the Saddam problem bubbled beneath the more immediate argument over how to liberate Kuwait. For the Kuwait problem the ends were clear; the only debate was over the means. The Saddam problem was about both means and ends. Supporters of the maximalist approach, a minority during the Gulf Crisis, believed that US interests in the Gulf would never be safe without the removal of Saddam and the entire Baathist regime. These mostly neoconservative figures argued that the United States should declare his ouster as a major goal for the conflict.

The minimalist approach to the Saddam problem held sway in US politics during the Gulf Crisis, including within the Bush administration. The Bush team welcomed Saddam's ouster as a by-product of sanctions and war, but they contended that the United States could still achieve its goals in the region by containing and enfeebling him. If, as the administration expected, the devastation inflicted by sanctions and war prompted disgruntled Iraqi generals to remove Saddam, the United States would welcome this development and try to get his successor to accept UN demands.

The Bush administration decided against directly pursuing regime change because it believed the United States might become mired in an occupation, the coalition might fracture, and the region would become even less stable. They also doubted that Saddam's removal would make the handling of postwar Iraq significantly easier. Thus, regime change remained a vague hope throughout this crisis, not a policy. Instead, the policy was to hit Saddam as hard as possible during Desert Storm and then organize a multilateral containment regime that would use sanctions, diplomatic isolation, and the threat of renewed military force to box in Iraq until Saddam or his successor fully conceded to the UN's demands.

Constructive Engagement: From 1988 to August 1990

The Persian Gulf War has its roots in Saddam's efforts to maintain his domestic hold on power and his geopolitical status in the region after the bloody Iran–Iraq War (1980–1988). The United States supported Iraq in this conflict to prevent Iran from becoming the dominant power in the

Persian Gulf. This policy became known as "the tilt" because it was never an overt alliance. US assistance began in 1982 in response to major Iraqi setbacks in the conflict. Over the next six years, the United States provided agricultural and Export–Import Bank credits, licensing for dual-use technologies, and military intelligence on Iranian forces.

Through Operation Staunch, starting in 1983, the United States sought to limit international arms sales to Iran even as US allies like France and West Germany sold billions in arms to Iraq. The United States removed Iraq from the terrorist state sponsor list in 1983 and restored full diplomatic relations in 1984. Lastly, from 1987 to 1988, the United States deployed naval forces to the Gulf to protect Kuwaiti oil tankers from Iranian attacks. This move benefitted Iraq by protecting Kuwaiti shipping, a key source of revenue for Iraq.[5]

When the war ended in a bloody stalemate in August 1988, Iraq emerged as the preeminent military force in the Gulf and Iran had been drastically weakened, which raised a crucial new question for US policy: Should the tilt to Iraq continue? Many in Congress and the media argued that the strategic rationale for supporting Iraq ceased with the end of the conflict. These critics of engagement pointed out that Iraq had not in fact stopped its support for terrorism after 1983 and that Saddam had become the new threat to stability in the Gulf. Moreover, outrage erupted after Iraqi forces killed thousands of Kurdish civilians with chemical weapons in the city of Halabja in 1988. Both houses of Congress, with significant bipartisan backing, passed legislation in the fall of 1988 to sever aid to Iraq and impose sanctions.[6]

By contrast, the Bush administration solidified the tilt under a policy it called constructive engagement. In October 1989, Bush signed a new policy directive called National Security Directive 26 (NSD-26). This paper emerged from an interagency review of Iraq policy led by National Security Council analyst Richard Haass. The paper concluded: "Normal relations between the United States and Iraq would serve our longer-term interests and promote stability in both the Gulf and the Middle East. The United States Government should propose economic and political incentives for Iraq to moderate its behavior."[7] This policy aimed to bolster Iraq

[5] Bruce Jentleson, *With Friends Like These: Reagan, Bush, and Saddam, 1982–1990* (New York: W. W. Norton, 1994), 42–67. See also Zachary Karabell, "Backfire: U.S. Policy toward Iraq, 1988–August 2, 1990," *Middle East Journal* 49, no. 1 (Winter, 1995): 30–31.

[6] Helen Dewar and Don Oberdorfer, "Senate Votes Sanctions against Iraq," *Washington Post*, September 10, 1988; Robert Pear, "House Approves Sanctions against Iraq," *New York Times*, September 28, 1990.

[7] "National Security Directive 26," October 2, 1989, George H. W. Bush Presidential Library and Museum Public Papers, 2, accessed October 21, 2016, https://bush41library.tamu.edu/files/nsd/nsd26.pdf.

as a bulwark against Iranian and Soviet power in the region and expand trade ties while downplaying criticism of the regime to incentivize moderate behavior. The Bush administration also assumed that Iraq was so exhausted and indebted from the Iran–Iraq War that it would focus on reconstruction, creating an opening for the United States to nudge Saddam toward restraint.[8] NSD-26 recommended warning Iraq that the United States would respond with sanctions to the use of chemical or biological weapons or the pursuit of nuclear weapons.[9] However, in practice, the policy became more carrot than stick, despite mounting evidence of Iraqi development of WMD and its abuse of US export credit programs.[10]

Constructive engagement shaped US policy toward Iraq from its inception to the Iraqi invasion of Kuwait in 1990. It also sparked a tense public debate on how to deal with Iraq. Critics in Congress and the press blasted the policy as inhumane and unrealistic. Columnists like Jim Hoagland and William Safire as well as legislators as varied as Claiborne Pell (D-RI) and Jesse Helms (R-NC) accused Iraq of committing genocide against the Kurds and continuing to build WMD.[11] Congressional opposition, however, was inconsistent and often hypocritical. Efforts to sanction Iraq frequently died because of procedural and partisan squabbles. Furthermore, lawmakers from agrarian states whose constituencies benefitted from agricultural credits for Iraq either opposed or watered-down bills that punished Iraq.

Doubts about constructive engagement accelerated in the spring of 1990 in response to a series of troubling Iraqi actions. In March, the Iraqi government executed British journalist Farzad Bazoft on false charges of espionage. Later that month, British and American agents halted the export of specialized equipment for the production of nuclear weapons and a "supergun," an experimental long-range artillery piece. On April 2, Saddam threatened to strike Israel with chemical weapons if it launched a preemptive attack on Iraqi weapons facilities, saying "we will make fire eat half of Israel if it tries to do anything against Iraq."[12] Finally, the State

---

[8] Jentleson, *With Friends Like These*, 97.   [9] "NSD 26," Bush Public Papers, 2.

[10] Joseph Stieb, "U.S. Financial Aid for Iraq under the Engagement Policy, 1988–1990," *International History Review*, published online September 21, 2018, www.tandfonline.com/doi/full/10.1080/07075332.2018.1504226.

[11] Jim Hoagland, "Iraq is the One Place Where Sanctions Might Work," *Washington Post*, September 15, 1988, A25; Julie Johnson, "U.S. Asserts Iraq Used Poison Gas against the Kurds," *New York Times*, September 9, 1988, A1; Editorial, "Too Tough on Iraq," *Washington Post*, September 20, 1988, A20. William Safire, "Free the Kurds," *New York Times*, November 23, 1989, A27; Editorial, "Hardly a Peep on Poison Gas," *New York Times*, September 10, 1988, A26.

[12] Jeff Gerth, "Atom Bomb Parts Seized in Britain En Route to Iraq," *New York Times*, March 29, 1990, A1. Alan Cowell, "Iraq Chief, Boasting of Poison Gas, Warns of Disaster if Israelis Strike," *New York Times*, April 3, 1990, A1; Freedman and Karsh, *The Gulf Conflict*, 34.

Department issued several reports in the spring of 1990 determining that Iraq's human rights practices had not improved since the end of the Iran–Iraq War.[13] Critics of constructive engagement in Congress and the media responded to this string of provocations by labeling Bush's policy as appeasement, calling for sanctions, and challenging the policy's core assumption that Saddam could be moderated.[14]

Internally, the Bush administration made minor adjustments to constructive engagement in the spring of 1990. On April 10, National Security Advisor Brent Scowcroft and his assistant Richard Haass wrote a memo to Bush arguing that although the policy had not pushed Iraq toward moderation thus far, the United States had little choice but to continue this approach. Cutting off economic links would barely hurt the Iraqi economy since other states would simply fill those gaps. In addition, punishing Iraq might backfire by feeding Saddam's sense of a US-led conspiracy against him.[15]

At the State Department, Secretary of State James Baker, Policy Planning Director Dennis Ross, and Under Secretary of State Robert Kimmitt concluded in early April that engagement was failing and that the United States needed to shift to punishing Iraqi misbehavior. They instructed April Glaspie, the ambassador to Iraq, to inform Saddam that additional threatening behavior would put Iraq "on a collision course" with the United States and compel the withdrawal of US aid. In late May, the United States suspended agricultural credits for Iraq, but the administration explained this move as a response to allegations of Iraqi misuse of the credits instead of reprimand for foreign policy misbehavior.[16]

Despite these mild alterations to engagement, in public the administration continued to defend the policy in the spring and early summer of 1990, thereby undermining warnings to Saddam. John Kelly appeared before several Congressional hearings to defend the administration's policy and push back on renewed calls for sanctions. While he admitted that Iraq's actions were troubling, he argued that sanctions would have little impact because no allies would join the effort, which meant that sanctions would only hurt US exporters. In line with NSD-26, he added,

[13] Jentleson, *With Friends Like These*, 145.
[14] William Safire, "Country of Concern," *New York Times*, April 9, 1990, A19; Jim Hoagland, "Soft on Saddam," *Washington Post*, April 10, 1990, A23.
[15] Memorandum, Brent Scowcroft to George H. W. Bush, April 10, 1990, OA/ID CF00209-011, National Security Council, Peter Rodman Files, George Bush Presidential Library, 2–3.
[16] James Baker, *The Politics of Diplomacy: Revolution, War, and Peace 1989–1992* (New York: G. P. Putnam's Sons, 1995), 268–269; Telegram, James Baker to US Embassy in Baghdad, April 12, 1990, OA/ID 45486-001, White House Counsel's Office, George Bush Presidential Library.

"Sanctions would not improve our ability to exercise a restraining influence on Iraqi actions."[17] Secretary Baker likewise told a Congressional hearing that sanctions were "a bit premature" and that US allies in the Middle East continued to support a flexible approach toward Iraq.[18]

The official policy may have been creeping toward a tougher line on Iraq, but it remained tethered to the assumptions of NSD-26 as Iraq escalated its threats against its neighbors in the summer of 1990. On July 15, Iraqi troops started to deploy on the border with Kuwait. The next day Tariq Aziz, the Iraqi foreign minister, accused Kuwait and the United Arab Emirates of intentionally overproducing oil in order to cripple the Iraqi economy. He demanded the raising of oil prices, a moratorium on Iraq's massive wartime loans, and the creation of a fund through which the Gulf States would repay Iraq for defending them against Iran.[19]

Critics of the administration pointed to this escalation as evidence for the failure of engagement. The House and Senate passed bills on July 27 to cut off economic aid to Iraq, but the administration continued to oppose these efforts.[20] Republican Senator Alphonse D'Amato (R-NY) cried, "We've waited for Hussein to take a more humane course and it has not been done. He is a butcher, a torturer, a manipulator."[21] Many former opponents of severing aid to Iraq now voted to punish Saddam, including Senator Nancy Kassebaum (R-KS) who said that despite her reservations about hurting food exporters, "there comes a time when I think we have to stand up and be counted."[22] Meanwhile, the administration generally assumed that Iraq was blustering in order to exact concessions from Kuwait but did not want a conflict because of its exhaustion from the Iran–Iraq War.[23] Saudi Arabia and Egypt encouraged this view and asked the United States to let them handle Saddam.

Critics of Bush's handling of preinvasion diplomacy later condemned Ambassador Glaspie for her conciliation of Saddam in a meeting on July

---

[17] Subcommittee on Europe and the Middle East of the House Committee on Foreign Affairs, *United States–Iraqi Relations*, 101st Cong., 2nd sess., April 26, 1990, 2–4; Senate Committee on Foreign Relations, *United States Policy Toward Iraq: Human Rights, Weapons Proliferation, and International Law*, 101st Cong., 2nd sess., June 15, 1990, 5–9.

[18] Baker, *The Politics of Diplomacy*, 270.

[19] Freedman and Karsh, *The Gulf Conflict*, 47–50.

[20] Guy Gugliotta, "Trade Sanctions Voted by Senate Against Iraq," *Washington Post*, July 28, 1990, A15.

[21] Steven Holmes, "Congress Backs Curbs against Iraq," *New York Times*, July 28, 1990, A5.

[22] *Cong. Rec.*, 101st Cong., 2nd sess., July 27, 1990, 19806.

[23] Memorandum, Richard Haass to Brent Scowcroft, July 25, 1990, OA/ID CF01937, National Security Council, Richard Haass Working Files, George Bush Presidential Library; Telegram, April Glaspie to James Baker, July 18, 1990, OA/ID 01937-003, National Security Council, Richard Haass Working Files, George Bush Presidential Library.

25. Glaspie offered the dictator multiple assurances of the US desire for good relations with Iraq and issued no clear warning of what the United States would do if Iraq invaded Kuwait. In a message to James Baker on the meeting, she noted Saddam's emphasis that he "wants peaceful settlement is surely sincere."[24] Whatever her faults in this meeting, she was following a policy that required officials to pepper nebulous warnings with reassurances that the United States still sought Iraqi friendship. For example, a cable from Bush to the Iraqi government on July 28 read: "We believe that differences are best resolved by peaceful means and not by threats involving military force or conflict. My administration continues to desire better relations with Iraq."[25] US messages repeatedly stated that the United States had no defense treaties with Kuwait or positions on Iraq–Kuwait border disputes.[26] Two days before the invasion, John Kelly reiterated the administration's desire for good relations with Iraq while refusing to speculate on what the United States would do if Iraq invaded Kuwait.[27] Despite some internal reconsideration of engagement, the Bush administration stuck to NSD-26 and missed any chance to deter Saddam.

Responding to the Invasion of Kuwait, August–November 1990

The Iraqi invasion and annexation of Kuwait in August 1990 shattered every assumption underpinning constructive engagement: that Iraq was too exhausted from the war with Iran to try to dominate the Persian Gulf; that Western and conservative Arab support for his war effort had mellowed Saddam in the 1980s; and that Saddam could be positively incentivized to align with US policies. Bush immediately started building an international coalition to condemn the invasion, stop further Iraqi aggression, and create a legal basis for action against Iraq. This effort led to the passing of a number of Security Council resolutions in the early fall that established the UN's demands for Iraq and the tools to enforce them. Resolution 660 on August 2 called for Iraq to "immediately and unconditionally" withdraw its forces from Kuwait and allow the restoration of

---

[24] Telegram, April Glaspie to James Baker, July 25, 1990, OA/ID 011937-002, National Security Council, Robert Gates Working Files, George Bush Presidential Library.

[25] David Hoffman and Helen Dewar, "State Department, Panel, Spar Over Envoy," *Washington Post*, July 13, 1991, A1, 14.

[26] Janice Gross Stein, "Deterrence and Compellence in the Gulf, 1990–91: A Failed or Impossible Task?" *International Security* 17, no. 2 (October, 1992): 150–152.

[27] Subcommittee on Europe and the Middle East of the House Committee on Foreign Affairs, *Developments in the Middle East: July 1990*, 101st Cong., 2nd sess., July 31, 1990, 2, 14.

the Kuwaiti government. Four days later, Resolution 661 froze Iraqi assets and imposed economic sanctions on Iraq, with exceptions for food and medicine.[28]

The United States also forged a military and political response to the invasion, starting with the deployment on August 8 of naval, air, and ground forces to the Gulf to protect Saudi Arabia from Iraqi forces menacing its border. In a speech announcing the deployment, Bush called for the "immediate, unconditional, and complete withdrawal of all Iraqi forces from Kuwait" and the restoration of the Kuwaiti government. He committed the United States, "as has been the case with every President from President Roosevelt to President Reagan," to the "security and stability of the Gulf." He framed the deployment of US forces as a measure to defend Saudi Arabia and enforce the sanctions but emphasized that the United States would demand the full implementation of the UN demands.[29]

By the end of August, Bush had established the basic policy of using sanctions and diplomatic isolation to coerce Saddam into leaving Kuwait. In making the case for action, he identified several core interests and values at stake. One interest was the free flow of oil from the region to global markets. Maintaining access to the energy resources of the Gulf had been a declared policy goal since World War II. By seizing Kuwait, Saddam gained control of about one-fifth of global oil reserves, and he could compel the Gulf States to obey his commands on oil prices.[30] Defense Secretary Richard Cheney warned that this situation "gave him a strangle hold on our economy and on that of most of the other nations of the world as well."[31] A surge in oil prices could lead to a global recession that might threaten recent trends toward democracy in Eastern Europe, Latin America, and Southeast Asia. Moreover, Saddam would use these gains to feed his military machine and aggressive ambitions.

Another major part of Bush's argument for action was the possibility of bolstering collective security, international law, and the United Nations as the primary mechanisms for stopping aggression in the post–Cold War

---

[28] Security Council Resolutions found in Cerf and Sifry, *The Gulf War Reader*, 137–143.

[29] George H. W. Bush, "Address to the Nation Announcing the Deployment of United States Armed Forces to Saudi Arabia," August 8, 1990, George Bush Presidential Library and Museum Public Papers, accessed November 12, 2016, https://bush41library.tamu.edu/archives/public-papers/2147.

[30] Hal Brands, *From Berlin to Baghdad: America's Search for Purpose in the Post-Cold War World* (Lexington, KY: University Press of Kentucky, 2008), 46–47; Michael Palmer, *Guardians of the Gulf: A History of America's Expanding Role in the Persian Gulf, 1883–1992* (New York: Simon & Schuster, 1992).

[31] Senate Armed Services Committee, *Crisis in the Persian Gulf Region: U.S. Policy Options and Implications*, 101st Cong., 2nd sess., September 11, 1990, 11.

world. Bush labeled this vision the "new world order," which he defined as the "community of nations" cooperating "to condemn and repel lawless aggression."[32] To the White House, the world in 1990 was in "a critical juncture" between the Cold War and a new, undetermined order. James Baker called the Gulf Crisis "a political test of how the post–Cold War world will work."[33] In Bush's words, Saddam had launched "a ruthless assault on the very essence of international order and civilized ideals."[34] Allowing Saddam to keep Kuwait would signal that the international community was willing to accept the violent eradication of a UN member, encouraging more aggression around the world. If, however, the United States and its allies thwarted Saddam, it could be the first step in creating a more peaceful, lawful, and cooperative international system.

The USSR's support for early US actions against Iraq further raised the administration's hopes of bolstering collective security in the post–Cold War world. The superpower rivalry had usually prevented the Security Council from enforcing international law, but the Cold War had faded by the time Saddam invaded Kuwait. Mikhail Gorbachev's government promptly denounced Iraq, accusing their former clients of acting like "feudal lords."[35] If the United States and USSR could collaborate in foiling Iraq, Bush believed this would open new options for the cooperative management of international affairs. As he told Gorbachev in early September: "I want to go to the American people tomorrow night to close the book on the Cold War and offer them the vision of this new world order in which we will cooperate."[36]

The Bush team believed the goal of setting precedents for a new world order made it vital to maintain multilateral consensus throughout the crisis. In pragmatic terms, the United States needed wide participation in the embargo from Iraq's neighbors and major trading partners to give the threat of force any teeth. Allied forces needed bases in Saudi Arabia, Turkey, and elsewhere. Bush also aimed to set a precedent for multilateral

---

[32] George H. W. Bush, "Address before a Joint Session of the Congress on the State of the Union," January 29, 1991, The American Presidency Project, accessed April 18, 2017, www.presidency.ucsb.edu/ws/?pid=19253.

[33] House Committee on Foreign Affairs, *Crisis in the Persian Gulf*, 101st Cong., 2nd sess., September 4, 1990, 7.

[34] George H. W. Bush, "Remarks at the Annual Conference of the Veterans of Foreign Wars in Baltimore, Maryland," August 20, 1990, George Bush Presidential Library and Museum Public Papers, accessed November 14, 2016, https://bush41library.tamu.edu/archives/public-papers/2171.

[35] Freedman and Karsh, *The Gulf Conflict*, 78–79.

[36] George H. W. Bush and Brent Scowcroft, *A World Transformed* (New York: Knopf, 1998), 364; Minutes, Meeting of George Bush and Mikhail Gorbachev, September 9, 1990, OA/ID CF 01478-021, National Security Council, Richard Haass Files, Working Files, George Bush Presidential Library, 2.

responses to aggression that would seek UN approval and use force only after pursuing nonviolent means. Getting Iraq out of Kuwait by any means was not adequate. The United States had to achieve this goal in a way that demonstrated the effectiveness of collective security. One crucial element of this effort to create a "model for the use of force" was that Saddam must gain nothing from his crimes: no concessions, no incentives, no deals.[37] Only a full denial of any gains for Saddam would firmly establish the principle that aggression does not pay. This would set a powerful precedent that would deter future conquerors and offer a model for responding to aggression.

The fall of 1990 brought a whirlwind of diplomatic, political, and military action that left little time for long-term thinking about how to address the Iraqi threat beyond the Kuwait problem. Key officials, including US Ambassador to the UN Thomas Pickering and CIA Director William Webster, identified an important dilemma in the stated policy: If sanctions and military pressure convinced Saddam to leave Kuwait voluntarily, he would escape with his military machine and WMD programs intact. The Kuwait problem would be solved for the moment, but the United States would have done little to solve the Saddam problem. He would retain his ability, and probably his intention, to bully his neighbors once again. On August 2, Pickering argued that the US needed "to find a broader basis to ensure that Iraq does not return to the status quo ante in a position where its considerable military muscle can be a source of intimidation and threat to Kuwait, Saudi Arabia, Jordan, or other states in the region."[38] In October, Webster warned that the region would not be secure unless Saddam was overthrown, "some countervailing force" in the area contained him, or his WMD programs and military strength were decimated.[39]

The Bush administration consequently aimed to weaken Saddam during this crisis and/or impose a set of strictures on him afterward to prevent him from keeping or reconstituting his military strength. In effect, from the beginning the United States had committed itself to a new, higher standard of success, one that the Security Council had not endorsed nor had the administration publicly stated as a goal. The lead conceptual developer of this early iteration of a postwar containment strategy was Richard Haass, who served as Senior Director for Near East and South Asian Affairs for the NSC, working closely with Brent Scowcroft.

---

[37] Bush and Scowcroft, *A World Transformed*, 491.

[38] Telegram, Timothy Pickering to James Baker, August 2, 1990, OA/ID CP 01478-028, National Security Council, Richard Haass Files, George Bush Presidential Library, 3.

[39] Walter Mossberg and Andy Pasztor, "CIA Director Says Gulf Can't Be Secure as Long as Saddam Hussein Rules," *Wall Street Journal*, October 26, 1990, A16.

Haass bookends the history of the containment of Iraq because he later served as Director of Policy Planning for the State Department under Colin Powell in the second Bush administration, where he privately criticized the rush to war. Haass was a key original developer of the containment strategy within the Bush administration, and he continued to defend it as a viable alternative up to the 2003 invasion. A Rhodes Scholar and a Ph.D. in international relations, Haass served in the Defense and State Departments under Carter and Reagan before joining Scowcroft's staff. Haass supported a US foreign policy that sought to construct a multilateral international order built on rules like state sovereignty and nonaggression and backed by US leadership.[40] He also demonstrated realist tendencies; he believed that geopolitical competition would persist after the Cold War, that global institutions ultimately could not restrain this competition by "governing" international politics, and that the United States should use force to protect well-defined national interests rather than to spread its ideals.[41] For these reasons, he described the Gulf War as a "war of necessity" because it both reinforced the principle of sovereignty and served a specific US interest. The 2003 Iraq War, however, he opposed as an unnecessary "war of choice" motivated by the fantasies of democratic crusaders.[42]

In August 1990, Haass spelled out the core conundrum of the Gulf Crisis: "It is not clear that an outcome that leaves Saddam in power and Iraq's industrial and war-making capability intact constitutes a viable much less optimal outcome from our perspective." Haass noted that if the situation in the Gulf returned to the status quo ante, Saddam would return to aggression in a few years, but this time he would have nuclear and biological weapons. In this case, coping with Saddam 2.0 would require at the minimum a full containment strategy and a permanent military presence in the region.[43] Haass' reasoning suggests that some kind of containment strategy was already percolating through the administration's thinking as it dealt with the Gulf Crisis. Bush and his top advisors entered the crisis believing that the containment of the Soviet Union had been "extraordinarily successful." A February 1989 National Security Review signed by Bush declared: "Containment is being

---

[40] Richard Haass, *The Reluctant Sheriff: The United States after the Cold War* (New York: Council on Foreign Relations Books, 1997), 6–8, 69–70.

[41] Haass, *Reluctant Sheriff*, 43–44, 50, 61–63.

[42] Richard Haass, *War of Necessity, War of Choice: A Memoir of Two Iraq Wars* (New York: Simon & Schuster, 2009), 111.

[43] Working Paper, "The Gulf Crisis: Thoughts, Scenarios, Opinions," Richard Haass, August 19, 1990, OA/ID CF00946, National Security Files, Subject Files, Robert Gates Files, George Bush Presidential Library, 1–3.

vindicated as the peoples of the world reject the outmoded dogma of Marxism-Leninism in a search for prosperity and freedom."[44]

Haass and other top officials envisioned an Iraqi containment strategy as requiring a peacekeeping force on the border, a naval presence, the prepositioning of military equipment, regular exercises in the region, the elimination of Iraq's ballistic missile and nuclear weapons programs, and "covert efforts designed to keep the regime in Baghdad on the defensive."[45] Bush suggested this kind of post-crisis structure to British Prime Minister Margaret Thatcher on October 18, saying: "we are talking about containing Iraq."[46] Bush believed that the new factors in the post–Cold War world would make multilateral containment feasible, especially the new cooperative potential between the United States and the USSR and the international community's recognition of Iraq as a manifest threat to the global economy.[47]

In an odd twist, the need for a future containment strategy led many US officials to see war as preferable to a diplomatic solution. In Haass' words, a punishing war "would greatly ease the post-war challenge of containing Iraq and maintaining security in the Gulf" by allowing the United States to degrade Saddam's military and WMD programs.[48] Scowcroft concurred, saying that if the United States had to use force to eject Saddam from Kuwait, it should "reduce the Iraqi military as much as possible" in order to "reduce the threat Saddam posed to his neighbors."[49]

The administration anticipated that many European and Arab allies might see this policy as "moving the goalpost" on Iraq, but they nevertheless believed they had to pursue this goal while preserving the sanctioning coalition, knowing that any unilateral containment regime would fail.

This exploration of the Saddam problem led the Bush foreign policy team to consider a new question: Would the Middle East ever be stable as long as Saddam Hussein remained in power? Top officials were usually pessimistic on this question, but they did not definitively decide if Saddam had to be removed for the United States to achieve its objectives

[44] Hal Brands, *Making the Unipolar Moment: U.S. Foreign Policy and the Rise of the Post-Cold War Order* (Ithaca, NY: Cornell University Press, 2016), 277.
[45] Memorandum, Richard Haass to Brent Scowcroft, August 27, 1990, OA/ID CP 00946, National Security Council, Subject Files, Robert Gates Files, George Bush Presidential Library, 3.
[46] Talking Points, "Themes for Call to PM Thatcher," October 18, 1990, OA/ID CF 01584-031, National Security Council, Richard Haass Files, Working Files, George Bush Presidential Library, 2.
[47] Andrew Rosenthal, "Neutralizing Iraq's Threat: For Bush, Toppling Hussein Isn't Required," *New York Times*, August 29, 1990, A1.
[48] Memorandum, Richard Haass to Brent Scowcroft, August 27, 1990, 4.
[49] Bush and Scowcroft, *A World Transformed*, 383.

beyond the current crisis.[50] There were hints that top policy-makers thought that United States might not be able to achieve its goals while Saddam was still around. In an August 4 NSC meeting, Baker said, "Our strategy is threefold: to keep Saddam out, to make him a pariah, and to topple him through sanctions and covert actions."[51] On August 6, Bush told the NSC: "All will not be tranquil until Saddam Hussein is history."[52]

The Bush administration believed the removal of Saddam Hussein would probably make Iraq easier to control after the crisis but never identified regime change as a policy goal. They framed it as a hope rather than an objective even though they expected that Saddam would have to be removed eventually for the region to return to stability. For example, when Senator Al Gore asked Cheney if the removal of Saddam was a US goal, Cheney said no but added: "I think it would be fair to say, Senator, we probably would not have any objection were that to occur."[53] As Chairman of the Joint Chiefs of Staff, Colin Powell, said after the war: "We hoped that Saddam would not survive the coming fury. But his elimination was not a stated objective. What we hoped for, frankly, in a postwar Gulf region was an Iraq still standing, with Saddam overthrown."[54] Instead of regime change, the administration focused on enforcing the Security Council resolutions and weakening Iraqi military capabilities in the process.

While the administration had decided early in the crisis to not pursue regime change directly, statements of those like Powell and Cheney show they cautiously welcomed the toppling of Saddam as by-product of the war for Kuwait. The NSC Deputies Committee, including Richard Haass, concluded in the fall of 1990 that the United States might be able to create the conditions in which regime change could happen via a military coup.[55] They reasoned that if the coalition pounded Iraqi forces, destroyed key pillars of the regime like the Republican Guard, and crippled the Iraqi communications system, these actions, combined with

---

[50] Gideon Rose, *How Wars End: Why We Always Fight the Last Battle: A History of American Intervention from World War I to Afghanistan* (New York: Simon & Schuster, 2010), 202.

[51] Minutes of NSC Meeting on Iraqi invasion of Kuwait, August 4, 1990, OA/ID 01478-029, National Security Council, Richard Haass Files, Working Files, George Bush Presidential Library.

[52] Minutes of NSC Meeting on Iraqi Invasion of Kuwait, August 6, 1990, OA/ID 01478-030, National Security Council, Richard Haass Files, Working Files, George Bush Presidential Library.

[53] See Cheney and Baker testimonies in Senate Armed Services Committee, *Crisis in the Persian Gulf Region*, September 11, 1990, 13; House Committee on Foreign Affairs, *Crisis in the Persian Gulf*, September 4, 1990, 13.

[54] Colin Powell, *My American Journey* (New York: Random House, 1995), 363.

[55] Bush and Scowcroft, *A World Transformed*, 383–384.

sanctions, might prompt top generals to remove Saddam. Robert Gates, then the Deputy National Security Advisor, described this approach as such: "We wanted to create circumstances that would encourage the Iraqi military to take Saddam out."[56] A more pragmatic successor might concede to UN demands in order to avoid further destruction and to solidify his domestic position. Bush also ordered the CIA to develop a covert component to the coup option that would cultivate sources of discontent with Saddam within the regime.[57]

Although the Bush administration was thinking about how to weaken or indirectly topple Saddam in the long run, they tried to minimize open discussion of broadening the war's scope. They wanted to avoid scaring the public, the Democrats, and the international coalition into thinking the administration planned to expand US objectives beyond those of the Security Council resolutions. In the fall of 1990, Bush had not yet convinced the American people, Congress, or the coalition that a war to liberate Kuwait was necessary, much less a war to cripple Saddam Hussein. Bush's sanctions-based strategy had broad public backing, with one poll from after the invasion showing 83 percent support.[58] Sanctions were also popular in both parties in Congress, although Democratic leaders like Sam Nunn (D-GA) and George Mitchell (D-ME) warned Bush that they opposed offensive military action for the time being.[59]

By the late fall of 1990, the basic structure of US policy on the Saddam problem had emerged. If Saddam relented without violence, the United States would install a containment regime to ensure that he could not rebuild his WMD and military strength. If war became necessary to oust him from Kuwait, the United States would strike hard at Iraqi forces, essential pillars of the regime, and WMD programs in order to force him out of Kuwait and weaken him in the long run. If sanctions and/or war led to his overthrow, the United States would welcome this outcome, but they did not see it as necessary for achieving their short- or long-term goals.

The Debate Heats Up: November 1990–January 1991

By late October 1990, the Bush administration had started to doubt that sanctions alone would compel Saddam to leave Kuwait. President Bush held a Cabinet meeting on October 30 to decide whether to stay with the

[56] Christian Alfonsi, *Circle in the Sand: Why We Went Back to Iraq* (New York: Doubleday, 2006), 192.

[57] Bob Woodward, *The Commanders* (New York: Simon & Schuster, 1991), 237, 282.

[58] Rosita Thomas, *American Public Opinion on the Iraq–Kuwait Crisis until January 15* (CRS Report No. 91–109) (Washington DC: Congressional Research Service, 1991), 17.

[59] Bush and Scowcroft, *A World Transformed*, 389.

sanctions-based policy or start building an offensive military option. The Cabinet noted that sanctions had been in place for almost three months and appeared to be having little effect on Saddam's decision-making. The CIA had reported in late September that sanctions would not force Iraq from Kuwait nor cause the shutdown of vital industries "in the short or medium term."[60] Most of Bush's foreign policy advisors agreed that sanctions might force Saddam's hand eventually, but not within an acceptable time frame. The United States could not sustain hundreds of thousands of troops in the desert indefinitely, and the best time period for offensive ground operations would end around March of 1991 when the heat started to increase.[61] The political climate in the Middle East posed an equally difficult problem. Recent fighting between Israelis and Palestinians opened the possibility that Saddam might use this crisis to divide the coalition. The haj was set to begin in the spring, and the mere presence of US troops posed political dangers for Saudi Arabia.[62] All of these factors militated against a strategy of sanctions and attrition.

On November 8, Bush announced the addition of another 200,000 troops to the Desert Shield force to "ensure that the coalition has an adequate offensive military option." The Cabinet simultaneously agreed to pursue a new Security Council resolution that would authorize the use of force against Iraq. They hoped that the creation of a viable offensive force and the setting of a deadline would convince Saddam of the coalition's resolve and get him to back down.[63] After several weeks of negotiations, the Security Council passed Resolution 678 on November 29. The resolution determined that Iraq had refused to comply with the Security Council's previous demands and offered Iraq "one final opportunity" to do so. If by January 15, 1991, Iraq did not begin the full implementation of these demands, the coalition would be authorized to use "all necessary means" to force Iraq from Kuwait. This resolution also called for the restoration of "international peace and security" in the region, a general enough goal to justify the broader US goal of weakening of Iraq through military action.[64]

One noteworthy skeptic of the push away from sanctions was Colin Powell, the Chairman of the Joint Chiefs of Staff. Powell was a combat veteran of the Vietnam War and a believer in using force only as a last

---

[60] Freedman and Karsh, *The Gulf Conflict*, 196.
[61] Brent Scowcroft's Notes, Meeting on the Gulf, October 30, 1990, OA/ID CF 01584-031, National Security Council, Richard Haass Files, Working Files, George Bush Presidential Library, 1–2; Bush and Scowcroft, *A World Transformed*, 394.
[62] Phebe Marr, *The Modern History of Iraq* (Boulder, CO: Westview Press, 2012), 234.
[63] Baker, *The Politics of Diplomacy*, 302.
[64] Cerf and Sifry, *The Gulf War Reader*, 155–156.

resort and only in defense of precisely defined national interests. He was not opposed to the use of force against Iraq, but he feared that Bush might not be hearing the full case for sanctions from advisors like Cheney and Scowcroft, who had expressed their skepticism of this route early in the crisis. Powell later explained: "My thinking was that it would be great if sanctions would do the job because then we would avoid a war with unknown consequences and therefore we should give sanctions as much of a ride as was politically possible."[65] State Department personnel remembered Powell as "a very reluctant warrior" who advocated the sanctions strategy to Bush and other top civilian officials.[66] Powell told Bush in late September: "There is a case here for the containment or strangulation policy. ... It may take a year, it may take two years, but it will work some day."[67] Bush, Cheney, and Scowcroft all disagreed, saying that there were too many risks in waiting that long, and Powell did not press his point once Bush decided to take the offensive route.

In late 1990 and early 1991, administration officials accelerated a campaign to convince Congress and the public that the United States could not wait indefinitely for sanctions to work and had to prepare for war. They sought Congressional authorization for the use of force before the January 15 deadline. James Baker told a Congressional hearing that sanctions were not having the desired political effect: "so far, all available evidence suggest they have had little, if any, effect on his inclination to withdraw from Kuwait."[68] Cheney and Webster noted that Saddam could endure the sanctions for years by directing resources to power bases like the Sunni population and the military while starving the rest of the population.[69] Adding to this urgency was the sense that, as the world waited for sanctions, Iraq was dismantling the nation of Kuwait to the point where there might be no country left to save.

The administration also argued that waiting for sanctions to work posed great risks to the coalition's unity. They emphasized that sanctions hurt countries like Jordan, Turkey, and Eastern European nations that relied on trade with Iraq. The longer the sanctions regime lasted, the more

---

[65] Colin Powell, interview by Frontline, PBS, 1995, accessed January 25, 2017, www.pbs .org/wgbh/pages/frontline/gulf/oral/powell/1.html; Woodward, *The Commanders*, 38.

[66] Dennis Ross, interview by Andrew Carpendale, February 9, 1994, Box 173, Folder 8, MC 197, James A. Baker III Papers at the Seeley G. Mudd Library, 12; Robert Zoellick, interview by Andrew Carpendale, July 27, 1993, Box 173, Folder 8, MC 197, James A. Baker III Papers at the Seeley G. Mudd Library, 12.

[67] Woodward, *The Commanders*, 41–42, 300–303; Powell, *My American Journey*, 467.

[68] House Committee on Foreign Affairs, *Update on the Situation in the Persian Gulf*, 101st Cong., 2nd sess., December 6, 1990, 5.

[69] House Committee on Foreign Affairs, *Situation in the Persian Gulf*, 5; Senate Armed Services Committee, *Crisis in the Persian Gulf Region*, December 3, 1990, 647–648.

that cheating would increase. Moreover, many Arab members of the coalition felt growing pressure from large segments of their population that sympathized with Saddam's challenge to the West and the wealthy Gulf States.[70] The contingency of Israel being dragged into the conflict, possibly by Saddam's own actions, would make it politically impossible for these states to stay in the coalition. The United States also feared that the longer the standoff lasted, the more likely that the Soviets, Arabs, or Europeans would offer Saddam some kind of incentive or partial reward for complying with the United Nations.[71]

As the January 15 deadline approached, the Bush administration increasingly stressed the long-term threat of Saddam as a nuclear power to defend the shift to an offensive strategy. Speaking to coalition forces in Saudi Arabia on Thanksgiving, Bush claimed: "Those who would measure the timetable for Saddam's atomic program in years may be seriously underestimating the reality of that situation and the gravity of the threat. Every day that passes brings Saddam one step closer to realizing his goal of a nuclear weapons arsenal." Bush then said that no one knew exactly when Saddam would acquire nuclear weapons but warned that "[h]e has never possessed a weapon that he didn't use."[72] Bush, a World War II combat veteran, peppered these warnings with comparisons of Saddam to Hitler. He contended: "A half century ago, our nation and the world paid dearly for appeasing an aggressor who should, and could, have been stopped. We are not going to make that mistake again."[73] Bush and others emphasized that the United States could either defeat Saddam now without nuclear weapons or fight him later when he had a nuclear arsenal.

These claims advanced a much more alarmist view of the Iraqi nuclear program than the intelligence community's assessments. An interagency review estimated in the fall of 1990 that Iraq was five to ten years from a large nuclear weapons program and that it could build a small nuclear weapon at some point between a few months and a few years.[74] Nevertheless, the growing emphasis on nuclear weapons bolstered the case for war. A CBS News Poll on November 19 found that 54 percent of

---

[70] House Armed Services Committee, *Crisis in the Persian Gulf: Sanctions, Diplomacy, and War*, 101st Cong., 2nd sess., December 14, 1990, 525–526.

[71] Telegram, Chas Freeman to James Baker, October 29, 1990, OA/ID CF 01584-032, National Security Council, Richard Haass Files, Working Files, George Bush Presidential Library, 5.

[72] George H. W. Bush, "Remarks to United States Army Troops Near Dhahran, Saudi Arabia," November 22, 1990, The American Presidency Project, accessed March 13, 2017, www.presidency.ucsb.edu/ws/index.php?pid=19088

[73] R. W. Apple, "Bush Invokes U.S. Values: Confrontation in the Gulf," *New York Times*, August 16, 1990, A1.

[74] W. R. Doerner and J. O. Jackson, "When Will Saddam Get the Bomb?" *Time*, December 10, 1990, 38.

Americans thought preventing Saddam from building nuclear weapons was a good reason for war. In contrast, 56 percent found restoring the Kuwaiti government and defending Saudi Arabia to be an inadequate reason, and 62 percent thought protecting the source of much of the world's oil also did not justify the use of force.[75] The Hitler comparison also played well in public, with one poll in August 1990 reporting that 61 percent of Americans agreed that Saddam was like Hitler and the United States needed to stop him quickly.[76]

Nevertheless, some top officials believed that this rhetoric raised expectations beyond the defined set of objectives. After all, the United States fought the war against Hitler with total means and for total ends, in marked contrast to the planned war against Iraq. Haass, for one, believed that "making the comparison would add pressure on us to go beyond our mission and remove the regime."[77] Powell later recalled similar unease with comparing Saddam to Hitler because "in so demonizing him ... you raised expectations that you would do something about him at the end of the day."[78] Haass and Powell feared that the mismatch between rhetoric and policy might tarnish whatever the United States achieved in the conflict, and later events would bear out this prediction.

The massive troop surge in November 1990 intensified domestic opposition to Bush's Iraq policy. Democrats in Congress had backed the sanctions-based strategy, but they believed this shift, combined with the January 15 deadline, altered US strategy in perilous ways. Led by Sam Nunn and Claiborne Pell, Democrats invited prominent foreign policy figures to speak in a series of Congressional hearings on behalf of the sanctions strategy and against a shift to the use of force.[79] Defenders of the sanctions-based approach came from many backgrounds, including several former Chairmen of the Joint Chiefs of Staff, former Defense Secretaries James Schlesinger and Robert S. McNamara, and former Carter National Security Advisor Zbigniew Brzezinksi. Democrats and these allies contended that war against Iraq was premature and that the United States should give sanctions more time. They agreed with Bush that Saddam should receive no rewards or incentives for withdrawing from Kuwait in order to reaffirm the principle that aggression does not pay. They also acknowledged the importance of establishing precedents of effective

---

[75] Freedman and Karsh, *The Gulf Conflict*, 227.

[76] H. W. Brands, "Neither Munich nor Vietnam: The Gulf War of 1991," in *The Power of the Past: History and Statecraft*, ed. Hal Brands and Jeremi Suri (Washington, DC: Brookings Institution Press, 2015), 81–86.

[77] Haass, *War of Necessity*, 77.   [78] Powell, interview by Frontline, 1995.

[79] Other prominent figures who argued for sticking with sanctions included Frank Carlucci, William Crowe, David Jones, McGeorge Bundy, Paul Nitze, Richard Murphy, Arthur Schlesinger, Edward Luttwak, and Kenneth Waltz.

collective security, countering Saddam's bid to dominate oil resources, defending human rights and state sovereignty, and stripping him of his WMD programs.

Democrats argued, however, that sanctions were still the best means of achieving those ends. They believed the sanctions would deny spare parts to the military, shut down key industries, drain Iraq's cash reserves, and force the rationing of food.[80] Saddam could only shuffle resources around so much before he became unable to pay off the key constituent groups that sustained his regime. At that point, projected by sanctions advocates to be between six months and a year, he would have to choose between withdrawing from Kuwait and facing internal revolt.[81] If the embargo failed and the United States had to use force, Iraq would be even weaker due to this extended economic isolation.[82] Democrats believed the coalition had time on its side and a chance to defeat Saddam without a risky conflict. Some Democrats pointed to the containment of the USSR as a model for how to deal with Iraq, claiming that if the United States outlasted this superpower, they could also wear down Iraq.[83]

Democrats and their allies also condemned what they saw as Bush's heedless rush to war. They contended that a war would cause thousands of American casualties, break up the international coalition, and turn Arab public opinion against the United States. Vietnam in particular loomed large over the Democrats' anxieties on Iraq. Many Democrats had personal connections to Vietnam, either as veterans or as politicians who opposed the war. As Congressman Richard Durbin (D-IL) put it, "We are products of the Vietnam experience. ... We are really touched by the possibility that we may be repeating that experience."[84] Vietnam veterans like John Kerry and Robert Kerrey, the latter of whom lost part of his leg in combat, cited their experiences as a warning against rushing into wars, particularly when the United States seemed to be fighting for countries that would not protect themselves.[85]

---

[80] Senate Committee on Foreign Relations, *U.S. Policy in the Persian Gulf*, December 4, 1990, 1–2.
[81] See testimony of Senator Sam Nunn and Claiborne Pell: Senate Armed Services Committee, *Crisis in the Persian Gulf Region*, November 27, 1990, 108–109; *Cong. Rec.*, 102nd Cong., 1st sess., January 4, 1991, 330; David Rogers, "Pro-Defense Nunn Counsels U.S. Not to Let Slip too Quickly Those Hard-to-Stop Dogs of War," *Wall Street Journal*, December 4, 1990, A20; Editorial, "How to Choke Iraq," *New York Times*, December 7, 1990, A34.
[82] See argument of Senator George Mitchell, *Cong. Rec.*, 102nd Cong., 1st sess., 409.
[83] See testimony of William Quandt and Senator Paul Sarbanes: Senate Committee on Foreign Relations, *U.S. Policy in the Persian Gulf, Part 2*, December 12, 1990, 128–130.
[84] E. J. Dionne, "Gulf Crisis Rekindles Democrats' Old Debate but with New Focus," *Washington Post*, January 3, 1991, A16.
[85] See testimony of Senators Robert Kerrey and John Kerry: *Cong., Rec.*, 101st Cong., 2nd sess., October 24, 1990, 33377; *Cong. Rec.*, 102nd Cong., 1nd sess., January 11, 1991, 846–849.

In legal terms, Democrats claimed that Bush had exceeded his constitutional authority by doubling the number of troops and signing Security
Council Resolution 678 because these steps effectively put the country on
a course for war before Congress had authorized the use of force. They
demanded that Bush seek Congressional approval before launching a war
to liberate Kuwait.[86] Democrats also argued that in spite of the broad
international support for Bush's policies, the United States would end up
bearing a disproportionate share of the fighting and the casualties given
the small military contributions of most coalition partners. Senator
Joseph Biden (D-DE), for instance, argued that this burden-sharing
problem undermined Bush's push for collective security, saying: "A
New World Order in the United Nations and collective security adds up
to 'We will hold your coat, United States. You go get them; we give you
the authority to do it'."[87]

On the issue of WMD, Democrats emphasized that the United States
could keep sanctions on Iraq after the withdrawal from Kuwait to
compel Saddam to undo these programs. They and other critics of
Bush also objected to his portrayal of Saddam's nuclear program as an
imminent threat to the United States. The United States had to be
concerned with Iraq's WMD, but this was not an immediate *casus belli*.
For instance, Zbigniew Brzezinski contended that even if Iraq built a
small nuclear weapons program in spite of sanctions, the United States
could deter them just as they had deterred far more powerful nuclear
states. Furthermore, nuclear experts noted that Saddam would still be
five to ten years away from a large nuclear arsenal even if trade restrictions were not in place.[88]

In the meantime, Saddam could create a crude, Hiroshima-sized
device, but nuclear experts emphasized that he could neither test this
device nor deliver it with ballistic missiles. These specialists also
doubted that Saddam Hussein was irrational enough to use a nuclear
weapon and bring destruction down upon his head.[89] They and experts
on Iraq such as Phebe Marr and Efraim Karsh portrayed Saddam as a

---

[86] Ruth Marcus, "Congress and the President Clash Over Who Decides on Going to War,"
Washington Post, December 14, 1990, A46.

[87] Senate Committee on Foreign Relations, *U.S. Policy in the Persian Gulf*, December 4,
1990, 27. See also the testimonies of Robert Kerrey and Zbigniew Brzezinski: Senate
Armed Services Committee, *Crisis in the Persian Gulf Region*, December 3, 1990, 751;
Senate Committee on Foreign Relations, *U.S. Policy in the Persian Gulf*, December 5,
1990, 168.

[88] Senate Committee on Foreign Relations, *U.S. Policy in the Persian Gulf, Part 1*, December
5, 1990, 156.

[89] See testimonies of Gary Milhollin and Leonard Spector as well as letter from Union of
Concerned Scientists: Senate Armed Services Committee, *Crisis in the Persian Gulf
Region*, December 3, 1990, 33–35.

power-hungry, ruthless, but mostly rational survivor who lacked a "Masada complex."[90] Saddam's invasion of Kuwait was a gamble, they argued, but it was not irrational because the conciliatory US engagement policy gave Saddam good reason to think he could get away with the invasion. Saddam's life was "a ceaseless struggle for survival" in which he always prioritized domestic power. Even if he could acquire nuclear weapons, the odds were exceedingly small that he would throw his lifelong struggle away by using them.[91]

A large minority of Democrats, however, broke with their party and supported Bush's case for war. Many of these legislators were members of the Democratic Leadership Council, a political organization whose members included Senators Al Gore and Chuck Robb, representatives Stephen Solarz and Les Aspin, and the then Arkansas Governor Bill Clinton. The DLC's official purpose was to pull the party back toward the political center after the leftward tilt of the 1970s.[92] While the DLC was more focused on domestic affairs, in foreign policy its members were more hawkish, conservative, pro-free trade, and pro-Israel than the average Democrat, and they tended to support tougher lines on Iraq. They particularly wanted to shed the Democrats' post-McGovern and post-Carter image of weakness on defense by embracing more active military interventionism.[93]

DLC member Les Aspin shifted many Democrats toward the administration's side through his position as the Chairman of the House Armed Services Committee, which published several reports declaring the low likelihood that sanctions would force Saddam out of Kuwait. Aspin thought that the United States would have to contain Iraq for years to come and that this task would be easier if the Kuwait crisis was resolved through force rather than diplomacy.[94] Since Democrats controlled both houses of Congress, these defections were crucial to the passage of the authorization to use force in January 1991. In the Senate, the vote was 52–47 in favor of authorization, with ten Democrats crossing the aisle. Eighty-six Democrats voted for the authorization in the

---

[90] See testimony of Phebe Marr: House Armed Services Committee, *Crisis in the Persian Gulf*, December 4, 1990, 24, 39; Efraim Karsh, "Myths about Hussein and Iraq," *New York Times*, August 13, 1990, A15.

[91] Efraim Karsh and Inari Rautsi, "Why Saddam Hussein Invaded Kuwait," *Survival* 33, no. 1 (January, 1991): 19, 29.

[92] Kenneth Baer, *Reinventing Democrats: The Politics of Liberalism from Reagan to Clinton* (Lawrence, KS: The University Press of Kansas, 2000), 36–93.

[93] Julian Zelizer, *Arsenal of Democracy: The Politics of National Security – From World War II to the War on Terrorism* (New York: Basic Books, 2010), 378–379.

[94] See the reports of the House Armed Services Committee under Les Aspin's name: House Armed Services Committee, *Crisis in the Persian Gulf*, January 8, 1991, 852–917.

House, enabling that resolution to pass by a more comfortable 250–183.[95]

Possibly the most significant Democrat who supported the war was Representative Stephen Solarz of New York. Solarz was a DLC member and staunch supporter of Israel who saw Saddam as an irrational tyrant on the brink of attaining nuclear weapons. He viewed the Gulf Crisis in stark moral terms, drawing the memory of World War II to conclude that "the great lesson of our time" is that "evil exists and when evil is on the march, it must be confronted."[96] He had advocated a policy of punishing Iraq since the chemical weapons attacks on the Kurds in 1988. He also warned Democrats against looking like the weaker party, writing: "The Democrats must ponder the political consequences of a reflexive refusal even to consider the use of force."[97]

Solarz and the neoconservative intellectual Richard Perle led the formation of the Committee for Peace and Security in the Gulf in the fall of 1990. This organization's main goal was to secure endorsements from a diverse mix of politicians and intellectuals to help convince the public and other Democrats to support Bush's policy. They particularly emphasized the need to destroy Saddam's ability to threaten Israel.[98] Janet Mullins, James Baker's assistant for legislative affairs, later declared that Solarz and this committee were "[t]he single greatest force to gather up the conservative Democrats who ended up voting with us in the House."[99]

The political debate throughout the Gulf Crisis centered on whether the United States should give sanctions more time to drive Saddam from Kuwait or shift to the use of force. The Democrats and other critics put forth a policy of sanctions and isolation to address both the short-term Kuwait problem and the long-term Iraqi threat. Bush and the Republicans countered that the United States could not indefinitely wait for sanctions to work and had to shift to the use of force. Although they diverged on how to tackle the Kuwait problem, these camps agreed

---

[95] "H. J. Res.77 (102nd): Authorization for Use of Military Force against Iraq Resolution," GovTrack.us, accessed March 16, 2017, www.govtrack.us/congress/votes/102-1991/h9.

[96] Stephen Solarz, *Journeys to War and Peace: A Congressional Memoir* (Waltham, MA: Brandeis University Press, 2011), 200.

[97] Stephen Solarz, "The Case for Intervention," in Cerf and Sifry, *The Gulf War Reader*, 282.

[98] Committee for Peace and Security in the Gulf, "Why We Are in the Gulf," December 10, 1990, OA/ID 03417-002, Kristen Gear Files, White House Office of Public Affairs, George Bush Presidential Library, 1–4.
    Same Box, Folder: Supportive Groups/Persian Gulf OA/ID 03417-002, Committee for Peace and Security in the Gulf, "Why We Are in the Gulf," December 10, 1990, 1–4.

[99] Janet Mullins, interview by Andrew Carpendale, September 28, 1993, MC 197, Box 173, Folder 6, James A. Baker III Papers at the Seeley G. Mudd Library, 6.

that Saddam needed to be weakened over the course of this conflict and then vigilantly contained in the aftermath.

Planning for Containment during Desert Storm: December to February 1991

President Bush made one last-ditch effort to avert war by sending James Baker to meet with Iraqi foreign minister Tariq Aziz on January 8, 1991. Bush expected the Iraqis to stonewall, but he believed that a final public effort at a nonviolent resolution would help rally domestic and international opinion to his side. Baker delivered a letter to Saddam through Aziz that communicated the coalition's insistence that Iraq fully comply with the Security Council's demands and that there would be no negotiation on any terms. The letter clarified that the coalition would use force to expel Iraq from Kuwait if the withdrawal did not start before January 15. Aziz called the letter an insult to a sovereign nation and refused to even take it back to Saddam.[100] On January 12, both houses of Congress voted to authorize the use of force to fulfill the Security Council resolutions. On January 15, the deadline set by Resolution 678 expired. The next day, Operation Desert Storm commenced with a massive bombing campaign against Iraq.

As the war began in the winter of 1991, the Bush administration expanded its thinking and planning for long-term policy on Iraq. In January 1991, the administration issued National Security Directive 54 (NSD-54), which set out objectives for the war and its aftermath. It identified the goals of the conflict as pushing Iraqi troops out of Kuwait, restoring Kuwait's government, and promoting "the security and the stability of the Persian Gulf."[101] The administration derived legal sanction for this last objective from Security Council Resolution 678's call for the restoring of "international peace and security in the area."[102]

NSD-54 then stated that "to achieve the above purposes" the United States would seek the destruction of Iraq's WMD programs, its "command, control, and communications capabilities," and the Republican Guard as "an effective fighting force."[103] The assault on these pillars of the Iraqi state aimed to liberate Kuwait and seek the postwar goal of

---

[100] Special to the *New York Times*, "Confrontation in the Gulf: Text of Letter from Bush to Hussein," *New York Times*, January 13, 1991, A1.

[101] "National Security Directive 54," George Bush Presidential Library and Museum Public Papers, accessed November 27, 2016, https://bush41library.tamu.edu/files/nsd/nsd54.pdf, 1.

[102] Cerf and Sifry, *The Gulf War Reader*, 156; Bob Kimmitt, interview by Andrew Carpendale, October 14, 1993, MC 197, Box 173, Folder 4, James A. Baker III Papers at the Seeley G. Mudd Library, 13.

[103] "NSD 54," Bush Library Public Papers, 2.

weakening and containing Iraq. In addition, NSD-54 defined the conditions under which the United States would pursue regime change. It would "become an explicit objective of the United States to replace the current leadership of Iraq" if Iraq used WMD, supported terrorist attacks on United States or coalition partners "anywhere in the world," or destroyed Kuwait's oil fields.[104]

As the United States planned for the aftermath of the war, top officials discussed how to build a containment regime under the legally sanctioned goal of restoring stability in the region. This goal would require eliminating Iraq's WMD programs and restraining its military strength. Richard Haass and Assistant Secretary of State Richard Clarke wrote that if the war did not destroy Iraq's WMD facilities, the United States had to demand access to those facilities after the war to render them inoperable.[105] Because this goal was not explicitly covered by the UN resolutions that authorized Desert Storm, the United States would have to seek a new resolution that would maintain sanctions until Iraq was disarmed. Moreover, US officials saw recreating the regional balance of power as essential for containing Iraq. In fact, Haass and others viewed the collapse of this balance at the end of the Iran–Iraq War as a precondition of Saddam's bid for regional supremacy.[106]

To achieve this regional balance, the United States would have to foster cooperation among the Gulf States and strengthen their militaries so that the United States would not have to play such a direct security role.[107] In addition, the United States needed to maintain the military capability to intervene rapidly in case of renewed aggression by Iran or Iraq. The Bush administration preferred to minimize the US presence in the postwar security system because of expense and the political pitfalls, both at home and in the region, of maintaining ground forces in the Gulf.[108] The pre-positioning of equipment, stationing of naval and air forces, and occasional joint exercises with the Gulf States would maintain the ability to respond to emergencies while limiting the US presence. Nevertheless,

---

[104] "NSD 54," Bush Library Public Papers, 3.
[105] Memorandum, Richard Haass to NSC Deputies, January 19, 1991, OA/ID CF 00946, National Security Council, Subject Files, Robert Gates Files, George Bush Presidential Library, 3; Memorandum, Richard Clarke to NSC Deputies, January 21, 1991, OA/ID CF 00946, National Security Council, Subject Files, Robert Gates Files, George Bush Presidential Library, 1; Memorandum, Richard Clarke to Reginald Bartholomew, September 20, 1990, Digital National Security Archive, Iraqgate, 1980–1994 Collection, 2–4.
[106] Working Paper, "Post-War Security Structures in the Gulf," Richard Haass, February 8, 1991, OA/ID CF 01584, National Security Council, Richard Haass Files, Working Files, George Bush Presidential Library.
[107] Memorandum, Richard Haass to NSC Deputies, January 25, 1991, 1, 3.
[108] Haass, "Post-War Security Structures in the Gulf," February 8, 1991, 1, 7; Alfonsi, *Circle in the Sand*, 148–150.

they acknowledged the need for an increased level of US involvement, or as Haass put it: "As the current crisis makes painfully clear, the era of keeping the Gulf at arm's length or managing its security on the cheap is over."[109]

As early as December 1990, the United States had announced that it would keep sanctions in place to enforce Iraqi disarmament after the resolution of the Kuwait crisis, whether it ended through war or voluntary withdrawal.[110] Policy staff in the State Department and NSC envisioned that the United States would seek a new Security Council resolution that would link the lifting of sanctions to progress in the disarmament of Iraq. Scowcroft and Haass recommended this approach throughout the winter of 1990–1991.[111] Haass spelled out the conditions for lifting sanctions:

We could also make clear what would be required from Iraq-Iraqi payment of reparations and signing of an Iraqi-Kuwait peace treaty, reductions in its conventional arms, pull-back of remaining arms away from the Kuwait border, elimination of chemical and biological arms, inspections of all nuclear facilities, and so on-in order for sanctions to be phased out.[112]

Richard Clarke echoed this thinking in counseling that the United States "develop a plan for a phased lifting of sanctions in response to Iraqi steps toward dismantlement of these programs."[113] Policy planners thus envisioned a flexible postwar policy in which Iraq, whether or not Saddam remained in charge, could earn the "gradual phase-out of sanctions" by disarming and cooperating with the United Nations, which would be taken as evidence of his changed intentions.[114] The United States would also have to convince the coalition that the destruction of Iraq's WMD and the limitation of its conventional strength were necessary for achieving postwar stability. Planners predicted that many members of the coalition would see this shift as "moving the goalposts" on victory in Iraq, which might cause difficulties in sustaining the coalition.[115] With this flexible approach, they

---

[109] Working Paper, "Post-Crisis Security Arrangements in the Gulf," Richard Haass, December 28, 1990, OA/ID CF 00946, National Security Council, Subject Files, Robert Gates Files, George Bush Presidential Library.

[110] "U.S. Said to Want Sanctions Kept after a Pullout," New York Times, December 14, 1990, A29.

[111] Memorandum, Brent Scowcroft to George Bush, February 25, 1991, OA/ID CF 01584-005, National Security Council, Richard Haass Files, Working Files, George Bush Presidential Library, 1.

[112] Haass, "Post-Crisis Security Arrangements in the Gulf," December 28, 1990, 3.

[113] Memorandum, Richard Clarke to NSC Deputies, January 21, 1991, 5, 8.

[114] Working Paper, "Arms Control after the War," Richard Haass, February 8, 1991, OA/ID CF 01584-006, National Security Council, Richard Haass Files, Working Files, George Bush Presidential Library, 3; Haass, War of Necessity, 142.

[115] Haass, "Post-Crisis Security Arrangements in the Gulf," December 28, 1990, 3; Memorandum, Richard Haass to NSC Deputies, January 19, 1991, 2.

argued that the United States could avoid rupturing the coalition with an overly punitive "Versailles"-style peace.[116]

As the administration planned for the war's aftermath, they reaffirmed the decision to not seek regime change directly. Top US officials recall no significant dissension on this point.[117] Their basic position on regime change was that Saddam's demise might be desirable if it made dealing with postwar Iraq easier but that it was irresponsible to pursue this goal directly. Officials repeatedly said the United States "would not weep" if Saddam fell from power but that this was not an objective.[118] The only way to guarantee this outcome seemed to be an occupation of some or all of Iraq, and Bush officials overwhelmingly rejected this option. They believed US troops would likely face guerrilla resistance from Baathist elements, what Robert Gates called "the Vietnam scenario."[119] Scowcroft summoned the ghost of another intractable war, Korea, to highlight the dangers of expanding objectives once the original set of goals had been achieved.[120] The military leadership echoed this concern, preferring the pursuit of limited, well-defined war aims over the nightmare of occupying Iraq.[121] Furthermore, there was no guarantee that the United States could actually capture Saddam Hussein, who could hide out in his labyrinthine security system. Scowcroft and Powell, for instance, recalled how difficult it was to capture Manuel Noriega in Panama during the previous winter, a leader of a smaller country with a weaker security apparatus.[122]

In addition, if the United States occupied Iraq, it would face the complex task of nation-building in a devastated society that Americans knew little about. In the meantime, the administration predicted that Arab public opinion would turn against the United States as imperial occupiers, fueling instability and extremism in the region.[123] Moreover, the administration had not prepared Congress, the public, or the coalition for a major expansion of war aims. The administration believed that invading Iraq would shatter the coalition and the domestic consensus around the conflict, undermining the goals of bolstering multilateralism and the United Nations as problem-solving mechanisms of the post–Cold War world.[124]

---

[116] Haass, "Arms Control after the War," February 8, 1991, 3.
[117] Haass, War of Necessity, 131.   [118] Baker, The Politics of Diplomacy, 408.
[119] Alfonsi, Circle in the Sand, 145.
[120] Bartholomew Sparrow, The Strategist: Brent Scowcroft and the Call of National Security (New York: Public Affairs, 2015), 415.
[121] Rick Atkinson, Crusade: The Untold Story of the Persian Gulf War (New York: Mariner Books, 1994), 299.
[122] Powell, interview by Frontline, 1995.
[123] Bush and Scowcroft, A World Transformed, 433, 464.
[124] Powell, interview by Frontline, 1995; Peter Cary, Brian Duffy, and Joseph Galloway, Triumph without Victory: The History of the Persian Gulf War (New York: Times Books, 1993), 142–143.

Another reason for the Bush administration's rejection of regime change was concern about the territorial integrity of Iraq and its place in the regional balance of power. The administration believed that a debilitated Saddam who nonetheless remained in power could preserve the political unity and territorial integrity of Iraq, albeit by brutal means. Many in the administration feared that if Saddam fell from power, his successors might not be able to keep the country intact, especially if restive Kurds and Shias launched rebellions. Scowcroft and Haass voiced this concern often, saying that Iraq could collapse without Saddam at the helm because no one else had his cult of personality and proven ability to sustain civil order.[125] The administration knew it would be hard to extract US forces from an Iraq mired in chaos, which made them doubt whether the demise of Saddam would really serve US interests.

A weakened but intact Saddam could also preserve enough Iraqi strength to balance Iranian power, a long-standing US objective in the region. If Iraq collapsed into civil war, it would be unable to check Iranian expansion. In addition, Iran would be poised to interfere in the conflict by backing Shia forces. As an NSC memo warned in January of 1991: "Political and military collapse could make Iraq vulnerable to the predatory ambitions of its immediate neighbors."[126] This contingency could bring about the ascension of a pro-Iranian Shia government in Iraq that would upend the regional balance of power, forcing the United States to protect allies like Saudi Arabia from a powerful and hostile Shia bloc. The CIA repeatedly warned that the Shia had threatened the stability of Iraq since the tribal revolts in the 1920s and that a Shia Iraqi government would probably align with Iranian policies.[127]

Moreover, Saudi Arabia, Kuwait, and other regional allies preferred a defanged Sunni regime, even one under Saddam, to the rise of a Shia-dominated Iraq. They wanted the Sunni to remain in charge of Iraq in order to stifle Shia political forces that might empower Iran and destabilize the Gulf States domestically. They encouraged Bush's tendency toward restraint on the regime change question.[128] The administration

---

[125] Minutes, National Security Council Meetings, August 3, 1990, OA/ID 01478, National Security Council, Richard Haass Files, Working Files, George Bush Presidential Library, 9; Working Paper, "Immediate Post-War Requirements," Richard Haass, January 21, 1991, OA/ID CF 01584-020, National Security Council, Richard Haass Files, Working Files, George Bush Presidential Library, 6.

[126] Haass, "Post-War Requirements," 8; Sparrow, *The Strategist*, 416.

[127] CIA Report: Political and Personality Handbook of Iraq, January 1991, CIA.gov, accessed February 6, 2017, www.cia.gov/library/readingroom/docs/DOC_0000227795.pdf, 2.

[128] US News and World Report, *Triumph without Victory: The Unreported History of the Persian Gulf War* (New York: Times Books, 1992), 395; Norman Friedman, *Desert Victory: The War for Kuwait* (Annapolis: Naval Institute Press, 1992), 58.

wanted Iraq to emerge from the crisis with enough strength to defend itself but not enough to threaten its neighbors, a balancing act they referred to as "Goldilocks outcome."[129] A cable from US Ambassador to Saudi Arabia Chas Freeman to Baker captured this approach, saying the United States should: "preserve its [Iraq's] capacity to defend itself in the post-crisis environment and thereby avoid the destabilizing vacuum of power in Iraq."[130]

Pessimism about Middle Eastern politics also contributed to the dread of becoming bogged down in Iraq. The Bush administration viewed Iraq and the entire Middle East as awash with religious and secular radicalism, ancient ethnic and religious conflicts, anti-Americanism, and political violence. All sides of the debate before Desert Storm shared the sense that the Middle East was a hostile, unstable place that the United States did not understand. James Schlesinger, an opponent of the war, told Congress that Saddam's overthrow would not address the deeper problem of the region: "The Middle East is quite unstable inherently. If Saddam Hussein were to be removed lock, stock, and barrel, the Middle East will not be stable."[131] Another opponent of the war, the liberal intellectual Arthur Schlesinger portrayed the region as "characterized from time immemorial by artificial borders, tribal antagonisms, religious fanaticisms, and desperate inequalities."[132] Martin Indyk, a supporter of Desert Storm who later served in the Clinton administration, reasoned that the United States should shape its policy with minimal regard for Arab public opinion because "[t]hey all hate us anyhow. I mean, they always did, they always will."[133] Most players in the Iraq debate concurred that the United States should remain distant from this strange, violent region, further dampening enthusiasm for regime change.

This skepticism toward the Arab world's potential for democracy enhanced the Bush administration's desire to avoid the nation-building project that regime change might require. A CIA handbook published just after Desert Storm described Iraqis as having a reputation among Arabs for being "self-confident and proud," "stubborn," "loath to

---

[129] Haass, *War of Necessity*, 126.

[130] Telegram, Chas Freeman to James Baker, December 15, 1990, OA/ID CF 08514-025, National Security Council, Richard Haass Files, Working Files, George Bush Presidential Library, 10.

[131] Senate Armed Services Committee, *Crisis in the Persian Gulf Region*, November 27, 1990, 135.

[132] Senate Committee on Foreign Relations, *U.S. Policy in the Persian Gulf*, December 4, 1990, 9.

[133] House Armed Services Committee, *Crisis in the Persian Gulf*, December 6, 1990, 242.

change their opinion," "suspicious," "conspiratorial," "brutal," and "persistent."[134] Back in February 1991, Haass wrote: "The prospects for democratization in the Arab world must be assessed as bleak."[135] To support this assessment, he later contended: "the lack of civil society, the lack of experience with democracy, the sectarian divisions, none of that suggested to me that Iraq was poised to become democratic if the lid was taken off."[136] US diplomat Edward Djerejian also described the chances of democracy in Iraq as "very improbable," pointing to obstacles like "the brutal repression of the regime" and "the lack of civil society."[137] Iraq historian Phebe Marr supported this reluctance to consider political transformation in Iraq, telling Congress: "Our knowledge to undertake social or political engineering – such as 'replacing Saddam' – is really extremely difficult. ... The fact that we would have a finger in a pie such as this is disturbing to me."[138]

The administration's enthusiasm for the demise of Saddam was further dampened by the belief that any successor who seized power, most likely a general, would have emerged from the same corrupted political culture as Saddam. Thus, he would most likely share Saddam's hatred of the United States, his Baathist ideology, and his expansionist goals for Iraq. For instance, a Defense Intelligence Agency (DIA) report suggested that any successor "would resume pursuit of weapons of mass destruction to support its ambitions" and be hostile to the United States, Israel, and the Gulf States.[139] As a high official in the Baathist system, he would also be implicated in human rights abuses.

Working with this kind of leader would create problems in domestic politics and lend an unsavory taste to the war's end. Powell and Scowcroft both doubted that any of Saddam's likely successors would be more reasonable, although they expected him to be weaker, which posed problems for Iraq's territorial integrity and the regional balance of power.[140] Powell mocked the idea that if Saddam fell "he would have necessarily been replaced by a Jeffersonian in some sort of desert democracy where people read *The Federalist Papers* along with the Koran."[141] The United States would demand that any successor to Saddam adhere to the

[134] Political and Personality Handbook of Iraq, January 1991, CIA.gov, 7.
[135] Paper, "The Middle East in the Post-War Period: Political Stability and Openness," Richard Haass, February 8, 1991, OA/ID 01584-003, National Security Council, Richard Haass Files, Working Files, George Bush Presidential Library, 2.
[136] Richard Haass, phone interview by Joseph Stieb, October 4, 2017.
[137] Edward Djerejian, phone interview by Joseph Stieb, October 20, 2017.
[138] Senate Armed Services Committee, *U.S. Policy Options and Implications*, November 29, 1990, 346.
[139] Alfonsi, *Circle in the Sand*, 156.   [140] Alfonsi, *Circle in the Sand*, 68.
[141] Powell, *My American Journey*, 513.

Security Council resolutions, but they had reason to doubt that Saddam's overthrow would ease the postwar management of Iraq enough to justify the risks of directly seeking regime change.

The expectation that Saddam would fall from power soon after the war further dissuaded Bush from seeking regime change directly. They struggled to imagine how Saddam could overcome an overwhelming military catastrophe on top of sanctions and the recent costs of war with Iran. For instance, Bush wrote in his diary on January 31:

> Seeing their troops and equipment getting destroyed, they've got to do something about it. ... It seems to me that the more suffering the people of Iraq go through, the more likely it is that somebody will stand up and do that which should have been done a long time ago-take the guy out of there.[142]

A DIA report from January 1991 likewise anticipated that military defeat of Iraqi forces would probably "lead to the fall of Saddam Hussein."[143] The expectation of Saddam's imminent demise also bolstered the administration's view that containment would suffice to fulfill US goals after the conflict. If Saddam was likely to be toppled, the United States could deal with a weaker successor who would need to end Iraq's isolation in order to survive at home, making him more likely to comply with the United Nations.

Nevertheless, most of the predictions that Saddam Hussein would be overthrown after the war were based not on hard evidence but on incredulity at the idea that Saddam could put his country through these catastrophes and not be overthrown. There was, in fact, little evidence from August 1990 to February 1991 that Saddam's grip on power was in jeopardy. Intelligence agencies and the State Department repeatedly noted that the opposition was weak and fragmented by ethnicity and ideology. Opposition groups also lacked a real presence in Iraq because of Saddam's effective security apparatus.[144] Over the previous two decades, Saddam had weeded out potential rivals with incredible severity and surrounded himself with dependent lackeys.[145] Moreover, the CIA reported in January that despite the damage inflicted by bombing and sanctions, "the regime appears fully in control. There have been no credible reports of unrest since the war began." This report noted that Saddam had put only his most loyal forces in

---

[142] Bush and Scowcroft, *A World Transformed*, 464; Haass, interview by Frontline, 1995.

[143] Alfonsi, *Circle in the Sand*, 156.

[144] Glenn Frankel, "Suppressed at Home and Dismissed Abroad: Prophetic Iraqi Opposition Considered Too Far-Flung, Fractious to Engineer Saddam's Overthrow," *Washington Post*, August 27, 1990, A13.

[145] On Saddam's methods of rule, see Efraim Karsh and Inari Rautsi, *Saddam Hussein: A Political Biography* (New York: Grove Press, 2002).

Baghdad, mostly from the Republican Guard, to reduce the chances of a coup or rebellion.[146]

The Bush administration steeled themselves for a messy, less than satisfying ending to Desert Storm. As Haass told Bush in January: "I don't think we're going to get our battleship Missouri here." On February 20, Bush expressed the central dilemma of the aftermath of the conflict: "Our goal is not the elimination of Saddam Hussein, yet in many ways it's the only answer in order to get a new start for Iraq in the family of nations."[147] Nevertheless, Bush dreaded the consequences of this removal occurring too precipitously, wanted to keep the United States out of Iraq, and did not see Saddam's ouster as a panacea for postwar problems. The ousting of Saddam thus remained a vague, qualified hope rather than a policy objective. The policy was to prepare a multilateral containment regime that would keep Iraq from threatening its neighbors and compel Saddam or his successor to comply with the United Nations, especially on the destruction of his WMD.

Regime Change Advocates during the Gulf Crisis

Most members of the political and policy establishments agreed with Bush that the best way to deal with Iraq beyond the crisis over Kuwait was to focus on enforcing the Security Council resolutions and weakening Saddam in the process. There were, however, some prominent figures, mostly conservatives and neoconservatives, who argued from the start of the crisis for the pursuit of regime change as a direct objective. Most major newspapers had at least one prominent writer who called for regime change, including A. M. Rosenthal and William Safire of the *New York Times*, Jim Hoagland and Charles Krauthammer of the *Washington Post*, and the editorial board of the *Wall Street Journal*.[148] The editors of the *National Review* called for regime change as an explicit policy goal, as did several prominent neoconservative intellectuals such as Richard Perle, Joshua Muravchik, Frank Gaffney, Laurie Mylroie, and Norman Podhoretz.[149] A fair number of Congressmen and Senators joined this

---

[146] CIA Report, Iraq: Domestic Impact of War, January 25, 1991, CIA.gov, accessed February 6, 2017, www.cia.gov/library/readingroom/document/iraq-domestic-impact-war, 1–2.

[147] Alfonsi, *Circle in the Sand*, 167.

[148] A. M. Rosenthal, "Making a Killer," *New York Times*, August 5, 1990, E19; Jim Hoagland, "Stopping Saddam's Drive for Dominance," *Washington Post*, August 5, 1990, D1; Charles Krauthammer, "It's Not Just Oil: If Saddam Hadn't Shot His Way into Kuwait, We Wouldn't be in Saudi Arabia," *Washington Post*, August 17, 1990, A27.

[149] Editorial, "Quick on the Draw," *National Review*, September 3, 1990, 11. Frank Gaffney, "Get It Over With," *New Republic*, December 10, 1990, 19–20.

crowd, including Alphonse D'Amato, Richard Lugar, William Dickinson, and Mark Sanford.[150]

Regime change advocates identified the same basic Saddam problem as the Bush administration, but they concluded that in order for the United States to achieve its goals in the region, Saddam absolutely had to be toppled. As Congressman Dickinson (R-AL) put it, "Achieving long-term stability in the region ultimately means removing Saddam Hussein and his power base, because Saddam Hussein is not a man capable of making fundamental changes in himself or his national policy goals."[151] This definition of victory meant that regime change should be a specific objective in the Gulf Crisis, not merely a by-product of the effort to liberate Kuwait.

The main reasons why early regime change advocates believed Saddam must be removed during the crisis were his WMD and ballistic missile programs as well as his record of aggression. They believed that even if this crisis ended with the liberation of Kuwait and the degrading of the Iraqi military, Saddam would eventually return to regional prominence with nuclear weapons, making his next act of aggression far harder to stop. Imagine, they argued, if Israel had not destroyed the Iraqi nuclear reactor at Osirak in 1981: the United States would be facing a nuclear-armed Iraq in the current crisis, maybe making the liberation of Kuwait impossible.[152] The only way to prevent a nuclear-armed Saddam from dominating the Gulf in a few years was to ensure that he did not survive the current crisis.[153] As William Safire concluded: "We must rid ourselves of Saddam Hussein before he achieves the means to rid himself of us."[154]

Another important difference between regime change advocates and the Bush administration centered on what kind of regime change each side would accept. Bush preferred a coup that would put a more pliable authoritarian in charge, fearing the pitfalls of pursuing deeper political transformation in Iraq. In contrast, most regime change advocates

[150] Alfonse D'Amato, "Yes, Hussein Must be Ousted," *New York Times*, August 24, 1990, A29; David Hoffman and Gwen Ifill, "Bush Wins Support on the Hill: Mideast Mission Has Lawmakers Anxious," *Washington Post*, August 29, 1990, A1.

[151] House Armed Services Committee, *Crisis in the Persian Gulf*, December 4, 1990, 6.

[152] Alfonse D'Amato, "Saddam Must be Ousted," *New York Times*, August 24, 1990.

[153] For representative regime change arguments, see Editorial, "The Stakes in the Gulf," *Wall Street Journal*, August 15, 1990, A8; Charles Krauthammer, "The Case for Destroying Saddam," *Washington Post*, November 25, 1990, C7; Joshua Muravchik, *Exporting Democracy: Fulfilling America's Destiny* (Washington, DC: AEI Press, 1991); Richard Perle, "In the Gulf, the Danger of a Diplomatic Solution," *Washington Post*, September 23, 1990, E21.

[154] William Safire, "The Phony War," *New York Times*, October 1, 1990, A21.

wanted not just to topple Saddam but also to root out the entire Baathist system and replace it with a democracy.

The concept of "the regime," especially Iraq as a totalitarian regime, played a crucial role in this maximalist desire, especially among neoconservatives and liberals. Within these traditions, the root source of a state's external behavior was the nature of its political system and ideology, or its regime. Different regime types affected both state behavior and the cultural and moral character of the population.[155] Democratic regimes that possessed mechanisms of accountability for their leaders and embraced liberal values were highly likely to act cooperatively rather than aggressively. In contrast, authoritarian and totalitarian regimes almost inevitably acted belligerently because their leaders embraced messianic, bellicose, or Manichean worldviews and were not accountable to the people or other branches of government. In addition, authoritarian and totalitarian regimes states often started wars to justify or distract from oppression at home.[156]

The idea of the United States as a champion of liberal democracy against the unique menace of totalitarianism had deep roots in its political culture, especially in liberal and neoconservative discourses. The political theorist David Ciepley treats totalitarianism as the "defining Other" of US political culture since the mid-twentieth century and a sort of photographic negative of whatever values and institutions are defined as "American."[157] While US scholars have contested the definition of totalitarianism since the term's inception, Ciepley contends that most Americans involved in this conversation define totalitarianism as "state control of both body and mind" or regimes that acknowledge no limit to their authority over politics, economics, social life, and thought.[158]

The concept of totalitarianism itself derives from the 1920s, but it first became popularized in the United States shortly after World War II. For thinkers like Arthur Schlesinger and the theologian Reinhold Niebuhr,

---

[155] Michael MacDonald, *Overreach: Delusions of Regime Change in Iraq* (Cambridge: Harvard University Press, 2014), 108–109; Tony Smith, *Why Wilson Matters: The Origin of American Liberal Internationalism and Its Crisis Today* (Princeton, NJ: Princeton University Press, 2017), 10.

[156] For overviews of neoconservative thought on the concept of the regime, see MacDonald, *Overreach*, 107–110; Gary Dorrien, *Imperial Designs: Neoconservatism and the New Pax Americana* (New York: Routledge, 2004), 120–121; Francis Fukuyama, *America at the Crossroads: Democracy, Power, and the Neoconservative Legacy* (New Haven: Yale University Press, 2006), 25–29.

[157] David Ciepley, *Liberalism in the Shadow of Totalitarianism* (Cambridge, MA: Harvard University Press, 2006), 1–2.

[158] Ciepley, *Shadow of Totalitarianism*, 2. For other influential theoretical treatments of totalitarianism, see Hannah Arendt, *The Origins of Totalitarianism* (New York: Schocken Books, 1951); Carl Friedrich and Zbigniew Brzezinski, *Totalitarian Dictatorship and Autocracy* (Cambridge, MA: Harvard University Press, 1956); Juan Linz, *Totalitarian and Authoritarian Regimes*, 2nd ed. (Boulder, CO: Rienner Publishers, 2000).

Nazi fascism and Soviet communism could be understood as two versions of a historically unique phenomenon of governments that sought total control over their populations.[159] Liberal groups like Schlesinger's Americans for Democratic Action (ADA) fervently backed the Cold War as a struggle to defend liberalism against Soviet totalitarianism. Influential novels like Arthur Koestler's *Darkness at Noon* and George Orwell's *1984*, widely read intellectual works by Carl Friedrich, Zbigniew Brzezinksi, and Hannah Arendt, and widespread usage by politicians including President Truman embedded totalitarianism into the US political lexicon. In the 1960s, the New Left increasingly criticized this idea as politically loaded, but it was revived by neoconservatives and some liberals in the late 1970s and 1980s as the Cold War reheated.[160]

Prominent among these was the political thinker Jeane Kirkpatrick, who served as Ronald Reagan's Ambassador to the United Nations from 1981 to 1985. In an influential 1979 essay for *Commentary* magazine, Kirkpatrick made a hard distinction between totalitarian and authoritarian regimes. Totalitarian regimes could be revolutionary theocracies like Iran or communist dictatorships like the USSR. They held in common the desire to bring about utopian transformations of politics, society, and ordinary life through the use of terror and mass reeducation. Totalitarian states sought to "cure the false consciousness" of their citizens and convert them into atomized, loyal ideologues. According to Kirkpatrick, they were also incapable of transforming themselves into more liberal, democratic states; they had to either collapse from within or be defeated from without. Authoritarian states like Iran under the Shah, in contrast, generally respect "habitual" ways of life, family relations, and religion, and they used violence mainly to stay in power rather than to revolutionize society. Citing Spain and Portugal as examples, Kirkpatrick held that because authoritarian regimes leave room for civil society, they are capable of evolving into democracies over time, unlike totalitarian states. The lesson for US foreign policy was that totalitarian states had to be uncompromisingly opposed while it was justifiable to work with authoritarian states.[161]

---

[159] Arthur Schlesinger, Jr., *The Vital Center: The Politics of Freedom*, 3rd ed. (New Brunswick, NJ: Transaction Publishers, 1998), 51–67; Reinhold Niebuhr, *The Children of Light and the Children of Darkness: A Vindication of Democracy and a Critique of Its Traditional Defense*, 2nd ed. (New York: Scribner, 1960).

[160] Abbott Gleason, *Totalitarianism: The Inner History of the Cold War* (New York: Oxford University Press, 1995), 35–42, 72–76, 129, 180–192. Sheila Fitzpatrick and Michael Geyer, eds., *Beyond Totalitarianism: Stalinism and Nazism Compared* (New York: Cambridge University Press, 2008), 3–8.

[161] Jeane Kirkpatrick, "Dictatorships and Double Standards," *Commentary*, November 1979, accessed January 17, 2019, www.commentarymagazine.com/articles/dictatorships-double-standards/.

Kirkpatrick's essay epitomized a deeper discourse among neoconservatives and many liberals in the 1970s and 1980s about regime type as a determinant of foreign policy behavior. Writers like Richard Perle, Irving Kristol, and Norman Podhoretz portrayed totalitarian states as uniquely, almost pathologically aggressive abroad and extreme at home. They employed these concepts in their criticism of détente by arguing that no compromise was possible with the totalitarian Soviet Union.[162] This discourse carried over into the Iraq debate in the 1990s. For Iraq to be labelled as totalitarian meant that it was ideologically fanatical and incapable of internally generated change. For regime change advocates, this meant that more hands-off strategies like containment could not address the heart of the problem: the regime. The framing of Iraq as totalitarian, moreover, appealed to a long-standing narrative of the United States as engaged in an ongoing struggle against totalitarianism, whether it came in the form of Nazi Germany, the Soviet Union, or modern "rogue states" like Iraq.

Regime change advocates also drew heavily on the work of Arab intellectuals like Kanan Makiya and Fouad Ajami about Arab political culture to support their case. Makiya had a particularly personal connection to the cause of regime change in Iraq. Born in Baghdad but trained as an architect at the Massachusetts Institute of Technology, Makiya published the book *Republic of Fear* in 1989 under the pseudonym "Samir al-Khalil" to protect his family members in Iraq from retaliation. This book denounced the Baathist regime as genocidal and totalitarian, and it surged in popularity after the Gulf Crisis began. During the 1990s, he published two books on Baathist crimes and helped create and translate an archive of documents on the regime at Harvard.[163] A secular Shia and self-described political "universalist," Makiya became a prominent liberal voice for the Iraqi National Congress, the lead exile opposition group, after the Gulf War, and he exerted enormous influence on the public discourse on Iraq up to the 2003 invasion.[164] Makiya strongly believed that the United States must help Iraqis topple Saddam, eradicate the Baathist regime, and enable democracy to take root. Containment, for

---

[162] John Ehrman, *The Rise of Neoconservatism: Intellectuals and Foreign Affairs: 1945–1994* (New Haven: Yale University Press, 1995), 115–116; Gleason, *Totalitarianism*, 190–193.

[163] Kanan Makiya, *Republic of Fear: The Politics of Modern Iraq*, 2nd ed. (Berkeley, CA: University of California Press, 1998); Kanan Makiya, *Cruelty and Silence: War, Tyranny, Uprising, and the Arab World* (New York: W. W. Norton, 1993).

[164] Dexter Filkins, "Regrets Only," *New York Times*, October 7, 2007, E52; George Packer, *The Assassins' Gate: America in Iraq* (New York: Farrar, Straus, and Giroux, 2005), 11–12, 68–74.

Makiya, was not merely ineffective but an immoral "realpolitik" that meant "accepting that there will always be a dictatorship" in Iraq.[165]

Makiya and Ajami argued that the core cause of Iraq's aggression was "the enormous, uncontrolled capacity for violence of the modern police state of Iraq," which they called "the warfare state." Iraqi politics, in Ajami's words, were defined by a swollen, totalitarian state at home, a cult of personality, self-delusion, utopian dreams, and extreme violence. Saddam was both a product and a producer of this milieu. The sickness of Iraqi politics reflected the "rotten" nature of a Middle Eastern world still under the sway of the false, dying hopes of Arab nationalism. In this political culture, force had become the ultima ratio of politics, and totalitarian ideologies had swallowed the rights of the minority and the individual. Ajami and Makiya pointed to the popularity of Saddam's invasion of Kuwait among many Arabs as evidence of the sickness of Arab politics, the enduring appeal of the strongman figure, and the desperation of the impoverished, humiliated Arab masses. Although they later changed this argument, they claimed during the Gulf Crisis that no "foreign savior" could pull the Arabs or the Iraqis from this morass. Nevertheless, they hoped that Saddam's fall might yield an improvement in Iraqi politics that would act, in Makiya's phrasing, as a "the fragile, razor-thin wedge of freedom" that could upend the authoritarian Arab order and empower democratic forces in the region.[166]

Within the frame of mind set by these ideas about regime type and political culture, the best and possibly sole way of eliminating the Iraqi threat was to transform its regime, which could not happen with Saddam or any other Baathist still in power. Regime change advocates in the United States echoed Ajami and Makiya's arguments to make the case that until its regime was transformed, Iraq would remain a source of trouble. Laurie Mylroie argued that Iraq needed push around its neighbors in order to justify domestic oppression and extort the wealth required to sustain authority at home.[167] The *New Republic* editors, major boosters of the Gulf War and regime change, saw Iraqi aggression as part of a deeper rot in Middle Eastern politics: "The distinctive aggression against

[165] Kanan Makiya, phone interview by author, November 1, 2017.

[166] Samir al-Khalil, "In the Mideast, Does Democracy Have a Chance?" *New York Times*, October 14, 1990, SM30; Fouad Ajami, "Into the Dangerous Twilight," *U.S. News and World Report*, March 11, 1991, 24; Fouad Ajami, *The Dream Palace of the Arabs: A Generation's Odyssey* (New York: Vintage Books, 1999), especially 169–171, and "The Summer of Arab Discontent," *Foreign Affairs* 69, no. 5 (Winter, 1990): 1–20; Makiya, *Cruelty and Silence*, 231–253.

[167] Judith Miller and Laurie Mylroie, *Saddam Hussein and the Crisis in the Gulf* (New York: Times Books, 1990), 53–54.

Kuwait is an expression of deep resentments in an Arab body politic that has never found a way to channel resentments into realistic hopes and reasonable programs."[168]

Regime change boosters identified democracy as the solution to this problem, which meant that the United States should seek to remove Saddam and the Baathist system. For example, columnist Flora Lewis of *The New York Times* argued that "a prerequisite for achieving the longer-range goal of a security balance in the region" entailed "ousting the regime and opening a chance for victims of one of the world's nastiest dictatorships to develop democratically."[169] A. M. Rosenthal reasoned that the United States should break the cycle of Arab violence and tyranny by implanting democracy in Iraq.[170] Many politicians and commentators recommended that Bush expand contacts with the Iraqi opposition to start building an alternative leadership.[171]

Furthermore, many regime change advocates believed the United States had to pursue regime change now because any attempt to contain Saddam after the crisis would be doomed from the start. Charles Krauthammer contended that the states surrounding Iraq were too weak and quarrelsome to rely on as part of a containment policy. The United States would have to take the lead in watching Saddam, which would require leaving a large force in the region.[172] Senator D'Amato and others argued that the United States could never get Saddam, an inveterate deal breaker, to commit to an arrangement that would destroy his WMD and limit his military.[173] Furthermore, regime change advocates noted that containment would rely on deterring Saddam from aggression, but they doubted that Saddam was rational enough to be deterred. For instance, William Safire argued: "A threat from us of massive retaliation is meaningless; a deterrent to a rational leader is an incentive to a martyr."[174] In keeping with the regime concept, advocates of this approach concluded that the United

[168] Editorial, "Tough Duty," *New Republic*, December 10, 1990, 9.

[169] Flora Lewis, "Eliminate Saddam Hussein: The Best Way to Long-Term Peace," *New York Times*, January 22, 1991, A23; Jim Hoagland, "Back Democracy in Iraq," *Washington Post*, February 26, 1991, A21.

[170] A. M. Rosenthal, "Neither God nor Infidel," *New York Times*, February 15, 1991, A35.

[171] Mark Sanford, Senate Committee on Foreign Relations, *U.S. Policy in the Persian Gulf*, December 5, 1990, 162; Flora Lewis, "Embolden Hussein's Opponents," *New York Times*, November 24, 1990, A21; Laurie Mylroie, "Post-War Issues: The Future of Iraq," Washington Institute for Near East Policy, Policy Watch Paper 71, February 27, 1991, accessed January 21, 2017, www.washingtoninstitute.org/policy-analysis/view/p ost-war-issues-the-future-of-iraq.

[172] Charles Krauthammer, "Why Containing Saddam Is Not Enough," *Washington Post*, September 7, 1990, A15.

[173] D'Amato, "Hussein Must be Ousted," *New York Times*, August 24 1990.

[174] Safire, "The Phony War," *New York Times*, October 1, 1990.

States could not devise a policy of constraints, threats, or incentives that would change Iraqi behavior. Iraq's actions stemmed inexorably from the nature of the Baathist regime and the psychology of its leader, and only uprooting that regime could address that core problem.

During the Gulf Crisis, regime change advocates rarely spelled out how the United States would achieve these ends. Among major media outlets, only the *Wall Street Journal* editorial board recommended that the United States "take Baghdad and install a MacArthur regency."[175] Neoconservative activist Frank Gaffney also went far beyond the norm in calling for the United States to start arming Shiites, Kurds, and disaffected military personnel in order to start an internal rebellion against the Baathists.[176] Nonetheless, even regime change advocates mostly shared Bush's reservations about involvement in internal Iraqi affairs and did not advocate anything close to an invasion. Richard Perle did not even like the idea of a ground war, preferring the less risky use of air power to undermine the regime.[177] Like these regime change boosters, the US public pined for grand outcomes in Iraq but did not identify clear ways of achieving these goals. A Gallup poll in August 1990 found that 73 percent of respondents thought that removing Saddam's government from power should be a coalition goal.[178] This outlook held steady throughout the crisis, as two polls in February 1991 found that 90 percent thought Saddam should be brought to trial at the conflict's end and 70 percent favored assassinating Saddam. Nevertheless, polling data also suggest that Americans did not want to occupy Iraq after the conflict.[179] Not until after Desert Storm, when Saddam appeared to be teetering on the brink of overthrow, did regime change advocates start to level a more effective argument against the Bush's policy in terms of how regime change could be achieved.

Conclusion

Regime change advocates during the Gulf Crisis contended that the real imperative was preventing a nuclear Iraq from dominating this vital region. Saddam's gamble of invading Kuwait gave the United States the

---

[175] Editorial, "Goals in the Gulf," *Wall Street Journal,* August 29, 1990, A10.

[176] Gaffney, "Get It Over With," *New Republic,* December 10, 1990, 19–20. For similar calls, see Mylroie, "The Future of Iraq," Washington Institute for Near East Policy, February 27, 1991; Krauthammer, "It's Not Just Oil," *Washington Post,* August 27, 1990.

[177] Senate Armed Services Committee, *Crisis in the Persian Gulf Region,* November 29, 1990, 374.

[178] Thomas, *American Public Opinion on the Iraq–Kuwait Crisis,* 5.

[179] Polling data from Freedman and Karsh, *The Gulf Conflict,* 412.

opportunity to eliminate him once and for all; that was the priority, not the liberation of Kuwait. In Krauthammer's phrasing: "Liberating Kuwait is the means. Defeating Saddam is the end."[180]

The *casus belli* of regime change advocates inverted Bush's thinking. Bush fought the war primarily to liberate Kuwait, prevent Saddam from controlling energy resources, and shape the post–Cold War international system in a positive manner. Bush also sought to degrade Saddam's strength in order to make him or his successor easier to contain after the war. However, his administration avoided pursuing this ancillary goal too openly or directly lest it jeopardize more important priorities, such as bolstering a multilateral approach to countering aggression or staying out of Middle Eastern politics. Unlike with regime change advocates, weakening Saddam was not the single priority but one of many goals that had to be balanced. Bush prepared to contain Iraq and enforce the writ of the United Nations regardless of who held the reins of power in Baghdad. The focus was, in Haass' words, on the "external behavior" of the Iraqi state rather than the "domestic trajectory" of Iraqi politics.[181]

The argument for regime change during the Gulf Crisis is nevertheless important to the broader story of Iraq policy in the later 1990s. Regime change advocates put forth the problem of the regime as a powerful argument against the administration's pursuit of limited ends during the conflict as well as their budding containment strategy. The Bush administration had not yet answered to itself or the nation whether Saddam, much less the Baathist system, had to be removed to satisfy US goals.

In a sense, this uncertainty inhered in the administration's realist approach to global politics. It aimed not to transform the politics of a region or a state but to restore balance and stability, sustain international cooperation, and minimize the expenditure of lives and resources. While it acknowledged the brutal nature of Iraq's regime, the enormous task of reconstituting a nation's political system, especially by force, was anathema to its worldview.[182] Nevertheless, to Bush's chagrin, the war itself and its messy aftermath would only bolster the suspicion that the root of Iraq's misbehavior was the regime itself, a problem that neither the toppling of any given leader nor a containment policy could resolve. The regime problem would form the heart of the argument against containment in the coming years.

---

[180] Charles Krauthammer, "Rush to Diplomacy: How to Disguise Defeat," *Washington Post*, January 4, 1991, A17.

[181] Richard Haass, interview by Joseph Stieb, October 4, 2017.

[182] Sparrow, *The Strategist*, 555–556; Alfonsi, *Circle in the Sand*, 68, 158–163.

The Fallout from Victory: Containment
and Its Critics, 1991–1992

Introduction

By mid-March 1991, an elderly woman named Daisy Lucas from
Martinsburg, West Virginia, wrote to her senators, Robert Byrd (D)
and Jay Rockefeller (D), with a message for President Bush about the
recently concluded war in the Persian Gulf. Lucas praised Bush's hand-
ling of the crisis but lamented that Bush had not toppled Saddam, saying:
"In fact, he should not be in power at all, kick his butt out. Let him suffer
like the Kuwaitis have suffered."[1] Representative Stephen Solarz
(D-MA), a staunch supporter of Desert Storm, had a similar experience.
Solarz had taught his four-year-old granddaughter Leah the name of
Saddam Hussein, and during a visit he asked her "And what did
Grandpa do to Saddam Hussein?" She replied, "You gave him
a spanking, but you should have thrown him in the trash can."[2] Bush
himself shared this feeling of an anticlimax, telling a press conference on
March 1: "I haven't yet felt this wonderfully euphoric feeling that many of
the American people feel. ... I feel much better about it today than I did
yesterday. But I think it's that I want to see an end."[3]

Americans across the political spectrum shared the mixed emotions of
Mrs. Lucas, Leah, and the president about a stunning military victory
with a messy political aftermath. Saddam Hussein's survival and his
crushing of Kurdish and Shia revolts in the spring of 1991 further contributed to a sense that Desert Storm was a missed opportunity to remove
a major threat to US regional interests. By April 1991, polls showed that

---

[1] Letter, Daisy Lucas to Robert Byrd and Jay Rockefeller, March 4, 1991, George Bush
Presidential Museum and Public Papers, accessed November 27, 2016, https://bush41li
brary.tamu.edu/files/persian-gulf/41-CO072-211871–225130/41-co072-222050.pdf.
[2] Stephen Solarz, *Journeys to War and Peace: A Congressional Memoir* (Waltham, MA:
Brandeis University Press, 2011), 202.
[3] George H. W. Bush, "The President's News Conference on the Persian Gulf Conflict,"
March 1, 1991, George Bush Presidential Library and Museum Public Papers, accessed
November 14, 2016, https://bush41library.tamu.edu/archives/public-papers/2755, 7.

55 percent of Americans thought that the United States should not have ended the war with Saddam still in power, a number that surged to 69 percent by June and 82 percent by January 1992.[4] There was wider backing for greater intervention on behalf of the rebels than Bush was willing to undertake, including 78 percent favoring attacking Iraqi helicopters that were fighting the rebels and 63 percent recommending arming the rebels.[5]

The events of the spring of 1991 tarnished the success of the Gulf War and added new momentum to those who believed the United States should directly pursue regime change in Iraq. During the Gulf Crisis, these critics held that Iraq would threaten regional stability as long as Saddam and the Baathists remained in power. The last stages of Desert Storm and the rebellions that followed offered these critics new opportunities to press the administration to take bolder action toward regime change. These opportunities included the ending of hostilities before coalition troops had fully surrounded Republican Guard units in Kuwait, the charitable ceasefire terms offered to the Iraqi military at the March 3 Safwan meeting, and the lack of support for the postwar rebellions. Bush's failure to seize these opportunities led to the breaking of the political coalition that had united behind the Gulf War. In early 1991, Democrats and neoconservatives, along with some Republicans, were blasting Bush's handling of the end of the war and his new policy of containment, which was installed under a pall of disappointment and anger in domestic politics. Combined with partisan recrimination about Iraq policy before the war, this firestorm of criticism pushed the president to seek tougher policies on Iraq and, in the longer term, biased the political discourse against restrained and flexible approaches.

As this maelstrom raged, Bush and the international coalition established a postwar policy on Iraq through a series of Security Council resolutions in early 1991. These resolutions formed the central mechanisms of containment for the next decade. In resolution 687, the Security Council stated that the sanctions on Iraq established in August 1990 would remain in place until Iraq completely destroyed all chemical, biological, and nuclear weapons, equipment, and materials as well as ballistic missiles with ranges over 150 km. Once Iraq had fulfilled these

---

[4] Richard Morin, "Majority in Poll Says U.S. Ended Attack on Iraq Prematurely," *Washington Post*, April 5, 1991, A14; Andrew Rosenthal, "Support for President Amid Some Questions: Poll Finds Strong War Support, but Some Erosion," *New York Times*, June 11, 1991, A1; "A Year after Desert Storm: What the War Didn't Resolve," *Washington Post*, January 12, 1992, C1.

[5] Morin, "Majority in Poll," *Washington Post*, April 5, 1991.

and several other obligations, the sanctions would be lifted and relations with Iraq would be progressively normalized.

Bush, however, took a decidedly different route by declaring in March 1991 that sanctions would remain in place until Saddam was out of power and Iraq had complied with the UN demands.[6] Shortly after Desert Storm, key Bush officials came to believe that the possibility of Saddam fully complying with the United Nations and becoming a nonthreatening actor was so unlikely that his removal would ultimately be necessary for recreating regional stability. The atmosphere of criticism and anger at home about how the war ended contributed to this policy shift.

For the remainder of Bush's presidency, containment was suspended between conflicting goals. The United States sought to contain Iraq and compel its compliance with the United Nations, but it also aimed to set the conditions to encourage a coup against Saddam. However, several factors restrained the more direct pursuit of regime change: the desire to avoid involvement in Iraqi politics, the fear of ethnic fragmentation, and the goal of maintaining the coalition's unity in order to enforce the Security Council resolutions. Bush's policy was stuck between domestic political demands to intensify action against Saddam and the calls of key allies to focus on compliance with the United Nations. The long-term effect of this tension was to open fissures within the international coalition that Saddam skillfully exploited.

As his domestic critics lamented, Bush never prioritized regime change within this web of conflicting goals. He focused on containing Saddam and enforcing the Security Council resolutions, in large part because he considered Saddam to be defanged for the moment. His administration sought regime change only insofar as it maintained the pressures that might foment a coup. As Saddam repeatedly challenged the inspections, Bush focused on preserving coalition unity and forcing Saddam into compliance rather than, as domestic critics demanded, using confrontations as pretexts to destabilize the Baathist regime. Bush continued to manage the Saddam problem, but numerous camps in US politics were shifting toward the consensus that this problem could not be managed indefinitely and that the United States needed to find a more permanent solution.

---

[6] George H. W. Bush, "The President's News Conference with Prime Minister Brian Mulroney of Canada in Ottawa," March 13, 1991, George Bush Presidential Library, accessed November 14, 2016, https://bush41library.tamu.edu/archives/public-papers/27 95%3cint_u%3e.

Ending Desert Storm

The wave of regret and second-guessing that followed Desert Storm gave rise to an enduring school of criticism of Bush's handling of the end of the conflict. These critics contend that Bush had established regime change as an unstated goal of the Gulf War but never developed a plan for how to, in scholar Thomas Mahnken's words, "translate a lopsided battlefield victory into a durable postwar settlement" with Saddam out of power.[7] Bernard Trainor and Michael Gordon similarly argue that there was an "absence of a clear political strategy for postwar Iraq."[8] These scholars argue that excessive caution and a lack of planning led the administration to miss opportunities to weaken or topple Saddam. They add that once it became clear that Saddam would survive the end of the war, Bush cobbled together a flawed containment policy.[9] This school of thought can be described as the "Triumph without Victory" thesis, after a book that *US News and World Report* published on conflict in 1992.

One major argument with in this thesis is that its proponents mistakenly attribute a policy objective to the Bush administration that it did not endorse during the crisis. Regime change had been a tentative hope, not a hidden objective of the Gulf War. US policy had focused on enforcing the Security Council resolutions, keeping the coalition intact, and weakening the Iraqi military. The second problem with this thesis is that the Bush administration in fact had a plan for how to move from war's end to an acceptable postwar settlement. The plan was to install a containment system on an enfeebled Iraq that would remove its WMD capabilities and maintain its military and economic weakness. Following this strategy, the administration simply was not in the mindset to maximize every feasible way of exerting pressure on the Iraqi state, such as destroying as many

---

[7] Thomas Mahnken, "A Squandered Opportunity," in *The Gulf War of 1991 Reconsidered*, ed. Andrew Bacevich and Efraim Inbar (Portland, OR: Frank Cass, 2003), 122.

[8] Michael Gordon and Bernard Trainor, *The Generals' War: The Inside Story of the Conflict in the Gulf* (Boston: Little, Brown, and Company, 1995), 476.

[9] For scholarly variations of this argument, see Robert Divine, "The Persian Gulf War Revisited: Tactical Victory, Strategic Failure," *Diplomatic History* 24, no. 1 (Winter, 2000): 129–138; Mahnken, "A Squandered Opportunity," 121–148; Gideon Rose, *How Wars End: Why We Always Fight the Last Battle: A History of American Intervention from World War I to Afghanistan* (New York: Simon & Schuster, 2010), 226, 230, 234; Christian Alfonsi, *Circle in the Sand: Why We Went Back to Iraq* (New York: Doubleday, 2006), 173, 188, 191; Kenneth Pollack, *The Threatening Storm: The Case for Invading Iraq* (New York: Random House, 2002), 52–53; Gordon and Trainor, *The Generals' War*, 461, 473; Steven Hurst, *The United States and Iraq since 1979: Hegemony, Oil, and War* (Edinburgh: University of Edinburgh Press, 2009), 105; Peter Cary, Brian Duffy, and Joseph Galloway, *Triumph without Victory: The History of the Persian Gulf War* (New York: Times Books, 1993), 400; Paul Wolfowitz, "Victory Came Too Easily: Review of Rick Atkinson," *The National Interest*, April 1, 1994, 87–92.

military units as possible, occupying Iraqi territory to weaken the regime, or supplying arms to the rebels. The United States planned to impose containment on Iraq after the war regardless of who was in power, so it perceived no need take these risky, maximalist actions.

The United States launched the Desert Storm ground campaign on February 24, 1991. This was preceded by more than a month of intensive coalition air assaults on both deployed Iraqi units and key pillars of the Baathist regime, including communications facilities, supply lines, WMD and ballistic missile sites, the civilian telephone and water systems, and oil production sites.[10] The ground offensive commenced with a Marine thrust into Kuwait from the south, which succeeded almost instantly. Iraqi troops fled Kuwait City on February 26, and Saddam ordered a retreat from Kuwait the next day. Nevertheless, the rapid success of the initial assault into Kuwait created a problem for the coalition's original plan to encircle and destroy the Republican Guard units in the Kuwaiti theater of operations (KTO). Although they suffered heavy damage, the allied assault had pushed these units into Iraq rather than fixing them in place for the flanking strike from US forces positioned in the desert west of Kuwait.[11] At 2100 hours in Riyadh, CENTCOM Commander Norman Schwarzkopf announced that the United States had achieved its mission of liberating Kuwait. Nevertheless, it was still uncertain whether the United States had demolished these Republican Guard forces, which were crucial pillars of the Baathist regime's ability to maintain power at home.[12]

After Schwarzkopf's announcement, President Bush held a Cabinet meeting to determine whether to end hostilities in Iraq. Powell told the Cabinet that at this point the United States had achieved its objectives by liberating Kuwait and degrading Iraqi military power. He emphasized that there were virtually no coherent Iraqi units left in the KTO. Bush, Cheney, and Scowcroft agreed, but Bush asked Powell to call Schwarzkopf and confirm that hostilities could be ended. In a phone call on February 27, Schwarzkopf confirmed that the Republican Guard was surrounded and asked for another day to finish off these units. Powell relayed this request back to Bush, but the Bush Cabinet decided to end

---

[10] Norman Friedman, *Desert Victory: The War for Kuwait* (Annapolis: Naval Institute Press, 1992), 180–183; John Olsen, *John Warden and the Renaissance of American Air Power* (Washington, DC: Potomac Books, 2007), 108–112, 146–151; Richard Reynolds, *Heart of the Storm: The Genesis of the Air Campaign against Iraq* (Maxwell Air Force Base, AL: Air University Press, 1995), 16–19.

[11] For early military histories of the Persian Gulf War, see Gordon and Trainor, *The Generals' War*; Rick Atkinson, *Crusade: The Untold Story of the Persian Gulf War* (Boston: Houghton Mifflin, 1993); Cary, Duffy, and Galloway, *Triumph without Victory.*

[12] Atkinson, *Crusade*, 471.

the war at the 100-hour mark on February 28, almost a day short of Schwarzkopf's request.[13]

Bush did this because of concerns that coalition forces were slaughtering too many Iraqis and because the coalition had achieved its main objectives. Powell called Schwarzkopf back to relay this decision and see if he had any reservations. Despite some of his later comments, Schwarzkopf agreed that they had achieved their objectives, including the degrading of Iraqi military capabilities.[14] However, soon after the unilateral ceasefire declaration on February 28, it became clear that the US military had overestimated the level of damage to the Republican Guard. About half of the Republican Guard troops and armor in the KTO had escaped to Iraq, including roughly 800 tanks and 1,400 armored personnel carriers.[15]

During the last hours of the ground war, the Bush administration was increasingly aware that American forces were inflicting massive losses on the retreating Iraqis, especially on the so-called Highway of Death between Kuwait City and Basra. Top Bush officials felt that continuing this carnage was unethical and ignoble and they feared it would tarnish the public's view of the victory. Moreover, Arab allies like Saudi Arabia and Egypt were pressuring Bush to end the fighting soon because the mass destruction of Iraqi forces was unpopular with their populations.[16] As Scowcroft later said, "I think it was stopped when it was stopped because we believed that we had achieved our objectives and that to continue the war would have been an unnecessary slaughter."[17] The broadly shared belief that Saddam would fall from power after the war further bolstered this perception.[18]

---

[13] Atkinson, *Crusade*, 471–476; Richard Cheney, interview by Frontline, PBS, 1995, accessed January 25, 2017, www.pbs.org/wgbh/pages/frontline/gulf/oral/cheney/1.html; Colin Powell, *My American Journey* (New York: Random House, 1995), 505–506; William Allison, *The Gulf War, 1990–1991* (New York: Palgrave Macmillan, 2012), 139–142.

[14] Powell, *My American Journey*, 509. Norman Schwarzkopf, *It Doesn't Take a Hero: The Autobiography of General H. Norman Schwarzkopf* (New York: Bantam Books, 1992), 470–471.

[15] Atkinson, *Crusade*, 476; Gordon and Trainor, *The Generals' War*, x; Joseph Galloway and Brian Duffy, "A Desert Storm Accounting," *US News and World Report*, March 16, 1992, 35.

[16] James Baker, *The Politics of Diplomacy: Revolution, War, and Peace 1989–1992* (New York: G. P. Putnam's Sons, 1995), 436; Atkinson, *Crusade*, 453; Gordon and Trainor, *The Generals' War*, 416; Cary, Duffy, and Galloway, *Triumph without Victory*, 395.

[17] Brent Scowcroft, interview by Frontline, PBS, 1995, accessed January 25, 2017, www.pbs.org/wgbh/pages/frontline/gulf/oral/scowcroft/1.html; Powell, *My American Journey*, 505.

[18] Andrew Rosenthal, "U.S. Expecting Hussein to Be Out by Year's End," *New York Times*, March 18, 1991, A8.

Once the fighting ended on February 28, the United States needed a ceasefire agreement with the Iraqi government to transition to a postwar settlement. On March 1, Schwarzkopf met with two Iraqi generals at Safwan, a town in southeastern Iraq near the Kuwaiti border. Bush had sent him little instruction for the meeting beyond strictly military issues such as separating Iraqi and coalition forces. Throughout Desert Storm, Bush had tried to avoid micromanaging the generals' conduct of the war, and he viewed the ceasefire negotiations as the military's domain. Schwarzkopf therefore offered terms so lenient they surprised the Iraqi generals. After agreeing on a buffer zone between their forces, Schwarzkopf demanded that Iraq ground all planes in order to avoid further conflict or confusion in the air. The Iraqi generals then requested the United States allow them to fly helicopters to ferry officials from place to place given the extensive damage to Iraq's infrastructure. Schwarzkopf, in a spirit of chivalrous magnanimity, agreed to this request, even allowing Iraqi officials to fly armed helicopters for this purpose. Finally, Schwarzkopf reassured the Iraqi generals that the United States had no intention of occupying southern Iraq and would withdraw its soldiers as quickly as possible.[19]

Many critics of Bush's handling of the war's ending have pointed to Safwan as another missed opportunities to humiliate and destabilize the Iraqi government. US forces at the time occupied large parts of southern Iraq, including key oil fields. Some have suggested that Bush should have demanded that Saddam himself appear at Safwan to accept the surrender terms in order to debase the dictator and inspire a coup.[20] Still more critics have argued that the United States should have preserved strategic uncertainty about its willingness to march to Baghdad in the hope of prompting Iraqi generals to move against Saddam. Indeed, both Scowcroft and Undersecretary of Defense for Policy Paul Wolfowitz thought that the concession on helicopters was too indulgent and would allow the Baathist regime to remain in power.[21]

Detractors of the Safwan agreement saw the lack of direction from Bush to Schwarzkopf as evidence that Bush lacked a plan to translate military victory into political success. However, this criticism misreads the administration's priorities and its approach to the end of the war. The

---

[19] Gordon and Trainor, *The Generals' War*, 444–447.

[20] Gordon and Trainor, *The Generals' War*, 444; Alfonsi, *Circle in the Sand*, 186–187; Mahnken, "Squandered Opportunity," 138, 142; Wolfowitz, "Victory Came Too Easily," *The National Interest*, April 1, 1994, 91–92. Charles Freedman, interview by Charles Stewart Kennedy, Association for Diplomatic Studies and Training Foreign Affairs Oral History Project, Library of Congress, April 14, 1995, 459; Mahnken, "Squandered Opportunity," 142.

[21] Gordon and Trainor, *The Generals' War*, 448; Scowcroft, interview by Frontline, 1995.

Bush Cabinet did discuss whether to demand that Saddam appear at Safwan to surrender, but they determined that if Saddam refused, the United States would face the unpleasant choice of backing down and empowering Saddam or resuming fighting. Resuming hostilities, however, would expand the coalition's war aims from liberating Kuwait to forcing Saddam into a symbolic surrender at greater cost to both sides. The administration further reasoned that the renewal of hostilities would sink US forces deeper into Iraq while alienating the coalition, most of which viewed the conflict's main objectives as completed.[22]

On a deeper level, Bush's failure to push for harsher terms at Safwan cohered with the plan for containing Iraq, which prioritized disarmament, coalition unity, and the withdrawal of US forces. Bush had only ever sought regime change as a by-product of the Gulf War, and he saw any direct moves toward regime change as hazardous and unnecessary.[23] Moreover, because it did not believe Saddam's immediate ouster was necessary for the United States to achieve its goals in the region, the administration did not seize every opportunity to maximize the likelihood that Saddam would fall, such as grounding Iraqi helicopters. Far from lacking a plan to terminate the war, the administration planned to quickly extract US forces, preserve Iraq's territorial integrity, and maintain the coalition as a foundation of containment.

Installing Containment: March–June 1991

In spring and early summer of 1991, the challenges facing US Iraq policy metastasized as the Bush administration attempted to establish a containment policy in the midst of chaos and rebellion in Iraq. The Bush administration installed containment through a series of Security Council resolutions that imposed demands on Iraq while using sanctions to ensure compliance. At the same time, it established a policy of indirect regime change through economic pressure and signals to the Iraqi

---

[22] George H. W. Bush and Brent Scowcroft, *A World Transformed* (New York: Knopf, 1998), 489–490; Baker, *The Politics of Diplomacy*, 409–410. One exception to the belief that the conflict was successfully concluded came from Turkey's President, Turgut Ozal, who pressed for additional steps, like the coalition seizure of Basra, to try to topple Saddam. See Memorandum of Telephone Conversation, George H. W. Bush and Turgut Ozal, February 26, 1991, George H. W. Bush Presidential Library, accessed September 7, 2020, https://bush41library.tamu.edu/files/memcons-telcons/1991–02-2 6–Ozal.pdf; Memorandum of Telephone Conversation, George H. W. Bush and Turgut Ozal, April 20, 1991, George H. W. Bush Presidential Library, accessed September 7, 2020, https://bush41library.tamu.edu/files/memcons-telcons/1991–04-2 0–Ozal.pdf.

[23] Haass, "Post-Crisis Security Arrangements in the Gulf," December 28, 1990, 3; Memorandum, Richard Haass to NSC Deputies, January 19, 1991, 2.

military that Saddam's removal would lead to the easing of sanctions. This restrained policy, however, was challenged by the unexpected Kurdish and Shia rebellions of March 1991. Bush decided to not support these rebellions, but growing domestic criticism and the near-genocidal Iraqi assault on Kurdish civilians led the United States and its allies to establish an NFZ and a humanitarian effort in Northern Iraq. As the administration struggled to contain Iraq, avoid more entanglements, and placate domestic critics, it gravitated to the position that Saddam would have to be removed to achieve stability in the region.

After the Safwan accords, top Bush administration officials examined how to move from the ceasefire terms to a postwar settlement that would lay the groundwork for containment and disarmament. Richard Haass at the NSC wrote that the United States should demand the destruction of Iraqi WMD and ballistic missile programs, Iraqi recognition of the border with Kuwait, a system for compensating Kuwaitis, and Iraqi acceptance of peacekeepers on the border. In Haass' formulation, sanctions would remain in place until Saddam or another Iraqi leader fulfilled these terms. However, he noted that this approach would "remove much of our leverage to see that Saddam is removed." He therefore proposed a strategy in which the United States would state that certain sanctions, such as the ban on oil exports, would be lifted only when Saddam was out of power. He also suggested communicating to Iraqi generals that "we would be willing to waive some compensation claims or be more relaxed toward prosecuting war crimes if there were a leadership change."[24] Undersecretary of State Robert Kimmitt echoed this approach, writing on February 24 that if Saddam survived the war, "we would be much slower in lifting the oil export limitations in the trade embargo, because we want to deny Saddam the means to rearm."[25]

This strategy targeted Baathist elites with a mix of pressures and incentives to encourage a coup against Saddam, although Haass and Kimmitt warned against direct measures to take Saddam down. Bush communicated this concept in a press conference in July 1991: "If the military talked him into stepping aside and getting out of there, I'd give them a real break as far as US policy goes."[26] This method of "turning the screw," as Haass later described it, formed a baseline approach of indirect

---

[24] Memorandum, from Richard Haass to Brent Scowcroft, March 7, 1991, OA/ID CF01585-018, National Security Council, Richard Haass Files, Working Files, George Bush Presidential Library, 2.

[25] Notes used in conjunction w/2/24/91 appearance on "This Week w/David Brinkley," James Baker, February 24, 1991, MC 197, Box 109, Folder 10, James A. Baker III Papers at the Seeley G. Mudd Library.

[26] Barton Gellman, "U.S. Officials Reiterate Possibility of Attack on Iraq over Arms Issue," *Washington Post*, August 3, 1991, A16.

regime change on which the administration would theoretically add new pressures and incentives throughout the next two years.[27]

The United States and its allies established a postwar settlement on April 3, 1991, with the passage of Security Council Resolution 687. This resolution issued demands that Iraq had to satisfy to have the sanctions removed. They included the revelation and destruction of all WMD and ballistic missile programs, reparations payments for Kuwait, the recognition of the Kuwaiti border, peacekeepers along the border, and the return of Kuwaiti nationals. To supervise the destruction of WMD, Resolution 687 established the United Nations Special Commission (UNSCOM), an international team of weapons experts given unconditional authority for the "immediate on-site inspection" of Iraqi weapons programs.[28] The International Atomic Energy Agency (IAEA), in turn, would supervise the destruction of Iraqi nuclear sites. Resolution 687 put the impetus on Iraq to reveal all of its weapons programs, which the inspectors would document and destroy. Once the inspectors were satisfied, Resolution 687 permitted the lifting of sanctions after a Security Council vote. To make sure Iraq did not rebuild its WMD programs, this resolution established UNSCOM as a long-term monitoring and verification agency.[29]

Immediately following Desert Storm, Bush administration officials made a series of statements that the United States would neither lift sanctions nor normalize relations with Iraq while Saddam was still in power. On March 13, 1991, Bush told reporters it would be "impossible to have normalized relations with Iraq while Saddam is in there. . . . [I]t is hard to see how an Iraq with him at the helm can rejoin the family of peace-loving nations."[30] Bush repeated this policy again on April 26 as he discussed how to address the Kurdish humanitarian disaster, saying: "[T]here will not be normal relations with this man as long as I'm President of the United States."[31] Again in May he said: "My view is we don't want to lift these sanctions as long as Saddam Hussein is in power."[32] This became a common refrain from administration officials

---

[27] Memorandum, Richard Haass to Brent Scowcroft, May 24, 1991, OA/ID CF01585, National Security Council, Richard Haass Files, Working Files, George Bush Presidential Library, 1.

[28] Cary, Duffy, and Galloway, *Triumph without Victory*, 432–434.

[29] Cary, Duffy, and Galloway, *Triumph without Victory*, 434.

[30] George H. W. Bush, "The President's News Conference with Prime Minister Brian Mulroney of Canada in Ottawa," March 13, 1991, George Bush Presidential Library, accessed November 14, 2016, https://bush41library.tamu.edu/archives/public-papers/2795.

[31] Andrew Rosenthal, "Once Kurds Are Safe, U.S. Will Leave Iraq, Bush Says," *New York Times*, April 27, 1991, 4.

[32] Patrick Tyler, "Bush Links End of Trading Ban to Hussein Exit," *New York Times*, May 29, 1991, A1.

for the remainder of his presidency.[33] This position, of course, assumed that Saddam was not likely to survive for long under economic and diplomatic isolation.[34]

This stance against normalization contrasted with the administration's plans during the Gulf Crisis to permit the reintegration of Iraq, whether Saddam remained in power or not, into the family of nations once it complied with the UN demands. However, throughout this period many Bush officials, including the President, doubted that Saddam would ever cease his crusade to dominate the Gulf and cooperate with US demands. Saddam's actions during Desert Storm and its aftermath, including the lobbing of missiles at Israel, the enormous environmental damage caused by the destruction of oil wells in Kuwait, and his brutal crushing of the postwar rebellions, pushed the administration toward rejecting normalization with a Saddam-led Iraq. Bush made this point to German foreign minister Hans Dietrich Genscher on March 1: "How can we negotiate with Iraq as long as he is there? With all of the atrocities and the damage he has done to the environment, it will be impossible for us to do anything constructive with Iraq as long as he is there."[35] Bush put the point even more starkly to Turkish Prime Minister Turgat Ozal, saying: "We have got to get him out. He cannot remain." Nevertheless, Bush agonized over lacking a clear means to remove Saddam, telling Ozal: "We have no interest in dismembering Iraq or getting involved in civil war."[36]

Despite these declarations against normalization, containment remained Bush's priority in the spring and summer of 1991. The Bush team recognized the tension between opposing normalization, creating conditions for a coup, and ensuring Iraqi weakness and compliance with the United Nations. Bush, Baker, and others reasoned that sanctions and inspections were the best way to "put Saddam Hussein in that cage" where he could not recover and threaten regional stability.[37] Neither of these tools of containment would be feasible without full the cooperation of the allies, who needed to eschew trade with Iraq while backing intrusive weapons inspections. Many members of the sanctioning coalition,

---

[33] See other statements by CIA Director Robert Gates in Tyler, "Bush Links End of Trading Ban," *New York Times,* May 7, 1991.

[34] Alfonsi, *Circle in the Sand,* 236.

[35] Memorandum of Conversation, Hans-Dietrich Genscher and George Bush, March 1, 1991, OA/ID 91108–005, Brent Scowcroft Collection, Presidential Correspondence Files, Presidential Memcons Files, George Bush Presidential Library. See similar thoughts by Scowcroft: Bush and Scowcroft, *A World Transformed,* 471.

[36] Memorandum of Telephone Conversation, George H. W. Bush and Turgut Ozal, April 20, 1991, George H. W. Bush Presidential Library, accessed April 26, 2020, https://bush41library.tamu.edu/files/memcons-telcons/1991–04-20–Ozal.pdf.

[37] Baker, *Politics of Diplomacy,* 441.

including France, Russia, and China, saw the purpose of sanctions strictly in terms of compelling Iraqi compliance, and they intended to renew relations with Saddam if he acquiesced to the UN's terms.[38] Javier Perez de Cuellar, the UN Secretary-General, illustrated this viewpoint: "If the objective of pursuing sanctions is to topple the Iraqi regime, then I do not agree."[39]

Top US officials recognized the lack of international support for regime change as a major constraint on Iraq policy. They repeatedly stressed that the primary function of sanctions was to compel Iraq to satisfy Resolution 687.[40] Keeping the focus on containment also bolstered the broader goal of sustaining a New World Order where challenges to international security were addressed through multilateral institutions.[41] Baker probably came closest to clearly delineating US priorities on April 17, 1991: "We must do all we can to continue to quarantine and ostracize the Saddam regime. That means we must never normalize relations with an Iraqi government controlled by Saddam. And it means that UN sanctions must not be relaxed so long as Saddam is in power."[42]

Despite its plans for containment, the Bush administration was blindsided by the eruption of Shia and Kurdish rebellions in March 1991. These uprisings stemmed from deep resentment of Sunni Baathist oppression of these sectarian groups as well as the devastation of the war and sanctions. Returning soldiers sparked the revolt in the south by attacking government forces and buildings in Basra. Although Iranian-aligned groups contributed to the revolt, most rebels lacked meaningful connection to foreign nations. The southern rebellion was concentrated in the cities and featured brutal street fighting and terrible atrocities by both sides.[43]

Bush came under heavy criticism in the spring of 1991 and afterward for failing to help the rebels even after making several calls for the Iraqi people to revolt against Saddam. The clearest exhortation came during Desert Storm on February 15 when Bush told an audience in Massachusetts: "And there's another way for the bloodshed to stop, and that is for the Iraqi military and the Iraqi people to take matters into their

---

[38] Sarah Graham-Brown, *Sanctioning Saddam: The Politics of Intervention in Iraq* (New York: I. B. Tauris, 1999), 59–60.

[39] Lawrence Freedman and Efraim Karsh, *The Gulf Conflict, 1990–1991: Diplomacy and War in the New World Order* (Princeton, NJ: Princeton University Press, 1993), 416.

[40] Richard Haass, *War of Necessity, War of Choice: A Memoir of Two Iraq Wars* (New York, Simon & Schuster, 2009), 142.

[41] Pollack, *The Threatening Storm*, 212.

[42] Notes from April 17, 1991, EC Ministerial Working Dinner, James Baker, April 17, 1991, MC 197, Box 110, Folder 2, James A. Baker III Papers at the Seeley G. Mudd Library.

[43] Phebe Marr, *The Modern History of Iraq* (Boulder, CO: Westview Press, 2012), 241–245.

own hands and force Saddam Hussein, the dictator, to step aside, and then comply with the United Nations resolutions and rejoin the family of peace-loving nations."[44] Bush later said that he made this statement "impulsively" and that he did not intend to encourage the Iraqi people to revolt. Rather, he aimed to signal to the Iraqi military that if they overthrew Saddam and complied with the United Nations' demands, the war would be halted and the sanctions eventually removed.[45]

As controversial as this call for rebellion later became, it largely aligned with administration policy before and after February 1991. On August 11, 1990, Bush said to reporters: "I hope that the Iraqi people do something about it so that their leader will live by the norms of international behavior that will be acceptable to other nations."[46] When Baker saw a transcript of Bush's remarks in Massachusetts, he simply noted in the text: "Statement of fact."[47] Baker meant that since August 1990, US policy had always treated a coup as a way to resolve the crisis. That did not mean, in the administration's view, that the United States was encouraging a massive revolt or promising aid to coup plotters or rebels. The disjunction occurred in its public language rather than in its strategic thinking.

For a brief period in March, it appeared that Saddam's regime was in severe jeopardy, as the rebels may have controlled large parts of fourteen of Iraq's eighteen provinces.[48] The rebellions created a major dilemma for the Bush team, which wanted Saddam to fall but intended to remain out of Iraqi politics. The administration decided against supporting the rebels for several reasons. First, the top officials did not think that the rebels would succeed. A CIA report in mid-March concluded that unless uprisings occurred in the Sunni-dominated core of the country around Baghdad or in the military, Saddam would manage to defeat the rebels.[49]

---

[44] George H. W. Bush, "Remarks to Raytheon Missile Systems Plant Employees in Andover, Massachusetts," February 15, 1991, George Bush Presidential Library, accessed November 14, 2016, https://bush41library.tamu.edu/archives/public-papers /2711.

[45] Bush and Scowcroft, *A World Transformed*, 472.

[46] "Confrontation in the Gulf: Excepts from Statements by Bush on Strategy in the Gulf," *New York Times*, August 12, 1990. For similar statements, see Cheney and Baker testimonies in Senate Armed Services Committee, *Crisis in the Persian Gulf Region*, September 11, 1990, 13; House Committee on Foreign Affairs, *Crisis in the Persian Gulf*, September 4, 1990, 13.

[47] "Copy of 2/15/91 Remarks by POTUS to Raytheon Missile Systems Plant Employees," James Baker's Notes, February 15, 1991, MC 197, Box 109, Folder 10, James A. Baker III Papers at the Seeley J. Mudd Library.

[48] Marr, *Modern History of Iraq*, 242.

[49] CIA Report, "Iraq: Implications of Insurrection and Prospects for Saddam's Survival," March 16, 1991, CIA.gov, accessed February 6, 2017, https://www.cia.gov/library/read ingroom/document/0001441917, 7.

The report noted that Saddam had thoroughly cultivated the loyalty of the top brass of the security forces through a mix of perks and punishments, making the defection of entire units unlikely. Saddam had also surrounded the capital with fiercely loyal Republican Guard units with leaders drawn from the Tikriti elite that controlled the Baath Party.[50]

Second, the administration believed that any step toward helping the rebels would likely embroil US troops in fighting and/or an occupation of Iraqi territory. They held that the US military had achieved its objectives in the Gulf and that backing the rebels would expand objectives unnecessarily, breaking up a coalition that had no interest in overthrowing Saddam. Many in the media and Congress called for the United States to reverse the agreement at Safwan to allow Iraqi helicopters to fly now that Saddam was using them against the rebels. Top Bush officials, however, saw shooting down the helicopters as the first step toward intractable involvement in the Iraqi civil war. State Department spokeswoman Margaret Tutweiler spelled out the slippery-slope dilemma of grounding Iraqi helicopters:

Once you make that decision [shooting down helicopters], then why aren't you taking on tanks? Why aren't you taking on artillery? How are you going to determine who is going to lead this country? Why would you be putting American lives at risk to interject yourself in something that was never a stated goal or objective either militarily or politically, to somehow change the Iraqi leadership?[51]

In sum, the administration, especially Powell, thought that direct military intervention would transform a successful war for clear goals into a desert version of Vietnam, draining US resources, lives, and credibility for uncertain purposes.[52]

The third reason that Bush decided against helping the rebels was the fear that a victory by the Shia rebels would transform Iraq into an Iranian client, creating a powerful Shia bloc against US allies like Saudi Arabia and Egypt. Iran voiced support for the Shia rebels and sent some militia forces to fight in southern Iraq. Many rebels carried portraits of Ayatollah Khomeini and used Iranian revolutionary slogans. Iranian involvement was too moderate to tip the balance against Saddam, but it sufficed to frighten the Bush administration into suspecting that a victorious Shia

---

[50] CIA Report, March 16, 1991, CIA.gov, 7–8.
[51] Ann Devroy and Al Kamen, "Bush, Aides Keep Quiet on Rebels: Defense of Policy Viewed as Risky," April 3, 1991, A1.
[52] "'Wait and See' on Iraq: Bush Views Aiding Rebels as Potential Morass," *Washington Post*, March 29, 1991, A1; Atkinson, *Crusade*, 490–491. Alfonsi, *Circle in the Sand*, 218. Baker, *Politics of Diplomacy*, 440.

rebellion would benefit Iran.[53] The administration recognized that most Shia rebels were not literal agents of Iran, but they nonetheless anticipated that a Shia-dominated Iraq would follow pro-Iranian policies and possibly emulate its theocratic style of government.

Finally, the Bush administration avoided helping the rebels because it thought a prolonged civil war might cause a "Lebanon-style power vacuum" in Iraq. The war might break the country into warring ethnic fragments or provoke interventions from regional powers like Iran, Turkey, and Syria. The CIA cautioned that Iran, for instance, might step in to bolster the Shia rebels, while Turkey might intervene to quash the formation of an independent Kurdish state.[54] US support for the rebels would only help them last longer against the government, magnifying the danger of ethnic division. Furthermore, a sense that this civil war was a resumption of timeless sectarian blood feuds in Iraqi history fed the sense that the United States should stay out. For example, one senior Bush official told a reporter: "The Kurds and Shi'ites were fighting the Sunnis for years before we got there, and they'll continue killing each other long after we've gone."[55]

In fact, the Bush administration later concluded that the rebellions saved Saddam rather than bringing about his downfall. The expectation in US policy was that once the war ended a faction of the military or Baath Party would move against Saddam after realizing how much his gamble had cost the country. The revolts, however, pinned the military down in fighting against the rebels and gave them common cause with Saddam in protecting the Sunni core and their own positions of power.[56] Siding with Saddam became their path to survival, giving Saddam, in Baker's words, "a pretty solid basis to argue to his army 'stick with me or we'll all be out'."[57] One Bush official later said: "The uprisings made it inevitable that there would not be a coup."[58]

The Baathist regime had crushed both rebellions by early April. In the south, the Iraqi government executed tens of thousands in retribution. In the north, terrified Kurds, expecting a massacre, fled by the millions

[53] Marr, *Modern History of Iraq*, 246.
[54] CIA Report, March 16, 1991, CIA.gov, 4–5; Baker, *Politics of Diplomacy*, 437.
[55] G. J. Church and D. Goodgame, "Keeping Hands Off," *Time*, April 8, 1991, 22.
[56] Andrew Rosenthal, "What the U.S. Wants to Happen in Iraq Remains Unclear," *New York Times*, March 24, 1991, E3.
[57] James Baker, interview by Frontline, PBS, 1995, accessed January 25, 2017, www.pbs.org/wgbh/pages/frontline/gulf/oral/baker/1.html.
[58] Ann Devroy and Al Kamen, "Saddam's Power Seen Increasing: U.S. Officials No Longer Regard His Ouster as Likely This Year," *Washington Post*, April 20, 1991, A1; Marr, *Modern History of Iraq*, 246–247; Gordon and Trainor, *The Generals' War*, 456; Bush and Scowcroft, *A World Transformed*, 489.

toward the Turkish and Iranian borders. They suffered Iraqi air attacks and lacked food, clothing, and shelter as they moved into the mountains. Soon these refugees were dying at a rate of 500–1000 per day while receiving little help from Turkey.[59]

The administration hesitated to intervene, viewing the Kurds as another nasty, feuding assemblage of factions within the unpleasant scene of Iraqi politics.[60] One State Department official reflected this perspective in saying: "They're nice people, and they're cute, but they're really just bandits. They spend as much time fighting each other as central authority. They're losers."[61] John Kelly, the Assistant Secretary for Near Eastern Affairs, later said that while the media latched onto the Kurds for "feel good articles," his office tried to limit contact with them because "many have a lot of blood on their hands and are certainly no great defenders of human rights."[62] Furthermore, Powell and other senior military officers disliked the idea of an indefinite presence in Iraqi territory.[63]

Several factors nonetheless prevailed upon Bush to help the Kurds. In early April, James Baker visited the refugee camps on the Turkish border, witnessing a "human nightmare." An emotionally stirred Baker called Bush on the plane out of Turkey and told him: "There's a true disaster in the making if we don't move fast. . . . We've got to do something and we've got to do it now. If we don't, literally thousands of people are going to die."[64] Baker pressed for a massive humanitarian effort and the use of US forces to create safe havens for the refugees.[65] Great Britain, France, and Turkey called for aid for the Kurds, as did many in Congress and large portions of the American public.[66]

For these reasons, on April 16 Bush started Operation Provide Comfort, a massive humanitarian effort in which US troops deployed to northern Iraq as coalition air power created a safe zone for the refugees. The United States and the United Nations funneled immense quantities

[59] Marr, *Modern History of Iraq*, 253–255.

[60] Church and Goodgame, "Keeping Hands Off," *Time*, April 8, 1991, 22.

[61] Christopher Dickey, "Could the Rebels Really Rule?" *Newsweek*, April 15, 1991, 27.

[62] John Kelly, interview by Charles Stewart Kennedy, Association for Diplomatic Studies and Training Foreign Affairs Oral History Project, Library of Congress, December 12, 1995, 303.

[63] Stephen Budiansky, "Saddam's Revenge," *U.S. News and World Report*, April 15, 1991, 26.

[64] Baker, *Politics of Diplomacy*, 433–434.   [65] Baker, *Politics of Diplomacy*, 434.

[66] Gerald Seib, "Mideast Mess: How Miscalculations Spawned U.S. Policy toward Postwar Iraq," *Wall Street Journal*, May 3, 1991, A1.

Memorandum of Telephone Conversation, William Clinton and Tony Blair, February 23, 1998, nationalarchives.gov, accessed March 25, 2018, www.archives.gov /files/declassification/iscap/pdf/2013–090-doc39.pdf.

of aid to the refugees, and by the end of June they had facilitated the return of most of these refugees to their homes. At this point, the coalition troops withdrew from northern Iraq, while the NFZ remained in place to deter Iraqi military incursions into Kurdish territory and to safeguard UN aid activities.[67] The United States, Great Britain, and France also formed a legal basis for these actions by passing Security Council Resolution 688 on April 5, 1991. This resolution condemned the atrocities against the Kurds, required that Iraq permit humanitarian agencies to operate in Kurdish areas, and insisted that "the human and political rights of all Iraqis are respected."[68] This last statement created a mandate for the continuation of the NFZ beyond the current crisis to guarantee the safety of the Kurds, although the United States would use it to justify other military interventions in Iraq in the coming years.[69]

President Bush stressed that this intervention was strictly humanitarian and that no US forces would take part in Iraq's civil war. He said in mid-April: "I do not want one single soldier or airman shoved into a civil war in Iraq that's been going on for ages."[70] The administration also aimed to avoid being dragged into intra-Kurdish politics, fearing that the Kurds might try to bait the Iraqi military into a fight to force the United States to intervene on their side.[71] A central part of US strategy throughout the crisis had been to preserve Iraqi territorial integrity and avoid a prolonged presence there. By mid-April, despite every attempt to avoid intervention, the United States now had ground and air units protecting a large swath of Iraqi territory, all without a clear sense of when that mission could end.

By May 1991, it was clear that Saddam would most likely survive these postwar uprisings. While Bush still anticipated that Saddam would fall to a coup within a year, this realization prompted the United States to seek more ways to "turn the screw" and incentivize the generals and political elites to move against Saddam.[72] Aside from keeping the sanctions intact while Saddam remained in power, Richard Haass wrote that the United States should encourage all members of the coalition to cut off ties to the

---

[67] Marr, *Modern History of Iraq*, 255–258.

[68] Cary, Duffy, and Galloway, *Triumph without Victory*, 437.

[69] David Malone, *The International Struggle over Iraq: Politics in the U.N. Security Council 1980–2005* (New York: Oxford University Press, 2006), 90, 95.

[70] Maureen Dowd, "Bush Stands Firm on Military Policy in Iraqi Civil War: No Backing for Rebels," *New York Times*, April 14, 1991, 1.

[71] Memorandum, Richard Haass to Brent Scowcroft, "Keeping the Pressure on Saddam Hussein's Regime: Strategy and Actions," May 24, 1991, OA/ID CF01585, National Security Council, Richard Haass Files, Working Files, George Bush Presidential Library, 3.

[72] Patrick Tyler, "Hussein's Ouster is U.S. Goal, But at What Cost to the Iraqis?" *New York Times*, April 28, 1991, E1.

regime to increase its diplomatic isolation.[73] The Iraqi people, Haass wrote, needed to absorb "the message that only Saddam's removal will lead to substantial improvement in their lives and livelihoods."[74] Haass further projected that deliberate infringements on Iraq's sovereignty, including inspections, reparations, and the presence of coalition forces in northern Iraq, created "a grinding irritant to the highly developed nationalism of Iraq's educated classes and the Baathist military leadership."[75]

Visa restrictions, the denial of aid from global financial organizations, and the freezing of Iraqi assets would compound the Iraqi elite's deprivation and humiliation. In meetings with Iraqi officials, the United States and its allies reinforced the fact that "relations are not normal because of Saddam's continued role" while promising aid and sanctions relief in exchange for Saddam's removal.[76] The administration hoped that combining these pressures with the chance of their relaxation once Saddam was gone would drive the Iraqi elite to decapitate the regime. In early May, Bush accelerated a covert action program to make contacts in the Iraqi military. This program involved funneling aid to exile groups like the Iraqi National Accord (INA), composed of top military officers who had fled Iraq.[77]

The Fallout from Victory: Political Backlash at Home, March–June 1991

By the summer of 1991, President Bush held that his Iraq policy since Desert Storm had largely succeeded despite some messy endings. War and sanctions had degraded the Iraqi military and ejected it from Kuwait. A CIA report calculated that "Iraq's ground forces do not constitute a regional threat" and would not recover prewar strength until the late 1990s at the earliest.[78] CIA analysts also concluded that "Iraq has not abandoned its regional ambitions, but the immediate need to devote its

---

[73] Memorandum, Haass to Scowcroft, "Keeping the Pressure," May 24, 1991, 2.

[74] Memorandum, Richard Haass to Brent Scowcroft, "Impact on International Isolation on Iraqi and Saddam Husayn," May 24, 1991, OA/ID CF01585, National Security Council, Richard Haass Files, Working Files, George Bush Presidential Library, 1.

[75] Memorandum, Haass to Scowcroft, "Keeping the Pressure," May 24, 1991, 1.

[76] Memorandum, Haass to Scowcroft, "Keeping the Pressure," May 24, 1991, 1–3.

[77] Richard Bonin, *Arrows of the Night: Ahmad Chalabi's Long Journey to Triumph in Iraq* (New York: Doubleday, 2011), 64; Andrew Cockburn and Patrick Cockburn, *Out of the Ashes: The Resurrection of Saddam Hussein* (New York: Harper Collins, 1999), 31; *ABC News Special Report,* "Unfinished Business: The CIA and Saddam Hussein," directed by Peter Jennings, ABC News, 1997, accessed January 22, 2019, www.youtube.com/watch? v=lZHHAI-eq2I.

[78] CIA Report: Iraq's Ground Forces: An Assessment, May 1991, US Intelligence on the Middle East, accessed February 14, 2017, http://primarysources.brillonline.com/brows e/us-intelligence-on-the-middle-east/cia-report-iraqs-ground-forces-an-assessment-may -1991-secret-cia;umeoumeob0908, 5.

resources to reconstruction, reestablishing domestic stability, securing its borders, and repairing severed political and economic ties to the international community restricts its policy options."[79] At the same time, the CIA judged that the Iraqi military could defend Iraq against one regional opponent, suggesting that the United States had achieved the "Goldilocks outcome" of a weakened Iraq that could balance Iranian power.[80]

Furthermore, the administration destroyed much of Saddam's WMD programs and compelled him to let weapons inspectors into Iraq, the first of which arrived in June 1991. While US forces remained engaged in Operation Provide Comfort, they had avoided becoming embroiled in the postwar rebellions and had saved countless Kurdish lives. The coalition continued to support inspections and sanctions, although the United States differed from its allies about the conditions for lifting sanctions. Bush defended these achievements in an interview in June: "Don't change the goalposts, I tell my critics. The goalposts were, aggression will not stand. And aggression didn't stand. And it was an enormous victory."[81]

The domestic political reaction to the events of the spring of 1991, however, challenged these declarations of victory. In a politicized version of the Triumph without Victory thesis, Americans from across the political and ideological spectrum believed there was a window of opportunity to solve the Saddam problem by removing him from power. He appeared to be teetering on the edge of oblivion, and advocates of a tougher line wanted Bush to give him a final push. These "simple solutionists," as Colin Powell derisively labeled them, identified many ways this could be done: backing the rebels by attacking Iraqi forces, occupying southern Iraq until Saddam was removed, holding on to oil fields in southern Iraq, and passing a Security Council resolution declaring Saddam's ouster as a coalition goal.[82]

---

[79] CIA Report: Iran–Iraq: Renewed Rivalry, July 1991, US Intelligence on the Middle East, accessed February 14, 2017, http://primarysources.brillonline.com/browse/us-intelligence-on-the-middle-east/cia-report-iraniraq-renewed-rivalry-july-1991-secret-cia;umeoumeob09089, 3.

[80] CIA Report, Iraq's Ground Forces, May 1991, US Intelligence on the Middle East, 5; Quote about the Goldilocks Outcome is taken from Haass, *War of Necessity*, 126.

[81] George Bush, interview by Linda Douglas, July 15, 1991, George Bush Presidential Library, accessed November 13, 2016, https://bush41library.tamu.edu/archives/public-papers/3099.

[82] Powell, *My American Journey*, 511. For suggestions made about how to help the rebels in the spring of 1991, see also Editorial, "George Bush's Elbe," *Wall Street Journal*, March 12, 1991, A14; Laurie Mylroie, "Help the Iraqi Resistance," *Wall Street Journal*, March 26, 1991, A22; Charles Krauthammer, "It's Time to Finish Saddam," *Washington Post*, March 29, 1991, A21; Editorial, "Desert Shame," *The New Republic*, April 29, 1991, 7–8.

The loudest critics of Bush's handling of the end of the war were likely to be neoconservatives or Democrats. They were much more numerous than those who had called for regime change during the Gulf Crisis, as the broad feeling of missed opportunity at the end of the war only intensified a thirst for total victory. Two convictions united the diverse critics. First, they pointed to the nature of the Iraqi regime to bolster the argument that Saddam needed to be removed from power now while the opportunity lasted. The core of their argument was that the Baathist regime and ideology, as well as Saddam personally, were immutable in their brutality, hostility, and desire to dominate the Gulf. As the *New York Times* columnist A. M. Rosenthal wrote in March: "As long as the man who brought about war is still in power, the peace will not be secure. It was precisely Iraq's most intimate internal affair – the character of its Government – that forced us into war."[83] In April, Senator Joseph Liebermann (D-CT) called for the pursuit of "final victory" over Saddam using "all reasonable diplomatic, economic, and military means to achieve his removal from power." He reasoned: "Until that end is realized, the peace and stability of the region will not have been fully accomplished."[84]

The United States, these critics argued, needed to go beyond hoping for a coup and declare a democratic Iraq as a short-term priority. Otherwise, there would be persistent aggression and human rights abuses from Iraq, even if another Baathist replaced Saddam. Senator Al Gore (D-TN) reflected this logic in a letter to Scowcroft on April 3 calling for an NFZ against Iraqi helicopters: "Saddam's external behavior is of a piece with the internal character of his regime."[85] Democratic Senators Robert Kerrey (NE), Claiborne Pell (RI), Lee Hamilton (IN), Ted Kennedy (MA), and Gore all advocated openly making democracy a goal in Iraq, citing "history's sweep toward democracy" in the past few decades. Kerrey would become a particularly passionate liberal advocate of regime change in the coming years. Kerrey was a Navy SEAL and Medal of Honor Winner who was wounded several times in Vietnam. Kerrey later forged close ties with Iraqi opposition figures and supported the 2003 US invasion. Like many liberals, he came to couch his argument for regime change less in terms of geopolitics than in universalistic ethical standards. During Desert Storm, he claimed that "[y]earning for democratic processes is a natural and universal human characteristic – that is what our

---

[83] A. M. Rosenthal, "How to Lose the Peace," *New York Times*, March 12, 1991, A23.
[84] *Cong. Rec.,* 102nd Cong., 1st sess., April 9, 1991, 7643.
[85] Letter, Al Gore to George Bush, April 5, 1991, George Bush Presidential Papers. See also Gore, *Cong. Rec.,* 102nd Cong., 1st sess., April 18, 1991, 8644–8648.

Founders taught. It is a fundamental aspect of human dignity which cuts across all national, religious, ethnic, and economic barriers."[86]

The second conviction uniting these critics was a sense of responsibility for inspiring the rebels who were being slaughtered as coalition forces stood by. Peter Galbraith, an influential liberal aide to Claiborne Pell, accused Bush of being unprepared for the postwar rebellions and then irresponsibly calling for an uprising. Galbraith, who had traveled to Kurdistan in March 1991, concluded that the United States had "lost an opportunity to overthrow Saddam Hussein in mid-March" by failing to cultivate ties with opposition groups during the crisis or to support the rebels.[87] Galbraith later promised that "had the United States continued on to Baghdad, we would have been received with kisses and as liberators every step of the way."[88] Stephen Solarz similarly declared it "morally and politically unacceptable to stand by and do nothing while Saddam brutally crushes a revolt we helped inspire."[89]

Numerous prominent Congressmen and senators, including some who had opposed the war, demanded that Bush take action to stop the killing and the refugee crisis, especially in Kurdistan.[90] Al D'Amato, Joseph Liebermann, Lee Hamilton, Ted Kennedy, Al Gore, and Gregory Mitchell all called for US intervention. They emphasized that the Shia rebels were not Iranian pawns, even arguing that the Iraqi Shia tradition "opposes all religious involvement in politics."[91] In this view, the United States was wasting a chance to build a better Iraq by

---

[86] Kerrey quote is from *Cong. Rec.*, 102nd Cong., 1st sess., February 27, 1991, 4403. Also see statements advocating democracy as a policy goal in Iraq from Pell and Kennedy: *Cong. Rec.*, 102nd Cong., 1st sess., March 7, 1991, 5377; *Cong. Rec.*, 102nd Cong., 1st sess., May 22, 1991, 12090.

[87] "Civil War in Iraq," A Staff Report to the Senate Committee on Foreign Relations, S. Rpt. 102–127, 102nd Cong., 1st Sess., May 1991 (US Government Printing Office, Washington, DC, 1991), 1–2.

[88] Peter Galbraith, Speech to Women's National Democratic Club, Records of the US Senate, Foreign Relations Committee, Subject Files, Persian Gulf-Iraq Invasion of Kuwait, War Powers, Box 100, Folder Iraq 1992 (2 of 2), National Archives, 11.

[89] George Lardner, Jr., "Solarz Wants U.N. to Demand Saddam Resign," *Washington Post*, April 11, 1991, A32. See also Stephen Solarz, "Get Involved: U.N. Must Oust Saddam," *Wall Street Journal*, April 17, 1991, A14.

[90] Lardner, Jr., "Solarz Wants U.N. to Demand Saddam Resign," *Washington Post*, April 11, 1991, A32. Senate Subcommittee on Immigration and Refugee Affairs of the Senate Committee on the Judiciary, *Refugee Crisis in the Persian Gulf*, 101st Cong., 1st sess., April 15 and May 20, 1991.

[91] Krauthammer, "It's Time to Finish Saddam," *Washington Post*, March 29, 1991. See also Mylroie, "Help the Iraqi Resistance," *Wall Street Journal*, March 26, 1991; "Civil War in Iraq," A Staff Report to the Senate Committee on Foreign Relations, May 1991, 11.

betraying pro-democracy forces out of sheer myopia, cynicism, and an outsized fear of becoming enmeshed in Iraqi affairs.[92]

Bush also came under fire for his management of the ending of hostilities, especially the Safwan accords. Conservative columnist Charles Krauthammer accused Bush of a naïve mercy in halting the war before the Republican Guard was crushed, saying: "He spared the lives of soldiers who went on to massacre civilians."[93] Others called for the United States to renege on the Safwan accords, reproaching Schwarzkopf for letting himself be hoodwinked.[94] Few in Congress actually called for major deployments of ground forces or extended occupation of Iraqi territory to help the rebels. The belief was that a selective use of US power at the right pressure point could tip the conflict in the rebels' favor.[95]

Despite this surge of criticism, many politicians and media figures continued to support Bush's avoidance of postwar involvement in Iraq beyond Operation Provide Comfort. These skeptics of regime change repeatedly asked what the United States would do if the first step toward involvement, such as shooting down helicopters, failed to tip balance in the rebels' favor. Columnist Leslie Gelb of the *New York Times* argued that "the logic of intervention leads on, inevitably, to capturing Baghdad" and governing Iraq, something outside of US interests and abilities. He and other skeptics highlighted the risk of Iraq fragmenting if the United States prolonged the civil strife by joining sides.[96] The public generally supported avoiding involvement in Iraqi affairs, with only 29 percent in the spring of 1991 favoring the resumption of ground operations to help the rebels.[97]

Some supporters of intervention and regime change accused these skeptics of treating Middle Eastern peoples as too mentally or culturally backward to embrace democracy and pluralism. The Iraqi opposition leader Ahmed Chalabi, for instance, claimed: "These realists dismiss people in our part of the world as savages who have been killing each other for centuries."[98]

---

[92] Editorial, "Ashes in Our Mouths," *The National Review*, April 29, 1991, 12–13. See also William Safire, "Follow the Kurds to Save Iraq," *New York Times*, March 28, 1991, A25.

[93] Krauthammer, "It's Time to Finish Saddam, *Washington Post*, March 29, 1991.

[94] A. M. Rosenthal, "Reverse the Reversals," *New York Times*, March 29, 1991, A23.

[95] Guy Gugliotta and Tom Kenworthy, "Congress Is Reluctant to Intervene in Iraq: U.S. Options Seen as Limited, Public Called Unenthusiastic," *Washington Post*, April 3, 1991, A28.

[96] Leslie Gelb, "A Unified, Weak Iraq: Not Another Lebanon," *New York Times*, March 20, 1991, A29; Editorial, "How Can the U.S. Stand Idly By?" *New York Times*, April 2, 1991, A18.

[97] Peter Hahn, *Missions Accomplished?: The United States and Iraq since World War I* (New York: Oxford University Press, 2012), 108.

[98] Ahmed Chalabi, "Democracy Is 'Realism' for Iraq," *The Defense Democrat: A Newsletter on Foreign Affairs and National Defense*, April 1991, 1; Safire, "Follow the Kurds," *New York Times*, March 28, 1991.

Skeptics of intervention retorted that it would be foolish to assume that the United States knew how to reengineer Iraqi politics or that a post-Baathist Iraq would blossom into a liberal democracy. One of these skeptics, the conservative writer George Will, pointed out the inconsistency of other conservatives who opposed "social engineering" at home but would take that task on in a foreign country that Americans did not understand. He also argued that there was no evidence that the Iraqis possessed "the social, institutional, and moral preconditions" for constitutional democracy. He and other skeptics of intervention lambasted these "imperial conservatives" as naive do-gooders sending US troops into a quagmire.[99] Iraq historian Phebe Marr likewise argued that the entire region had no history of democracy and suffered from vast social and economic problems. She recommended that the United States focus on its containing Iraq and creating the conditions for Saddam's downfall rather than transformative crusades.[100]

Another casualty of the fallout from victory was the credibility of Bush's New World Order. Bush officials had employed high-minded rhetoric about human rights, international law, and morality in arguing for the war, and their moral outrage at Saddam was genuine. After Desert Storm, however, the administration stood by as Saddam, whom Bush had compared to Hitler, recovered from defeat and massacred thousands of civilians. For Bush, letting the Iraqis settle their own affairs after the war did not contradict the justification for the war, which was to counter aggression rather than address other states' internal problems. As he said in early April: "The United States and these other countries with us in this coalition did not go there to settle all the internal affairs of Iraq."[101]

Neoconservative and liberal detractors faulted Bush's foreign policy realism and multilateralism for the shortcomings of his Iraq policy. Bush and Scowcroft saw global politics in terms of the interactions of states and the pursuit of the national interest. For them, the Gulf War was largely about defending the principles of state sovereignty and nonaggression. Moreover, they greatly valued international institutions and collective action as ways to counter aggression, and they accepted that coalitional enterprises imposed restraints on policy. Bush's reluctance to intervene in

---

[99] George Will, "The Imperial Conservative," *Washington Post*, April 18, 1991, A21. See also Leslie Gelb, "A Unified, Weak Iraq," *New York Times*, March 20, 1991; "Don't Intervene," *New York Times*, March 31, 1991, E13; Editorial, "Direct Help for the Kurds," *Washington Post*, March 29, 1991, A20; Daniel Pipes, "Why America Can't Save the Kurds," *Wall Street Journal*, April 11, 1991, A15.

[100] Senate Subcommittee on Near Eastern and South Asian Affairs of the Senate Committee on Foreign Relations, *The Middle East*, 102nd Cong., 1st sess., May 9, 1991, 81–83, 90.

[101] Thomas Friedman, "Decision Not to Help Iraqi Rebels Puts U.S. in an Awkward Position," *New York Times*, April 4, 1991, A1.

the former Yugoslavia, where fighting broke out soon after Desert Storm, reflected this sense that force should be used only when a clear national interest is at stake.[102]

This restrained form of multilateral realism conflicted sharply with neoconservative visions for post–Cold War US foreign policy. Underlying their dissatisfaction with Bush was a conviction that US power and values could topple tyrants and transform nations if only political leaders had the courage to exercise that power. Neoconservatives like Charles Krauthammer believed that the United States should use its post–Cold War primacy, what he termed the "Unipolar Moment," to "shape a world order congenial to our interests and values."[103] Neoconservatives like Krauthammer and Joshua Muravchik argued that there was global momentum behind democratization in the post–Cold War world that the United States should support Iraqi democracy.[104] They accused Bush of failing to seize opportunities to reshape rogue nations like Iraq, which thereby undermined the moral credibility the United States needed for the benign exercise of hegemony.[105]

In addition, neoconservatives and liberal hawks accused Bush of a Kissinger-like willingness to work within existing geopolitical realities rather than press for transformation. The "murky, fantasy realpolitik" of restoring a weakened but still dictatorial Iraq to balance the equally autocratic Iran would only cause more instability. The region did not need a realist balance of power but a democratic revolution because democracies do not act aggressively or terrorize their own people.[106] In fact, most neoconservatives blamed the failure to remove Saddam on

[102] Hal Brands, *From Berlin to Baghdad: America's Search for Purpose in the Post–Cold War World* (Lexington: University Press of Kentucky, 1994), 88–91; Bartholmew Sparrow, *The Strategist: Brent Scowcroft and the Call of National Security* (New York: Public Affairs, 2015), 555–556; Derek Chollet and James Goldgeier, *America between the Wars: From 11/9 to 9/11: The Misunderstood Years between the Fall of the Berlin Wall and the Start of the War on Terror* (New York: Public Affairs, 2008), 10–12, 30–31.

[103] Charles Krauthammer, "Bless Our Pax Americana," *Washington Post*, March 22, 1991, A25; Charles Krauthammer, "The Unipolar Moment," *Foreign Affairs* 70, no. 1 (Winter, 1990/1991): 23–33.

[104] Joshua Muravchik, "Right to Intervene," *Washington Post*, April 23, 1991, A19. For Muravchik's complete defense of a foreign policy centered on democracy promotion, see *Exporting Democracy: Fulfilling America's Destiny* (Washington, DC, AEI Press, 1991); Gary Dorrien, *Imperial Designs: Neoconservatism and the New Pax Americana* (New York: Routledge, 2004), 69–114.

[105] Charles Krauthammer, "Tiananmen II," *Washington Post*, April 5, 1991, A19; Krauthammer, "It's Time to Finish Saddam," *Washington Post*, March 29, 1991, A21; See also William Safire, "Bush's Moral Crisis," *New York Times*, April 1, 1991, A17.

[106] Fred Hoffman and Albert Wohlstetter, "The Bitter End by Fred Hoffman and Albert Wohlstetter," *The New Republic*, April 29, 1991, 20–24.

Bush's multilateralism and commitment to the United Nations, which they saw as pointless restraints on US might. If US allies did not support a foreign policy based on exporting democracy and toppling tyrants, so be it: unrestrained US power would suffice to bring about these changes.[107] Liberals in particular criticized Bush's approach and argued that the United States should use its overwhelming power to defend human rights and address humanitarian crises. As the editors of the *New Republic* lamented: "In his new world, states may be gently criticized for brutalizing people within their borders, but no decisive action can be taken against them for doing so."[108] This explosion of criticism shows that Bush's restrained, multilateral approach to foreign policy was at a fundamental ideological disadvantage in a country flooded with a sense of confidence and momentum from its Cold War and Gulf War triumphs. As a strategy of restraint and multilateral cooperation, containment was sure to face legitimacy problems in this atmosphere.

The fallout from victory was worsened by reemergence of partisan politics in early 1991 from their wartime hibernation. Both parties attacked political weaknesses in the other's approach to Iraq. Democrats seized on Saddam's invasion to reprimand the failure of the engagement policy, which many of them had critiqued for years. They claimed that Bush's "appeasement" merely convinced Saddam he could get away with seizing Kuwait and that imposing sanctions beforehand might have convinced Saddam to stay his hand. If Bush had taken a tougher stand with Iraq, these critics argued, the war might have been prevented.[109] When former US ambassador to Iraq April Glaspie appeared before Congressional hearings in the spring, Democrats blasted her for failing to warn Saddam that the United States would oppose an invasion of Kuwait. When Glaspie said that she had given Saddam "repeated and crystal warnings," Congressman Tom Lantos (D-CA) responded: "I am appalled by the frighteningly flawed judgment you

---

[107] Brands, *From Berlin to Baghdad*, 77. For overviews of neoconservative foreign policy thought at the end of the Cold War, see Barry Posen and Andrew Ross, "Competing Visions for U.S. Grand Strategy," *International Security* 21, no. 3 (Winter, 1996/1997): 32–43; Richard Immerman, *Empire for Liberty: A History of American Imperialism from Benjamin Franklin to Paul Wolfowitz* (Princeton, NJ: Princeton University Press, 2010), 209–210.

[108] Editorial, "Desert Shame," *The New Republic*, April 29, 1991, 7; see also Richard Cohen, "A Moral Failure," *Washington Post*, April 5, 1991, A19.

[109] See statements by Berman and Lantos, House Committee on Foreign Affairs, *Sanctions against Iraq*, 101st Cong., 2nd sess., August 1–2, 1990, 20, 42. For a summary of Democratic criticism, see John Goshko and Jeffrey Smith, "State Dept. Assailed on Iraq Policy: Democrats Cite Failure to Avert Invasion," *Washington Post*, September 19, 1990, A1.

displayed. .... To say in retrospect that Saddam Hussein absolutely knew that we would move in a military way is simply absurd."[110]

The Democrats also seized on the "Iraqgate" controversy of 1991 and 1992 to undermine Bush's political position on Iraq. This scandal had actually emerged in 1989 when federal prosecutors found that the Atlanta branch of the Italian Banca Nazionale del Lavoro (BNL) had issued $5 billion in illegal credits to Iraq. The branch's manager, Christopher Drogoul, had made some of these loans through a US export credit program for Iraq, the Commodity Credit Corporation (CCC), which had been a key plank of the engagement strategy. These loans vastly exceeded the limits set by the CCC program, and Drogoul received $2.5 million in kickbacks from Iraq for his services. After the Gulf War, evidence started to trickle out that Iraq had abused virtually every US aid program, adding to the sense that the Bush administration had erred in sticking to engagement for so long.[111]

Congressional Democrats launched extensive investigations and held numerous hearings about this scandal. Henry Gonzalez (D-TX) and Sam Gejdenson (D-CT) accused top Bush officials of knowing about the abuses of aid programs, including Iraqi purchases of weapons with CCC-derived funds and Iraqi imports of materials and equipment with potential use in WMD programs. They argued that top US officials allowed these activities to continue in order to woo Iraq into the US orbit. They also claimed that Bush had established a team to cover up their knowledge of these abuses.[112] Gejdenson was uncompromising in his accusations, saying in May 1992: "This administration used every vehicle within the government to make sure that Saddam Hussein got what he wanted. It

[110] Subcommittee on Europe and the Middle East of the House Committee on Foreign Affairs, *United States-Iraqi Relations*, 102nd Cong., 1st sess., March 21, 1991, 14.
[111] Bruce Jentleson, *With Friends Like These: Reagan, Bush, and Saddam, 1982–1990* (New York: W. W. Norton, 1994), 123–127; Kenneth Timmerman, *The Death Lobby: How the West Armed Iraq* (Boston: Houghton Mifflin, 1991), 225–246; George Lardner and R. Jeffrey Smith, "CIA Shared Data with Iraq Until Kuwait Invasion," *Washington Post*, April 28, 1992, 16; Elaine Sciolino, "U.S. Documents Raise Questions over Iraq Policy," *New York Times*, June 7, 1992, A1; John Fialka and Peter Truell, "As 'Iraqgate' Unfolds, New Evidence Raises Questions of Cover-Up," *Wall Street Journal*, October 9, 1992, A1.
[112] See statements by Gonzalez and Gejdenson: Subcommittee on International Economic Policy and Trade of the House Committee on Foreign Affairs, *United States Exports of Sensitive Technology to Iraq*, 102nd Cong., 1st sess., April 8, 1991, 1–2, 91–93; House Committee on Banking, Finance, and Urban Affairs, *The Banca Nazionale Del Lavoro (BNL) Scandal and the Department of Agriculture's Commodity Credit Corporation (CCC) Program for Iraq, Part 1*, 102nd Cong., 2nd sess., May 21, 1992, 646–663; Elaine Sciolino, "Bush's Greatest Glory Fades as Questions on Iraq Persist," *New York Times*, June 27, 1992, A1; "Export Controls: Gejdenson Alleges Iraq Cover-Up," *Congressional Quarterly Weekly*, April 13, 1991, 905–906.

clearly emboldened Saddam Hussein."[113] These investigations ginned up little evidence of legal or ethical wrongdoing by US officials, but the public airing of just how far the engagement strategy had gone to appeal to Saddam became a significant headache for Bush.[114]

The Republicans in turn defended themselves against Democratic charges that the Gulf Crisis was partially their fault. They argued that engagement was a sensible policy at the time and accused the Democrats of trying to criminalize and politicize a policy error.[115] They seized on the overwhelming Democratic skepticism about the war to blast them as weak on defense. Only ten Democrats in the Senate and eighty-six in the House had voted to authorize the use of force against Iraq, and they had frequently predicted that the war would cause thousands of US casualties. Afterward, Democrats had to defend their skepticism about a war that proved a massive, low-cost success.[116]

The Republicans determined to make the Democrats pay for their votes on the war. Shortly after the vote to authorize the use of force in January 1991, Clayton Yeutter, soon to become chairman of the Republican National Committee, warned that the Republicans would make the vote a "very significant factor" in the 1992 election. Some Republicans began wearing buttons declaring "I Voted With the President."[117] Moreover, the National Republican Senatorial Committee sent out a fundraising letter labeling Democratic opponents of the war as "appeasement-before-country liberals."[118] Senator Phil Gramm (R-TX), the chairman of this committee, said on March 1 that the Democratic vote against the war fit "the pattern of Jimmy Carter, Walter Mondale, and Michael Dukakis. It says to the nation once again

---

[113] Gejdenson statement found in House Committee on Banking, Finance, and Urban Affairs, *White House Efforts to Thwart Congressional Investigations of Pre-War Iraq Policy: The Case of the Rostow Gang*, 102nd Cong., 2nd sess., May 29, 1992, 8.

[114] Murray Waas and Douglas Frantz, "Abuses in U.S. Aid to Iraqis Ignored," *Los Angeles Times*, March 22, 1992, A1. Moreover, columnists Jim Hoagland and William Safire became obsessed with Iraqgate, writing dozens of columns on the topic in the early 1990s. See Jim Hoagland, "Engulfed," *Washington Post*, October 11, 1992, C2; William Safire, "Crimes of Iraqgate," *New York Times*, May 18, 1992, A17.

[115] Brent Scowcroft, "We Didn't Coddle Saddam," *Washington Post*, October 19, 1992, A27; Lawrence Eagleburger, House Committee on Banking, Finance, and Urban Affairs, May 21, 1992, 65.

[116] Carroll Doherty and Pat Towell, "Democrats Try to Bury Image of Foreign Policy Weakness," *Congressional Quarterly Weekly*, March 23, 1991, 752–759; Stephen Solarz, "Don't Argue with Victory," *New York Times*, March 18, 1991, A15; Lee Hamilton, "Who Voted Wrong?" *Washington Post*, March 10, 1991.

[117] Carroll Doherty, "Parties Split into Postwar Camps after Giving Victory Cheer," *Congressional Quarterly Weekly*, April 27, 1991, 611–613.

[118] Thomas Edsall, "Political Warfare Erupts over Gulf," *Washington Post*, January 25, 1991, A4.

that the Democrats cannot be trusted to define the destiny of America."[119]

In sum, both parties were unclean on Iraq policy, but each tried to exploit the other side's errors, creating an escalatory political dynamic that shifted the public discourse on Iraq toward harsher policies. Both sides distanced themselves from the engagement policy, reinforcing for the remainder of the decade the "lesson" that any attempts to incentivize Saddam to behave were doomed. This perception became an important part of the regime change consensus.

By the summer of 1991, once it was clear that Saddam had survived the postwar challenges, Bush's critics derided his failure to bring down the Iraqi leader. In July, the *New Republic* editors asserted: "What's happened in Iraq since our grand 'victory' isn't a bit of rain at a Fourth of July picnic; it's a deluge, washing the guests, the food, and the marching band out to sea."[120] Saddam was only 54 years old, critics noted, and had proven himself a dogged survivor. The question suffusing political debates was whether Desert Storm had positively changed the struggle with Saddam or whether it had merely postponed a day of reckoning. The conversation now shifted to containment. Those who criticized Bush's restrained approach to the end of the war would now demand a hard-line approach to Iraqi compliance, oppose any normalization, and push for ever tougher measures in order to bring down Saddam and his regime.

Enforcing Containment: June 1991–November 1992

Starting in June 1991, the United States set out to enforce a containment policy based on sanctions, inspections, the NFZ in Northern Iraq, and pressure the Iraqi state to spark a coup. It continued to prioritize containment and Iraqi compliance with the UN resolutions, especially on WMD disarmament. Saddam countered US efforts to contain and overthrow him with a two-part strategy. In the short term, he sought to prevent the sanctions from destabilizing his regime and to convince the inspectors that he was complying in order to get the sanctions lifted. In the long term, he tried to break up the sanctioning coalition by provoking confrontations and encouraging countries like France, Russia, and China to defect from the coalition, which would undermine sanctions and inspections. Saddam even established

---

[119] David Broder and Thomas Edsall, "GOP Seeking to Exploit Public Support for Bush," *Washington Post*, March 1, 1991, A33.
[120] Editorial, "Staying There," *The New Republic*, July 29, 1991, 5.

a committee under Tariq Aziz to harass the inspectors and conceal important materials and information.[121]

The IAEA and UNSCOM began inspections in June 1991. The IAEA quickly unmasked Iraq's undeclared uranium enrichment program, followed by the discovery in July of several kilograms of highly enriched uranium and stores of uranium ore.[122] The IAEA concluded that Saddam had been much closer to an advanced nuclear weapons capacity than most experts estimated before Desert Storm. Hans Blix, the head of the IAEA, said that Iraq might have been two to three years from producing enriched uranium by centrifuge, which would have enabled it to make several nuclear weapons per year.[123] David Kay of the IAEA described the Iraqi program as one with "technical vision and direction that, if it had proceeded unhindered by the Gulf War, would have resulted in Iraq, in a relatively short period of time, joining the ranks of the nuclear weapons states."[124] In the meantime, UNSCOM uncovered and oversaw the destruction of significant quantities of ballistic missiles, chemical weapons, and, after its revelation in 1992, implements of a biological warfare program.[125]

These successes in uncovering and destroying Iraqi WMD programs came in spite of frequent interference from Iraqi officials and the withholding of key documents that would enable the inspectors to deduce the extent and nature of Iraqi programs. The Iraqi campaign of obstruction led to frequent confrontations with the international coalition. US officials read each of these episodes as a test, thinking that if Saddam received some slack, he would lose respect for the coalition and continue to push.[126] The first of these challenges occurred in the summer of 1991 when Saddam repeatedly refused to let UN personnel into suspected nuclear facilities and inspectors caught Iraqi agents smuggling nuclear

---

[121] Department of Central Intelligence, Iraq Survey Group, *Key Findings*, September 30, 2004, cia.gov, accessed July 15, 2018, www.cia.gov/library/reports/general-reports-1/ir aq_wmd_2004/, 1–3; Cockburn and Cockburn, *Out of the Ashes*, 103–104.

[122] Richard Krasno and James Sutterlin, *The United Nations and Iraq: Defanging the Viper* (Westport, CT: Praeger, 2003), 50–52; Pollack, *The Threatening Storm*, 62.

[123] David Kay, "Denial and Deception Practices of WMD Proliferators: Iraq and Beyond," *The Washington Quarterly* 18, no. 1 (Winter, 1995): 86; "Promise of a Saddam Surprise," *The Economist*, January 25, 1992, 69.

[124] Senate Committee on Foreign Relations, *Nuclear Proliferation: Learning from the Iraq Experience*, 102nd Cong., 1st sess., October 17, 1991, 16.

[125] Krasno and Sutterlin, *Defanging the Viper*, 60–66; Pollack, *The Threatening Storm*, 63.

[126] See, for examples, Proposed Agenda Meeting with the President, James Baker, April 19, 1992, MC 197, Box 115, Folder 9, James A. Baker III Papers at the Seeley G. Mudd Library, 1; Proposed Agenda Meeting with the President James Baker, April 24, 1992, MC 196, Box 115, Folder 9, James A. Baker III Papers at the Seeley G. Mudd Library, 5.

equipment out of a building.[127] Bush threatened air strikes against Iraq in order to induce cooperation. During this crisis, Bush reiterated his call for the Iraqi military to overthrow Saddam, promising leniency if they succeeded: "Before the war started I made very clear ... that our argument was not with the people of Iraq – it wasn't even with the regime in Iraq – it was with Saddam Hussein."[128] Colin Powell and the Joint Chiefs of Staff cautioned Bush against coercive strikes because they feared they would achieve little and lead the military into deeper involvement.[129] Moreover, key members of the coalition vacillated over the use of force, including France, Egypt, and Turkey.[130] The Iraqi government reversed itself in July and allowed the inspectors into the suspected sites, which by this point had been cleaned of illegal materials.

It did not take long for the Iraqi government to obstruct inspections once again. In September 1991, Saddam detained forty inspectors for about 12 hours after they discovered hidden Iraqi documents on nuclear weapons. He also protested the inspectors' use of helicopters to move freely around Iraq. Bush again accused Iraq of failing to comply with the United Nations and of secretly trying to reconstruct its nuclear weapons program.[131] The administration determined that Saddam was not a current threat, but it stressed the need to demonstrate that the United States and the coalition would not bend on its commitment to disarmament.[132] The inspectors themselves resolved this showdown through a compromise that allowed them to make copies of documents from these buildings.

On January 28, 1992, UNSCOM director Rolf Ekeus reported that Iraq was in material breach of Security Council Resolution 687 because of its persistent obstruction of inspections. Iraqi agents had destroyed large quantities of missiles and chemical weapons, but the inspectors still had not received documentation showing what weapons and equipment the Iraqis actually had possessed. This situation left uncertainty as to what the Iraqis

---

[127] John Yang and John Goshko, "Bush Says Iraq Violates Cease-Fire; Pentagon Preparing Range of Options," *Washington Post*, June 29, 1991, A1.

[128] George H. W. Bush, "The President's News Conference with the French President Francois Mitterand," July 14, 1991, George Bush Presidential Library, accessed November 17, 2016, https://bush41library.tamu.edu/archives/public-papers/3188, 10.

[129] Memorandum, Richard Haass to Brent Scowcroft, July 10, 1991, OA/ID CF01585-006, National Security Council, Richard Haass Files, Working Files, George Bush Presidential Library, 1.

[130] Krasno and Sutterlin, *Defanging the Viper*, 57–59; Patrick Tyler, "U.S. Faces Trouble Maintaining Unity of Allies on Iraq," *New York Times*, July 28, 1991, A1.

[131] Paul Lewis, "Baghdad Detains 40 UN Inspectors Who Find A-Plans," *New York Times*, September 24, 1991, A1.

[132] Andrew Rosenthal, "The Bush-Hussein Duel: U.S. Aides Admit Iraq Is No Armed Threat but Say That Control Must Be Established," *New York Times*, September 26, 1991, A1.

had unilaterally destroyed and what they still possessed.[133] The Iraqi government by this point had issued six "Full, Final, and Complete Declarations" of its weapons programs, draining the inspectors' patience.[134]

Once again, the Bush administration drew up plans for air strikes on suspected WMD sites to coerce Iraq into compliance. Powell, however, argued against these strikes, saying that they would do little to change Saddam's behavior while creating significant military risks. Powell considered these types of limited and "surgical" strikes to be politicians' ways of convincing critics they were addressing the problem without having a clear aim for the use of force. Baker and Scowcroft disagreed, saying that the United States needed to strike Iraq to demonstrate resolve and end the cycle of confrontation.[135] Baker later expressed his frustration to Bush about Powell's opposition to the use of force: "You know well that Saddam respects force, not exhortations. But there is a profound allergy at JCS to back-up that entails the use of force."[136] Cheney emphasized that the administration did not want to run risks to overthrow Saddam, saying in January: "It's an irritant that he's still in power in Baghdad, but I don't think it's the kind of thing that merits, for example, risking additional military casualties – American casualties – to get him out of there."[137] Saddam backed down in late March and promised to cooperate with the inspections, but this promise again did not last.

In July 1992, UNSCOM personnel sought to enter the Ministry of Agriculture to uncover documents on ballistic missile development. The Iraqi government refused to let them in, leading to a seventeen-day standoff in the parking lot in which government agents threatened the inspectors and mobs pelted them with rocks and rotten vegetables.[138] Scowcroft and Haass reasoned that the United States had to show Saddam that he could not "defy the UN with impunity" or he would continue his intransigence.[139] The lack of international enthusiasm for

---

[133] "Losing Patience," *The Economist*, February 15, 1992, 70.

[134] Cockburn and Cockburn, *Out of the Ashes*, 107.

[135] Barton Gellman and Ann Devroy, "Powell Said to Oppose New Strike on Iraq," *Washington Post*, March 20, 1992, A1; Colin Powell, "U.S. Forces: Challenges Ahead," *Foreign Affairs* 71, no. 5 (Winter, 1992): 37–42.

[136] Baker, Proposed Agenda Meeting with the President, April 24, 1992, 5.

[137] R. Jeffrey Smith, "White House Prepares to Step Up Pressure on Iraq," *Washington Post*, February 9, 1992, A1.

[138] Jon Alterman, "Coercive Diplomacy against Iraq, 1990–98," in *The United States and Coercive Diplomacy*, ed. Robert Art and Patrick Cronin (Washington, DC: United States Institute of Peace, 2003), 285; Scott Ritter, *Endgame: Solving the Iraqi Crisis* (New York: Simon & Schuster, 2002), 37.

[139] NSC Meeting Notes, Richard Haass, July 23, 1992, OA/ID CF 01404–002, National Security Council, Richard Haass Files, Presidential Meeting Files, George Bush Presidential Library, 2.

military action, however, balanced against the desire to punish Saddam.[140] Bush dreaded that a punitive attack would further weaken the coalition without definitively changing Iraqi willingness to cooperate.[141] On July 26, Iraq backed down and agreed to allow UN personnel into the Agriculture Ministry. He did so, however, largely because of a deal made with Rolf Ekeus that allowed the Iraqi government to remove US and British personnel from the team that would inspect this ministry. The Bush administration was displeased with Ekeus for compromising on UNSCOM's right to determine the national composition of the inspectors, but it accepted this deal as international backing for a strike crumpled once Saddam conceded.[142]

After the confrontation at the Agriculture Ministry, the Bush administration developed plans for sustained air strikes on Iraq and the creation of a no-fly zone in southern Iraq in response to the next inspections crisis. The purpose of this escalation would be to further destabilize the regime, punish it more effectively for obstructing inspectors, and protect Shia civilians in the south. The leak of the planned air campaign right before the start of the Republican National Convention led to accusations that Bush was trying to make political gains by striking Iraq, and the administration withdrew those plans.[143]

On August 26, the United States, Great Britain, and France responded to Saddam's continued aerial assaults on the Shia with Operation Southern Watch, a new NFZ over southern Iraq. The southern zone was not a "safe haven" like the northern zone because the United States only denied air access to government aircraft, allowing Saddam to retain an administrative and security presence on the ground.[144] The United States also hoped that the denial of Saddam's aircraft in the southern zone would further undermine his legitimacy at home and possibly spark

---

[140] NSC Deputies Committee Meeting Notes, Brent Scowcroft, July 27, 1992, OA/ID CF 01404–004, National Security Council, Richard Haass Files, Presidential Meeting Files, George Bush Presidential Library, 1.

[141] NSC Meeting Notes, Richard Haass, July 23, 1992, George Bush Presidential Library, 2.

[142] This overview of major crises does not capture the true extent of the harassment and noncooperation that Iraqi personnel inflicted on the inspections teams. For example, Tim Trevan, a biological weapons expert in UNSCOM, logged over 200 minor and major incidents in a nine-month period in 1992. See Tim Trevan, *Saddam's Secrets; The Hunt for Iraq's Hidden Weapons* (London: Harper Collins, 1999), 220; Michael Gordon, "Iraq Won Its Point on U.N. Inspections, Top U.S. Aides Say," *New York Times*, July 28, 1992, A1.

[143] Liam O'Brien, "Winning Back the Peace: The George H.W. Bush Administration and the Creation of Operation Southern Watch, August 1992," *International History Review*, accessed April 27, 2020, www.tandfonline.com/doi/full/10.1080/07075332 .2020.1741423, 2–6.

[144] Malone, *International Struggle over Iraq*, 99.

a coup.[145] Scowcroft told Bush that one of the strengths of the NFZ was that it "communicated a sense of momentum moving away from Saddam."[146] The new NFZ established in Operation Southern Watch, however, garnered even less international support than the NFZ in the north. This southern NFZ lacked specific UN approval, and many countries began to suspect the United States was stretching existing resolutions beyond their original meaning in order to pressure Saddam. Moreover, countries like China, India, and Russia did not want to sponsor a policy that involved the violation of sovereignty to protect oppressed minorities.[147] Great Britain and France were the only two major allies who participated in Operation Southern Watch.[148]

Meanwhile, the economic sanctions and embargo of Iraq were devastating the Iraqi economy. Iraq lost billions of dollars in export revenue because of the severing of oil sales, and its industrial output declined by 50 percent. Inflation surged to more than 5,000 percent as per capita income plummeted.[149] Unemployment also increased as the Iraqi state laid off hundreds of thousands of workers and soldiers to save money.[150] This economic decline, combined with the massive damage done to infrastructure during the war, ravaged public health. The sanctions technically did not prohibit food imports, but bureaucratic delays, corruption, and the Baathist regime's deliberate denial of resources to rebellious populations drastically lowered ordinary Iraqis' access to basic staples, causing a surge in malnutrition.[151]

The United States maintained a hard line on sanctions by exercising its veto power on the committee responsible for determining permissible imports to Iraq, which allowed any Security Council member to veto any trade item. The United States and Great Britain used this veto to stop Iraq from importing crucial goods for agriculture and public health, including insecticides, refrigeration equipment, and chlorine, because of

---

[145] John Lancaster, "U.S. Moves to Toughen Iraq Stance: Flight Ban Is Called 1st Step in Campaign to Pressure Saddam," *Washington Post*, August 29, 1992, A1.

[146] Memorandum, Brent Scowcroft to George Bush, August 26, 1990, OAID CF01404-012, National Security Council, Richard Haass Files, Presidential Meeting Files, George Bush Presidential Library, 1.

[147] Gerald Seib, "Bush Faces Tricky Decisions in Trying to Get Tougher with Saddam Hussein," *Wall Street Journal*, August 3, 1992, A13; "The Push for a Southern Haven," *The Economist*, August 8, 1992, 48.

[148] John Lancaster, "Allies Endorse U.S. Plan for 'No Fly' Zone in Iraq," *Washington Post*, August 19, 1992, A1.

[149] David Cortright and George A. Lopez, "Are Sanctions Just? The Problematic Case of Iraq," *Journal of International Affairs* 52, no. 2 (Spring, 1999): 741; Marr, *Modern History of Iraq*, 268–270.

[150] Graham-Brown, *Sanctioning Saddam*, 161.

[151] Joy Gordon, "Sanctions as Siege Warfare," *The Nation*, March 22, 1999, 18–22.

possible applications in WMD research or production.[152] The damage to Iraq's electric, water, and sanitation systems increased childhood mortality, mainly from diarrhea, hunger, and respiratory diseases. Crime, black markets, prostitution, and other social ills also surged.[153] The Bush administration acknowledged that this situation threatened the sanctions regime by creating a humanitarian imperative to ease sanctions. For instance, Baker wrote in early 1992: "It will be harder to maintain sanctions as Arab and regional opinion increasingly objects to the perceived hardships inflicted on ordinary Iraqis."[154]

In response to growing outrage about this situation, the United States led the passage of Security Council Resolutions 706 and 712 in August and September of 1991. These resolutions allowed Iraq to sell $1.6 billion in oil over a renewable six-month period for the import of food, medicine, and other humanitarian goods. The United Nations would control these funds in an escrow account so that the Iraqi government could not access them directly. These resolutions formed the basis of the oil-for-food plan of the mid-late 1990s, but in 1991 Saddam Hussein rejected them as infringements of Iraqi sovereignty.[155] Citing these resolutions, the Bush administration argued that Saddam was responsible for this suffering and that the sanctions should not be lifted.[156]

Although Iraqi citizens suffered immensely, Saddam managed to insulate his key political supporters in the army, security services, and the Sunni minority from the impact of sanctions through smuggling, the use of goods stolen from Kuwait, and other means.[157] In historian Charles Tripp's phrasing, he continued to convince these groups with a mixture of threats and rewards that "his leadership was better for their interests than that of any imaginable alternative and that they would lose everything if he were to be overthrown and a new dispensation of power established in

[152] Joy Gordon, *Invisible War: The United States and the Iraq Sanctions* (Cambridge, MA: Harvard University Press, 2010), 49–55, 191–199.

[153] Gordon, *Invisible War*, 86–103; Sarah Graham-Brown and Chris Toensing, "A Backgrounder on Inspections and Sanctions," in *The Iraq War Reader: History, Documents, Opinions*, ed. Christopher Cerf and Micah Sifry (New York: Simon & Schuster, 2003), 168–169; "When Sanctions Don't Work," *The Economist*, April 8, 2000, 25.

[154] Proposed Agenda Meeting with the President, James Baker, May 28, 1992, MC 197, Box 115, Folder 9, James A. Baker III Papers at the Seeley J. Mudd Library, 3.

[155] Marr, *Modern History of Iraq*, 270.

[156] See statements of Timothy Pickering and John Wolf: House Subcommittees on Europe and the Middle East and Human Rights and International Organizations of the House Committee on Foreign Affairs, *U.N. Role in the Persian Gulf and Iraqi Compliance with U. N. Resolutions*, 102nd Cong., 1st sess., October 21, 1991, 160–163, 181–187.

[157] Lisa Blaydes, *State of Repression: Iraq under Saddam Hussein* (Princeton, NJ: Princeton University Press, 2018), 117–122; Department of Central Intelligence, Iraq Survey Group, *Key Findings*, September 30, 2004, 1–3.

Baghdad."[158] In September 1991, the CIA concluded: "[T]he odds are that Saddam will still be ruling over Iraq one year from now. Only significant erosion of support from key groups would alter this judgment."[159] A National Intelligence Estimate in June 1992 reported that Saddam was much stronger than last spring and would likely survive another year, although it noted that he relied on a shrinking set of loyalists and family members.[160]

As it maneuvered through these crises, the Bush administration frequently revisited the basic tenets of its Iraq policy. Each time, however, it found no better strategy than what it was already doing. Issues like the Middle East Peace Process and the Bosnian Crisis seized the administration's attention, and it largely felt that the Iraq problem should not monopolize time and resources. Richard Haass later recalled: "It was a continuing problem, but a problem within bounds. We weren't solving the problem, we were at best managing it."[161] Moreover, Bush had ordered the CIA to seek out contacts in the Iraqi military to foment a coup, but these efforts amounted to little in Bush's last two years.[162]

A major part of the administration's unwillingness to go beyond the current policy was that it perceived the exiled Iraqi opposition to be weak, disunited, and untrustworthy.[163] The two major external opposition groups were the Iraqi National Congress (INC) under Ahmed Chalabi and the INA under Ayad Allawi. The INC formed as a political umbrella group in June 1992 to coordinate the major opposition groups, build a presence in Iraq, and ultimately challenge the regime. It managed to unite various opposition groups behind an agenda of replacing the Baathists with a federal democratic government, although the INC leadership exerted minimal authority over the disparate groups.[164] The INA, in contrast, was composed of former regime officials and military officers who aimed to use contacts in the Iraqi government to launch a coup.

[158] Charles Tripp, *A History of Iraq* (New York: Cambridge University Press, 2007), 264.

[159] CIA Report, National Intelligence Estimate 36: "Saddam Husayn's Prospects for Survival over the Next Year," September 1991, National Security Archive Online, accessed February 6, 2017, http://nsarchive.gwu.edu/NSAEBB/NSAEBB167/08.pdf, 7.

[160] CIA Report, National Intelligence Estimate 97–92: "Saddam Husayn: Likely to Hang On," June 1992, National Security Archive Online, accessed February 6, 2017, http://nsarchive.gwu.edu/NSAEBB/NSAEBB167/10.pdf, 3; Elaine Sciolino, "U.S. Reports a Stronger Saddam Hussein," *New York Times*, June 16, 1992, A3.

[161] Richard Haass, interview by Joseph Stieb, October 4, 2017.

[162] Haass, *War of Necessity*, 149.   [163] Haass, *War of Necessity*, 149.

[164] For an account of the formation of the INC and early contacts with the Bush administration, see Hamid Bayati, *From Dictatorship to Democracy: An Insider's Account of the Iraqi Opposition to Saddam* (Philadelphia: University of Pennsylvania Press, 2011), 38–42. For a summary of the opposition groups, see Dilip Hiro, *Neighbors, Not Friends: Iraq and Iran after the Gulf Wars* (New York: Routledge, 2001), 58–60.

Within Iraq, the main opposition groups were the Patriotic Union of Kurdistan (PUK) under Jalal Talabani, the Kurdish Democratic Party (KDP) under Massoud Barzani, and an Iran-backed Shia group called the Supreme Council for the Islamic Revolution in Iraq (SCIRI).

Ahmed Chalabi would emerge as the most significant figure in the Iraqi opposition in the coming decade. Chalabi's family held elite positions in the old Iraqi monarchy, and they fled Iraq during the 1958 Revolution when he was a teenager. Chalabi went to the Massachusetts Institute of Technology as an undergraduate and later received a Ph.D. in mathematics from the University of Chicago. He started a career in banking in Jordan in the 1970s, but he had to flee Jordan in 1989 under charges of bank fraud. After helping found the INC in 1992, he became a skilled political networker who connected the INC to elite neoconservative and Republican intellectuals and policy-makers. Like Kanan Makiya and other exiles, Chalabi portrayed Iraq as a budding democracy that simply needed liberation from Saddam to emerge. While the INC would have little success in challenging Saddam inside Iraq, it became a highly successful lobbying and awareness group that helped push the US political discourse toward regime change.[165]

The Bush administration generally viewed the opposition as fractious and unreliable. Of these groups, US intelligence worked most closely with the INA by providing money and CIA agents in order to foster contacts in the Iraqi elite.[166] It encouraged INC efforts to unite the opposition, and Baker even met with INC leaders in July 1992 to voice support for its efforts. Still, the administration supplied the INC with only about $20 million in its first year.[167] The CIA in particular saw the INC as liability because of its squabbling members and its inability to project power into Iraq.[168] US officials doubted Chalabi because he often exaggerated his influence inside Iraq, and he was on the run from bank fraud charges in Jordan.[169] State Department analyst Wayne White called Chalabi and his entourage "political dilettantes" who reminded him of a "used car salesman."[170] Haass wrote to Dennis Ross that in principle it

---

[165] For Chalabi's background, see Aram Roston, *The Man Who Pushed America to War: The Extraordinary Life, Adventures, and Obsessions of Ahmad Chalabi* (New York: Nation Books, 2008); Bonin, *Arrows of the Night*.

[166] Cockburn and Cockburn, *Out of the Ashes*, 57.   [167] Bonin, *Arrows of the Night*, 78.

[168] Jane Mayer, "The Manipulator," *The New Yorker*, June 7, 2004, 29; Cockburn and Cockburn, *Out of the Ashes*, 166.

[169] David Mack, interview by Charles Stuart Kennedy, Association for Diplomatic Studies and Training Foreign Affairs Oral History Project, Library of Congress, February 4, 1997, 374.

[170] Wayne White, interview by Charles Stuart Kennedy, Association for Diplomatic Studies and Training Foreign Affairs Oral History Project, Library of Congress, April 21, 2005, 206–207.

would be desirable to give a higher profile to the opposition, but "our efforts to encourage opposition unity continue to be undermined by the weaknesses and rivalries of the opposition."[171] Any regime change strategy that centered on these groups, the administration concluded, would have little chance of succeeding and might drag the United States into fighting inside Iraq.

Richard Haass noted that, in this period, US Iraq policy closely resembled "classic containment in its emphasis on limiting Iraq's capability and reach and in its secondary interest in fostering regime change."[172] The administration increasingly felt, in Baker's words, that "the tide is running against us" in the struggle to maintain sanctions and inspections, leaving few officials eager to prioritize the even tougher effort to overthrow Saddam.[173] As Scowcroft wrote in July 1992, the United States needed to distinguish between "the objective (full compliance) and the desirable outcome (Saddam's ouster)."[174] Bush's Iraq policy never strayed from that hierarchy of goals. Its stance against normalization of relations with a Saddam-led Iraq, moreover, persisted from 1991 to 1992. If anything, the frustration of dealing with Iraqi intransigence hardened this position, as did mounting political pressure at home.[175]

Early Critics of Containment: 1991–1992

Bush's struggle to make Saddam comply with the Security Council resolutions took place in an atmosphere of intense scrutiny from the media and Congress. The political conversation on containment for this period and the remainder of the 1990s can be categorized into three schools: conditionalist, inevitable decline, and humanitarian. For the most part, the first two schools operated within the regime change consensus because they held that no normalization with Saddam was possible, that he would never fundamentally change his intentions, and that he would have to be removed at some point. They diverged, however, on how much the United States

---

[171] Memorandum, Richard Haass to Dennis Ross, March 31, 1992, OA/ID CF01585-015, Working Files, Richard Haass Files, George Bush Presidential Library, 1.

[172] Haass, *War of Necessity*, 148. Haass says something similar, in Memorandum, Haass to Ross, March 31, 1992, 1.

[173] Proposed Agenda Meeting with the President, James Baker, May 28, 1992, 3.

[174] NSC Meeting Notes, Richard Haass, July 25, 1992, OA/ID CF 01404–003, National Security Council, Presidential Meeting Files, Richard Haass Files, George Bush Presidential Library, 4.

[175] For examples of this hardening, see Memorandum, Haass to Ross, March 31, 1992, 1–3; Testimony of Edward Djerejian, Assistant Secretary for Near Eastern Affairs at the State Department in House Subcommittee on Europe and the Middle East of the House Committee on Foreign Affairs, *Developments in the Middle East*, 102nd Cong., 2nd sess., June 24, 1992, 8.

should risk to remove him and whether containment and regime change could be pursued simultaneously or were incompatible. The humanitarian school, in contrast, operated outside of the regime change consensus because of its focus on alleviating the Iraqi health crisis.

I call the first approach conditionalist because their support for containment hinged on how effectively the policy was enforced and whether it could plausibly lead to regime change, preserved the coalition, and adjusted the policy as circumstances changed. Conditionalists could be described as both critics and defenders of containment, depending on its effectiveness and future prospects. This school consisted mostly of centrist Democrats, self-identified realists, defense experts, and media institutions like the *New York Times* and *Washington Post* editorial boards. They argued that the containment could serve as a way to manage the Iraqi threat and enforce the UN resolutions while low-risk ways of removing Saddam were pursued. They also generally supported Bush's stance against normalization with a Saddam-led Iraq. However, unlike members of the inevitable decline school, they believed that a more direct regime change policy might bog the United States down in Iraqi affairs and undermine the international coalition behind sanctions and inspections.[176] Furthermore, members of this school thought that while democratizing Iraq was a worthwhile goal, fundamentally reforming Iraqi politics was beyond US means or knowledge. Despite significant overlap with Bush's approach to Iraq, they frequently criticized his enforcement of containment, which they saw as overly cautious and inattentive.[177]

Centrist Democrats like Al Gore, Les Aspin, and Joseph Liebermann best represented the thinking of the conditional school of thought on containment in the early 1990s.[178] They had all voted in favor of Desert Storm, and they argued afterward that the United States should use sanctions, inspections, air power, and support for the opposition to maximize the likelihood of regime change. They strongly opposed normalization, with Gore arguing that the United States could sooner "housebreak a cobra" than have a constructive relationship with Saddam. However, they all accepted that the need to preserve the coalition imposed necessary constraints on Iraq policy.[179]

---

[176] Editorial, "The Quicksand in Iraq," *New York Times,* March 20, 1991, A28; Editorial, "Who Should Liberate Iraq?" *New York Times,* January 22, 1992, A20.

[177] For example, see Editorial, "Time to Punish Hussein-Again," *New York Times,* July 24, 1992, A24.

[178] Julian Zelizer, *Arsenal of Democracy: The Politics of National Security from World War II to the War on Terrorism* (New York: Basic Books, 2010), 378.

[179] *Cong. Rec.,* 102nd Cong., 1st sess., April 18, 1991, 8646; Alfonsi, *Circle in the Sand,* 214. Al Gore, "Defeating Hussein, Once and for All," *New York Times,* September 26, 1991, A27.

Gore in particular spoke extensively on Iraq from 1991 to 1992, supporting the administration when it demanded full compliance from Iraq and excoriating it for hesitation. In November 1991, he led every member of the House Select Committee on Intelligence in sending a letter to Bush that declared: "In our judgment, the current policy towards Iraq does not seem to be working." The letter called for greater willingness to use force to punish Saddam as well as a stronger effort to delegitimize the Baathist regime, including war crimes trials.[180] Another letter from mostly Democratic Congressmen to Bush in 1992 lamented Saddam's survival and called for additional steps to force him into compliance and possibly out of power, including the extension of the NFZ, greater aid to opposition groups, and a stated policy that the United States would use force against WMD sites if Saddam continued to obstruct inspectors.[181] For Gore and others in the conditional approach, containment was adequate as long as it remained a firm base upon which the United States pursued both Iraqi compliance with the United Nations and regime change.

The reaction of members of this conditional approach to the confrontation at the Agriculture Ministry in July 1992 captures their thinking well. Gore, Aspin, and others portrayed this case as an Iraqi victory that "made the nonnegotiable, negotiable" by giving Iraq a say in the national composition of the inspections teams and "opened the door for Iraq to negotiate many of the more onerous elements of the U.N. resolutions."[182] In Aspin's colorful phrasing, Iraq was winning "the war of nerves and inches" because of Bush's feckless policy of "threat and forget."[183] If Bush did not back strict enforcement of the resolutions, Saddam would continue to erode the coalition's resolve. The *New York Times* and *Washington Post* editorial boards and foreign policy expert Anthony Cordesman likewise called for Bush to respond to each inspection crisis with air strikes or other ways of punishing Saddam. Without this unrelenting pressure and continual support for inspections and sanctions, containment would eventually fall apart.[184]

---

[180] Alfonsi, *Circle in the Sand*, 274.
[181] Letter, Robert Torricelli, Stephen Solarz, Dante Fascell, et al. to George Bush, March 6, 1992, George Bush Presidential Library, November 28, 2016, accessed November 28, 2016, https://bush41library.tamu.edu/files/persian-gulf/41-CO072-302096–323770/41-co072-313772.pdf.
[182] Gore, "Defeating Hussein," *New York Times*, September 26, 1991.
[183] Quotes are from Aspin, *Cong. Rec.*, 102nd Cong., 2nd sess., July 28, 1992, 19686; Les Aspin, "Saddam Is Winning," *Washington Post*, August 11, 1992, A17; See Lieberman on same point: *Cong. Rec.*, 102nd Cong., 2nd sess., July 27, 1992, 19450.
[184] Editorial, "No Partial Deal for Iraq," *New York Times*, November 24, 1992, A14; Editorial, "Measured Force on Iraq," *New York Times*, September 19, 1991, A26; Anthony Cordesman, "How to Hit Iraq," *New York Times*, August 19, 1992; Editorial, "The Right Reply to Iraq," *Washington Post*, September 19, 1991, A20.

A second, more uncompromising set of actors defined containment from the outset as a policy that inherently could not work against regimes like Baathist Iraq and individuals like Saddam. I call this the "inevitable decline" school because, unlike the conditionalists, members of this approach believed containment was doomed to fail from the start. They mostly came from neoconservative circles, although they included some liberal hawks and conservatives. Whereas containment focused on limiting Iraqi capabilities, these critics argued that the real problem was not the regime's capabilities but its unchanging intent to develop and use those capabilities. Moreover, containment could not last because it relied on a fickle international coalition that did not share the US stance against normalization. Whereas members of the conditional school believed that containment could form a baseline for pursuing regime change, members of the inevitable decline school saw containment and regime change as incompatible strategies. Because Bush would not take the aggressive actions needed to topple Saddam for fear of harming the coalition, containment actually precluded the goal of regime change.

Critics in the inevitable decline school further claimed that the current policy could not remove Saddam because its main regime change mechanism was sanctions, which had not even forced Saddam out of Kuwait. Once the inspectors left and the sanctions were lifted, Saddam or any Baathist successor would return to building WMD.[185] Any policy that did not address the fundamental problem of the regime and its intentions was therefore dangerously inadequate. For example, *The Wall Street Journal* editors wrote in July 1991: "The real problem here is less the weapons than the regime sitting in power in Baghdad. ... The weapons are dangerous because the Baath Party is incorrigibly dangerous. So long as these people are in control, no amount of inspecting can ever guarantee that we have found it all."[186] Charles Krauthammer stressed the same set of problems: "The Iraqi bomb is today a problem of intent, not capability. The capability is there, and it is extremely difficult to destroy piece by piece. It can only be taken care of by going after intent: by producing a leadership in Baghdad willing to give it over to us."[187]

These critics pointed to Iraqi noncompliance with the inspections as evidence that the current regime would never comply and would

---

[185] William Safire, "Saddam's Deadline," *New York Times*, July 22, 1991, A15; Jim Hoagland, "Unfinished Business in the Gulf," *Washington Post*, September 12, 1991, A23; Editorial, "Ashes in Our Mouths (cont.)," *The National Review*, July 8, 1991, 17.

[186] Editorial, "Saddam's Compliance," *Wall Street Journal*, July 10, 1991, A12.

[187] Charles Krauthammer, "What to Do about Saddam," *Washington Post*, July 26, 1991, A23.

inevitably hide some WMD capabilities. They also mocked UNSCOM and the IAEA as bumbling "Inspector Clouseaus" and claimed that the inspections created a false sense of security.[188] In contrast to the conditionalists, they contended that containment was too feckless to be given a chance to work. With each confrontation, they pressed Bush to launch sustained air strikes on the Iraqi military, security services, and infrastructure in order to break his regime's hold.[189] Without concerted action, Saddam would simply keep up this "Baghdad Shuffle" until the exhausted coalition withdrew the inspectors.[190] Later in the decade, they developed a strategy for regime change called rollback, which will be discussed in a later chapter.[191]

The third school of thought on containment was the humanitarian school, which did not concur with the regime change consensus. Most of them came from the political and academic left, religious organizations, and humanitarian activism. Although they generally agreed that Iraq should be contained, they prioritized lifting sanctions to relieve the health crisis, noting that sanctions affected ordinary Iraqis far more than Saddam's regime. They frequently pointed out that most Iraqis had become dependent on government ration cards, allowing the state to control them further.[192] David Bonior (D-MI) argued that an enfeebled Iraqi people stood no chance against the Baathist security system, saying, "Saddam Hussein will not be brought down by starving the Iraqi people."[193]

In the House Select Committee on Hunger, Democratic Congressmen Byron Dorgan (ND), Timothy Penny (MN), and Jim McDermott (WA) heard dozens of testimonies about the suffering in Iraq and urged Bush to allow for normal commerce with the exception of military goods. At the

---

[188] Quote is from: Editorial, "Clouseau in Iraq," *Wall Street Journal*, August 12, 1991, A10. For a variation on this argument, see Albert Wohlstetter, "Wide Open Secret Coup," *The National Review*, March 16, 1992, 34–36.

[189] Safire, "Saddam's Deadline," *New York Times*, July 22, 1991, A15; Jim Hoagland, "Is It Time to Strike at Saddam Again?" *Washington Post*, March 27, 1992, A27; Editorial, "The President and Iraq," *Washington Post*, August 18, 1992, A12.

[190] Editorial, "Rethinking Iraq," *Wall Street Journal*, July 22, 1992, A12; Jim Hoagland, "Advantage Saddam Hussein," *Washington Post*, July 28, 1992, A19.

[191] For some calls for rollback in 1991 and 1992, see Gerald Seib, "Washington Insight: Shake-Up by Saddam Hussein Rekindles U.S. Hopes for Overthrow of Iraqi Leader," *Wall Street Journal*, November 11, 1991, A10. Charles Krauthammer, "Saddam Won," *Washington Post*, July 29, 1992, A23; Laurie Mylroie, "Still Standing," *The New Republic*, April 13, 1992, 11–12.

[192] Achim Rohde, *State–Society Relations in Ba'thist Iraq* (New York: Routledge Press, 2010), 68; Meghan O'Sullivan, *Shrewd Sanctions: Statecraft and State Sponsors of Terrorism* (Washington, DC, Brookings Institution Press, 2003), 137.

[193] International Task Force of the House Select Committee on Hunger, *Humanitarian Crisis in Iraq: Challenge for U.S. Policy*, 102nd Cong., 1st sess., November 13, 1991, 95.

minimum, they called for Iraq to be permitted to use its frozen assets to purchase essential goods abroad.[194] McDermott questioned the basic morality of the "turn the screw" policy: "We have to ask ourselves: at what point does the starvation of 18 million people take precedence over our attempts to remove one person from power?"[195] The humanitarian critics argued that this suffering stemmed mainly from the Desert Storm bombing campaign, which devastated crucial Iraqi infrastructure like power plants and water treatment facilities.[196] Furthermore, they argued that waiting for Saddam to accept Security Council Resolutions 706 and 712 was insufficient given the gravity of the humanitarian situation. Instead, the United States had to alleviate this suffering even if it meant weakening a cornerstone of containment.[197] Congressman Henry Gonzalez, for instance, wrote to Bush in May 1991 calling for an "immediate and massive international effort" to provide relief for the Iraqi people.[198] Of these three schools of thought, the humanitarian argument was the most distant from centers of power in politics and the media. The leadership of both major parties did little to support this criticism as they were both committed to tough policies on Iraq.[199] Nevertheless, this argument would gain traction over time as Saddam remained in power and the Iraqi people's suffering continued.

Conclusion

For the remainder of the decade, key figures in the Bush administration continued to defend Desert Storm as a limited victory and argue that containment was effectively managing the Iraqi threat. Colin Powell best spelled out this defense in September 1991:

There is also this romantic view that all we had to do was sail up the river valley to Baghdad and Saddam Hussein would be waiting at the gate, that all we had to do was snatch him, and that there was some Jeffersonian democrat waiting in the Baath Party to take over. I think the President showed great wisdom in not getting

---

[194] See testimonies of religious and humanitarian organizations in International Task Force of the House Select Committee, *Humanitarian Dilemma in Iraq*, 102nd Cong., 1st sess., August 1, 1991.

[195] House Select Committee on Hunger, *Humanitarian Crisis in Iraq*, November 13, 1991, 3.

[196] See testimony by Congressman Henry Gonzalez in *Cong. Rec.*, 102nd Cong., 1st sess., June 24, 1991, 16079.

[197] See testimonies of Tim Penny and Jim McDermott in House Committee on Hunger, *Humanitarian Crisis in Iraq*, November 13, 1991, 3–7; Phyllis Bennis and Michel Moushabeck, eds., *Beyond the Storm: A Gulf Crisis Reader* (Brooklyn: Olive Branch Press, 1991).

[198] Gordon, *Invisible War*, 149.   [199] Gordon, *Invisible War*, 141–142.

himself mired down in a Mesopotamian mess. I am confident that regional stability is intact. Saddam Hussein is threatening none of his neighbors.[200]

In an interview in 1996, Brent Scowcroft backed up Powell: "As long as we are alert and observant Saddam Hussein is not a threat to his neighbors. He's a nuisance, he's an annoyance, but he's not a threat."[201] Indeed, many parts of containment worked well in the early 1990s. The multinational coalition behind the Security Council resolutions remained intact and the sanctions prevented Saddam from rebuilding his military strength. The NFZs limited his ability to harm vulnerable populations and project force against his neighbors. Finally, the inspections had uncovered and destroyed most of his WMD capabilities.[202]

Bush may have won the policy battle over Iraq after the Gulf War, but he lost the political war to defend that policy. Few figures in politics and the media accepted the idea that Saddam was being contained and would continue to be in the future. Most of the political establishment supported the no-normalization stance because they thought Saddam had proven himself incapable of change, willing to do anything to augment his power, and impervious to positive incentives like those of the prewar engagement policy. This line of thinking about Iraq drew conceptual strength from the problem of the regime, or the belief that the nature of totalitarian regimes like the Baathist state drove them to be aggressive, anti-American, and oppressive.

The impossibility of redemption was the bitter "lesson" of Saddam's invasion of Kuwait. This lesson was then calcified by the anguish and disappointment of an incomplete victory and subsequent years of frustration in trying to compel Iraqi cooperation with the United Nations. The principle of no-normalization formed an absolute baseline of US political discourse for the rest of the decade, with few dissensions. Debates would rage over whether containment was working, whether the United States needed to seek democracy or could accept a more pliable strongman, or how much and what kind of direct action the United States should take to topple Saddam. All of these conversations nonetheless occurred on this calcified bedrock. For the rest of the decade, as Saddam remained in power and key pillars of containment weakened, more Americans shifted from the conditionalist approach to the inevitable decline perspective that

---

[200] Powell quote from Senate Armed Services Committee, *Nominations before the Senate Armed Services Committee*, 102nd Cong., 1st sess., September 27, 1991. 314. For a similar point, see Cheney testimony in House Committee on Foreign Affairs, *The Future of U.S. Foreign Policy in the Post–Cold War Era*, 102nd Cong., 2nd sess., March 24, 1992, 416.

[201] Scowcroft, interview by Frontline, 1995.   [202] Haass, *War of Necessity*, 151–152.

containment was not working, could not work, and was only postponing his resurrection.

The strength of Bush's argument for containment was that the United States lacked a low-risk means of toppling Saddam or handling the consequences of his ouster, which left containment as a reasonable way to manage the problem. This, however, was a defensive position with an indefinite but inexorable political expiration date. When it became clear that Saddam would survive the immediate postwar crises, the administration lost its most credible explanation for how containment would bring about his downfall. Furthermore, the administration had trapped itself by ruling out any form of normalization, even in the unlikely event of Iraqi compliance with the inspections, and domestic politics hemmed them in even further.

With Bush's defeat in 1992, he passed these dilemmas to William Jefferson Clinton.

3 The Long Watch: The High Years of Containment, 1993–1996

Introduction

Sergeant Gary Jordan of the US Army's 24th Infantry Division returned to Kuwait in October 1994 as part of the effort to deter Iraq from invading its tiny neighbor after Saddam positioned combat units on the border. A veteran of Desert Storm, Jordan could not help but voice frustration over his redeployment: "If we'd taken care of the problem the first time, we wouldn't have had a problem this time."[1] In Iraq at the same time, an anonymous waiter slipped a note to two reporters that read: "Dear sir, sorry to trouble you. I know you are very kind and therefore, when you leave the country, could you give me whatever medication you have. I'm poor and I have a big family. ... Any antibiotics would be a great help."[2] In Baghdad's hotels, foreign businessmen prepared huge oil contracts with the Iraqi government that awaited the end of sanctions. In the United States, Congressmen, columnists, and other critics grumbled that there was no way out of containment.

The containment of Iraq pleased no one involved, but in its first term the Clinton administration enforced and defended this policy as a way of managing the Saddam problem at reasonable cost. Clinton largely continued Bush's approach of using sanctions to compel Saddam's compliance with the United Nations, keep him weak, and create the conditions for a coup. Clinton's strategy for managing Saddam was to maintain the coalition, support weapons inspectors, preserve sanctions, enforce the no-fly zones (NFZ), and occasionally use or threaten to use force when Saddam challenged his confinement. The administration hoped that this approach would allow it to focus on other international priorities. It basically achieved these goals in the first term. The coalition, led by the

---

[1] Russell Watson, "But What about Next Time?" *Newsweek*, October 24, 1994, 28.
[2] Youssef Ibrahim, "Vote Leaves Iraqi as Winner and West at a Loss," *New York Times*, October 18, 1995, A1.

United States and Great Britain but including key countries like France, Russia, China, and the Arab states, suppressed Saddam's threats to his neighbors, unveiled and destroyed most of his weapons of mass destruction (WMD), inhibited his military recovery, and forced him to focus on survival at home. The administration held that for the time being there was no realistic alternative to containment because direct attempts at regime change would be ineffective, risky, and harmful to the international coalition.

These successes, however, did not erase key tensions in Clinton's Iraq policy, especially the increasingly incompatible demands by domestic and international actors. The political discourse on Iraq in Clinton's first term operated within the regime change consensus, or the belief that any true solution to the Saddam problem required his removal at the minimum and the transformation of his regime at the maximum. This belief had been solidified in US politics after the Gulf War, and it remained virtually unassailable under Clinton. This political discourse generated pressure on Clinton to intensify actions against Iraq, particularly the pursuit of regime change by coup and the maintenance of sanctions as long as Saddam remained in power.

The international coalition, however, pulled Clinton in the opposite direction. Countries like France, Russia, China, and most US allies in the Middle East would not countenance indefinite containment, much less the direct pursuit of regime change. They envisioned using sanctions as a temporary stick to compel Saddam's compliance with the inspectors, and they called for the lifting of sanctions once his compliance could be verified. Suspicious of overweening US power and keen to renew trade with Iraq, many coalition members criticized the US hard line and sought ways to normalize relations with Iraq. For Clinton, the core dilemma was that leaning too far to one side jeopardized the support of the other, as he needed both domestic backing and a united international coalition to maintain containment.

In order to deal with these irreconcilable audiences, the administration developed what might be called the "Clinton fudge."[3] Clinton officials intentionally avoided tying the lifting of sanctions to Saddam's overthrow, as Bush had done after Desert Storm. However, they demanded that Saddam comply with all Security Council resolutions passed after Desert Storm, including Resolution 688, which called for Iraq to "ensure

---

[3] Foreign policy scholar Laurie Mylroie called Clinton's policy on when to lift sanctions a "fudge." The "Clinton fudge" is my term. See Subcommittee on Europe and the Middle East of the House Committee on Foreign Affairs, *U.S. Policy toward Iraq 3 Years after the Gulf War*, 103rd Cong., 2nd sess., February 23, 1994, 19.

that the human and political rights of all Iraqi citizens are respected."[4] The administration argued that it was unlikely that Saddam would fully comply with these demands and that if he did he would fall from power because his totalitarian system hinged on terror and violence. Clinton officials justified this high bar of compliance by arguing for the need to be reassured of Saddam's changed intentions, not just his literal compliance, in order to safely lift sanctions. Thus, the Clinton fudge provided a formula to signal to domestic audiences that it was almost inconceivable that sanctions would be lifted with Saddam in power while telling the coalition that it was open to easing sanctions if Saddam met these standards. This intentionally ambiguous rhetorical strategy signaled a hard line to the domestic sphere and flexibility to the coalition, allowing Clinton to focus on other priorities. After all, Clinton ran for president on an economic platform and did not want foreign policy issues draining political capital.

Clinton's Iraq policy and this balancing act held together as long as several conditions prevailed. First, the administration needed to maintain the possibility that Saddam Hussein might be overthrown in a coup in order to protect Clinton's political flank. The hope for a coup preserved the possibility that containment itself could generate sufficient pressures to solve the Saddam problem without massive US intervention. If containment lacked this outlet and Saddam appeared firmly in power, the policy would seem indefinite, forcing the United States to choose between accepting his survival and actively pursuing regime change. Second, the United States needed to maintain coalition support for sanctions and inspections because without this cooperation Saddam could export oil and rebuild his WMD and conventional forces.

By the end of Clinton's first term the conditions necessary for preserving containment had been undermined. Between 1992 and 1996, Saddam survived coups, family betrayals, rebellions, and economic scarcity. By the end of 1996, he had crushed the US-backed Iraqi opposition and made his regime virtually immune to coups or rebellions. In addition, the coalition grew shakier as France, Russia, China, and US partners in the Middle East pressed to end inspections, renew trade with Iraq, and draw down the sanctions. At home, these two shifts accelerated the process of moving key policy-makers, politicians, and commentators from the conditional position to the inevitable declinist view that containment cannot work and must be replaced with a regime change policy. The

---

[4] United Nations Security Council Resolution 688, April 5, 1991, un.org, accessed May 10, 2017, https://daccess-ods.un.org/TMP/7304973.00624847.html, 32.

paradox of Clinton's first-term Iraq policy was that containment achieved many goals at a tolerable cost but became less tenable in the long term.

New President, Old Policy: Clinton Takes Over Containment

Iraq policy did not play a central role in the 1992 election, but it had a more important place than many scholars have acknowledged. The Clinton campaign focused on economic issues while seeking to neutralize Bush's experience and accomplishments in foreign affairs. They acknowledged that Desert Storm counted as a victory in the public eye but tried to tarnish Bush's victory by arguing that Iraq's invasion of Kuwait resulted from his coddling of Saddam beforehand. Al Gore, Clinton's running mate and a Gulf War supporter, cited Bush's support for export credit aid to Iraq and his muted reaction to Iraqi threats as reasons why Saddam thought he could get away with the invasion. In one speech, Gore stated: "His poor judgment, moral blindness, and bungling policies led directly to a war that never should have taken place."[5]

Clinton and Gore further attacked Bush's Iraq record by accusing him of betraying the Iraqi rebels after promising assistance against Saddam, adding that the United States missed an opportunity to bring Saddam down after the war.[6] One Democratic bumper sticker linked Bush's failure to topple Saddam with the faltering US economy by asking: "Saddam still has his job. What about you?"[7] Despite these attacks on Bush's performance, the Clinton campaign was vague about how it would change Iraq policy. Campaign officials discussed plans to support the opposition more concretely but did not promise significant changes to containment.[8] Clinton said in January 1992 that he probably would have voted for the authorization to use force against Iraq, although his record at that time was ambiguous.[9]

The Bush campaign retorted that Clinton lacked foreign policy experience and that Bush had dealt with Saddam successfully and prudently. They objected to Clinton's moral reproaches of Bush's handling of authoritarian regimes, arguing: "The objective is to change behavior,

---

[5] Albert Gore, "Speech before the Center for National Policy" (speech, Washington, DC, September 29, 1992) C-SPAN.org, accessed November 3, 2017, www.c-span.org/video/?32824–1/clinton-campaign-event.
[6] Christian Alfonsi, *Circle in the Sand: Why We Went Back to Iraq* (New York: Doubleday, 2006), 289.
[7] Mark Shields, "The Gulf Glow Fades," *Washington Post*, March 6, 1992, A23.
[8] Gore, "Speech before the Center for National Policy," September 29, 1992.
[9] Michael Kelly, "Clinton Defends Position on Iraqi War," *New York Times*, July 31, 1992, A13.

not make yourself feel good. Sometimes you isolate. Sometimes you must engage to change behavior."[10] They also deflected Clinton's Iraqgate accusations onto the Democrats by saying that most Democrats had supported aid to Iraq before 1990 but then voted against the use of force authorization for Desert Storm.[11]

Clinton's criticism of Bush's Iraq record fit into a larger strategy of depicting Bush as both too focused on foreign affairs and too uncertain about democracy and human rights abroad. Clinton accused Bush of "ambivalence about supporting democracy" and a willingness to partner with dictators like Saddam, Hosni Mubarak, and the Chinese communists.[12] He pledged that his foreign policy would prioritize multilateral institutions, expand free trade, and promote democracy and peaceful globalization.[13] This vision appealed to many intellectuals who were frustrated with Bush's pragmatic but uninspiring foreign policy. Many liberals, conservatives, and neoconservatives had criticized Bush for not prioritizing the spread of democracy in an age when it seemed the inevitable course of history.[14] The Clinton campaign, in turn, tried to cultivate these groups, especially neoconservatives, in order to undermine a key element of the Republican coalition.[15] The editors of the *New Republic* backed Clinton because they saw him as a new type of Democrat who believed in strong defense and the global assertion of US values. They accused Bush of failing to recognize the unique historical opportunities created by communism's collapse, writing: "Instead of embracing the democratic revolutions of the late 1980s and using them to formulate a clearly pro-democratic foreign policy, Bush lapsed into an incoherent realism."[16]

---

[10] Bush Debate Preparation Documents, James Baker, 1992, MC 197, Box 141, Folder 9, James A. Baker III Papers at the Seeley G. Mudd Library, 5.

[11] Brent Scowcroft, "We Didn't 'Coddle' Saddam," *Washington Post*, October 10, 1992, A27; Bush Debate Preparation Documents, Baker Library, 8.

[12] Thomas Friedman, "Clinton Asserts Bush Is Too Eager to Befriend the World's Dictators," *New York Times*, October 2, 1992, A1.

[13] Norman Ornstein, "Foreign Policy and the 1992 Election," *Foreign Affairs* 71, no. 3 (Summer, 1992): 1–16; Julian Zelizer, *Arsenal of Democracy: The Politics of National Security from World War II to the War on Terrorism* (New York: Basic Books, 2010), 383.

[14] Other prominent neoconservative and conservative supporters of Clinton in 1992 included Joshua Muravchik, Paul Nitze, Samuel Huntington, Edward Luttwak, Martin Peretz, and James Woolsey. For examples, see Editorial, "No Fly," *Wall Street Journal*, August 28, 1992, A10; Steven Rosenfeld, "Return of the Neocons," *Washington Post*, August 28, 1992, A23; Joshua Muravchik, "Conservatives for Clinton," *The New Republic*, November 2, 1992, 22.

[15] Derek Chollet, *America between the Wars: From 11/9 to 9/11: The Misunderstood Years between the Fall of the Berlin Wall and the Start of the War on Terror* (New York: Public Affairs, 2008), 35–36.

[16] Editorial, "Clinton for President," *The New Republic*, November 9, 1992, 8.

After Clinton won the 1992 election, he began building a foreign policy team and weighing how to handle challenges like Iraq. On January 5, 1993, Secretary of State Lawrence Eagleburger sent a memo to his successor Warren Christopher which outlined the Iraqi threat:

Saddam is anxious to break out of the system of postwar constraints imposed by the U.N. He will test you early in the new Administration, perhaps first with charm, and when that fails, with defiance. ... If you are not moving forward to keep the pressure on Saddam, you will find yourself sliding backward.[17]

Eagleburger portrayed Iraq as a maintenance problem that required active attention and pressure to prevent Saddam from chipping away at containment.

In fact, the pattern Eagleburger described manifested itself even before Clinton took office. In early January, Iraq started challenging the southern NFZ by sending surface-to-air missiles (SAMs) and combat aircraft into the southern zone and activating preexisting antiaircraft batteries, leading to US forces shooting down one Iraqi fighter.[18] On January 8, Iraqi officials announced that UN inspectors would have to fly into Iraq on chartered Iraqi aircraft rather than UN planes.[19] On January 11, Bush retaliated with air strikes on Iraqi SAM sites and other air defenses.[20] US officials made clear that the strike was intended to force Saddam's compliance rather than overthrow him. One official called the strikes "a spanking, not a beating."[21]

Some of Clinton's comments shortly after this confrontation muddled what his Iraq policy would be upon taking office. He told an interviewer that he backed the strikes and added:

The people of Iraq would be better off if they had a different leader. But my job is not to pick their rulers for them. I always tell everybody, "I'm a Baptist; I believe in deathbed conversions." If he wants a different relationship with the United States and the United Nations all he has to do is change his behavior.[22]

---

[17] Memorandum, Lawrence Eagleburger to Warren Christopher, January 5, 1993, State Department FOIA Reading Room, accessed October 14, 2017, https://foia.state.gov/Se arch/results.aspx, 14.

[18] Michael Gordon, "Iraq Is Reported to Move Missiles into Areas Patrolled by U.S. Jets," *New York Times*, January 5, 1993, A1.

[19] Frank Piral, "U.N. Condemns Iraq Move," *New York Times*, January 9, 1993, A6.

[20] Eric Schmitt, "Allied Strike: Swift and Unchallenged," *New York Times*, January 13, 1998, A8.

[21] Jill Smolowe, "A Spanking for Saddam," *Time*, January 25, 1993, 44.

[22] "Excerpts from an Interview with Clinton after the Air Strikes," *New York Times*, A10. For critics of the "Baptist" comment, see William Safire, "Stumbling into the Oval Office," *New York Times*, January 18, 1993, A17; A. M. Rosenthal, "Bill Clinton's War," *New York Times*, January 19, 1993, A21.

Clinton had never hinted that he would accept any normalization with Iraq during the campaign, but now he was suggesting that relations with Saddam could improve if he complied with the UN demands. His advisers were surprised and quickly urged him to withdraw this comment.[23] In the face of media and Congressional criticism, Clinton backtracked a few days later and reaffirmed that he had "no intention of normalizing relations" and that "there is no difference between my policy and the policy of the present administration." Clinton officials later said that he feared looking weak on Iraq going into his presidency but also saw a hard-line policy as risky. This anecdote nonetheless shows the influence of the regime change consensus, as Clinton suffered heavy political criticism for even suggesting that Saddam might be rehabilitated.[24]

The confrontation with Saddam continued on January 17 when Iraqi officials said they would not guarantee the safety of UN aircraft that flew into Iraqi airspace. Bush responded by launching 40 cruise missiles against a military complex outside of Baghdad and promising more strikes if Saddam continued his obstruction.[25] On January 19, the day before Clinton's inauguration, the Iraqis relented and promised to stop firing on coalition planes and allow inspectors to fly into Baghdad. They portrayed this move as a gesture of goodwill to a new president they hoped might take a softer approach.[26] Nevertheless, Iraqi antiaircraft sites continued to target US planes, and on January 22 Clinton retaliated with air strikes on antiaircraft installations near the northern NFZ. Soon thereafter, the Iraqis resumed compliance with the inspectors.[27] Eagleburger's prediction that Saddam would try to sway Clinton with hollow cooperation first and defiance second came true immediately, and the administration's firm response demonstrated a willingness to use force to deter Iraqi misbehavior.

Clinton entered office with little experience in foreign affairs or a clear conception of grand strategy. As members of the Democratic Leadership Council, he and Gore wanted to distance themselves from the left wing of the party and defy the Democratic Party's reputation as weak and inept on foreign policy. For Clinton, Gore, and other centrist Democrats,

---

[23] Martin Indyk, *Innocent Abroad: An Intimate Account of American Peace Diplomacy in the Middle East* (New York: Simon & Schuster, 2009), 31.

[24] Indyk, *Innocent Abroad*, 31; Thomas Friedman, "Clinton Affirms U.S. Policy on Iraq," *New York Times*, January 15, 1993, A1.

[25] Michael Gordon, "Clinton Backs Step: About 40 Rockets Fired from Navy Ships," *New York Times*, January 18, 1993, A1.

[26] Michael Gordon, "Iraq Says It Won't Attack Planes and Agree to U.N. Flight Terms," *New York Times*, January 20, 1993, A1.

[27] Elaine Sciolino, "New Iraqi Site Raided as White House Vows Firmness," *New York Times*, January 23, 1993, A3.

changing this perception would require more willingness to use US power to spread democracy and liberal values and defend the national interest.[28] The DLC's think tank, the Progressive Policy Institute, played a key role in helping Clinton formulate this foreign policy agenda.

At the White House, National Security Advisor Anthony Lake led an effort throughout 1993 to develop an overarching foreign policy framework that would also satisfy these political objectives. He and other Clinton advisors wanted to devise a more transformative vision than Bush's New World Order, which mainly sought to restore cooperation among the great powers in order to maintain international stability. Clinton and Lake believed that the cautious Bush had not recognized the opportunities created by globalization and the end of the Cold War. At the same time, the incoming administration believed their political mandate was for domestic issues, and they did not want any foreign policy issue dominating the agenda, especially not the intractable Iraq question.[29]

Lake delivered an address at Johns Hopkins on September 21, 1993, to lay out Clinton's conception of the US global role. He defined democracy, human rights, and market economics as the "core concepts" of US foreign policy and argued that in recent years these ideas were "more broadly accepted than ever." He made a case that these values had "universal appeal" and that in the wake of the Soviet defeat the United States had an unprecedented opportunity to spread their reach. In a Wilsonian fusion of interests and ideology, he claimed: "To the extent democracy and market economics hold sway in other nations, our own nation will be more secure, prosperous, and influential, while the broader world will be more humane and peaceful."[30] This statement reflected the deep belief of key figures in the Clinton administration in the democratic peace, or the idea that democracies generally acted less aggressively, did not go to war with each other, and cooperated more with other states. To explain this behavior, democratic peace theorists cited institutions and mechanisms like popular control of government, the separation of

---

[28] Sean Wilentz, *The Age of Reagan: A History, 1974–2008* (New York: Harper Collins, 2008), 318, 324–326; Chollet, *America between the Wars*, 31–37; Zelizer, *Arsenal of Democracy*, 378–380, 386, 396.

[29] Hal Brands, *From Berlin to Baghdad: America's Search for Purpose in the Post–Cold War World* (Lexington: University Press of Kentucky, 2008), 102–103, 134.

[30] Anthony Lake, "From Containment to Enlargement" (speech, Washington, DC, September 21, 1993), accessed April 15, 2017, www.mtholyoke.edu/acad/intrel/lakedoc .html. See also Michael Hunt, *The American Ascendancy: How the United States Gained and Wielded Global Dominance* (Chapel Hill, NC: University of North Carolina Press, 2007), 266–268, 272–274; John Lewis Gaddis, *Surprise, Security, and the American Experience* (Cambridge, MA: Harvard University Press, 2004), 77–79.

powers, and more liberal values. Clinton officials connected the democratic peace to free trade, reasoning that as nations built economic interdependence, they would have fewer reasons to fight, and would mutually gain in prosperity.[31]

For Lake, the end of the Cold War meant that the United States should shift from containing the threat to capitalist democracies to enlarging this community. The United States would pursue this goal by example, exhortation, and material support for democratic and market forces. It would also pursue these ends in partnership with allies and multilateral institutions in order to bolster democratic collective security and international law. Lake labeled this approach the "strategy of enlargement."[32] The great threat to this vision was not a single state like the Soviet Union or an ideology like communism but a category of states, what Lake called "backlash" or "rogue" states. These were mostly medium-sized regional powers like Iraq, Iran, Libya, Cuba, and North Korea. Lake defined them as dictatorial regimes that oppressed their own people, fomented ethnic hatred, backed terrorist groups, and pursued WMD. These countries lacked superpower resources but acted aggressively in their regions and defied international norms.[33] They could not pose a global threat to US power and the mission of democratic enlargement like the Soviet Union did, but they could disrupt these goals at the regional level.

According to Lake, these states faced a dilemma in a globalizing, post–Cold War world. If they opened their societies to market forces and mass communication, they would jeopardize their hold on power by enabling internal resistance and exposing their people to the outside world. Thus, backlash states severed or limited their people's access to information and trade, which stunted economic growth and increased their isolation. The US role in dealing with these states was: "as the only superpower ... to neutralize, contain, and through selective pressure possibly transform these backlash states into responsible members of the international

---

[31] Barry Posen and Andrew Ross, "Competing Visions for U.S. Grand Strategy," *International Security* 21, no. 3 (Winter, 1996–1997): 23–24; Brands, *Berlin to Baghdad*, 106. For a theoretical examination of the democratic peace concept, see Bruce Russett and Zeev Maoz, "Normative and Structural Causes of the Democratic Peace, 1946–1986," *American Political Science Review* 87, no. 3 (September, 1993): 624–638. For a historical examination of its role in the history of US foreign policy, see Tony Smith, *Why Wilson Matters: The Origin of American Liberal Internationalism and Its Crisis Today* (Princeton, NJ: Princeton University Press, 2017).

[32] Lake, "Containment to Enlargement," September 21, 1993. See also William Perry, "Defense in an Age of Hope," *Foreign Affairs* 75, no. 6 (November–December, 1996): 64–79.

[33] Anthony Lake, "Confronting Backlash States," *Foreign Affairs* 73, no. 2 (March–April, 1994): 46. See also, Michael Klare, *Rogue States and Nuclear Outlaws: America's Search for a New Foreign Policy* (New York: Hill and Wang, 1995), 24–26.

community."[34] The tools of this approach were deterrence, nonproliferation, sanctions, isolation, and military force, if needed. The backlash states, if contained, would either succumb to global trends or remain pariahs.[35]

Within this framework, the Clinton administration defined US goals in the Middle East as fostering a community of "like-minded states that share our goals of free markets, broad democratic values, and controls on proliferation."[36] Crucial US interests were preserving access to oil, achieving an Israeli–Palestinian peace deal, and countering Islamic extremism.[37] They particularly emphasized the Middle East Peace Process (MEPP) as the best way to ease tensions and encourage political reform.[38] Backlash states like Iraq and Iran could threaten these objectives through their pursuit of WMD, sponsorship of terrorist groups, opposition to democratization and the MEPP, and ability to threaten US allies and trade interests.

To deal with these threats, the Clinton administration developed a policy called dual containment that aimed to limit the regional influence of both Iraq and Iran. The architect of this policy was Martin Indyk, the NSC's Director of Near Eastern and South Asian Affairs. Indyk founded the policy on the premise that "we do not accept the argument that we should continue the old balance of power game, building up one to balance the other," as the United States had done in the Gulf during the Cold War. He argued that this strategy had set the stage for Iraqi aggression because the United States was mistakenly trying to build up Saddam as a bulwark of stability in the region. The solution under dual containment was for the United States to provide stability in the Gulf by containing both Iran and Iraq. Indyk reasoned that this strategy was feasible in the USSR's absence because Iran or Iraq could not look to another superpower for help. Iran and Iraq would also be easier to contain after a decade of war and economic decline.[39]

Aside from containing Iran as well, the Clinton administration's approach to containment deviated little from his predecessor. Clinton officials agreed that Saddam would probably never fully comply with the UN demands and that normalizing relations with a Saddam-led Iraq was

---

[34] Lake, "Backlash States," 45–46.

[35] Lake, "Containment to Enlargement," September 21, 1993.

[36] Anthony Lake, "The Middle East Moment," *Washington Post*, July 24, 1994, C1.

[37] Martin Indyk, "Address to the Soref Symposium" (speech, Washington, DC, May 20, 1993), accessed November 14, 2017, www.washingtoninstitute.org/policy-analysis/view/the-clinton-administrations-approach-to-the-middle-east

[38] Brands, *Berlin to Baghdad*, 184.

[39] Indyk, "Address to the Soref Symposium"; Lake, "Backlash States," 49; Indyk, *Innocent Abroad*, 36.

probably impossible.[40] They saw him as inflexibly committed to rebuilding his conventional and unconventional arsenals, escaping sanctions, and seeking regional domination. One intelligence estimate backed up this statement in saying: "Whether the sanctions remain in effect or not, Baghdad will pursue the following goals, objectives, and policies as long as Saddam remains in power."[41] Indyk reasoned further that "Saddam Hussein will continue to probe for daylight between the positions of President Clinton and his predecessor." Making him comply with the United Nations would require constant parrying of his threats as well as patient "hand-holding" of a divided coalition. There was a broad sense that the policy of using sanctions to enforce compliance and possibly oust Saddam would not work indefinitely because "Saddam Hussein is still in control, the sanctions are eroding, and international support is dissipating."[42]

The Clinton administration was somewhat split on how to compel Saddam's compliance while preserving the coalition. Officials like Indyk, Gore, Defense Secretary Les Aspin, and UN Ambassador Madeleine Albright recommended a tougher policy of "low tolerance" for noncompliance. Under this approach, the United States would respond immediately to Iraqi misbehavior with escalating strikes on military targets or the expansion of the NFZs.[43] The prevailing view within the administration, however, was that Saddam was more of a nuisance than a serious military threat. Chairman of the Joint Chiefs of Staff (JCS) Colin Powell, Lake, and Christopher saw containment as a cost-effective strategy for managing Saddam while they pursued a full docket of other foreign policy problems.[44] They referred to Saddam as a "rash," a "migraine," or a "toothache," all periodic problems that are not life-threatening.[45] Lake recalled that Clinton did not see Iraq as a top issue

[40] Memorandum to Martin Indyk, Unknown Author, January 1993, OA/ID 255, National Security Council, Near East and South Asian Affairs, Martin Indyk Files, William Clinton Presidential Library, 1.

[41] CIA Report, National Intelligence Estimate 93–42, "Prospects for Iraq; Saddam and Beyond," December 1993, accessed April 10, 2018, http://primarysources .brillonline.com/reader/open?rotate=1&searchTerms=iraq&starEnabled=1&shareLin k=, 25.

[42] Quotations Are from Unknown Author, Draft Outline: Iraq, January 26 Principal Committee Meeting, January 19, 1993, OA/ID 255, National Security Council Near East and South Asian Affairs, Martin Indyk Files, William Clinton Presidential Library, 1.

[43] Same Box, Same Folder, January 19, 1993, Draft Outline: Iraq, January 26 Principals Committee Meeting, 7 photos; Indyk, *Innocent Abroad*, 36.

[44] Sciolino, "New Iraqi Site Raided as White House Vows Firmness," *New York Times*, January 23, 1993, A3.

[45] The term "rash" was used by an anonymous senior official in Thomas Lippman, "Iraqi Defiance Expected to Continue," *Washington Post*, September 22, 1996, A27.

and that "Iraq, it seemed to us, was not going to be soluble at any reasonable cost any point soon. I recall describing it ... as a dull toothache that you just have to keep dealing with and make sure it doesn't get worse. But you can't fix it."[46] Another Clinton official described Iraq as a "second-tier issue" for his foreign policy team.[47]

Furthermore, Clinton had seen Bush's intractable struggle of wills with Saddam and wanted to avoid this draining and politically distracting contest.[48] Clinton officials stressed "de-personalizing" the conflict with Iraq by focusing on compliance rather than ousting Saddam, which they viewed as too risky for several reasons.[49] Like the Bush administration, they feared that Saddam's removal might lead to massive revenge attacks by the Shia and Kurds against the Sunni and that in the general chaos Iran would expand its influence in the region.[50] The bloodshed that followed Yugoslavia's collapse in 1991 reinforced this dread about the dissolution of multiethnic states.[51]

The Clinton approach to regime change remained roughly the same as Bush's: maintain isolation and economic pressure and hope that a disgruntled general launches a coup.[52] Iraqi society, according to one intelligence report, was portrayed as "cowed ... making a popular revolt an unlikely means of regime change."[53] In the absence of a popular revolt, the United States had to dangle promises of sanctions relief to elite Iraqis as incentives to act.[54] The administration generally believed that Saddam would not remain in power much longer under these pressures. One 1993 intelligence report, for instance, claimed: "If enforcement of the sanctions continues unabated, there is a better than even chance that Saddam will

"Toothache" was Powell's term and "migraine" was Albright's. See Indyk, *Innocent Abroad*, 38; Madeleine Albright, *Madam Secretary: A Memoir* (New York: Harper Collins, 2013), 274.

[46] Anthony Lake, interview by Russell Riely, William J. Clinton Presidential History Project, Miller Center, November 6, 2004, accessed October 5, 2017, https://millercenter.org/the-presidency/presidential-oral-histories/anthony-lake-oral-history-2004-national-security-advisor, 24.

[47] Michael Mazarr, *Leap of Faith: Hubris, Negligence, and America's Greatest Foreign Policy Tragedy* (New York: Public Affairs, 2019), 58.

[48] Kenneth Pollack, *The Threatening Storm: The Case for Invading Iraq* (New York: Random House, 2002), 65.

[49] Paul Lewis, "U.S. and Britain Softening Emphasis on Ousting Iraqi," *New York Times*, March 30, 1993, A3.

[50] Richard Bonin, *Arrows of the Night: Ahmad Chalabi's Long Journey to Triumph in Iraq* (New York: Doubleday, 2011), 86.

[51] Indyk, *Innocent Abroad*, 38.   [52] Mazarr, *Leap of Faith*, 60.

[53] National Intelligence Estimate, "Prospects for Iraq," December 1993, 24.

[54] Elaine Sciolino, "Clinton to Scale Down Program to Oust Iraqi Leader," *New York Times*, April 11, 1993, A3; Indyk, *Innocent Abroad*, 36–38.

be ousted during the next three years."[55] In the meantime, containment and compliance would remain the priorities. As the then CIA Iraq analyst Kenneth Pollack put it: "They were much more committed to containment as an end in itself. They embraced it consciously."[56]

One key question on Iraq that the administration had to answer in its first months was, as one NSC memo put it: "What are the precise terms under which the United States will agree to lift economic sanctions against Iraq, and must these terms include a change of regime in Baghdad?"[57] In keeping with the regime change consensus and the strategy of enlargement, Clinton officials contended that "the ultimate political solution for all of Iraq is the formation of a democratic government in Baghdad that can both be representative of the Iraqi people and maintain peaceful relations with its neighbors."[58] Nevertheless, they recognized that voicing this viewpoint at the United Nations or openly stressing regime change efforts jeopardized the coalition. Key partners like France, Germany, and Russia saw sanctions as a way to compel cooperation with WMD disarmament with the ultimate goal of returning Iraq to its normal status in the world with or without regime change.[59] However, at home, Congress, most foreign policy commenters, and the public generally, opposed normalization and supported tougher regime change efforts. One poll from January 1993 found that 65 percent of respondents would support renewed US military action to force Saddam from power.[60]

Clinton's rhetorical strategy, the Clinton fudge, helped him balance these contradictory forces and prevent Iraq from absorbing political capital. Clinton officials provided deliberate nonanswers to the questions about what terms Iraq had to meet for the United States to support the easing of sanctions. Bush had declared that the United States would not lift sanctions while Saddam was in power, but the Clinton administration saw that these statements created problems with the coalition, thereby creating a need for more rhetorical flexibility. One example of the Clinton fudge came from White House spokeswoman Dee Dee Myers, who was

---

[55] National Intelligence Estimate, "Prospects for Iraq," December 1993, v; Indyk, *Innocent Abroad*, 38–39.

[56] Kenneth Pollack, interview by author, November 6, 2017.

[57] Draft Outline, January 26 Principals Committee Meeting, 4.

[58] Quotation is from Robert Pelletreau in House Committee on International Relations, *Middle East Overview and U.S. Assistance to the Palestinians*, 104th Cong., 1st sess., April 6, 1995, 70.

[59] Frederic Bozo, *A History of the Iraq Crisis: France, the United States, and Iraq, 1991–2003* (Washington, DC: Woodrow Wilson Center Press, 2016), 40–44.

[60] *Newsweek* Telephone Survey, January 25, 1993, Polling the Nations, accessed November 25, 2017, http://poll.orspub.com.libproxy.lib.unc.edu/search.php?action.

asked in March 1993 if Clinton would deviate from Bush's position on the lifting of sanctions. She replied:

Our position is that Iraq has to comply with all U.N. resolutions, including those of giving up weapons of mass destruction and stopping violence against his own people. . . . We don't believe that can be achieved with Hussein, with Saddam in power. And therefore there's no practical difference.[61]

Clinton officials frequently argued, in Assistant Secretary of State for Near Eastern Affairs Robert Pelletreau's words, that "repression and terrorism are the only pillars of Saddam's regime" to support the claim that he would inevitably fall from power if he complied with all UN resolutions, especially those regarding human rights.[62] This claim drew on the discourse on Iraq as a totalitarian state, portraying coercion, ideology, and terror as the sole bases of Baathist rule. This view also ignored intelligence assessments arguing that Saddam stayed in power also because of patronage, clan networks, nationalist and xenophobic appeals, and the Sunni fear of Shia and Kurdish retaliation if the regime collapsed.[63] One National Intelligence Estimate from December 1993, for instance, asserted that "Saddam Husayn currently has sufficient economic and security resources, along with the skill to marshal and deploy them, to maintain his hold on power."[64]

With this rhetorical strategy, Clinton officials signaled hypothetical willingness to lift sanctions without regime change in the event of Saddam's full compliance. In October 1994, for example, Clinton said: "I think that the Iraqis are quite well aware of what the United Nations expected them to do to lift the sanctions. And if they do it, then no one will stand in the way of lifting the sanctions."[65] Mark Parris, Richard Haass' successor as NSC Director for Near East and South Asian Affairs, explained that this approach was designed to keep the sanctions intact while signaling to the coalition openness to lifting them in order to create time for sanctions and covert action to overthrow Saddam.[66] Anthony

---

[61] Dee Dee Myers, "Press Briefing," March 28, 1993, The American Presidency Project, accessed September 27, 2017, www.presidency.ucsb.edu/ws/index.php?pid=59938&st=iraq&st1=.

[62] House Committee on International Relations, *Overview of U.S. Policy in the Middle East*, 104th Cong., 1st sess., August 2, 1995, 100.

[63] CIA Report, National Intelligence Estimate 97–2, "Saddam Husayn: Likely to Hang On," June 1992, National Security Archive Online, accessed February 6, 2017, http://nsarchive.gwu.edu/NSAEBB/NSAEBB167/10.pdf, 3.

[64] National Intelligence Estimate, "Prospects for Iraq," December 1993, v.

[65] "President's News Conference," October 7, 1994, The American Presidency Project, accessed September 27, 2017, www.presidency.ucsb.edu/ws/index.php?pid=49247&st=iraq&st1.

[66] Indyk, *Innocent Abroad*, 37.

Lake later admitted that the Clinton fudge was a "roundabout way" of saying that sanctions would not be lifted until Saddam was gone without making regime change the explicit goal.[67]

Clinton's continuation of Bush's approach to Iraq was bolstered by the view that Iraq remained economically and militarily feeble. Intelligence reports judged Iraq's military to be weaker than before 1991 because of the draining effects of sanctions, a morale crisis, and its inability to import high-tech equipment and spare parts. Edward Djerejian, the Assistant Secretary of State for Near Eastern Affairs, argued that the sanctions kept Saddam focused on survival by raising his people's anger and reducing his ability to pay off key supporters.[68] The CIA likewise judged: "The weaknesses of the postwar Iraqi military far outweigh its strengths, and Baghdad's military power will decline – or at least not increase – as long as UN sanctions remain in effect."[69] These conditions seemed likely to hold for the near future, so Clinton tried to sideline Iraq and focus on foreign policy priorities like the MEPP.

Although Clinton's approach to the Persian Gulf proceeded under the dual containment label, its rather different readings of each society and regime led to quite different types of containment policies. The Clinton administration saw Iran as a backlash state and a threat to US regional interests. Aside from being an oppressive theocracy, Iran sponsored terrorist groups like Hezbollah, threatened Israel and Saudi Arabia, opposed the MEPP, and pursued WMD. Nevertheless, several key factors differentiated Iran from Iraq in US thinking. First, the Iranian government possessed domestic legitimacy that Saddam lacked. While revolutionary fervor had declined from years of war, stagnation, and repression, the government had real credibility among the Iranian people, who would not accept foreign regime change efforts. The Iranian people had a deep and coherent collective identity, unlike the relatively new, multiethnic Iraqi state.[70] Second, Iran had countervailing political institutions, some of which were partially democratic, that distributed political power rather than concentrating it in a single dictator. Third, the United States had no significant Iranian opposition groups to support,

[67] Lake, interview by Russell Riely, 4.

[68] Subcommittee on Europe and the Middle East of the House Committee on Foreign Affairs, *Developments in the Middle East*, 103rd Cong., 1st sess., March 9, 1993, 24–25; Intelligence assessments backed up this claim. See National Intelligence Estimate, "Prospects for Iraq," December 1993, v.

[69] CIA Report, "Iraq's Military Capabilities," September 12, 1994, CIA.gov, accessed December 31, 2017, 1.

[70] Douglas Little, *Us versus Them: The United States, Radical Islam, and the Rise of the Green Threat* (Chapel Hill, NC: The University of North Carolina Press, 2016), 108; Indyk, *Innocent Abroad*, 39.

and the Iranian Revolutionary Guards kept the regime secure from internal and external challenges.[71] Finally, unlike Iraq, Iran was not openly aggressive, which reduced the urgency of the Iranian threat.[72]

These factors ruled out covert attempts to remove the Iranian regime. Instead, the administration had to treat the regime as a given and try to modify its behavior while preventing it from destabilizing or dominating the region. Still, Clinton opposed the EU's policy of "critical dialogue" that tried to build trade and diplomatic relations with Iran to incentivize better behavior. Clinton officials believed this approach rewarded Iranian misbehavior and strengthened the regime.[73] Instead, the administration would punish Iran with sanctions and diplomatic isolation until it ceased objectionable behavior like the pursuit of WMD. Clinton preserved unilateral sanctions on Iran and pressured allies to cease commercial dealings with Iran. The United States told Iran that it did not seek the regime's overthrow and would ease sanctions and seek better relations once Iran halted its negative behavior.[74]

In contrast to the Iran policy, Indyk stated in his 1993 speech introducing dual containment that the United States would not "seek or expect a reconciliation with Saddam Hussein's regime. . . . [T]he current regime in Iraq is a criminal regime, beyond the pale of international society and, in our judgment, irredeemable."[75] In contrast to his views on Iraq, Indyk stated about Iran: "We are not opposed to the Islamic government in Iran but to these specific aspects of its behavior. . . . [W]e will not normalize relations with Iran until and unless Iran's policies change, across the board."[76] Because of the domestic legitimacy of Iran's regime and the greater possibility of outside pressures creating internal change in a less centralized authoritarian state, the administration could envision a "way out" of containing Iran based on behavior change rather than regime change. In Iraq, however, it viewed the only likely outlet as a coup or assassination because Saddam and his totally different regime were so deeply entrenched and the Iraqi people so weak, impoverished, and divided. Thus, dual containment featured a rigid approach to Iraq that

---

[71] Robert Litwak, *Rogue States and U.S. Foreign Policy: Containment after the Cold War* (Washington, DC: Woodrow Wilson Center Press, 2000), 159; Indyk, *Innocent Abroad*, 39.

[72] Lake, "Backlash States," 9.   [73] Litwak, *Rogue States*, 207.

[74] Indyk, *Innocent Abroad*, 40–41; Martin Indyk, interview by Daniel Pipes, November 15, 1993, *Middle East Quarterly*, accessed October 26, 2017, www.meforum.org/219/perspectives-from-the-white-house.

[75] Indyk, "Address to the Soref Symposium," May 20, 1993.

[76] Indyk, "Address to the Soref Symposium," May 20, 1993. See also Lake, "Backlash States," 9–11; Edward Djerejian testimony in Subcommittee on Europe and the Middle East of the House Committee on Foreign Affairs, *Developments in the Middle East*, July 27, 1993, 8–9.

walled off the possibility of normalization and a more flexible approach to Iran that imposed pressures in order to induce long-term behavioral change.

By the end of 1993, Clinton officials had advanced the interlocking strategic concepts of enlargement, backlash states, and dual containment. Their approach to Iraq mostly continued that of George H. W. Bush, although it stressed compliance with UN resolutions and avoided divisive statements about regime change. Like Bush, Clinton believed that Saddam Hussein had to be removed for the United States to achieve its regional goals and eventually restore relations with Iraq. Nevertheless, the administration did not clearly answer whether Saddam had to be removed soon or whether the United States needed to take risks to achieve that goal. It carried this ambiguous strategy into a series of confrontations with Iraq during the first term.

A Chronic Migraine: Crisis after Crisis, 1993–1996

Clinton carried a somewhat ambiguous approach into a series of confrontations with Iraq in his first term. He believed that preserving containment required firm responses to Saddam's provocations and strict enforcement of the Security Council Resolutions, but he did not want to make Iraq a high-profile issue of his first term. His first major crisis on Iraq came in June 1993 when US and Kuwaiti intelligence found evidence that Iraqi agents had plotted an assassination attempt against former President Bush during his visit to Kuwait in April 1993. Kuwaiti intelligence foiled the plan, but Clinton was nonetheless outraged by Saddam's attempt to kill his predecessor. He responded by launching cruise missiles at the Iraqi secret police headquarters in Baghdad on June 26 as retaliation and to deter future Iraqi support for terrorism.[77] The administration legally justified this attack not in terms of any Security Council resolution but with Article 51 of the UN charter, which grants each state the right to self-defense.[78] This approach enabled Clinton to avoid a Security Council vote on the use of force, which would have been troublesome because some coalition members were skeptical about the evidence on the Iraqi plot. He described the strikes as a "firm and commensurate response" and contended that "Saddam Hussein has demonstrated repeatedly that he will resort to terrorism and aggression

---

[77] Alfonsi, *Circle in the Sand*, 341–342; Tim Weiner, "Attack Is Aimed at the Heart of Iraq's Spy Network," *New York Times*, June 27, 1993, A1.

[78] Letter, William Clinton to the Speaker of the House, June 28, 1993, OA/ID 4057, National Security Council, Mary DeRosa Files, Clinton Presidential Records, William Clinton Presidential Library, 1.

if left unchecked."[79] A *Newsweek* poll found that 71 percent of Americans supported Clinton's actions.[80]

Containment faced a different set of challenges as the UN weapons inspectors made significant progress in locating and destroying proscribed Iraqi weapons programs in 1993 and early 1994. In November 1993, UNSCOM achieved a major victory when Iraq agreed to Security Council Resolution 715's requirement that inspectors be allowed to establish long-term monitoring of sites linked to WMD or ballistic missiles.[81] The monitoring system included remote cameras at research facilities, the sealing of equipment, chemical sensors, aerial surveillance, import inspections, and unannounced visits to suspected sites.[82] UNSCOM reported increased Iraqi cooperation on WMD and the rapid destruction or sealing of weapons sites, equipment, and materials. UNSCOM Chief Rolf Ekeus said that once he felt comfortable reporting that Iraq was in full compliance, the Security Council should vote to lift the ban on oil exports as required by Resolution 687. This move would allow billions of dollars to flow into Iraqi coffers even though the trade embargo would remain for everything except food and medicine.[83]

Ekeus' interpretation of when to lift the oil export embargo reflected the consensus view of the Security Council. France, Russia, China, and others pointed to Paragraph 22 of Resolution 687, which stated that once the inspectors verified compliance with the disarmament requirements of the resolution, the "prohibitions against the import of commodities and products originating in Iraq ... shall have no further force or effect."[84] These countries' interpretation reflected their view that the point of sanctions was to change Iraq's behavior on WMD and then allow the renewal of normal relations. They did not accept the US use of sanctions to try to force Saddam from power or contain him indefinitely.[85]

---

[79] William Clinton, "Address to the Nation on the Strike on Iraqi Intelligence Headquarters" (speech, Washington, DC, June 26, 1993), the American Presidency Project, accessed October 12, 2017, www.presidency.ucsb.edu/ws/index .php?pid=46758&st=iraq&st1=.

[80] Russell Watson, "A New Kind of Containment," *Newsweek*, July 12, 1993, 30.

[81] Paul Lewis, "Bowing to U.N., Iraq Will Permit Arms Monitors," *New York Times*, November 27, 1993, A1.

[82] Tim Trevan, *Saddam's Secrets: The Hunt for Iraq's Hidden Weapons* (London: Harper Collins, 1999), 257–259 Carlyle Murphy, "U.N. Inspectors in Iraq Prepare to Shift to Monitoring Role," *Washington Post*, July 14, 1994, A18.

[83] Paul Lewis, "U.N. Is Holding Talks on Lifting Its 3-Year Ban on Iraqi Oil Sales," *New York Times*, September 6, 1993, A2.

[84] United Nations Security Council Resolution 687, April 8, 1991, un.org, accessed May 10, 2017, www.un.org/Depts/unmovic/documents/687.pdf, 14.

[85] Sarah Graham-Brown, *Sanctioning Saddam: The Politics of Intervention in Iraq* (New York: I. B. Tauris, 1999), 59–60.

France, Russia, China, and other countries further claimed that the United Nations needed to send an "encouraging gesture from the international community" by sticking to the letter of Resolution 687.[86] They feared that Iraq would simply cease compliance if the Security Council refused to recognize even partial compliance. As the inspectors made progress, these nations repeatedly introduced text into UN sanctions reviews noting Iraqi cooperation. The United States and Great Britain blocked these amendments, arguing that they would "only confirm to the Iraqi regime that its policy of defiance was working."[87] On a more fundamental level, France, Russia, and China viewed the US hard line on Iraq as evidence of its unilateral and hegemonic behavior in the aftermath of the Cold War. These and other countries were anxious that the unipolarity of the post–Cold War world would lead the United States into uncompromising, righteous crusading.[88] France had been dedicated to an independent defense posture and the moderate checking of US power since the 1960s, and these tendencies only increased in the mid-late 1990s with the rise of Jacques Chirac.[89] Many countries saw the United States as a self-appointed, unilateral enforcer of the Security Council resolutions, and they held the US requirement that Iraq comply with Resolution 688's call for human rights protections as improper interference in Iraq's internal affairs. China in particular opposed this resolution because it did not want to set a precedent of UN punishment for human rights abuses.[90]

France, Russia, China, and other countries also had strong economic interests in resuming Iraqi oil exports and renewing their lucrative trade connections. In the short term, they believed that restoring Iraqi oil income would enable the repayment of billions in Iraqi debt. Turkey, which started calling for the phased lifting of sanctions in 1993, lost around $27.3 billion in trade with Iraq between 1991 and 1996, especially from pipeline closures.[91] Moreover, China's rapid industrialization required immense quantities of oil, and it envisioned Iraq as a major source. Oil companies from all three nations had already started to

[86] Paul Lewis, "U.N. Council Split on Iraq, Keeps Its Ban," *New York Times*, May 18, 1994, A10.

[87] Quotation is from Robert Pelletreau in Subcommittee on Europe and the Middle East of the House Committee on Foreign Affairs, *Developments in the Middle East, March 1994*, 103rd Cong., 2nd sess., March 1, 1994, 58. See also Paul Lewis, "U.N.'s Team in Iraq Sees Arms Gains," *New York Times*, July 26, 1994, A3.

[88] Bozo, *Iraq Crisis*, 7; David Malone, *The International Struggle Over Iraq: Politics in the UN Security Council 1980–2005* (New York: Oxford University Press, 2006), 87–95.

[89] Philip H. Gordon and Jeremy Shapiro, *Allies at War: America, Europe, and the Crisis over Iraq* (New York: McGraw-Hill, 2004), 27–28.

[90] Graham-Brown, *Sanctioning Saddam*, 79; Bozo, *Iraq Crisis*, 40.

[91] Graham-Brown, *Sanctioning Saddam*, 68.

negotiate contracts with Iraq, although they could not sign anything until the lifting of the embargo.[92]

The United States and Great Britain, however, applied a much higher standard to Iraq before they would consider lifting the oil export ban. Even if Ekeus verified Iraqi cooperation, US officials held that Saddam would still have to establish "a demonstrable track record of compliance" before they would consider acting on the embargo.[93] Clinton officials also argued that Iraq had to account for "long-standing gaps and inconsistencies" in its reports to inspectors, including its foreign procurement network for WMD-related materials, biological weapons programs, and missing ballistic missile equipment.[94] The administration further insisted that Iraq comply with all of the Security Council resolutions, including recognizing Kuwaiti sovereignty and respecting human rights.

The Clinton administration demanded such a high level of compliance because it believed that the United States needed evidence of Saddam's changing intentions, not just his literal compliance. Because it had taken so much effort to get Saddam to cooperate even partially, the administration felt justified in demanding evidence that he would not start building WMD and threatening his neighbors once he had oil revenue again. Resolution 687 supplied some justification for this focus on intentions because it called for "the need to be assured of Iraq's peaceful intentions in the light of its unlawful invasion and occupation of Iraq."[95] One US official stated that even if Iraq complied with the WMD provisions of Resolution 687, "the overall pattern of Iraq's behavior ... is still one of generalized non-compliance," making it "difficult to believe Baghdad is sincere."[96]

The Clinton administration interpreted Saddam's intentions from his behavior. It saw Iraq's grudging, inconsistent, and opportunistic cooperation as evidence of unchanged intentions, meaning that Iraq merely desired to escape sanctions and return to its old ways.[97] Aside from demanding compliance with all UN resolutions, the United States also requested a six to twelve-month period of Iraqi cooperation with UN monitoring to test its intentions before lifting the export ban. Albright

---

[92] Dilip Hiro, *Neighbors, Not Friends: Iraq and Iran after the Gulf Wars* (New York: Routledge, 2001), 75.

[93] Lewis, "U.N. Is Holding Talks on Lifting Its 3-Year Ban on Iraqi Oil Sales," *New York Times*, September 6, 1993, A2.

[94] Trevan, *Saddam's Secrets*, 252. Lewis, "Bowing to U.N., Iraq Will Permit Arms Monitors," *New York Times*, November 27, 1993, A1.

[95] United Nations Security Council Resolution 687, 11.

[96] Paul Lewis, "U.S. Is Hardening Its Stand on Iraq," *New York Times*, December 9, 1993, A1.

[97] Warren Christopher, "Wobbly on Iraq," *New York Times*, April 29, 1994, A27.

described this period as a test of Iraq's "readiness to rejoin society."[98] Iraqi improvement on human rights would further signal changed intentions. Albright and other officials noted that Iraq was actually regressing on human rights, including new practices of punishing deserters and petty criminals with branding, blinding, and amputation.[99] Moreover, Clinton officials feared that once the export ban was lifted, France, Russia, and China would block any effort to reinstall the ban because they would be importing oil and receiving debt repayment.[100]

The conflict over lifting the embargo accelerated in the summer of 1994 when Ekeus announced that the monitoring system was ready and that he was close to verifying Iraqi compliance on WMD.[101] France, Russia, and China began to push for a timetable for lifting sanctions and threatened to call for a Security Council vote on the matter. In September, however, Ekeus reported that he could not yet verify compliance, citing missing information and materials. Saddam tried to bully his way out of this impasse by mobilizing Republican Guard divisions totaling 64,000 troops on the Kuwaiti border in October 1994. He threatened to invade if the Security Council did not lift sanctions immediately.[102]

Clinton responded swiftly to this threat by surging US ground forces in Kuwait up to about 50,000 and sending a second aircraft carrier to the Gulf.[103] On October 10, the NSC met at the White House to discuss the crisis. Defense Secretary William Perry and Martin Indyk recommended calling for Iraqi withdrawal from the border and the creation of a no-drive zone (NDZ) for Iraqi military vehicles below the 32nd parallel. This option, they contended, would intensify pressure on Saddam, contain him more effectively, and inhibit assaults on the Shia population. However, Albright and JCS Chairman John Shalikashvili argued that an NDZ would put an immense burden on the military because it would have to respond to any vehicle the Iraqis sent to this area, giving Saddam the ability to provoke the United States at will. Moreover, they argued

---

[98] Lewis, "Hardening Its Stand," *New York Times*, December 19, 1993.

[99] Max van der Stoel, "Report on the Situation of Human Rights in Iraq," February 15, 1995, repository.un.org, accessed November 20, 2017, http://repository.un.org/bit stream/handle/11176/213156/E_CN.4_1995_56-EN.pdf?sequence=3&isAllowed=y, 9–11.

[100] Lewis, "Hardening Its Stand," *New York Times*, December 19, 1993.

[101] Charles Duelfer, *Hide and Seek: The Search for Truth in Iraq* (New York: Public Affairs, 2009), 105; Murphy, "U.N. Inspectors in Iraq Prepare to Shift to Monitoring Role," *Washington Post*, July 14, 1994, A18.

[102] Indyk, *Innocent Abroad*, 153.

[103] W. Eric Herr, "Operation Vigilant Warrior: Conventional Deterrence Theory, Doctrine, and Practice," MA Thesis, School of Advance Air Power Studies, 1996, htt ps://apps.dtic.mil/dtic/tr/fulltext/u2/a360732.pdf, 27–28; Douglas Jehl, "Clinton's Line in the Sand," *New York Times*, October 10, 1994, A1.

that the coalition would oppose this idea as an overreach into Iraqi territory. They claimed that containment was basically working and that there was no good reason to experiment with dangerous innovations.[104] Clinton concurred with the more limited approach, in large part because he wanted to put Saddam back in the box and return his attention to the MEPP.[105]

In public, Clinton officials warned Iraq that the United States would again use force if his troops set foot in Kuwait.[106] Perry said quite bluntly: "We're talking about military action" to prevent Saddam from underestimating US willpower as he did in 1990.[107] Clinton viewed the threat as another test of the U.N. Security Council's resolve to enforce the resolutions and keep Saddam in the box. He said shortly after the crisis: "I guess he figured that if he mounted a provocation, I would send Jimmy Carter over there to make a deal, and he could wheedle something out of us."[108]

Saddam's actions backfired in the international arena, even among nations like France, Russia, China that wanted sanctions relief.[109] Swift US diplomacy plus the overt nature of Saddam's threat left him isolated, and the Security Council unanimously voted on October 15 to condemn Iraq and demand the withdrawal of its forces.[110] The next day, Iraq started to recall its forces. Iraq also announced it would formally recognize Kuwaiti sovereignty and its current borders, fulfilling one major obligation of the Security Council resolutions.[111] The United States and Great Britain tried to deter Saddam from further threats like this by sending him demarches on October 20 warning that they would "use military force to stop any new buildup of Iraqi troops south of the 32nd parallel."[112] Clinton received widespread praise at home for resolving this crisis. Seventy-four percent of respondents in one poll supported the

---

[104] Pollack, *The Threatening Storm*, 70.

[105] Chollet, *America between the Wars*, 184; Indyk, *Innocent Abroad*, 154–157; Elaine Sciolino, "U.S. Offers Plan to Avoid Threat from Iraq Again," *New York Times*, October 13, 1994, A1.

[106] Michael Gordon, "U.S. Sends Force as Iraqi Soldiers Threaten Kuwait," *New York Times*, October 8, 1994, A1.

[107] Michael Gordon, "U.S. Warns Iraq to Complete Pullback," *New York Times*, October 15, 1994, A7.

[108] Taylor Branch, ed., *The Clinton Tapes: Wrestling History with the President* (New York: Simon & Schuster, 2009), 207.

[109] Steven Greenhouse, "Arab States Withholding Their Support for Baghdad," *New York Times*, October 11, 1994, A13.

[110] Barbara Crossette, "Security Council Condemns Iraqis' Threat to Kuwait," *New York Times*, October 16, 1994, A12; Hiro, *Neighbors, Not Friends*, 80–81.

[111] Youssef Ibrahim, "Iraq Signals Acceptance of U.N. Move," *New York Times*, October 17, 1994, A10.

[112] Herr, "Operation Vigilant Warrior," 33.

troop deployment, and his overall approval rating for Iraq policy increased to 69 percent in another survey.[113]

Saddam's reckless threat saved Clinton from having to confront significant problems in the containment policy. His blatantly hostile troop movements allowed for a deterrent response with conventional forces that briefly reunited the coalition. If Saddam had not threatened Kuwait, the United States may have had to veto an attempt by France, Russia, and China to lift the oil embargo. A veto would have preserved the sanctions but may have endangered the coalition by confirming the suspicion that the United States intended to punish Iraq indefinitely.

Unfortunately, containment had other implications, especially the massive economic and humanitarian damage caused by sanctions. By 1996, Iraq's GDP had fallen to $10.6 billion compared to $66.2 billion in 1989. The health crisis in Iraq had only worsened by the mid-1990s, particularly when the Iraqi state cut food rations by a third.[114] The United Nations estimated that by 1996, in the worst-hit areas of Iraq in the south, as many as 34 percent of all children were underweight and at least 10 percent were wasting.[115] While Congress remained supportive of sanctions, US partners on the Security Council and in the Middle East were growing restive. Sanctions were especially unpopular among the populations of US allies in the Middle East, who largely blamed the United States for the health crisis.[116] Like the Bush administration, Clinton officials blamed Saddam for this crisis because of his failure to import adequate food and medicine and his denial of basic goods and services to disloyal populations. Saddam had the money to provide relief, but he chose to spend it on his security services and internal clients. Nevertheless, Iraq's inability to export oil and obtain hard currency under sanctions inhibited the importing of basic goods.[117]

Preventing sanctions from undermining the coalition required the United States to find a way to allow more essential goods to be imported into Iraq without permitting cash to flow to the state. The solution came

---

[113] Seventy-four percent is from Gallup Telephone Survey, October 19, 1994. Sixty-nine percent is from NBC Telephone Survey, October 1994. Both surveys accessed in Polling the Nations, accessed November 25, 2017, http://poll.orspub.com.libproxy.lib .unc.edu/search.php?action.

[114] Joy Gordon, *Invisible War: The United States and the Iraq Sanctions* (Cambridge, MA: Harvard University Press, 2010), 21, 36.

[115] Lisa Blaydes, *State of Repression: Iraq under Saddam Hussein* (Princeton, NJ: Princeton University, Press, 2018), 123.

[116] Graham-Brown, *Sanctioning Saddam*, 70–74, 179–190; Gordon, *Invisible War*, 148–149.

[117] Eric Rouleau, "America's Unyielding Policy toward Iraq," *Foreign Affairs* 74, no. 1 (January–February, 1995): 63.

with the passage of Security Council Resolution 986 in April 1995. This plan expanded the oil-for-food offerings of Resolutions 706 and 712 by permitting Iraq to sell $2 billion in oil every six months. The proceeds went to an escrow account controlled by the Security Council. Iraq could then submit requests to a Security Council-appointed panel to release funds to pay for imports of essential goods. Resolution 986 further mandated surveillance over the distribution of these goods inside Iraq to ensure that they reached the neediest populations as well as full UN control over distribution in the Kurdish areas. Some of the money in the escrow account would also be funneled to Kurdish relief, Kuwaiti reparations, and the inspectors' operating costs.[118] While Iraq initially dismissed Resolution 986 as a violation of its sovereignty, its economic crisis impelled it to cave to US terms in May 1996.[119]

Oil-for-food came to play several important roles in sustaining containment. It deflected criticism about sanctions' humanitarian effects, enabling the United States to continue demanding a high standard of compliance on inspections. Oil-for-food also put the burden of guilt for Iraqis' suffering on Saddam because at any point he could accept this resolution and import vital goods. Albright, for example, quipped that this program prevented Saddam from shedding "crocodile tears" for his people while using their suffering to undermine sanctions.[120] Robert Pelletreau explained the strategic utility of oil-for-food to Congress in 1996: "Implementation of this resolution is not a precursor to lifting sanctions. It is a humanitarian exception that preserves and even reinforces the sanctions regime."[121]

The question of Iraqi compliance with inspections took an odd turn in August 1995 with the defection to Jordan of Saddam's son-in-law Hussein Kamel, who was one of the most powerful members of Saddam's inner circle. He and his brother's marriages to Saddam's daughters formed key links between Saddam and the powerful al-Majid clan that had been a pillar of his regime for decades. Kamel worked his way up through the security service, and by the 1990s he had become the director of the Iraqi military industrialization agency

---

[118] United Nations Security Council 986, April 14, 1995, accessed December 2, 2017, http://unscr.com/en/resolutions/986.

[119] Barbara Crossette, "Accord Reached by Iraq and U.N." *New York Times*, May 21, 1996, A1; Paul Lewis, "U.N. and Iraq Suspend Talks on Limited Oil Sales," *New York Times*, April 25, 1996, A10.

[120] Elaine Sciolino, "U.S. Says It's Won U.N. Votes to Keep Sanctions on Iraq," *New York Times*, March 5, 1995, A1.

[121] House Committee on International Relations, *Developments in the Middle East*, 104th Cong., 2nd sess., June 12, 1996, 4.

and the team dedicated to concealing information from inspectors.[122] Kamel had a long-standing dispute with Saddam's erratic son Uday, who felt threatened by Kamel's political ascension. Uday attacked Kamel in the state media and tried to take control of several of his economic holdings. Saddam appeared to be siding with his son, so on August 7, 1995, Kamel, his brother, and their wives fled in the night to Jordan. Once in Amman, he pledged to work to overthrow Saddam and offered inside information about Iraqi WMD programs to the United Nations. Kamel eventually returned to Baghdad on a promise of clemency from Saddam, but members of his own clan killed him days after his return in an attempt to regain favor with Saddam.[123]

Before Kamel's defection, Rolf Ekeus suspected Iraq of retaining a major biological weapons program, and he resisted calls to certify compliance until Iraq came clean.[124] Iraq had denied the existence of this program since 1991, but thanks to persistent scrutiny from UNSCOM, the Iraqi government confessed in July 1995 to possessing an offensive biological weapons program before the Gulf War that included botulism and anthrax.[125] Now that Kamel appeared poised to spill the beans, Saddam decided to preempt him and show UNSCOM his full biological weapons program.[126] Iraqi officials led inspectors to a chicken shack outside Baghdad that featured millions of pages of information about a massive biological weapons program. Iraq had tried to preserve this program from inspectors by hiding infrastructure, selectively destroying materials and equipment, and covertly continuing research.

These unprecedented revelations included the fact that Iraq had created Scud warheads that could deliver biological weapons. Iraq had also possessed ten times the amount of anthrax than it had previously claimed as well as an undisclosed crash nuclear weapons program started after the invasion of Kuwait.[127] Finally, this trove divulged the existence of

---

[122] Andrew Cockburn and Patrick Cockburn, *Out of the Ashes: The Resurrection of Saddam Hussein* (New York: Harper Collins, 1999), 200.

[123] Douglas Jehl, "Iraqi Defectors Killed 3 Days after Returning," *New York Times*, February 24, 1996, A1; Cockburn and Cockburn, *Out of the Ashes*, 144–163, 191–210.

[124] Barbara Crossette, "Iraq Hides Biological Warfare Effort, Report Says," *New York Times*, April 12, 1995, A8; Trevan, *Saddam's Secrets*, 288.

[125] United Nations Special Commission, "UNSCOM Final Compendium," January 29, 1999, accessed March 16, 2018, http://web .archive.org/web/20051124075332/http://www.iraqwatch.org:80/un/UNSCOM/dis armament.htm, 7; Trevan, *Saddam's Secrets*, 288–290. Barbara Crossette, "Iraq Admits It Produced Germ Arsenal," *New York Times*, July 6, 1995, A3.

[126] "Iraq Rushes to Preempt Defectors' Arms Disclosures," *Washington Post*, August 15, 1995, A13.

[127] United Nations Special Commission, "UNSCOM Final Compendium," January 29, 1999; Department of Central Intelligence, Iraq Survey Group, *Key Findings*, September 30, 2004, CIA.gov, accessed July 15, 2018, www.cia.gov/library/reports/ge

Kamel's official concealment team.[128] The chicken shack documents now gave UNSCOM a huge quantity of data that had to be painstakingly cataloged. This task was made even harder by Iraq's claim that it had unilaterally destroyed all of its biological weapons materials after the Gulf War.[129]

The Clinton administration portrayed Hussein Kamel's defection as a sign of containment's effectiveness in dividing the Iraqi elite and keeping Saddam occupied with domestic problems.[130] A CIA report from earlier in 1995 noted that members of the Iraqi elite, including the Republican Guard, were feeling the impact of sanctions and selling personal possessions to buy basic goods.[131] Mark Parris argued after the defection: "We have seen over the past several years a steady deterioration in the coherence of the Iraqi power structure."[132] While the role of containment in causing Kamel's defection was uncertain at best, this and other high-level defections did show significant dissension within the Iraqi elite. Although Kamel claimed that Iraq had fully disarmed, at the time Kamel's actions seemed to validate UNSCOM's suspicions that Iraq was hiding more information and material and eased pressure for sanctions relief at the United Nations.[133] However, as we will see, in the long term, they undermined containment by intensifying distrust for Iraq in the domestic political sphere.

Support of Iraqi opposition groups formed another significant aspect of Clinton's first-term Iraq policy. Vice President Gore in particular had called for greater support for the Iraqi National Congress (INC) during the 1992 campaign. Gore preferred the INC because of its pro-democracy platform, whereas the CIA's preferred group, the Iraqi National Accord (INA), promised a new strongman. He and Warren Christopher met with the INC in April 1993, but most top Clinton

neral-reports-1/iraq_wmd_2004/,1–2; R. Jeffrey Smith, "Iraq Admits Working on Biological Weapons Systems," *Washington Post*, August 19, 1995, A17; Trevan, *Saddam's Secrets*, 331, 341–342.

[128] Cockburn and Cockburn, *Out of the Ashes*, 200.

[129] Barbara Crossette, "Germ War Plan Underreported, Iraq Tells U.N.," *New York Times*, August 23, 1995, A1.

[130] Letter, William Clinton to Speaker of the House, October 23, 1995, OA/ID 1200000, National Security Council, Clinton Presidential Records, William Clinton Presidential Library, 2.

[131] CIA Report, "No Rest for Iraq's Weary," June 20, 1995, CIA.gov, accessed October 16, 2017, www.cia.gov/library/readingroom/document/0001435821.

[132] Background Briefing by Mark Parris, August 10, 1995, OA/ID 590000, National Security Council Cables, Clinton Presidential Records, William Clinton Presidential Library, 2. See also the testimony of US Assistant Secretary of State Toby Gati in Senate Select Committee on Intelligence, *Current and Projected National Security Threats to the United States and Its Interests Abroad*, 104th Cong., 2nd sess., February 22, 1996, 151.

[133] Indyk, *Innocent Abroad*, 165–166.

officials and the CIA doubted that the INC could unify the various opposition groups enough to challenge Saddam. Moreover, the administration suspected Shia opposition groups of connections to Iran and believed that Turkey would oppose support for Kurdish groups for fear of encouraging Kurdish separatism.[134] Clinton's foreign policy team put more trust in the INA, which they saw as more likely to remove Saddam through the "silver bullet solution" even if that might preclude democratization in Iraq.[135]

The Iraqi opposition launched several attempts to remove Saddam in Clinton's first term. Since 1991, CIA teams had assisted the INA, which was mostly based in Jordan, in making contacts in the military and Baath Party. Saddam faced several coup plots and minor rebellions but managed to unravel and crush them all.[136] The largest INA coup, which received CIA backing, was planned for June 1996, but Iraqi intelligence infiltrated it and executed hundreds of the conspirators. After this failure, the despairing CIA team in Amman gave up on a coup for the time being and returned to the United States.[137] One CIA official lamented the regime's tight security and the incompetence of the coup plotters: "There are two great realities that govern here. First, if we know about it, Saddam does. Second, if someone comes to us needing help [to mount a coup], they are probably incapable of pulling it off."[138]

Rather than seeking a coup that would put a new strongman in power, the INC under Ahmed Chalabi wanted to spark a rebellion from its base in the Kurdish zone of Northern Iraq.[139] The Clinton administration intended for the INC to unite the opposition groups and show domestic critics that Clinton was actively aiding the opposition. However, Chalabi quickly started forming his own scheme to topple Saddam.[140] His plan, which he called "End Game," was to attack Iraqi forces from the Kurdish zone to encourage defections and possibly spark a revolt from the

---

[134] Anthony Cordesman, *Iraq: Sanctions and Beyond* (Boulder, CO: Westview Press, 1997), 21, 34–35.

[135] Cockburn and Cockburn, *Out of the Ashes*, 174; *ABC News Special Report*, "Unfinished Business: The CIA and Saddam Hussein," directed by Peter Jennings, ABC News, 1997, accessed January 22, 2019, https://www.youtube.com/watch?v=lZHHAI-eq2I.

[136] Phebe Marr, *The Modern History of Iraq* (Boulder, CO: Westview Press, 2012), 270–271; Blaydes, *State of Repression*, 293–303.

[137] Kevin Fedarko, "Saddam's CIA Coup," *Time*, September 23, 1996, 42; Cockburn and Cockburn, *Out of the Ashes*, 226–229. For an overview of the 1996 coup plan, see Hiro, *Neighbors, Not Friends*, 102–108.

[138] R. Jeffrey Smith and David Ottaway, "Anti-Saddam Operation Cost CIA $100 Million," *Washington Post*, September 15, 1996, A1.

[139] Bonin, *Arrows of the Night*, 92.

[140] Aram Roston, *The Man Who Pushed America to War: The Extraordinary Life, Adventures, and Obsessions of Ahmad Chalabi* (New York: Nation Books, 2008), 120.

disaffected regular army.[141] The INC reconciled disputes between the KDP and PUK in 1994, creating the possibility that they could provide ground forces against Saddam. The defection of a high-level general named Wafiq al-Samarrai to the INC in 1994 bolstered the INC's optimism that the regime could be toppled. The INC hoped to use Samarrai's contacts inside the regime to foment a military uprising while opposition forces attacked government troops.[142]

Confusion was the order of the day when the INC launched its campaign against Iraqi forces in March 1995. Chalabi expected US assistance in this rebellion because of an August 1993 letter from Gore to the INC that issued vague statements of support, including: "I can assure you that the U.S. intends to live up to these commitments ... and give whatever additional support we can reasonably provide to encourage you in your struggle for a democratic Iraq."[143] The chief of the CIA mission in Iraq, Robert Baer, promised support for this plan, further convincing Chalabi that United States would help him with force.[144]

However, when the Clinton administration found that the INC, with Baer's support, was about to launch a coup attempt and ground offensive, it quickly tried to stop the risky plot, which the Joint Chiefs of Staff said would not work without significant US military intervention. Lake had previously told the CIA that it must request the White House's approval before supporting any rebellion. Now the administration had discovered the INC plan, by intercepting an Iranian transmission no less, just as it was about to commence. Moreover, US intelligence had reported that Iraqi security knew the attack was coming.[145] A furious Lake warned all opposition groups that the plan was compromised and "any decision to proceed will be on your own."[146]

[141] Elaine Sciolino, "A Failed Plot to Overthrow Hussein Is Reported in Iraq," *New York Times*, March 14, 1995, A6; Robert Baer, *See No Evil: The True Story of a Ground Solider in the CIA's War on Terrorism* (New York: Crown Publishers, 2002), 191; Roston, *Man Who Pushed*, 106; Cockburn and Cockburn, *Out of the Ashes*, 166–167; Jim Hoagland, "How the CIA's Secret War on Saddam Collapsed," *Washington Post*, June 26, 1997.

[142] Smith and Ottaway, "Anti-Saddam Operation Cost CIA $100 Million," *Washington Post*, September 15, 1996; Baer, *See No Evil*, 183; Cockburn and Cockburn, *Out of the Ashes*, 179.

[143] "Letter from Albert Gore to Ahmed Chalabi" in House Committee on International Relations, *U.S. Policy in the Persian Gulf*, 104th Cong., 2nd sess., September 25, 1996, 87–88.

[144] Alan Cooperman, "Rolling Up in Iraq," *U.S. News and World Report*, September 23, 1996, 50; *ABC News Special Report*, "Unfinished Business," 1997.

[145] Indyk, *Innocent Abroad*, 163; Bonin, *Arrows of the Night*, 97, 102; Cockburn and Cockburn, *Out of the Ashes*, 188; Mazarr, *Leap of Faith*, 60.

[146] Baer, *See No Evil*, 173.

The administration feared that a failed rebellion might force the United States to intervene to save its clients from annihilation.[147] Chalabi later admitted that he hoped for this exact situation: "I told them that if we attack, the United States will have to make a choice – whether or not to let us be slaughtered. I told them the Americans wouldn't let us be slaughtered."[148] With US support out of the question, Massoud Barzani pulled all KDP forces out of the offensive.[149] Chalabi decided to launch the attack anyway on March 6, claiming the coup plotters were already in motion. The INC offensive, composed mainly of PUK units, forced some Iraqi units into retreat and attracted several hundred defectors. However, no wider Iraqi military rebellion or coup ensued, and the offensive petered out.[150]

These failures soured relations between the administration and the opposition, especially the INC. The CIA came to see Chalabi and Samarrai as liars who provided faulty intelligence about Saddam's regime, collaborated with Iran, and wanted to draw the United States into direct fighting.[151] CIA analyst Bruce Riedel summarized the problems with the opposition in September 1996: "I don't know of any reputable analyst of the situation in Iraq who believes those opposition forces were on the verge of overthrowing the Saddam dictatorship. They have been weak since their inception ... and they remain weak and very badly divided."[152] After the failed March 1995 uprising, the CIA drastically cut its budget for the INC and by the end of 1996, it was refusing to communicate with Chalabi.[153] One CIA agent involved with the opposition issued a more explicit threat to Chalabi: "If I see you on the streets here in London and get the chance, I'll fucking run you over."[154] With the opposition in tatters, the only hope for regime change now seemed to be a direct war against Saddam, which the administration would not consider. These fiascoes thus bolstered the argument of

---

[147] Lake, interview by Russell Riely, 7; Indyk, *Innocent Abroad*, 160; Pollack, *The Threatening Storm*, 73.

[148] Bonin, *Arrows of the Night*, 101.

[149] Sciolino, "A Failed Plot to Overthrow Hussein Is Reported in Iraq" *New York Times*, March 14, 1995.

[150] Smith and Ottaway, "Anti-Saddam Operation Cost CIA $100 Million," *Washington Post*, September 15, 1996; Indyk, *Innocent Abroad*, 163; Baer, *See No Evil*, 207.

[151] Steven Hurst, *The United States and Iraq Since 1979: Hegemony, Oil, and War* (Edinburgh: Edinburgh University Press, 2009), 130; Lake, interview by Russell Riely, 7; Indyk, *Innocent Abroad*, 163; Bonin, *Arrows of the Night*, 110.

[152] Bruce Riedel, House Committee on National Security, *U.S. Policy toward Iraq*, 104th Cong., 2nd sess., September 26, 1996, 72.

[153] Bonin, *Arrows of the Night*, 111; Roston, *Man Who Pushed*, 119.

[154] Roston, *Man Who Pushed*, 120.

advisors like Warren Christopher, who wanted to eschew hazardous regime change efforts and focus on containment and compliance with the United Nations.[155]

The administration's hopes that Saddam would be toppled from within received another devastating blow in August 1996 when Saddam exploited intra-Kurdish fighting to crush the INC in Northern Iraq. The KDP and the PUK had long feuded over control of smuggling routes into Turkey and Iran. The PUK used arms and advisors from Iran to launch an offensive against the KDP in August 1996. Barzani countered by asking Saddam for help. Sensing a golden opportunity, Saddam allied with Barzani and rushed 40,000 troops into the Kurdish zone to attack the PUK. Aside from striking a major blow against the PUK, Saddam seized Erbil and destroyed the INC's headquarters in Iraq while executing hundreds of INC agents.[156] The CIA team in northern Iraq hastily fled the country, leaving behind communications equipment and intelligence documents.[157] Saddam thereby reasserted control over a semiautonomous region of Iraq, gained access to valuable smuggling routes, and proved to potential challengers that he still ruled Iraq.[158]

The Clinton administration had been debating throughout the first half of 1996 whether to increase pressure on Iraq. Mark Parris and Bruce Riedel argued in an NSC meeting that conditions were ripe to press for regime change because Saddam was still weak at home and the coalition would not get any stronger. The more cautious camp of Christopher and Lake argued in response that containment was managing the problem and allowing the administration to focus on priorities like the MEPP and the Balkan crisis. The hard-liners failed to convince any of Clinton's principal advisors, but Saddam's northern incursion in August 1996 resurrected the conversation. The foreign policy team agreed that a military response was necessary for this major provocation, but it saw intervention in the north as a hopeless tangle. The administration did not want to take sides in the intra-Kurdish fighting, and the Defense Department warned that US troops would be needed to expel Saddam's forces from the north. Their intention to launch an air strike, however, was stymied by Saudi Arabia and Turkey's refusal to support strikes or grant access to bases. Saudi Arabia feared public backlash for

---

[155] Hurst, *United States and Iraq*, 130; Indyk, *Innocent Abroad*, 163.
[156] Pollack, *The Threatening Storm*, 81–84.
[157] Tim Weiner, "Iraqi Offensive into Kurdish Zone Disrupts U.S. Plot to Oust Hussein," *New York Times*, September 7, 1996, A1.
[158] John Lancaster, "Saddam Took Risk for Domestic Gain," *Washington Post*, September 3, 1996, A11.

supporting the United States, while Turkey was pleased to see Saddam pound the PUK.[159]

Instead of an air campaign, US naval forces launched forty-four cruise missiles on September 3–4 against military targets in the south such as antiaircraft batteries and command centers.[160] Clinton also extended the southern NFZ northward to the outskirts of Baghdad to punish Saddam and restrain his ability to threaten his neighbors. After these strikes and further US threats, Saddam withdrew most of his forces from the north. Clinton framed this response as helping to "increase America's ability to contain Iraq over the long run" while tightening the "strategic straightjacket."[161] To address public confusion as to why the United States had retaliated in the south for actions in the north, officials argued that the most crucial US interests were in blocking Iraqi aggression toward the Gulf rather than interceding in intractable Kurdish feuds.[162] Polls suggested public approval of this response, with 69 percent in one poll supporting the missile attacks and 66 percent agreeing that the United States should limit Saddam's power inside Iraq.[163]

The crisis over Saddam's Kurdish incursion further undermined containment by widening fissures in the international coalition. Great Britain, Japan, and Germany supported the strikes, but France, Russia, and China believed Saddam's actions were part of a sovereign affair. These nations argued that neither Resolution 687 nor 688 authorized this attack and criticized the United States for failing to seek specific Security Council authorization.[164] The United States and Great Britain failed to convince their allies to pass a Security Council resolution merely rebuking Saddam's actions.[165] Russia's ambassador to the United Nations, Sergei Lavrov, called the attacks "disproportionate" and accused Clinton of using force to prove his toughness for the 1996

[159] Pollack, *The Threatening Storm*, 78–79, 82–83; Mike McCurry, "Press Briefing," September 4, 1996, The American Presidency Project, accessed September 27, 2017, www.presidency.ucsb.edu/ws/index.php?pid=48820&st=iraq&st1=.

[160] Steven Lee Myers, "Pentagon Says Command Site Was Struck," *New York Times*, September 3, 1996, A1.

[161] Quotation is from Clinton. See Alison Mitchell, "Clinton Rebuts G.O.P Attacks on Iraq Policy," *New York Times*, September 15, 1996, A1; Alison Mitchell, "U.S. Continuing Bid to Smash Air Defense," *New York Times*, September 4, 1996, A1.

[162] Press Briefing by Mike McCurry and Mark Parris, September 3, 1996, OA/ID 3604, National Security Council, James Baker Files, Clinton Presidential Records, William Clinton Presidential Library, 10.

[163] Janet Elder, "Most Americans Support Clinton on Iraq," *New York Times*, September 6, 1996, B11.

[164] Barbara Crossette, "Clinton Finds Little Support at the U.N. for Iraqi Strikes," *New York Times*, September 5, 1996, A10.

[165] John Goshko, "U.N. Drops Resolution Rebuking Iraq," *Washington Post*, September 7, 1996, A17.

election.[166] Moreover, Jacques Chirac, who became president of France in 1995, criticized the US attacks and withdrew from the southern NFZ in December 1996 in order to distance France from US policy.[167]

Like Bush, Clinton defended his first-term Iraq policy as the effective management of a weak and contained threat. The inspectors had destroyed most of Saddam's WMD and ballistic missile arsenals and sanctions had inhibited military reconstruction. Saddam had recognized Kuwaiti sovereignty and relented in most showdowns with the coalition.[168] After the elimination of the coup and rebellion options in 1996, Clinton had to double down on this management paradigm as regime change looked increasingly improbable. One senior official described the US role as: "We know he's going to knock on that door from time to time to see if there's anybody out there who still cares. He's got to recognize we're still here and we ain't going away."[169]

Nevertheless, the Clinton administration ended its first term with a deep sense of frustration about Iraq. In a memorandum to incoming Secretary of State Madeleine Albright, Robert Pelletreau wrote "Our policy of containment is time-consuming, fraught with repeated crises, and costly to maintain in terms of our relationships," leading to "containment fatigue within the international community." Pelletreau predicted that the United States would have to devote "regular, high level attention" to containing Saddam and preserving the coalition.[170] Moreover, for Americans and the international coalition to believe that this costly management might end someday, the administration needed to show that there was a way out of containment, especially if virtually everyone in the political and policy establishment believed Saddam's intentions would never change. Since the Gulf War, this way out had been the hope that sanctions and other pressures would force a coup or rebellion against Saddam. Clinton promised an inverse way out to the international community, promising the potential easing of sanctions if Saddam adhered to high standards of compliance. The management paradigm of containment depended on these pillars, but the steady weakening of the coalition and the loss of the possibility of internally generated regime change

---

[166] Adam Nagourney, "Muting His Criticism of Clinton, Dole Backs Troops in Iraq Raid," *New York Times*, September 4, 1996, A1; Craig Whitney, "From Allies, U.S. Hears Mild Applause or Silence," *New York Times*, September 4, 1996, A10.

[167] Craig Whitney, "France to Pull Its Planes Out of Patrols over Northern Iraq," *New York Times*, December 28, 1996, A5; Steven Erlanger, "Paris Offers Scant Backing, but London Is Supportive," *New York Times*, September 6, 1996, A17.

[168] Madeleine Albright in House Committee on International Relations, *U.S. Policy toward Iraq*, 104th Cong., 2nd sess., March 28, 1996, 1–6.

[169] Johanna McGeary, "Slamming Saddam Again," *Time*, September 16, 1996, 32.

[170] Chollet, *America between the Wars*, 188.

started to erode the domestic legitimacy of containment and empower its detractors.

Debating Containment at Home, 1993–1996

Iraq mainly became a prominent political issue during these occasional confrontations, and it garnered less public attention in this period than problems like the Balkan crisis or the MEPP. Nevertheless, events in this period promoted important long-term changes in the conversation about Iraq. Factors like the dwindling unity of the coalition, the collapse of the hope for a coup or indigenous rebellion, and the persistent limits of inspections weakened the conditionalist view that the United States could manage the Iraqi threat and that Saddam might be overthrown at low cost. These subtle but important shifts set the ground for the inevitable decline critique to become the politically dominant view of containment in Clinton's second term.

Conditionalists during Clinton's first term were mainly realists or liberals in foreign policy terms, and they included more Democrats now that a Democrat was in the White House. They still agreed with Clinton's basic framework, but they argued that he needed to strictly enforce the Security Council resolutions and intensify pressures on the regime to possibly spark a coup. They also supported adjusting the policy to meet changing conditions. One important point for the conditional school was that Clinton should react to Saddam's provocations with disproportionate punishments rather than proportional responses. They recognized that the coalition's willingness to sanction Saddam would not last forever and wanted to increase pressure on Saddam to facilitate his ouster. A mere slap on the wrist, such as a few dozen cruise missiles, inflicted no real damage on Saddam and did not deter him from aggression. Proportional responses also undermined deterrence by enabling Saddam to calculate just how far he could go and how much punishment he could receive.[171] The strategic analyst Anthony Cordesman, for instance, argued that "force is only effective when it is large enough to show that each new provocation or crisis will do Saddam far more harm than the provocation is worth."[172] Policy-makers and scholars like Cordesman, Henry Kissinger, Brent Scowcroft, and Zbigniew Brzezinski argued that the United States should have responded to Iraqi provocations like the 1996 northern incursion with massive, multiday air

---

[171] Michael Eisenstadt, "Target Iraq's Republican Guard," *The Middle East Quarterly* 3, no. 4 (December, 1996): 11–16.

[172] Anthony Cordesman, "The Folly of Proportionate Escalation," *Washington Post*, January 18, 1993, A29.

strikes against the key elements of the regime, including Republican Guard units, communications networks, suspected WMD sites, and Saddam's palaces.[173]

Members of the conditional approach varied on whether Clinton should demand full compliance with all Security Council resolutions before considering sanctions relief. Most believed that the United States should not lift sanctions on Iraq until Saddam fell, just as Bush and Clinton did. A significant body of conditionalists nonetheless argued that there were advantages to promising that the oil export ban would be lifted if UNSCOM certified Iraqi compliance on WMD. The *New York Times* editorial board held this position, arguing: "He should make plain that by full compliance Iraq, even under Saddam Hussein, can have the embargo lifted and recover its sovereignty."[174]

This kind of statement implied that the United States might have to accept some level of normalization with Saddam if he complied with the Security Council. Advocates of this viewpoint believed that not "raising the goalposts" on the terms of lifting sanctions was necessary both to keep the coalition intact and induce Iraqi cooperation. Historian and Iraq expert Amatzia Baram warned that the United States should "expect the worst" if Saddam is convinced that he can do nothing to reduce the sanctions.[175] These critics often accused Clinton of maintaining this hard line for short-term domestic political gain rather than sound strategy.[176]

Furthermore, conditionalists generally accepted containment as a reasonably effective and low-cost way to manage the Iraqi threat and compel compliance with the United Nations as long as Clinton enforced it rigorously. Richard Haass, for example, told Congress in September 1996: "Saddam Hussein's Iraq is significantly weaker today than it was at the start of this decade and is better understood as

---

[173] For examples, see Henry Kissinger, "No Objective, No Will," *Washington Post*, October 6, 1996, A47; testimonies of Richard Haass and Michael Eisenstadt in House Committee on National Security, *U.S. Policy toward Iraq*, September 26, 1996, 4, 6; John McCain, *Cong. Rec.*, 103rd Cong., 1st sess., September 11, 1996, 10279; Brent Scowcroft and Zbigniew Brzezinski, *Differentiated Containment: U.S. Policy toward Iran and Iraq* (New York: Council on Foreign Relations Press, 1997), 9.

[174] Editorial, "Hanging Tough Isn't Enough," *New York Times*, January 7, 1993, A16.

[175] Subcommittee on Europe and the Middle East, *3 Years after the Gulf War*, February 23, 1994, 3.

[176] Editorial, "To Contain Saddam Hussein," *Washington Post*, February 16, 1994, A18. See also Charles Maynes, "Clinton Is Right on Iraq," *New York Times*, January 19, 1993, A21; Editorial, "Now What about Iraq?" *New York Times*, January 21, 1993, A24; Editorial, "Sanctions on Iraq," *The Economist*, March 27, 1993, 15; Editorial, "Bill's Gulf Adventure," *The Nation*, October 21, 1994, 478–479.

constituting a dangerous nuisance rather than an actual strategic threat."[177] Regime change would be desirable, but as historian Phebe Marr argued, it was "likely to prove difficult and costly and can only take place at the hand of Iraqis inside Iraq."[178] Sixty percent of Americans, according to a 1996 poll, agreed that the United States should not put ground troops in Iraq to achieve regime change.[179]

Finally, members of the conditional perspective concurred with Clinton's multilateral approach to containment, saying that unilateral sanctions would not work and would make the United States look like a bully. They faulted Clinton mainly for not putting enough effort into preserving the coalition and for not pressing Iraq's neighbors to limit sanctions violations. Furthermore, they backed oil-for-food as a way of alleviating the Iraqi humanitarian crisis and justifying the maintenance of sanctions.[180] They acknowledged that the limitation of US goals on Iraq was deeply "unsatisfactory," as Scowcroft put it, because the United States could do little about Iraq's human rights abuses or Saddam's odious presence. Nevertheless, they claimed there was no other short-term, low-risk way of ousting Saddam, which made containment the best approach until conditions changed. Making regime change an explicit goal just bolstered Saddam's image in Iraq while disrupting the coalition.[181]

In contrast to the conditionalist approach, members of the inevitable decline school argued for a total revision of US policy and the open declaration of regime change as a goal. For each of Clinton's claims of success on Iraq, they created counter-narratives that emphasized Saddam's unchanged intentions and steady erosion of containment.

---

[177] House Committee on National Security, *U.S. Policy toward Iraq*, September 26, 1996, 4. For more on this line of argument, see Brent Scowcroft, "Why We Stopped the Gulf War," *Newsweek*, September 23, 1996, 17.

[178] House Committee on International Relations, *U.S. Policy toward Iraq*, March 28, 1996, 17.

[179] Yankelovich Partners Telephone Survey, September 6, 1996, Polling the Nations, accessed November 25, 2017, http://poll.orspub.com.libproxy.lib.unc.edu/search.php ?action.

[180] Scowcroft and Brzezinski, *Differentiated Containment*, 20.

[181] Scowcroft, "Why We Stopped the Gulf War," *Newsweek*, September 23, 1996, 17. For other supporters of this approach to Iraq during Clinton's first term, see Richard Haass testimony in House Committee on National Security, *U.S. Policy toward Iraq*, September 26, 1996, 5; Amatzia Baram testimony in Subcommittee on Europe and the Middle East, *3 Years after the Gulf War*, February 23, 1994, 9; Daniel Pipes Testimony in Subcommittee on Near Eastern and South Asian Affairs of the Senate Foreign Relations Committee, *U.S. Policy toward Iraq and Iran*, 104th Cong., 1st sess., March 2, 1995, 54; Cordesman, "Proportionate Escalation," *Washington Post*, January 18, 1993; Maynes, "Clinton Is Right," *New York Times*, January 19, 1993; Thomas Friedman, "Keep It Simple," *New York Times*, September 18, 1996, A21.

This group included neoconservatives, liberal hawks, and, with a Democrat in office, more conservative Republicans. These critics believed that the nature of Saddam's totalitarian regime and his personal psychology precluded meaningful change in Iraqi behavior. A totalitarian state could not be managed, as the *Wall Street Journal* editors claimed: "We will never be able to fully supervise or control a relatively large totalitarian state."[182] Rather than arguing that Saddam might escape the box down the road, they claimed he was already escaping containment. Saddam was "setting the agenda" by whittling away at international unity and provoking the United States whenever he wanted.[183] These critics pointed to each crisis between 1993 and 1996 not as evidence of the stresses imposed on Saddam, as Clinton portrayed them, but as signs of the growing cracks in containment and Saddam's belief that the coalition lacked the will to stop him.[184]

Inevitable decline critics like Charles Krauthammer mocked Clinton's missile strikes as "pinpricks" that conveyed "timidity" and encouraged Iraq to misbehave even more.[185] To mount a serious campaign to bring down Saddam, they recommended extensive punitive strikes, military training for the INC, war crimes tribunals, the formation of an NDZ in the south and an NFZ over the entire country, and permanent sanctions.[186] This group also opposed relenting on sanctions until Saddam was gone, even if that broke up the coalition. In fact, many inevitable decline critics, especially Republicans, denounced oil-for-food as a "foot in the door" for Saddam to destroy the entire sanctions regime.[187]

[182] Editorial, "Beyond Saddam," *Wall Street Journal*, January 13, 1993, A14; for similar arguments, see Jim Hoagland, "Saddam's Game," *Washington Post*, January 14, 1993, A29; A. M. Rosenthal, "Saddam Moves Along," *New York Times*, September 6, 1996, A27.

[183] Editorial, "Beyond Saddam," *Wall Street Journal*, January 13, 1994.

[184] Editorial, "End of Illusions," *Wall Street Journal*, January 14, 1993, A16.

[185] Charles Krauthammer, "The Pinprick Response to Aggression," *Washington Post*, September 5, 1996, A19.

[186] For examples of this argument, see Mylroie testimony in Subcommittee on Europe and the Middle East, *3 Years after the Gulf War*, February 23, 1994, 6, 14; Richard Perle testimony in House Committee on National Security, *U.S. Policy toward Iraq*, September 26, 1996, 19; A. M. Rosenthal, "Shrinking Saddam," *New York Times*, October 14, 1994, A35; Jim Hoagland, "Don't Let Saddam Get Away Again," *Washington Post*, October 16, 1994, C7; Paul Wolfowitz, "Clinton's Bay of Pigs," *Wall Street Journal*, September 27, 1996, A18; Editorial, "Dangerous Curves," *National Review*, November 7, 1994, 6; Fouad Ajami, "Hosing Down the Gulf's Arsonist," *U.S. News and World Report*, November 7, 1994, 48.

[187] Quote is from Senator Alphonse D'Amato (R-NY) in *Cong. Rec.*, 103rd Cong., 2nd sess., May 16, 1994, 5768. See also Robert Dole, "Statement by Senator Bob Dole on Iraq Sanctions Relief," May 20, 1996, The American Presidency Project, www.presidency.ucsb.edu/ws/index.php?pid=115384&st=iraq&st1; Patrick Clawson, "The

One key idea in the inevitable decline argument that emerged in Clinton's first term was that Saddam was fixated on revenge against the United States for Desert Storm. They believed that Saddam was not a rational survivor but a maniac obsessed with vengeance. In particular, a policy scholar named Laurie Mylroie relentlessly promoted this idea by spreading dubious theories that Saddam was behind most major anti-US terrorist attacks of the 1990s. Mylroie was a foreign policy scholar with a Ph.D. in political science from Harvard. During the 1980s she had supported the engagement policy toward Iraq, but after the invasion of Kuwait she turned sharply against Saddam and cowrote a book with journalist Judith Miller denouncing his regime.[188] After Saddam emerged damaged but intact from the Gulf War, she blamed Bush's "shallow realpolitik" for his failure to topple the dictator and became a firm regime change supporter.[189]

After the 1993 World Trade Center bombing, Mylroie published numerous papers and eventually a book claiming that Saddam was responsible for the 1993 terrorist attacks on the World Trade Center. There were some potential links between Iraq and this attack, including the fact that one minor figure in the conspiracy had fled to Iraq after the attack.[190] Mylroie, however, concocted a highly tendentious story that pinned responsibility on Saddam, including the unsubstantiated claim that the United States had not apprehended the real Ramzi Yousef, the al-Qaeda affiliated orchestrator of the 1993 bombing, whom she asserted was an Iraqi agent who had stolen the identity of a Kuwaiti citizen.[191]

Extensive investigations of this attack by the FBI, the State Department, and several US intelligence agencies found no evidence for her claims, but she nonetheless became widely influential in neoconservative and Republican circles.[192] Her conspiracy theory sustained the fear that Saddam would do anything to get back at the United States, or in

---

Stakes in the Iraq Oil Sales Dispute," Washington Institute for Near East Policy, Policy Watch Paper 200, May 14, 1996, accessed September 17, 2017, www .washingtoninstitute.org/policy-analysis/view/the-stakes-in-the-iraq-oil-sales-dispute.

[188] Judith Miller and Laurie Mylroie, *Saddam Hussein and the Crisis in the Gulf* (New York: Times Books, 1990).

[189] Laurie Mylroie, "How We Helped Saddam Survive," *Commentary*, July 1991, 15.

[190] Michael Isikoff and David Korn, *Hubris: The Inside Story of Spin, Scandal, and the Selling of the Iraq War* (New York: Three Rivers Press, 2007), 71.

[191] Laurie Mylroie, "Saddam's Fingerprints on N.Y. Bombings," *Washington Post*, June 28, 1993, A16. See also Laurie Mylroie, *Study of Revenge: Saddam Hussein's Unfinished War against America* (Washington DC: American Enterprise Institute Press, 2000); Laurie Mylroie, "The World Trade Center Bomb: Who Is Ramzi Yousef? And Why It Matters," *The National Interest* 42 (Winter, 1995/1996), 3–15.

[192] Mylroie's claims have been thoroughly debunked by experts and US intelligence agencies. See Peter Bergen, "Did One Woman's Obsession Take America to War?" *The Guardian*, accessed December 31, 2017, www.theguardian.com/world/2004/jul/05/iraq

Mylroie's words, "I am not sure now that I can say that there is anything that Saddam would not do."[193] This belief became a key part of the regime change consensus, as it implied that containment could not stop a WMD-armed madman who used terrorist groups to strike his greatest adversary.

These condemnations of Clinton's Iraq policy fit within a larger Republican and neoconservative political agenda as well as their case against his foreign policy. They claimed Clinton had inherited an unprecedentedly peaceful world with no superpower rivalry and then wasted this opportunity by cutting military spending, focusing on "international social work" in places like Haiti and Somalia, and neglecting core strategic regions like the Gulf.[194] In Iraq and elsewhere, these critics claimed that Clinton let himself be chained into inaction by UN procedures as well as irresolute or duplicitous partners rather than showing leadership and taking action.[195] They believed Clinton's weakness invited provocations from Saddam and other foes. For instance, Senator Robert Dole (R-KS), Clinton's challenger in the 1996 election, claimed after the 1996 Kurdish crisis: "The fact is that in the last few months Saddam Hussein has been testing American leadership and finding it lacking."[196]

Inevitable declinists seized on events like the Hussein Kamel affair and the crushing of the internal opposition to bolster their arguments. They contended that Kamel's revelations about the depths of Iraqi cheating on biological weapons meant that the United States was nowhere near a solution on Iraqi WMD. The discovery of the biological weapons program was largely dumb luck, they claimed, and if not for Kamel's actions, UNSCOM and the IAEA might have wrongly certified Iraqi compliance in 1996. Clinton had tried to portray this episode as a sign of his policy's success, but critics turned this claim on its head. They retorted that the real lessons of Hussein Kamel were that Saddam would never come clean on WMD and no matter how thoroughly the inspectors

.iraq; Richard Clarke, *Against All Enemies: Inside America's War on Terror* (New York: Free Press, 2004), 95.

[193] Mylroie, Subcommittee on Europe and the Middle East, *3 Years after the Gulf War*, February 23, 1994, 31.

[194] Quote is from Krauthammer, "Pinprick Response," *Washington Post*, September 5, 1996. See also Robert Kagan, "A Retreat from Power?" *Commentary*, July 1995, 19–25; Zalmay Khalilzad, "Losing the Moment? The United States and the World after the Cold War," *Washington Quarterly* 18, no. 2 (Spring, 1995), 85–107.

[195] Paul Wolfowitz, "Clinton's First Year," *Foreign Affairs* 73, no. 1 (January–February, 1994): 30–33.

[196] R. W. Apple, "What's Bad for Hussein Seems Good for Clinton," *New York Times*, September 5, 1996, A11.

searched he would always be hiding something.[197] How could the United States know that future Iraqi WMD disclosures were not "self-serving selective glimpses?"[198] Furthermore, inspectors like David Kay argued that virtually any modern industrial country could produce chemical and biological weapons from existing industrial and pharmaceutical infrastructure.[199] These persistent problems with inspections reinforced the idea that the true problem was, in Kay's words, the "motivation and intentions" of the regime itself rather than their capacity to generate and hide these programs.[200]

The crushing of the Iraqi opposition in 1996 further strengthened the inevitable decline case against containment. Few in the media or Congress doubted that Iraq had gained more in this showdown than it lost. Paul Wolfowitz called this crisis "Clinton's Bay of Pigs" and claimed that it signaled the failure of "inept covert operations" and the "passive containment policy."[201] Bob Dole and John McCain (R-AZ) said that Clinton's "weak leadership" and "vacillation" prompted Saddam to strike at the opposition.[202] These critics claimed the loss of the two main options for toppling Saddam meant that the United States must shift to a more open and aggressive regime change policy. Legislators like McCain, Trent Lott (R-MI), Robert Kerrey (D-NE), and Richard Lugar (R-IN) said that with the fading of the coup possibility the United States should "do more than just contain" and declare regime change as "an open objective."[203] The editors of the *New Republic* likewise argued that after September 1996 "the only solution to the threat posed by Saddam is the overthrow of Saddam."[204]

---

[197] For examples of this claim, see Mylroie testimony in Subcommittee on Europe and the Middle East, *3 Years after the Gulf War*, February 23, 1994, 20; William Safire, "Iraq's Threat: Biological Warfare," *New York Times*, February 16, 1995, A27.

[198] Quote is from Editorial, "Don't Take Iraq's Word for It," *New York Times*, August 24, 1995, A22.

[199] David Kay, "Denial and Deception Practices of WMD Proliferators: Iraq and Beyond," *Washington Quarterly* 18, no. 1 (Winter, 1995): 88–90. For a similar argument, see Michael Eisenstadt, "Still Not Bomb-Proof," *Washington Post*, February 26, 1996, A19.

[200] Kay, "Denial and Deception," 101; Editorial, "Four Years of Lies," *Washington Post*, July 7, 1995, A20.

[201] Wolfowitz, "Bay of Pigs," *Wall Street Journal*, September 27, 1996.

[202] The first quotation in this sentence is from Dole, and the second is from McCain. Both quotations found in Myers, "Pentagon Says Command Site Was Struck," *New York Times*, September 3, 1996. See also Editorial, "Where Are the Allies?" *Wall Street Journal*, September 4, 1996, A14.

[203] The first quotation is from Robert Kerrey in Senate Select Committee on Intelligence, *Iraq Report*, 104th Cong., 2nd sess., September 19, 1996, 21. The second quotation is from John McCain in *Cong. Rec.*, September 11, 1996, 10279. See also "G.O.P. Leaders Hit President on Iraq Policy," *Washington Post*, September 13, 1996, A33.

[204] Editorial, "Operation Desert Prick," *The New Republic*, September 30, 1996, 7; see also Michael Ledeen, "Bill Clinton's Bay of Pigs," *The Weekly Standard*, October 7, 1996, 29.

The simmering policy debate between the conditional and inevitable decline approaches to containment was not just over different means for reaching the same end. Each camp had distinct views of what end point for Iraq and Saddam would be tolerable for US security and national interests. For conditionalists, a weak Saddam was acceptable for the moment, a compliant successor was vastly more preferable, and a democratic Iraq was a laudable goal but not necessarily one the United States could achieve. Analysts like Cordesman stressed the bounds of US power and knowledge: "We cannot invade, occupy, or change the fundamental political character of either Iraq or Iran."[205] Furthermore, conditionalists held that containment could only work as a multilateral policy, which limited the United States' leeway to pursue regime change.

For inevitable declinists, multilateralism was a problem, not an asset because it inhibited the world's most powerful state from abandoning a futile containment policy and pursuing regime change directly and purposefully. Only his removal and the transformation of Iraq from a totalitarian dictatorship to a democracy would eliminate this menace. Because Iraq remained a secondary issue in Clinton's first term, the conditionalist view won in the Clinton administration and the larger political debate. However, the tools and assumptions of containment were being eroded by the dwindling unity of the coalition, the collapse of hope for a coup or indigenous rebellion, and the persistent limits of inspections.

Conclusion

Iraq played a minor role in the 1996 presidential election, which hinged on domestic politics. Dole and his running mate, Jack Kemp, occasionally attacked Clinton for not maintaining the coalition and hitting back weakly against Saddam's provocations.[206] Despite their criticism, Dole and Kemp did not make Iraq a central plank of their campaign or offer specific policy changes. While Iraq usually stayed on the political back burner in Clinton's first term, these were highly consequential years for the long-term trajectory of containment. In his memoir, Martin Indyk illuminated the larger significance of this period:

---

[205] Senate Committee on Armed Services, *The Situation in Iraq*, 104th Cong., 2nd sess., September 12, 1996, 39. See also A. M. Rosenthal, "On Clinton's Watch," *New York Times*, September 10, 1996, A27; Zalmay Khalilzad, "The U.S. Failure in Iraq," *Wall Street Journal*, September 10, 1996, A22.

[206] Dole, "Bob Dole on Iraq Sanctions Relief," May 20, 1996.

The policy of containment of the Soviet Union, first articulated by George Kennan, was based on the idea that the Soviet system was rotten to the core and would collapse of its own weight if the United States could only keep the pressure on it. Containment of Iraq was based on a similar calculation. But the Clinton administration's critical assumption was that the combination of sanctions and covert operations would force the collapse of Saddam's regime in five years, not the five decades that it took for the Soviet Union to collapse. And that would prove to be a fatally flawed judgment.[207]

Indyk's analysis highlights the importance of a theory of change in any containment policy. By their nature, containment strategies do not directly seek the overthrow of the target state, so strategists of containment must explain how they will create an atmosphere conducive to the target changing either its behavior or its ruling government lest containment start to appear indefinite.[208] The containment of the Soviet Union had a theory of change that resembled Clinton's approach to Iran: maintain economic pressures and block expansion so that forces within each society would create either regime or behavioral change.[209] In contrast, in the Iraq case behavioral change was considered virtually impossible, while regime change by invasion or assassination were unacceptable.

This impasse left regime change by coup or uprising as the only solution. Containment remained stable in political and policy terms only while these outlets remained viable. The crushing of the internal and external opposition in the mid-1990s discredited the idea that Saddam could be removed through these tools. Moreover, the steady dissolution of the coalition and Saddam's ongoing attempts to mask his WMD programs fed the idea that containment could not hold for much longer. The domestic audience and the international coalition were heading in opposite directions, and Clinton's rhetorical gymnastics – the Clinton fudge – on Iraq policy could not bridge this gap forever.

Clinton's first term was therefore a deceptively quiet time for containment. The policy achieved many successes, and it was most effective when Saddam made obvious, conventional threats to his neighbors. Nevertheless, containment's foundations were being hollowed out from within, and frustration with the policy was mounting at home. This hollowing out would shift the domestic political momentum

---

[207] Indyk, *Innocent Abroad*, 38–39.
[208] Robert Litwak, *Regime Change: U.S. Strategy through the Prism of 9/11* (Washington, DC: Woodrow Wilson Center Press, 2007), 87, 107.
[209] John Lewis Gaddis, *Strategies of Containment: A Critical Appraisal of American National Security Policy during the Cold War*, 2nd ed. (New York: Oxford University Press, 2005), 19–23, 35–43.

toward the inevitable decline critics of containment once Saddam intensified his challenges in the late 1990s. In Clinton's second term, the expanding inevitable decline group would try to wrest control of Iraq policy away from Clinton and decisively shift US policy toward regime change.

4 Saddam Must Go: Entrenching the Regime Change Consensus, 1997–2000

Introduction

On February 11, 1998, during yet another standoff with Iraq over inspections, National Security Advisor Sandy Berger met with a group that his staff labeled the "Iraq Influentials." The visitors included Paul Wolfowitz, Donald Rumsfeld, Richard Perle, William Kristol, and Francis Fukuyama, all of whom had been relentlessly criticizing Clinton's Iraq policy in the last few months. According to his notes, Berger tried to convince his guests that containment "has kept Saddam under pressure and muzzled," and that in each crisis sparked by Iraq, "we have consistently and firmly put Saddam back in his box." "Remember Aideed," his notes read, referring to the ill-fated US special forces raid against the Somali warlord Mohammed Farah Aidid in which 18 US soldiers were killed. He meant to warn his guests that even if the United States overthrew the Baathist regime, there was no guarantee they would enjoy a smooth aftermath.[1]

The "Influentials," led by Wolfowitz, responded with an attack on containment. Wolfowitz argued that the Clinton administration should "back out of containment rhetoric" now that they had the "xth demonstration that we can't live w. SH." Perle and Wolfowitz recommended a regime change strategy that was gaining political momentum: declare Saddam's regime to be illegitimate, build up US forces in the region, and back the Iraqi opposition's war against Saddam. Rumsfeld interjected that ground troops should be kept out of Iraq, citing the US intervention in Lebanon in the early 1980s as a warning about occupying Middle Eastern cities. The meeting was cordial, but neither side convinced the other to shift their views.[2]

---

[1] Memorandum, Steven Naplan to Sandy Berger, February 11, 1998, OA/ID 3108, National Security Council Office of Press and Communications, Matthew Gobush Files, William Clinton Presidential Library, 4–5.

[2] Notes, Influentials Session with Sandy Berger, February 11, 1998, OA/ID 3108, National Security Council Office of Press and Communications, Matthew Gobush Files, William Clinton Presidential Library, 2–4.

This meeting demonstrated the rising influence during Clinton's second term of a group of intellectuals, Iraqi exiles, and politicians who sought to discredit and replace containment with an active regime change strategy. The most devoted members of this movement were neoconservatives like Perle and Wolfowitz, Republican legislators, and the INC under Ahmed Chalabi. Numerous liberals and Democrats also backed this effort. Clinton's handling of repeated inspection crises in Iraq convinced his critics that he had no broader strategy beyond maintaining inspections and sanctions and mending the faltering coalition. They believed Clinton was shifting toward a strategy of limited containment and deterrence that would abandon serious efforts to remove Saddam and accept that he might develop some WMD.

This strengthened political movement focused on convincing Congress and the public that containment must be replaced with regime change. They argued that sanctions were collapsing, the coalition was not dependable, inspections had outlived their usefulness, and Saddam was still determined to build WMD. Moreover, they contended that as containment weakened, the United States had a narrow window of time to achieve regime change before Saddam reconstituted his WMD and military strength. Pursuing his ouster would require that the United States recognize regime change and containment as incompatible, in contrast to the Bush and Clinton approach of sporadically pursuing regime change from a baseline of containment. Containment required maintaining a diverse coalition, regime change advocates claimed, which precluded the bold steps that were needed to overthrow Saddam and uproot the Baathist system.

The culmination of this movement's efforts was the Iraq Liberation Act (ILA), which declared the removal of Saddam and his regime as an official US foreign policy goal in October 1998. Scholars usually ignore or downplay the ILA because it was a nonbinding resolution that did not meaningfully change actual policy.[3] In a wider historical frame, however, it is a deeply important signpost in the evolution of ideas about how to deal with Saddam. The ILA reflected a growing bipartisan consensus that containment could

---

[3] For work that examines Iraq policy in the 1990s but glosses over the Iraq Liberation Act, see James Mann, *Rise of the Vulcans: The History of Bush's War Cabinet* (New York: Viking, 2004), 216–234; Robert Litwak, *Rogue States and U.S. Foreign Policy: Containment after the Cold War* (Washington, DC: Woodrow Wilson Center Press, 2000) 135; Derek Chollet, *America between the Wars: From 11/9 to 9/11: The Misunderstood Years between the Fall of the Berlin Wall and the Start of the War on Terror* (New York: Public Affairs, 2008), 199. For two prominent works that do not mention the ILA at all, see Andrew Bacevich, *America's War for the Greater Middle East: A Military History* (New York: Random House, 2016); Peter Galbraith, *The End of Iraq: How American Incompetence Created a War Without End* (New York: Simon & Schuster, 2006).

not be rehabilitated because the coalition would always prefer a weaker policy, Saddam would always evade or obstruct inspectors, and sanctions would continue to collapse. The bill conveyed the political ascension of the belief that only regime change and democratization in Iraq could definitively solve this problem. This assertion of Congressional power to shift foreign policy priorities suggested that Clinton had lost control of the conversation about Iraq. Finally, the ILA debate showed how few people in the political discourse still defended containment. These outnumbered conditionalists were now limited mainly to ex-Bush administration officials, some Democrats, realist scholars, and military personnel. They tried to manage expectations about what could be achieved in Iraq, emphasize the containment's achievements, and adjust the policy to make it more sustainable.

In sum, the ILA signified the entrenching of the regime change consensus in US political and intellectual life. It signaled the political victory of the inevitable decline critique of containment, which stated that containment is not working and cannot work against a regime like Saddam's. These principles became a sort of common sense in US thinking about Iraq, a set virtually unquestionable assumptions that narrowed the range of ideas for dealing with Iraq. Finally, the pro-regime change argument benefitted from the development of the rollback strategy by the Iraqi opposition, which offered a concrete, if fantastical, alternative to containment.

By the end of 1998, Saddam's seemingly endless intransigence and growing tensions in the coalition deepened top Clinton administration officials' sense that only regime change could solve this threat. Nonetheless, the basic containment paradigm still guided their handling of confrontations with Iraq. They focused on maintaining inspections and sanctions, funneling essential supplies to the Iraqi people, and preserving the coalition. They continued to view containment and regime change as compatible, seeking ways to destabilize Saddam within the framework of sanctions and inspections. They resisted the ILA and signed it reluctantly, rhetorically endorsing its goals while doing the bare minimum to carry it out. By 2000, Iraq policy had reached an anticlimactic impasse, with a political discourse fixated on regime change facing an administration that saw no responsible path to this end.

The Inspection Crises and the Road to Operation Desert Fox, 1997–1998

The period from October 1997 to December 1998 witnessed an unprecedented string of confrontations between Iraq and the coalition. Iraq sought to impose restrictions on UNSCOM while asserting that it had completed disarmament and that sanctions should be lifted. UNSCOM resisted this obstruction, and the United States repeatedly threatened to use force to compel Iraq's compliance. Last-second agreements or temporary retreats by Iraq prevented US strikes in November 1997, February 1998, and November 1998, but Iraq quickly returned to non-cooperation after each reprieve. Clinton was torn between domestic political calls for toughness, the coalition's unwillingness to back up the inspections with force, and some UN members' undermining of the inspections. This year of confrontations with Iraq culminated in US and British air and missile strikes in Operation Desert Fox in December 1998 and the permanent ejection of the inspectors from Iraq.

In the first ten months of 1997, Clinton held that Iraq was still a minor threat, but he remained concerned about the growing challenge to containment. A CIA Report from early 1997 reflected this delicate stasis: "Although U.N. sanctions alone probably are not sufficient to bring down the regime, their maintenance is key to keeping pressure on Saddam and frustrating his ambitions for regional hegemony."[4] However, the international coalition, especially Middle Eastern nations, increasingly criticized the humanitarian effects of sanctions. One cable from State's Near Eastern Affairs Office (NEA) stated: "We are deeply concerned that the Iraqis appear to be gaining ground in influencing international perceptions of the sanctions regime."[5] Another intelligence assessment judged that Iraq had not abandoned its "regional hegemonistic political aspirations" and that it "remains strongly committed to retaining and acquiring weapons of mass destruction and will try to rapidly rebuild these programs once U.N. sanctions are lifted and inspections are halted."[6]

Weapons inspections continued their steady progress in 1997. UNSCOM director Rolf Ekeus reported advances on biological and chemical disarmament, although Iraqi obstruction persisted. In April 1997, Ekeus reported that "not much is unknown about Iraq's retained proscribed weapons capabilities," although "what is still not accounted for cannot be neglected."[7] In June, he reported: "We have

---

[4] CIA Report, "Iraq: Regime Prospects for 1997," December 31, 1996, in Senate Select Committee on Intelligence, *Postwar Findings about Iraq's WMD Programs and Links to Terrorism and How They Compare with Prewar Assessments*, 109th Cong., 2nd sess., September 8, 2006, S. Report 109–331, 384.

[5] Cable, State Department Near East Office to Various Embassies, March 29, 1997, Digital National Security Agency, Targeting Iraq, Part 1 Collection, 3.

[6] Defense Intelligence Agency Assessment, "Iraq's Weapons of Mass Destruction Programs," October 1997, Digital National Security Agency, Targeting Iraq, Part 1 Collection, 1.

[7] United Nations Special Commission, "3rd Report Under UNSCR 1051," April 11, 1997, accessed February 25, 2018, http://web.archive.org/web/20050313225009/http://www.ir aqwatch.org:80/un/UNSCOM/1051/sres97-301.html.

documentary evidence about orders from the leadership to preserve a strategic capability" on WMD.[8] Gaps remained regarding chemical weapons like VX, biological weapons and precursors, and ballistic missiles.[9]

The core problem was that in 1991 Iraq had unilaterally destroyed a great quantity of ballistic missiles, chemical and biological weapons and materials, and a variety of components and equipment. Iraqi officials wanted the inspectors to accept their assertions that these weapons were gone, but the inspectors demanded documentary and physical evidence that they had been destroyed because unaccounted weapons and materials could still be intact.[10] For example, in the summer of 1998, UNSCOM found evidence of Iraqi development of the chemical weapon VX. They knew Iraq had imported 600,000 kg of VX precursor and weaponized some of it, but Iraq never surrendered the materials nor provided evidence of their destruction. Inspectors called this gap in the record the "material balance."[11]

In July 1997, Richard Butler, an Australian arms control expert, replaced Ekeus as head of UNSCOM. Butler soon expanded UNSCOM's use of aerial surveillance, listening devices, and surprise inspections to expose ongoing concealment activities.[12] He hoped that these "counter-concealment operations" would expose the systematic Iraqi program to hide information and materials and harass the inspectors.[13] Such evidence, Butler thought, would show skeptical Security Council members that Iraq was far from complying, thereby sustaining the international will to maintain sanctions.[14] Verification of Iraqi compliance, he argued, was possible only if the Iraqi concealment

---

[8] Barbara Crossette, "Iraqis Still Defying Arms Ban, Departing U.N. Official Says," *New York Times*, June 25, 1997, A1.

[9] United Nations Special Commission, "3rd Report Under UNSCR 1051," April 11, 1997.

[10] United Nations Special Commission, "Ambassador Richard Butler's Presentation to the U.N. Security Council," June 3, 1998, accessed March 19, 2018, http://web.archive.org/web/20050314073650/http://www.iraqwatch.org:80/un/UNSCOM/s-1998–529.htm.

[11] Jean Krasno and James Sutterlin, *The United Nations and Iraq: Defanging the Viper* (Westport, CT: Praeger, 2003), 68; United Nations Special Commission, "6th Report Under UNSCR 1051," October 6, 1998, accessed February 25, 2018, http://web.arch ive.org/web/20060222203010/http://www.iraqwatch.org:80/un/Index_UNSCOM. html.

[12] Tim Trevan, *Saddam's Secrets: The Hunt for Iraq's Hidden Weapons* (London: Harper Collins, 1999), 358–360; Krasno and Sutterlin, *The United Nations and Iraq*, 73–5.

[13] United Nations Special Commission, "UNSCOM Final Compendium," January 29, 1999, accessed March 16, 2018, http://web.archive.org/web/20051124075332/http://w ww.iraqwatch.org:80/un/UNSCOM/disarmament.htm.

[14] Charles Duelfer, *Hide and Seek: The Search for Truth in Iraq* (New York: Public Affairs, 2009), 139–140.

strategy could be exposed to the point that the Iraqis agreed to stop.[15] In contrast to UNSCOM's struggles, the IAEA had achieved significant progress on nuclear disarmament. It concluded in October 1997 that nuclear inspections had "reached a point of diminishing returns" as there were "no indications that there remains in Iraq any physical capability for the production of amounts of weapon-usable nuclear material of any practical significance."[16]

Secretary of State Madeleine Albright gave a major speech at Georgetown University in March 1997 to issue a "wake-up call" to Saddam that the United States would still enforce the Security Council resolutions.[17] She listed Iraq's violations of these resolutions and noted how sanctions and inspections had weakened Iraq. Reaffirming containment, she asserted: "As long as the apparatus of sanctions, enforcement, inspections, and monitoring are in place, Iraq will remain trapped within a strategic box." She then restated the US approach to lifting sanctions in stark terms: "We do not agree with nations that argue that if Iraq complies with its obligations concerning weapons of mass destruction, sanctions should be lifted. Our view, which is unshakeable, is that Iraq must prove its peaceful intentions" by complying with every UN resolution.[18] The speech was less a policy shift than a reiteration of US resolve to Saddam as well as international partners who wanted to end inspections and the oil embargo.

In late 1997, Iraqi officials escalated their campaign to cripple inspections by creating a crisis that would further isolate the United States within the coalition and undermine Richard Butler's counter-concealment operations.[19] In early October, Iraqi Foreign Minister Tariq Aziz blocked inspectors from visiting a list of "sensitive sites" he claimed were vital for Iraqi security services. In response, the United States and Great Britain led the passage of a Security Council resolution condemning these actions and suspending the next sanctions review as punishment. US officials tried to get France, Russia, and China to agree to a travel ban on top Iraqi officials, but they would agree to threaten a ban

[15] United Nations Special Commission, "UNSCOM Final Compendium," January 29, 1999, appendix 4.

[16] International Atomic Energy Agency, "4th Consolidated Report Under UNSC 1051," October 8, 1998, accessed February 25, 1998, http://web.archive.org/web/2006121515 2301/http://www.iraqwatch.org:80/un/IAEA/s-1997–779.htm.

[17] Madeleine Albright, *Madam Secretary: A Memoir* (New York: Harper Collins, 2013), 277.

[18] Madeleine Albright, "Speech on Iraq at Georgetown University" (speech, Washington, DC, March 26, 1997), accessed March 29, 2018, https://awpc.cattcenter.iastate.edu/2 017/03/21/policy-speech-on-iraq-march-26–1997/.

[19] Gregory Koblentz, "Saddam versus the Inspectors: The Impact of Regime Security on the Verification of Iraq's WMD Disarmament," *Journal of Strategic Studies* 41, no. 3 (April, 2018): 372–409. See also Duelfer, *Hide and Seek*, 139.

only if UNSCOM continued to judge that Iraq was not cooperating by April 1998.[20] These nations also did not agree to threaten Iraq with "serious consequences," diplomatic code for military force.[21]

Aziz seized on this shaky response on October 29, 1997, by informing the Security Council that Iraq would only cooperate with UNSCOM if "no individuals of American nationality shall participate in any activity of the Special Commission inside Iraq" and if all US inspectors left Iraq within 24 hours.[22] Iraq also threatened to shoot down US U-2 spy planes participating in inspections.[23] UNSCOM and Clinton saw these threats as an attempt to divide the coalition and weaken the principle that Iraq had no say in the composition of the inspection teams.[24] Butler rejected the demand to exclude US inspectors, and a few days later he sent teams with US personnel on inspection missions. When Iraqi officials again prevented them from accessing suspected sites, Butler and the IAEA withdrew all inspectors in early November to ensure their safety.[25]

The United States struggled to mobilize the coalition and compel Iraq to readmit inspectors with full rights. The Clinton administration strongly preferred a diplomatic solution, fearing that an air or missile strike would make the ejection of inspectors permanent.[26] Furthermore, Clinton officials believed that acting unilaterally would only foment division in the coalition, which is what Saddam wanted.[27] The United States rallied France, Russia, and China to pass a Security Council resolution condemning Iraq, imposing a travel ban on top Iraqi officials, and warning of "serious consequences" if it failed to readmit the inspectors.[28] This stronger statement, combined with Russian diplomacy, convinced Iraq to let inspectors back in with full rights. In return, foreign minister Yevgeny

---

[20] United Nations Security Council Resolution 1134, October 23, 1997, unscr.org, accessed February 29, 2018, http://unscr.com/en/resolutions/1134

[21] Martin Indyk, *Innocent Abroad: An Intimate Account of American Peace Diplomacy in the Middle East* (New York: Simon & Schuster, 2009), 186; Richard Butler, *The Greatest Threat: Iraq, Weapons of Mass Destruction, and the Growing Crisis of Global Security* (New York: Public Affairs, 2000), 91.

[22] Butler, *The Greatest Threat*, 91.

[23] Barbara Crossette, "Iraq Threatens to Shoot Down U.S. Spy Planes," *New York Times*, November 4, 1997, A1.

[24] Butler, *The Greatest Threat*, 91.

[25] Butler, *The Greatest Threat*, 96–99, 102–103; Steven Lee Myers, "A Defiant Iraq Bars Entry to 3 UN Arms Inspectors," *New York Times*, October 30, 1997, A3.

[26] Kenneth Pollack, *The Threatening Storm: The Case for Invading Iraq* (New York: Random House, 2002), 88–89; Albright, *Madam Secretary*, 277; Elaine Sciolino, "How Tough Questions and Shrewd Mediating Brought Iraqi Showdown to an End," *New York Times*, November 23, 1997, A8.

[27] Steven Lee Myers, "U.S. Says It Is Prepared to Use Force on Iraq," *New York Times*, November 8, 1997, A6.

[28] United Nations Security Council Resolution 1137, November 12, 1997, accessed February 29, 2018, http://unscr.com/en/resolutions/1137.

Primakov told Iraq that Russia would push for "the speedy lifting of sanctions" while ensuring that future inspections respected "Iraq's sovereignty and security."[29]

Although inspectors resumed work in December, this crisis disturbed the Clinton administration. It viewed such crises as part of the cost of containment, but it acknowledged that it had taken several Iraqi acts of defiance to spark a united Security Council response. Moreover, Russian officials had openly communicated their desire to end inspections and lift sanctions without a full accounting of Iraqi WMD programs. Primakov, for instance, told Albright and Butler on separate occasions that the United States was exaggerating Iraqi noncompliance, urging the United States to be "more flexible, more understanding" about inspections.[30] The inspectors also had to account for materials that Iraq might have moved during the one-month hiatus and restore surveillance equipment that Iraqi officials had disabled.[31]

When the inspectors returned to Baghdad in mid-December, Iraqi personnel again obstructed their work. On January 13, 1998, Aziz introduced a new set of restrictions for the inspectors, including "presidential and sovereign sites" that were "of significance in terms of the security of the State." These sites related to the personal security of Saddam and his entourage, including private homes, office buildings, resorts, and intelligence facilities. The presidential sites were not merely buildings but entire compounds and the land around them. UNSCOM estimated that they encompassed 70 km^2 and 1,500 structures, plenty of space to hide proscribed weapons. Aziz demanded that these sites "not be allowed to be inspected or overflown under any circumstances" and reasserted that Iraq had given up all of its WMD programs.[32] In mid-January, Butler reported that Iraq had again ceased cooperating with UNSCOM by blocking inspection teams from visiting presidential sites. On January 22, Aziz ordered a total freeze on inspections, and UNSCOM and the IAEA left Iraq soon thereafter.[33]

[29] Duelfer, *Hide and Seek*, 128.

[30] Albright, *Madam Secretary*, 277; Butler, *The Greatest Threat*, 105–106; Barbara Crossette, "Russians Press U.N. to Relax Iraq Sanctions," *New York Times*, November 22, 1997, A1.

[31] Barbara Crossette, "While Diplomats Talk, Iraq Is Said to Hide Arms Evidence," *New York Times*, November 6, 1997, A3.

[32] United Nations Special Commission, "Baghdad Mission Report," December 17, 1997, accessed March 29, 2018, http://web.archive.org/web/20050314073646/http://www.ira qwatch.org:80/un/UNSCOM/s-1997-987.htm; Butler, *The Greatest Threat*, 114–115, 130.

[33] United Nations Special Commission, "Baghdad Mission Report," January 22, 1998, accessed March 29, 2018, http://web.archive.org/web/20050314073904/http://www.ira qwatch.org:80/un/UNSCOM/s-1998-58.htm; Barbara Crossette, "Iraq Bars Arms

Clinton responded by rushing troops and two aircraft carriers to the region and threatening to use force, alone if necessary, to compel compliance.[34] The administration believed that the efficacy of the inspections as well as US and UN credibility were at stake.[35] The military developed multiday bombing plans that targeted central pillars of the regime such as Republican Guard units and communications infrastructure.[36] However, Clinton's team lacked a clear sense of how long they would have to bomb Iraq and doubted that a limited offensive would force Saddam back into line.[37] One senior official stated: "We'd like to think we could start bombing and Saddam Hussein would throw his hands up and ask the United Nations inspectors back in, but no one believes it."[38] At one Cabinet meeting, Albright asked if the United States should openly declare that the purpose of a military strike would be regime change, but Berger and Chairman of the Joint Chiefs of Staff Hugh Shelton opposed the idea, saying that the only sure means of regime change was a land invasion.[39] The administration concluded that there was simply "no adequate substitute," in Defense Secretary William Cohen's words, for fully empowered inspections.[40] It stressed that the policy was still containment and that the goal of any strike would be to diminish Iraqi WMD capabilities and ensure total access for inspectors.[41]

During the winter of 1998, the United States and Great Britain again struggled to rally international support for tough diplomacy backed by the threat of force. French Prime Minister Jacques Chirac helpfully warned of "grave consequences" for Iraq if it did not readmit the inspectors.[42] In

Inspectors Again," *New York Times*, January 14, 1998, A1; Barbara Crossette, "Iraq Orders Freeze on Arms Inspectors," *New York Times*, January 22, 1998, A6.

[34] Tim Weiner, "Clinton's Warning to Iraqis: Time for Diplomacy May End," *New York Times*, January 22, 1998, A1.

[35] Steven Erlanger, "Countdown on Iraq: U.S. Weighs February Attack," *New York Times*, January 26, 1998, A1.

[36] Tim Weiner, "U.S. Lists Options on Use of Force in Iraq Standoff," *New York Times*, January 25, 1998, A1.

[37] Richard Newman, "Stalking Saddam," *U.S. News and World Report*, February 23, 1998, 18; Thomas Lippman and Barton Gellman, "If U.S. Military Strike Doesn't Sway Saddam, What's Next?" *Washington Post*, January 29, 1998, A1.

[38] Steven Lee Myers, "Albright Says U.S. Could Act Alone against Baghdad," *New York Times*, January 29, 1998, A6.

[39] Barton Gellman, "Raids May Strike at Power Structure," *Washington Post*, February 17, 1998, A1.

[40] Barton Gellman and Bradley Graham, "Cohen Says U.S. Would Not Seek to Topple Iraq," *Washington Post*, February 1, 1998, A22.

[41] Steven Erlanger, "Clinton and Blair Warn Iraq It Must Obey U.N. on Arms," *New York Times*, February 7, 1998, A1; James Bennet, "Clinton Describes Goals for a Strike on Iraqi Arsenals," *New York Times*, February 18, 1998, A1.

[42] Albright, *Madam Secretary*, 281; Craig Whitney, "Backing U.S., France Warns Iraqis to yield on Arms Inspections," *New York Times*, January 31, 1998, A6.

contrast, Russian and Chinese officials contradicted US statements by saying that negotiations were just starting and calling for an end to sanctions and more respect for Iraqi sovereignty.[43] Arab allies like Egypt, Jordan, and Saudi Arabia took ambiguous positions on the use of force and told US officials that limited attacks bolstered Saddam's credentials at home.[44] The Saudi government even denied US forces permission to launch planes from Saudi bases.[45] The lack of solid international support pushed the United States toward diplomacy over force. Even though this situation frustrated the administration, Clinton believed it was worthwhile for the United States to accept some of the strictures of coalition diplomacy because the US position as the sole superpower was a "luxury" that "won't last forever," which created a "moral responsibility to show restraint and seek partnerships and alliances."[46]

On February 17, 1998, UN Secretary General Kofi Annan announced that he would travel to Iraq to try to resolve the impasse. The Clinton administration backed the trip and said it would accept a deal if it imposed no limits on the inspectors' access rights.[47] On February 23, Annan and Aziz announced a "memorandum of understanding" (MOU) that allowed the inspectors to return with full rights. The MOU, however, imposed new burdens on the inspectors. Inspections would now be accompanied by senior UN diplomats appointed by Annan. The MOU also included "special considerations" for eight presidential sites, calling on inspectors to "take into consideration any observations the Iraqi representative may wish to make regarding entry into a particular structure." Finally, the MOU specified that "UNSCOM undertakes to respect the legitimate concerns of Iraq relating to national security, sovereignty, and dignity."[48] Annan also called the inspectors "cowboys" after the

---

[43] David Malone, *The International Struggle Over Iraq: Politics in the UN Security Council 1980–2005* (New York: Oxford University Press, 2006), 158; Steven Erlanger, "Washington and Moscow Show Split Over Iraq," *New York Times*, January 31, 1998, A6.

[44] Douglas Jehl, "On the Record, Arab Leaders Oppose U.S. Attacks on Iraq," *New York Times*, January 29, 1998, A6; Steven Erlanger, "Albright Receives Measured Support of Saudis on Iraq," *New York Times*, February 3, 1998, A1.

[45] Steven Lee Myers, "U.S. Will Not Ask to Use Saudi Bases for a Raid on Iraq," *New York Times*, February 9, 1998, A1.

[46] Steven Erlanger, "Clinton Says Iraq Is Promising Unconditional Access to Sites," *New York Times*, February 24, 1998, A5. William Clinton, interview by Jim Lehrer, *PBS News Hour*, January 21, 1998, accessed February 27, 2018, http://presidency.prox ied.lsit.ucsb.edu/ws/index.php?pid=56080&st=iraq&st1.

[47] Christopher Wren, "Annan to Go to Iraq to Seek a Solution to Arms Impasse," *New York Times*, February 18, 1998, A8.

[48] Kofi Annan, "Letter from the Secretary-General to the President of the Security Council," March 9, 1998, accessed March 28, 2018, http://www.un.org/Depts/unsco m/s98-208.htm

MOU was signed and described as Saddam someone he "can do business with."[49]

The inspectors, especially Butler, accepted the MOU but objected to Annan acting as a mediator between Iraq and the inspectors, treating them as equally responsible for the crisis, rather than advocating for inspectors' mission and safety. Butler argued that this deal would politicize and weaken UNSCOM by giving Iraq further excuses to block inspections.[50] Clinton agreed that Annan had gone too far in limiting the inspectors' autonomy, but he nonetheless accepted the pact to avoid military strikes and get inspectors back into Iraq.[51] He kept US forces in the region and cautioned that if Saddam reneged again, "everyone would understand that then the United States and hopefully all of allies would have the unilateral right to respond."[52] Clinton wanted the deal tested as soon as possible to see if Iraq would comply, telling Tony Blair on February 23: "We have to test the agreement soon. ... [S]how up at one of these sites and start looking around."[53]

As these inspection crises developed, the Clinton administration started to emphasize the WMD threat in new and frightening ways. This shift reflected its growing conviction that the dangers of WMD proliferation, rogue states, and terrorism were merging into a new problem that made denying WMD to states like Iraq even more essential. In an interview in January 1998, Clinton said that the Iraqi threat was not just that they might use WMD to pursue regional power but that "terrorists and drug runners and other bad actors . . . could just parade through Baghdad to pick up their stores if we don't take the strongest possible action."[54] Clinton further argued that if the coalition caved to Saddam's demands, "[h]e will conclude that the international community has lost its will. He will then conclude that he can go right on and do more to rebuild an arsenal of devastating destruction. And some day, some way, I guarantee you, he'll use the arsenal." Standing firm against Saddam would also deter other potential proliferators.[55] Back in November 1997, Clinton asked Americans to think of this crisis not as a "replay" of the Gulf War but "in

---

[49] Butler, *The Greatest Threat*, 144.

[50] Butler, *The Greatest Threat*, 141–148; Krasno and Sutterlin, *The United Nations and Iraq*, 131–132.

[51] Indyk, *Innocent Abroad*, 190.

[52] Erlanger, "Unconditional Access," *New York Times*, February 24, 1998.

[53] Memorandum of Telephone Conversation, William Clinton and Tony Blair, February 23, 1998, nationalarchives.gov, accessed March 25, 2018, www.archives.gov/files/declassification/iscap/pdf/2013–090-doc39.pdf.

[54] Clinton, interview by Jim Lehrer, *PBS News Hour,* January 21, 1998.

[55] William Clinton, "Text of Clinton Statement on Iraq," February 17, 1998, cnn.com, accessed February 27, 2018, www.cnn.com/ALLPOLITICS/1998/02/17/transcripts/clinton.iraq/.

terms of the innocent Japanese people that died in the subway when the sarin gas was released," referring to a 1995 terrorist attack on the Tokyo subway system that killed twelve people with sarin gas.[56]

Clinton's rhetoric raised the stakes of Iraq policy beyond the threat to US regional interests to the danger of a volatile, vengeful dictator who must not be permitted to build WMD lest he use them or hand them to terrorists. During the Gulf Crisis in 1990–1991, George H. W. Bush had portrayed Iraqi WMD as a serious threat to regional stability and Iraq's own people, but he did not link this problem to terrorism. After a decade with numerous terrorist attacks on the US homeland and institutions overseas, Clinton now linked Saddam's WMD to terrorist attacks like Tokyo, which transformed Iraq from a threat to national interests to a threat to national security.[57]

Al-Qaeda's bombings of the US embassies in Kenya and Tanzania on August 7, 1998, further reinforced this conviction. Clinton responded with missile strikes on suspected al-Qaeda targets in Sudan and Afghanistan later in August, calling al-Qaeda the "most dangerous, non-state terrorist actor in the world today."[58] Clinton's framing of the Iraqi threat as potentially connected to terrorism presaged the second Bush administration's concept of a "nexus" between rogue actors, WMD, and terrorism, which served as a major justification for the 2003 invasion of Iraq. Furthermore, this new threat resonated with the public, with one poll from February 1998 showing that 60 percent of respondents believed that if the United States attacked Saddam, he would use biological or chemical weapons on US targets and 75 percent expecting a terrorist attack directed by Iraq against Americans.[59]

From the signing of the MOU in February 1998 to the fall of 1998, the inspectors steadily uncovered more of Iraq's WMD programs. The IAEA reported in April that "Iraq has satisfactorily completed its undertaking to produce a consolidated version of its full, final, and complete declaration of its clandestine nuclear program."[60] UNSCOM, however, had a great deal

---

[56] John Lancaster and John Harris, "U.S. at a Crossroads on Iraq and Its Choices Appear Bleak," *Washington Post*, November 16, 1997, A1.

[57] Chollet, *America between the Wars*, 196–197; Madeleine Albright, "The Testing of American Foreign Policy," *Foreign Affairs* 77, no. 6 (November–December, 1998): 50–64; William Cohen, "In the Age of Terror Weapons," *Washington Post*, November 26, 1997, A19.

[58] Julian Zelizer, *Arsenal of Democracy: The Politics of National Security from World War II to the War on Terrorism* (New York: Basic Books, 2010), 415–416; Lawrence Wright, *The Looming Tower: Al-Qaeda and the Road to 9/11* (New York, Knopf, 2006), 272–286.

[59] Evan Thomas, "Did Saddam Blink?" *Newsweek*, March 2, 1998, 28.

[60] International Atomic Energy Agency, "5th Consolidated Report Under UNSCR 1051," April 9, 1998, accessed March 19, 2018, http://web.archive.org/web/20050313225012/http://www.iraqwatch.org:80/un/IAEA/s-1998–312.htm.

of rechecking to do because inspectors had been unable to operate in-country since October 1997.[61] Butler reported in June that Iraq was cooperating and that UNSCOM had established a viable monitoring system over key sites. However, gaps remained in the material balance of biological and chemical weapons programs. Despite Iraqi, Russian, and Chinese pleas, UNSCOM would not confirm that Iraq had fully disarmed.[62]

The Clinton administration found no clear alternative to containment in early and mid-1998 even as its key pillars wavered. The administration wanted a way out of the exhausting cycle of Iraqi provocation, US response, and a last-second deal. Openly shifting to a regime change strategy, though, did not seem to be the solution. Saddam was not an immediate threat, and sanctions still prevented his military's recovery.[63] Martin Indyk, now the Assistant Secretary of State for Near Eastern Affairs, reasoned that "there would be a cost to declaring such an objective because it could undermine the international support that we have for maintaining the sanctions regime." The use of excessive or unilateral force against Iraq, Indyk judged, would have the same effect, and US policy needed to work within those restrictions.[64] The intelligence agencies judged that a coup remained unlikely because, as one July 1998 study stated, "Saddam's domestic position appears to be as strong as it has been at any point since the Gulf War."[65] An exasperated Clinton summarized the policy stalemate, saying that Iraq was "the most difficult of problems because it is devoid of a sensible policy response."[66] The administration nonetheless tried to modulate public expectations by saying that unless the United States was willing to ignore the Iraqi threat or invade, "Saddam will be with us for some time," in Sandy Berger's phrasing.[67]

During the fall, Iraqi cooperation declined precipitously, culminating on October 31 when Iraq announced it was ending all cooperation with inspectors and demanded that they leave the country.[68] The United

---

[61] Duelfer, *Hide and Seek,* 146.

[62] United Nations Special Commission, "Ambassador Richard Butler's Presentation to the U.N. Security Council," June 3, 1998.

[63] Anthony Zinni, interview by Daniel Pipes and Patrick Clawson, *Middle East Quarterly,* June 17, 1998, accessed February 7, 2018, www.meforum.org/articles/other/anthony-zinni-avoid-a-military-showdown-with-iraq.

[64] Martin Indyk, Hearing of House Committee on International Relations, *Developments in the Middle East,* 105th Cong., 2nd sess., March 10, 1998, 16, 22.

[65] National Intelligence Council Briefing Paper, "Iraq: Prospects for Confrontation," July 17, 1998, Digital National Security Agency, Targeting Iraq, Part 1 Collection.

[66] Indyk, *Innocent Abroad,* 192–193.

[67] Samuel Berger, "Iraq: Securing America's Interests," *Washington Post,* March 1, 1998, C7.

[68] Barbara Crossette, "In a New Challenge to the UN, Iraq Halts Arms Monitoring," *New York Times,* November 1, 1998, A1.

States and Great Britain again moved forces to the region and called for Saddam to comply.[69] Clinton told Blair in early November that the coalition had to act quickly and decisively to preserve the inspections: "I really think that we have to take decisive action this time to respond to Saddam's challenge. It is clear to me that Saddam really wants to force the Council to lift sanctions without giving up his weapons of mass destruction and missile programs."[70] Berger likewise argued that weak or delayed action would "risk making the Council irrelevant and emboldening Saddam to further challenge the sanctions regime."[71] In addition, Iraq now found itself isolated at the United Nations, as the Arab states, France, and even Russia condemned its actions, although they did not back the threat of force.[72]

Clinton launched US warplanes against Iraqi government and military installations on November 15, 1998, in what was supposed to be an intensive three-day campaign. However, with US and British planes literally en route to their targets, Iraq announced that they would readmit the inspectors unconditionally.[73] Cohen and Albright wanted Clinton to persist, but Berger and a call from Tony Blair persuaded Clinton that attacking would wreck the coalition and make the United States appear aggressive now that Iraq was conceding.[74] One senior official said of this dilemma: "You can't shoot a man who's waving a white flag."[75] Clinton reluctantly recalled the strikes, and the inspectors soon returned to Baghdad with a mandate to report on Iraqi cooperation in a month. By showing restraint, the administration believed it had paved the diplomatic course for a military attack once Saddam reneged on inspections.[76] It agreed to "encourage UNSCOM and the IAEA to aggressively test Iraq's

[69] John Broder, "Clinton Is Sending Bombers and G.I.'s to the Persian Gulf," *New York Times*, November 12, 1998, A1.

[70] Memorandum of Telephone Conversation, William Clinton and Tony Blair, November 3, 1998, nationalarchives.gov, accessed March 25, 2018, www.archives.gov/files/declassification/iscap/pdf/2013–090-doc39.pdf.

[71] Memorandum, Samuel Berger and Leon Fuerth to William Cohen, November 3, 1998, Clinton Digital Library, Declassified Documents Concerning Iraq, accessed March 30, 2018, https://clinton.presidentiallibraries.us/items/show/16192.

[72] Steven Lee Myers, "U.S. Works to Win Allies' Support for Using Force against Iraq," *New York Times*, November 5, 1998, A15.

[73] Carla Robbins and Thomas Ricks, "Iraq Backs Down, Averting U.S. Airstrikes," *Wall Street Journal*, November 16, 1998, A3; Indyk, *Innocent Abroad*, 195.

[74] John Harris and Dana Priest, "Off-Again Airstrikes May Be On Again Soon, Officials Suspect," *Washington Post*, November 17, 1998, A35; Thomas Omestad, "The U.S. Strategy to Hammer Saddam," *U.S. News and World Report*, November 23, 1998, 18.

[75] Barton Gellman, "Mr. President, We're Going Ahead," *Washington Post*, December 20, 1998, A1.

[76] Steven Erlanger, "Clinton Accepts Iraq's Promise to Allow Weapons Inspectors," *New York Times*, November 16, 1998, A1.

unconditional commitment to full cooperation," even though it expected him to renege on this pledge.[77]

Saddam rapidly fulfilled Clinton's expectations when Iraqi officials blocked inspectors from viewing suspected sites on December 9. Many of the sites UNSCOM was allowed to visit had been sanitized since November, with equipment and materials moved from buildings once under UN monitoring. Butler reported to the Security Council on December 14 that Iraq was not complying and that he planned to remove the inspectors from Iraq.[78]

Clinton believed he needed to respond instantly to prevent Saddam from again escaping punishment via last-second diplomacy. He and his Cabinet uniformly wanted an immediate and major air campaign against Saddam. Iraq had evaded retaliation too many times, and it appeared that it would never cooperate with UNSCOM and that France, Russia, and China would continue to hamstring serious inspections. Thus, the administration did not make the readmission of inspectors a goal for the upcoming operation.[79] Clinton spelled out his rationale for the attack to Saudi Crown Prince: "Baghdad has repeatedly violated that commitment and consistently refused to provide documents and information, barred access and harassed inspectors, lied repeatedly, and destroyed documents. I hope you will agree that we can't continue this cycle."[80] Aside from punishing Iraq for these violations, Clinton hoped "to degrade [Saddam's] capacity to develop weapons of mass destruction and his ability to threaten his neighbors as much as possible."[81] They were not, as Cohen stated, "seeking to destabilize his regime" but to weaken him and uphold the credibility of the United States and the United Nations.[82]

---

[77] National Security Council, Summary of Conclusions for National Security Council Principals Committee Meeting on Iraq, November 15, 1998, Clinton Digital Library, Declassified Documents Concerning National Security Council, accessed March 29, 2018, https://clinton.presidentiallibraries.us/items/show/16197.

[78] Butler, *The Greatest Threat*, 204–209.

[79] Sandy Berger, "Press Briefing by National Security Advisor Sandy Berger," December 16, 1998, American Presidency Project, accessed February 27, 2018, www. presidency.ucsb.edu/ws/index.php?pid=48298&st=iraq&st1; Steven Erlanger, "U.S. Set to Give Up Arms Inspections for Curbing Iraq," *New York Times*, November 8, 1998, A1.

[80] Memorandum of Telephone Conversation, William Clinton and Crown Prince Abdullah, December 15, 1998, Clinton Digital Library, Declassified Documents Concerning Iraq, accessed March 29, 2018, https://clinton.presidentiallibraries.us/item s/show/16192.

[81] Douglas Little, *Us versus Them: The United States, Radical Islam, and the Rise of the Green Threat* (Chapel Hill, NC: The University of North Carolina Press, 2016), 113.

[82] Steven Lee Myers, "Pentagon Is Sticking to Timetable and Targets," *New York Times*, December 19, 1998, A8. Remarks by Madeleine Albright, December 17, 1998, OA/ID 1481, National Security Council, Samuel Berger Files, William Clinton Presidential Library, 1.

The ensuing Anglo-American air and missile campaign, titled Operation Desert Fox, lasted from December 16 to 19. It was the largest attack on Iraq since the Gulf War, including 415 cruise missiles and 650 air sorties. US Central Command (CENTCOM) developed a target list of about 100 sites or facilities, only 12 of which were related to WMD or ballistic missile production, mainly from fear of contaminating surrounding areas.[83] Other targets included command centers, air defense installations, Saddam's palaces, and Republican Guard sites.[84]

According to Pentagon assessments, the strikes hit 85 percent of the 100 targets on CENTCOM's list and diminished much of Saddam's missile development, Republican Guard, air defense, and communications facilities and equipment, much of which was hard to replace because of sanctions. The Pentagon estimated that Desert Fox set the Iraqi missile development program back by about two years.[85] The operation also rattled Saddam Hussein, who responded with a purge of the military and intelligence agencies.[86] Nonetheless, this operation did not fundamentally change Saddam's strategic intentions. For instance, the Iraq Survey Group found in 2004 that after Desert Fox and the withdrawal of UNSCOM, "the pace of ongoing missile programs accelerated" as Iraq poured resources into developing longer-range missiles.[87]

Operation Desert Fox drew broad support from an international coalition fed up with Saddam's intransigence, although Russia and China criticized the United States for "taking unprovoked military action," in Boris Yeltsin's words.[88] At home, Clinton feared that the world and the public would see the strikes as a distraction from the pending impeachment vote against him in the Senate. His missile strike against al-Qaeda targets in August had also coincided with Clinton's admission before a grand jury that he had had an inappropriate relationship with Monica Lewinsky. Republicans like Trent Lott insinuated that Clinton was using

[83] Mark Conversino, "Operation Desert Fox: Effectiveness with Unintended Effects," *Chronicles Online Journal, Air and Space Power Journal* (July, 2005), accessed May 15, 2018; Anthony Cordesman, "The Military Effectiveness of Desert Fox," Center for Strategic and International Studies, June 19, 2000, www.csis.org/analysis/military-effect iveness-desert-fox-warning-about-limits-revolution-military-affairs-and, 9.

[84] Conversino, "Operation Desert Fox"; Steven Lee Myers, "U.S. and Britain End Raids on Iraq, Calling Mission a Success," *New York Times*, December 20, 1998, A1.

[85] Cordesman, "Effectiveness of Desert Fox," 21–24; Anthony Zinni, Senate Armed Services Committee, *U.S. Policy on Iraq*, 106th Cong., 1st sess., January 28, 1999, 7–8.

[86] Pollack, *Threatening Storm*, 93; Thomas Ricks, *Fiasco: The American Military Adventure in Iraq* (New York: Penguin Press, 2006), 19; Cordesman, "Effectiveness of Desert Fox," 4.

[87] *Comprehensive Report of the Special Advisor to the DCI on Iraq's WMD*, September 30, 3004, vol. 2, cia.gov, www.cia.gov/library/reports/general-reports-1/iraq_wmd_2004/ch ap3.html.

[88] Thomas Lippman and William Drozdiak, "America's Allies Give Support to Attack," *Washington Post*, December 18, 1998, A55.

foreign policy to mask this scandal.[89] Nonetheless, Clinton received high approval ratings for his handling of Iraq policy, including a Gallup poll that found 74 percent of respondents approved of the strikes.[90] Still, the American public generally did not believe the strikes would have a positive long-term effect on the Iraq problem, with 60 percent in one poll saying that the strikes were a "temporary solution."[91]

Clinton's Iraq policy stood on uncertain ground at the end of 1998. The inspectors had departed Iraq and the coalition was more divided than ever. UNSCOM reported massive, unresolved gaps in the record on VX gas, biological and chemical precursors, unconventional missile warheads, various chemical agents, specialized aerosol generators, and Scud missiles. Iraq also retained teams of scientists who could quickly revive these programs, likely using dual-use facilities at which WMD development could be masked unless inspectors were on the ground.[92] The IAEA likewise had concerns about centrifuge and nuclear weapon designs and the Iraqi international procurement network for nuclear materials.[93] Without inspections, the administration believed, Saddam would surely start rebuilding his arsenal, and as sanctions weakened he would have more resources to do so. Moving forward, the Clinton administration would either have to develop a different version of containment or, as its increasingly powerful critics argued, shift to an open and concerted regime change strategy.

Making the Iraq Liberation Act, 1997–1998

Throughout the inspection crises of 1997–1998, the Clinton administration defined its objectives within the containment paradigm: preserve sanctions and inspections, maintain the coalition, and be ready to strike Iraq if it violates the Security Council resolutions or threatens its neighbors. During these years, criticism of containment intensified as three separate political strands coalesced into a movement powerful enough to

---

[89] Indyk, *Innocent Abroad*, 200.

[90] Gallup Telephone Survey, December 19, 1998, Polling the Nations, accessed March 8, 2018. http://poll.orspub.com.libproxy.lib.unc.edu/search.php?action. See also Pew Telephone Survey, December 21, 1998, Polling the Nations, accessed March 8, 2018, http://poll.orspub.com.libproxy.lib.unc.edu/search.php?action.

[91] Newsweek Telephone Survey, December 19, 1998, Polling the Nations, accessed March 8, 2018, http://poll.orspub.com.libproxy.lib.unc.edu/search.php?action.

[92] United Nations Special Commission, "UNSCOM Final Compendium," January 29, 1999, accessed March 16, 2018, http://web.archive.org/web/20051124075332/http://www.iraqwatch.org:80/un/UNSCOM/disarmament.htm.

[93] The International Atomic Energy Agency, "7th Consolidated Report Under UNSCR 1051, April 7, 1999, accessed March 19, 2018, http://web.archive.org/web/20050222025252/http://www.iraqwatch.org:80/un/iaea/s-1999-393.htm.

rally Congressional and media support to discredit containment and pass the Iraq Liberation Act. These strands were neoconservative intellectuals, Iraqi exiles, and a core of devoted Congressional staffers. The argument of this regime change movement was largely the same as in past years: the inevitable decline case that containment was not working and could not work against this type of regime. By 1998, however, events and trends had shifted to give their argument greater force, including the confrontations with Iraq, the growing international isolation of the United States, and expanding apprehension in the United States about the threat of ballistic missiles and WMD wielded by rogue states.

Skeptics of containment viewed the inspection crises from October 1997 to February 1998 as evidence of the policy's imminent collapse. Neoconservative writer David Wurmser complained that the United States had surrendered Iraq policy to "an amorphous, rudderless international community" that was protecting Saddam from retaliation and driving UN policy to the lowest common denominator.[94] Even containment's defenders mocked the imposition of a travel ban as punishment for Iraq's noncompliance in November 1997. The *Washington Post* editors, for example, wrote: "The world community, outraged, summons all of its courage and indignation and responds with ... a travel ban on some Iraqi officials. No more shopping at Harrod's for ... Tariq Aziz, that'll show 'em."[95] Critics of containment also feared that as Saddam defied the United Nations and secured power at home, many countries would treat him as a permanent fixture and try to curry favor with him. Neoconservative commentators William Kristol and Robert Kagan described this inevitable demise as such: "Over time, containment of Saddam becomes 'détente', and eventually détente becomes appeasement."[96]

This intractable cycle of crises intensified the inevitable declinists' conviction that only Saddam's removal would stop this draining dance. Paul Wolfowitz, for instance, argued in January 1998: "As long as he's around he's going to be back doing this, and we're going to have to be back doing it over and over again. I think we have to develop a new political strategy that's aimed at really liberating Iraq from this tyrannical

---

[94] David Wurmser, "Iraq Needs a Revolution," *Wall Street Journal*, November 12, 1997, A22.

[95] Editorial, "The U.N. Flinch," *Washington Post*, November 13, 1997, A22. See also Charles Krauthammer, "Munich on the Tigris," *Washington Post*, November 19, 1997, A21; A. M. Rosenthal, "Time for Repairs," *New York Times*, November 25, 1997, A25; John McCain, *Cong. Rec.*, 105th Cong., 1st sess., November 5, 1997, 11786.

[96] William Kristol and Robert Kagan, "A 'Great Victory' for Iraq," *Washington Post*, February 26, 1998, A20; Paul Wolfowitz, "Rebuilding the Anti-Saddam Coalition," *Wall Street Journal*, November 18, 1997, A22; Editorial, "No Substitute for Victory," *Weekly Standard*, February 16, 1998, 9.

monster."[97] Senator John McCain (R-AZ) put the point more starkly: "The nature of the regime of Saddam Hussein is impervious to any peaceful effort at resolution of the ongoing conflict."[98] Kofi Annan's lenient dealings with Iraq further fueled their sense that the mendacity of the United Nations and France, Russia, and China was crippling Iraq policy. For example, Senate Majority Leader Trent Lott (R-MS) told Clinton that Annan's "appeasement" signaled the "beginning of the unraveling of the inspection process" by granting Saddam the "right to determine the scope of the inspections and the makeup of inspection teams."[99]

In this context, a political effort coalesced to shift US policy from containment to regime change, bringing together Iraqi exile groups like the INC, a small group of Congressional staffers, and neoconservatives. Ahmed Chalabi's INC changed its strategy after being run out of Northern Iraq by Saddam's forces in 1996. Chalabi instead focused on convincing Congress and intellectual leaders to support regime change and back the INC.[100] He built a small core of supporters, including Perle, Wurmser, Wolfowitz, and former Congressman Stephen Solarz (D-NY), who helped make political connections and raise funds. They set out to, in Perle's words, create "a climate of opinion and a set of perceptions about Iraq" that would mobilize Congress and the public.[101] Chalabi and the INC provided Westernized, politically savvy opposition leaders who could be backed as an alternative to containment and possibly to Saddam himself. Meyrav Wurmser, David Wurmser's wife and a director of a conservative think tank on the Middle East, described Chalabi's significance: "Ahmad came, and all of a sudden, we had an angel. ... Here's proof: Arabs can be Democrats."[102] As INC official Nabeel Musawi told ABC News: "We want real change, we want

[97] Transcript, William Clinton interview with Jim Lehrer, January 30, 1998, OA/ID 3108, National Security Council Office of Press and Communications, Matthew Gobush Files, William Clinton Presidential Library, 1; see also Editorial, "Fair Strike," *New Republic*, February 16, 1998, 218–219; Editorial, "Tightening the Vise on Iraq," *New York Times*, February 3, 1998, A22.

[98] John McCain, *Cong. Rec.*, 105th Cong., 2nd sess., February 9, 1998, 473.

[99] Press Release, "Trent Lott Responds to Annan/Hussein Deal," February 25, 1998, OA/ID 1736, National Security Council Office of Legislative Affairs, Mara Rudman Files, Iraq (2), William Clinton Presidential Library, 1. See also William Kristol and Robert Kagan, "Bombing Iraq Isn't Enough," *New York Times*, January 30, 1998, A17; A. M. Rosenthal, "Annan's Bad Gamble," *New York Times*, February 27, 1998, A25.

[100] Richard Bonin, *Arrows of the Night: Ahmad Chalabi's Long Journey to Triumph in Iraq* (New York: Doubleday, 2011), 118.

[101] Bonin, *Arrows of the Night*, 125–126.

[102] Aram Roston, *The Man Who Pushed America to War: The Extraordinary Life, Adventures, and Obsessions of Ahmad Chalabi* (New York: Nation Books, 2008), 137.

democratic change, we want elections, we want parliaments, we want to live the way you do."[103]

The second source of the political campaign against containment was a group of Congressional staffers for influential legislators. The main players were Stephen Rademaker, the chief counsel to the House International Relations Committee, Danielle Pletka and Randy Scheunemann, foreign policy advisors to Jesse Helms (R-NC) and Trent Lott, respectively, and Chris Straub, an aide to Robert Kerrey (D-NE). They had long been dissatisfied with containment, and Clinton's weak response to the inspection crises of 1997 and 1998 tipped them into action. Scheunemann later recalled that after the Annan deal with Iraq in February 1998, "[w]e Republicans ... savaged Annan because it was clear ... that Iraq was only going to do the minimum amount necessary, and that Clinton was looking for a way out." As Clinton drifted into a weaker policy, it became critical, Scheunemann argued, to get an "on the record statement" of regime change.[104] Many in this group knew and were impressed by Chalabi. In fact, Rademaker first drafted what became the Iraq Liberation Act on February 19, 1998, after meeting with Chalabi in Congress, although they decided to wait to introduce the bill.[105] This group helped connect the INC to powerful legislators who eventually ushered the ILA through Congress.

Neoconservatives formed the third main group in the political campaign against containment. They had long criticized containment, but in 1997 and 1998 they organized more concertedly to influence the public debate and Congress. In June 1997, Kristol and Kagan formed the Project for a New American Century (PNAC) to promote an activist foreign policy against what they saw as Clinton's weak multilateralism. Their founding statement of principles included high defense spending, global US unipolarity, a more confrontational approach to geopolitical rivals, and the promotion of democracy and free markets.[106] Prominent signers of PNAC's founding statement included Richard Cheney, Donald Rumsfeld, Paul Wolfowitz, and Scooter Libby. PNAC rooted its worldview in the assumption that the main "present danger" facing the

---

[103] *ABC News Special Report*, "Unfinished Business: The CIA and Saddam Hussein," directed by Peter Jennings, ABC News, 1997, accessed January 22, 2019, www.you tube.com/watch?v=lZHHAI-eq2I.

[104] Randy Scheunemann, phone interview by author, March 31, 2018.

[105] Bonin, *Arrows of the Night*, 150.

[106] "Project for a New American Century Statement of Principles," in *The Iraq Papers*, ed. John Ehrenberg, J. Patrice McSherrey, Jose Sanchez, and Caroleen Sayej (New York: Oxford University Press, 2010), 19–20. See also Stefan Halper and Jonathan Clarke, *America Alone: The Neoconservatives and the Global Order* (New York: Cambridge University Press, 2004), 74–111; Chollet, *America between the Wars*, 171–177.

United States was not any specific threat but the risk that the United States would abandon its position of leadership in the liberal international system:

The United States, the world's dominant power on whom the maintenance of international peace and the support of liberal democratic principles depends, will shrink its responsibilities and – in a fit of absentmindedness, or parsimony, or indifference – allow the international order that it created and sustains to collapse.[107]

PNAC formed part of a web of neoconservative and conservative institutions that organized opposition to Clinton's foreign policy and the containment of Iraq. These groups included the American Enterprise Institute (AEI), the Heritage Foundation, and the short-lived Committee for Peace and Security in the Gulf (CPSG), founded by Stephen Solarz and Richard Perle.[108] These organizations made connections to the INC and lobbied the Republican-controlled Congress for tougher action on Iraq.

During January and February 1998, PNAC and the CPSG wrote public letters to Clinton that laid out the inevitable decline case for replacing containment with regime change. The CPSG letter argued: "It is clear that this danger cannot be eliminated as long as our objective is simply 'containment'" because "as the crises of recent weeks have demonstrated, these static policies are bound to erode, opening the way to Saddam's eventual return to a position of power . . . in the region."[109] Both letters argued that allowing Saddam to possess WMD was unacceptable because he had used them before, he could employ them as a shield to enable aggressive actions, and his very possession of WMD would destabilize the region by encouraging other states to seek WMD. Because containment hinged on unreliable allies and Saddam's own cooperation, the policy was "dangerously inadequate."[110] In line with the regime change consensus, the CPSG letter argued that "the problem is not only the specifics of Saddam's actions, but the continued existence

---

[107] Robert Kagan and William Kristol, "Introduction: National Interest and Global Responsibility," in *Present Dangers: Crisis and Opportunity in American Foreign and Defense Policy*, ed. Robert Kagan and William Kristol (San Francisco: Encounter Books, 2000), 4.

[108] "Overthrow Hussein, U.S. Group Advises," February 20, 1998, cnn.com, accessed May 5, 2018, www.cnn.com/WORLD/9802/20/iraq.war.presser/.

[109] Committee for Peace and Security in the Gulf, "Open Letter to the President," February 19, 1998, iraqwatch.org, www.iraqwatch.org/perspectives/rumsfeld-openletter.htm.

[110] Project for a New American Century, "Letter to Bill Clinton," January 26, 1998, informationclearinghouse.org, accessed May 5, 2018, www.informationclearinghouse.info/article5527.htm.

of the regime itself."[111] The PNAC letter drew many of the same signatories as the group's founding statement, including Rumsfeld and Wolfowitz, while the CPSG letter drew supporters like future Rumsfeld aide Douglas Feith and historian Bernard Lewis, all of whom pushed for war with Iraq in the second Bush administration.

One key innovation in the inevitable decline case in this period was the idea that containment and regime change had become incompatible strategies. Most of containment's critics had supported Bush and Clinton's covert regime change efforts and their attempts to maintain sanctions, inspections, and NFZs. By 1998, however, the chances of a coup were near zero and coalition partners were abandoning a tough line on Iraq. With inspections and sanctions jeopardized, inevitable declinists argued, the United States had an uncertain window of time to defeat Saddam before he gained WMD. Perle, for example, wrote: "If we do not develop a strategy for removing Saddam now, we may be unable to do so later. Once he is in possession of weapons of mass destruction, our options will have narrowed considerably."[112] Containment, with its emphasis on restraint and multilateralism, inhibited Clinton from taking the bold action needed to deal with the threat before it escalated. These critics also suspected that Clinton was moving toward a posture of deterrence and limited containment that would accept Saddam developing some WMD and give up on overthrowing him. Congressman Benjamin Gilman (R-NY) called this ostensible shift "a silent U-turn" toward "bowing to the wishes of the French, the Russians, and the Chinese, who want to help Iraq lower the bar on UNSCOM inspections."[113]

Regime change advocates believed they needed to arrest this drift, which meant getting the United States to openly declare a regime change policy and backing the opposition with military training even if that alienated the coalition partners. In fact, regime change boosters believed that many US partners did not support a tough policy on Iraq because they thought Clinton lacked the will to see it through. Adopting a bold regime change policy would rally the world behind the United States, as Wolfowitz argued: "A willingness to act unilaterally can be the most

---

[111] Project for a New American Century, "Letter to Bill Clinton," January 26, 1998.

[112] Richard Perle, "Iraq: Saddam Unbound," in Kagan and Kristol, *Present Dangers*, 106. For a similar version of this argument, see Project for a New American Century, "Letter to Newt Gingrich and Trent Lott," May 29, 1998, iraqwatch.org, accessed March 6, 2018, http://web.archive.org/web/20031011070800/http://newamericancentury.or g:80/iraqletter1998.htm. This letter was signed by Donald Rumsfeld, Paul Wolfowitz, Robert Kagan, William Kristol, Richard Perle, and John Bolton, among others.

[113] Benjamin Gilman, House Committee on International Relations, *Disarming Iraq: The Status of Weapons Inspections*, 105th Cong., 2nd sess., September 15, 1998, 2.

effective way of securing effective collective action."[114] Without such leadership, as another PNAC letter to Congress argued: "[T]hose nations living under the threat of Saddam's weapons of mass destruction can be expected to adopt policies of accommodation."[115]

The interlocking threat of rogue states with WMD and ballistic missiles further intensified the urgency of regime change, especially among conservatives and neoconservatives. Missile defense activists lobbied Clinton to withdraw from the Anti-Ballistic Missile Treaty, a 1972 pact between the United States and the Soviet Union that limited the number of defensive antiballistic missiles each state could deploy. They argued that this treaty was a Cold War relic that inhibited the United States from protecting US territory and bases from rogue states. They contended that these actors might not be deterrable and they would use those weapons to project power in strategic regions.[116] House Majority Leader Newt Gingrich (R-GA), for instance, argued to Clinton: "Our nation's policy of relying solely on offensive weapons to deter a nuclear missile attack from the Soviet Union has been overtaken by events. The Soviet Union no longer exists and our multiple adversaries ... no longer play by the familiar Cold War rules."[117]

In 1997, the Senate commissioned Donald Rumsfeld to lead a study of the ballistic missile threat. His team included Paul Wolfowitz and former CIA director R. James Woolsey. The report identified Iraq, Iran, and North Korea as active seekers of ballistic missiles who were within five years (ten for Iraq) of acquiring the ability to strike the United States. In a jab at the intelligence community, it concluded: "The threat to the U.S. posed by these emerging capabilities is broader, more mature and evolving more rapidly than has been reported ... by the Intelligence Community." The report warned that as these states developed stronger denial and deception techniques, the United States might have little warning before these missiles were deployed.[118]

---

[114] Wolfowitz, "Anti-Saddam Coalition," *Wall Street Journal*, November 18, 1997.

[115] Project for a New American Century, "Letter to Newt Gingrich and Trent Lott," May 29, 1998.

[116] Hal Brands, *From Berlin to Baghdad: America's Search for Purpose in the Post–Cold War World* (Lexington: University Press of Kentucky, 2008), 256–257; Frederick Kaplan, *Daydream Believers: How a Few Grand Ideas Wrecked American Power* (Hoboken, NJ: John Wiley & Sons, 2008), 78, 98–102.

[117] Newt Gingrich, Open Letter to Bill Clinton, January 20, 1998, Center for Security Policy, accessed February 14, 2018, www.centerforsecuritypolicy.org/1998/02/06/clinton-on-iraq-wrong-question-wrong-answer-its-not-the-weapons-its-the-regime-stupid-2/.

[118] "Executive Summary of the Report of the Commission to Assess the Ballistic Missile Threat to the United States," July 15, 1998, Federation of American Scientists, accessed January 5, 2018, https://fas.org/irp/threat/bm-threat.htm.

Furthermore, regime change advocates rooted their case in a specific interpretation of US strategy in the Cold War. Joshua Muravchik, a neoconservative working at AEI, wrote that contrary to the standard narrative, containment did not defeat the Soviets. In reality, communism was on the offensive in the 1970s until "Ronald Reagan succeeded in reversing this momentum by adopting a policy of 'containment-plus', the core of which was aid to anti-Communist insurgencies."[119] Wolfowitz broadened this point: "The communists, then, were defeated through our strong support of democracy, and by providing those willing to fight for their rights the means to win their freedom."[120] In this narrative, communism was destroyed "from outside the system" through Reagan's intensification of the Cold War in areas like Latin America and Afghanistan. As crucial aspects of the Cold War triumph, regime change advocates also cited Reagan's active human rights and democracy promotion, massive arms spending, moral rhetoric, support for anti-communist insurgencies, as well as his refusal to treat the USSR as a permanent fixture in international politics.[121]

Regime change boosters thus likened the containment of Iraq to détente in the Cold War. Many neoconservatives saw détente as an amoral reconciliation with a hostile, evil power that abused US trust to catch up militarily and spread its global reach. As with Iraq in the 1990s, neoconservatives during the 1970s struggled against what they viewed as the unprincipled realism of Kissinger, who sought to maintain a balance of power with the USSR while downplaying ideology. They also criticized the ostensibly feckless Mcgovernite liberals who opposed a strong military and an assertive foreign policy.[122] Many of the major critics of Iraqi containment had fought against détente as Congressional aides in the 1970s, including Perle, Wolfowitz, and Feith, who all worked for the anti-détente Senator Henry Jackson (D-WA).[123] The lesson of the Cold War

---

[119] Joshua Muravchik, "What to Do About Saddam Hussein," *Commentary*, June 1998, 40.

[120] Paul Wolfowitz, House Committee on International Relations, *U.S. Options in Confronting Iraq*, 105th Cong., 2nd sess., February 25, 1998, 39.

[121] Quote is from David Wurmser, *Tyranny's Ally: America's Failure to Defeat Saddam Hussein* (Washington, DC: AEI Press,1999), 63. See also Paul Wolfowitz, "Remembering the Future," *Foreign Affairs* 59 (Spring, 2000): 35–45; Joshua Muravchik, *Exporting Democracy: Fulfilling America's Destiny* (Washington, DC, AEI Press, 1991), 1–12; Michael Ledeen, *Freedom Betrayed: How America Led a Global Democratic Revolution, Won the Cold War, and Walked Away* (Washington, DC: AEI Press, 1996), 34–59.

[122] John Ehrman, *The Rise of Neoconservatism: Intellectuals and Foreign Affairs, 1945–1994* (New Haven: Yale University Press, 1995), 97–136; Jacob Heilbrunn, *They Knew They Were Right: The Rise of the Neocons* (New York: Doubleday, 2008), 99–106, 113–126; Halper and Clarke, *America Alone*, 55–58.

[123] George Packer, *The Assassins' Gate: America in Iraq* (New York: Farrar, Straus, and Giroux, 2005), 21–27.

for Iraq was that the Baathists, like the Soviets, could not be moderated via indirect pressures and therefore needed to be defeated with US military and moral power.[124]

A significant contingent of liberals and Democrats also turned against containment in the late 1990s following the rise of humanitarian interventionism and R2P, or the responsibility to protect. This doctrine held that a state's right to sovereignty depended on how it treated its people, and if it committed or failed to stop genocide and other humanitarian disasters, external powers had the right to intervene.[125] The 1990s was rife with genocide, ethnic cleansing, refugee crises, and other humanitarian problems, most notably in the Balkans and Rwanda. The United States intervened in Somalia, Kurdish Iraq, Bosnia, and Kosovo for humanitarian purposes, but interventionists like the academic Michael Ignatieff and the journalist Samantha Power blamed the United States for not acting more quickly and decisively in cases like 1994 Rwandan Genocide.[126]

Iraq was not a major focus of the humanitarian activists in the 1990s, but many liberal politicians and intellectuals were drawn to regime change in Iraq as part of the belief that the United States should use its military power to protect human rights and save lives. Legislators like Robert Kerrey and Joseph Liebermann embraced a humanitarian mission for Iraq, with Kerrey arguing in strongly moralistic terms that "[t]he existence of such a government is a daily affront to every freedom loving person, to everyone who is revolted by the degradation of our fellow human beings. I refuse to accept it."[127] Joseph Biden and John Kerry, among others, introduced concurrent resolutions in Congress calling for an international criminal tribunal to prosecute Baathist crimes, including genocide.[128] Another reason many liberals backed regime change was the belief that Saddam's brazen defiance of the Security Council undermined

---

[124] Wurmser, *Tyranny's Ally*, 63–65.

[125] One key document of humanitarian interventionist thought in the 1990s was Kofi Annan's speech on September 20, 1999, in which he argued for a new understanding of sovereignty: Kofi Annan, "Secretary-General Presents His Annual Report to the General Assembly," September 20, 1999, un.org, accessed March 2, 2018, www.un.org/press/en/1999/19990920.sgsm7136.html. See also Mark Mazower, *Governing the World: The History of an Idea* (New York: Penguin Press, 2012), 380.

[126] Samantha Power, *A Problem from Hell: America in the Age of Genocide* (New York: Basic Books, 2002), 503–516; Mazower, *Governing the World*, 378–405; Michael Walzer, *Just and Unjust Wars: A Moral Argument with Historical Illustrations* (New York: Basic Books, 2006), 101–108; Michael Ignatieff, "Intervention and State Failure," in *The New Killing Fields: Massacre and the Politics of Intervention*, ed. Nicolaus Mills and Kira Brunner (New York: Basic Books, 2002), 229–245.

[127] Robert Kerrey, *Cong. Rec.*, 105th Cong., 2nd sess., September 29, 1998, 1124.

[128] S. Con. Res. 78, 105th Cong., 2nd sess., March 13, 1998, 1907.

the credibility of the United Nations, an institution they wanted to strengthen in order to manage international relations and institutionalize humanitarian intervention.[129]

Regime change advocates of all political stripes sought to seize the moral high ground by stressing the centrality of democracy and human rights to their strategy. Containment at best could bring about a coup and a new dictator, they claimed, but only the uprooting of the Baathist system and its replacement with a democracy could ensure the rights of the Iraqi people as well as remove the security threat. Following the deterministic logic of regime-thinking, David Wurmser argued that the root of violence and tyranny in the Middle East was "the grip of centralized, totalitarian power and despotism."[130] Robert Kerrey similarly held: "We also know the dictatorships from this unbalanced state will inevitably threaten their neighbors. . . . We need to get rid of Iraqi dictatorship. Our long-range goal should be a democratic Iraq."[131] By contrast, a democratic Iraq could "transform the Middle East" into a land of "security, prosperity, and creative diversity" by showing other Arab peoples that they did not have to tolerate despotism.[132]

Regime change accused defenders of containment of believing that Arabs were unfit for democracy and undesiring of human rights.[133] Ahmed Chalabi claimed that containment's defenders held the "essentially racist view" that Arabs were "people who were querulous and cannot reasonably govern themselves . . . that they deserve what they get."[134] This universalist argument had broad appeal in a post–Cold War era that had just witnessed waves of democratization in Eastern Europe, Latin America, and East Asia. The INC, moreover, bolstered this argument by portraying Iraqi society as bursting with democratic and economic potential. Chalabi told a neoconservative think tank in a 1997 speech that "Iraq is blessed with a talented and industrious population. . . . [I]t may fairly be described as the western world's gateway to the non-Arab Muslim East."[135] The INC and its neoconservative allies

[129] Robert Kerrey, *Cong. Rec.*, 105th Cong., 1st sess., November 8, 1997, 12103; Richard Cohen, "The Limits of 'Whack-a-Mole,'" *Washington Post*, February 24, 1998, A21.

[130] Wurmser, *Tyranny's Ally*, 41.   [131] Kerrey, *Cong. Rec.*, November 8, 1997, 12103.

[132] Robert Kerrey, *Cong. Rec.*, 106th Cong., 2nd sess., March 2, 2000, 2053.

[133] James Woolsey, House Committee on Armed Services, *United States Policy toward Iraq*, 106th Cong., 1st sess., March 10, 1999, 5; Wurmser, *Tyranny's Ally*, 44.

[134] Ahmed Chalabi, interview, *PBS Frontline*, 2000, accessed March 23, 2018, www.pbs.org/wgbh/pages/frontline/shows/saddam/interviews/chalabi.html.   See   also Jim Hoagland, "Pretend Iraq Policy," *Washington Post*, July 2, 2000, B7.

[135] Ahmed Chalabi, "Creating a Post-Saddam Iraq," speech to the Jewish Institute for National Security Affairs, June 1997, jinsa.org, accessed September 14, 2018, www.jinsa.org/jinsa-reports/creating-post-saddam-iraq.

developed a narrative of Iraqi history in which Iraq had once been guided by a civic-minded elite under the Hashemite monarchy and that ethnic conflict had not arisen until the Baathist era. They stressed that Iraq had a large population of well-educated, middle-class professionals who did not support Saddam and could form the core of a vibrant democracy and capitalist economy once the Baathists were eliminated.[136]

Congressional Republicans, with the aid of hawkish Democrats, sustained the heat on Clinton's Iraq policy throughout 1998. They wrote dozens of letters and held hearings on Iraq, most of which allowed prominent critics like Wolfowitz and Perle space to broadcast their arguments. In the fall of 1998, as Saddam renewed his open rebellion against containment, the regime change movement rallied to pass the ILA. The bill passed 360–38 in the House on October 5 and unanimously in the Senate on October 7. Its sponsors in the House were Benjamin Gilman and Christopher Cox (R-CA), while in the Senate its sponsors were Trent Lott, Robert Kerrey, Joseph Lieberman, John McCain, and several other Republicans.[137]

The ILA's text reflected most of the main points of the case for regime change. It faulted Saddam for crimes against humanity, foreign aggression, and violations of various UN resolutions. It declared an open regime change policy with a democratic Iraq as its goal: "It should be the policy of the United States to support efforts to remove the regime headed by Saddam Hussein from power in Iraq and to promote the emergence of a democratic government to replace that regime." The ILA required that the president designate Iraqi opposition groups that would be eligible to receive aid as long as they represented a "broad spectrum" of Iraqi ethnic groups and committed to human rights, democracy, Iraq's territorial integrity, and peaceful relations with neighbors. It then authorized but did not require him to provide up to $97 million per year in broadcasting assistance, humanitarian aid, the use of military equipment, and military training. The act also urged the president to establish an international criminal tribunal for the Baathist leadership.[138]

---

[136] Ahmed Chalabi, "Democracy Is 'Realism' for Iraq," *The Defense Democrat: A Newsletter of Foreign Affairs and National Defense*, April 1991, 1; Ahmed Chalabi, "Iraq: Past as Prologue?" *Foreign Policy*, Summer 1991, 20–29; Wurmser, *Tyranny's Ally*, 128–129. For a scholarly counterpoint to this narrative, see Charles Tripp, *A History of Iraq* (New York: Cambridge University Press, 2007).

[137] *The Iraq Liberation Act of 1998*, Public Law 338, 105th Cong., 2nd sess. (October 31, 1998), congress.gov, accessed May 10, 2018, www.congress.gov/bill/105th-congress/h ouse-bill/4655. For more on the passage of the ILA, see Roston, *Man Who Pushed*, 154–156; Bonin, *Arrows of the Night*, 157–160.

[138] *The Iraq Liberation Act of 1998* (October 31, 1998).

Congressional aide Stephen Rademaker later described the purpose of the ILA as "to declare a policy, and then it was to authorize, not require, a policy approach for the president that was basically the application of the Reagan Doctrine to Iraq."[139] Rademaker further argued that the ILA did not call "for the U.S. to directly intervene in the of overthrow Saddam Hussein. ... It was not an AUMF [authorization to use military force]."[140] For that reason, the law included a caveat about the involvement of US military forces in bringing about regime change: "Nothing in this Act shall be construed to authorize or otherwise speak to the use of United States Armed Forces ... in carrying out this Act."[141] Congressional aide Randy Scheunemann later said that this rider was included to ensure "it was clear that we weren't trying to create a back door to US military intervention," which would have been far more controversial.[142] Thus, the ILA is best understood as an attempt to entrench certain principles about Iraq, such as the inadequacy of containment and the need for democracy, and to push Clinton toward a tougher approach. Its main sponsor in the House, Benjamin Gilman, described it as a way to "break this logjam" of repeated confrontations with no clear end point while establishing the principle that "Saddam is the problem, and there will be no permanent solution as long as his regime remains."[143]

Clinton signed the ILA on October 31, 1998, but he and most members of his administration opposed the open declaration of a regime change policy. Elizabeth Jones, the NEA's Principal Deputy Assistant Secretary, recalled that at the State Department:

We did everything we could to prevent that bill from being passed. We could not identify a way to assure that the people to whom that money was meant to go were legitimate and that the money would be properly used. This was because the person who had talked the Congress into setting money aside for the Iraq Liberation Act was Chalabi, who we all thought to be a charlatan.[144]

Jones claims that her office unsuccessfully argued to the NSC that Clinton should veto the bill. She also reports that they did convince Clinton to not hand cash to the INC but pay for its legitimate, independently verified expenses.[145] Furthermore, top administration officials met with Congressional leaders to argue that openly declaring a regime change policy would make maintaining sanctions and inspections even harder because

---

[139] Stephen Rademaker, interview by author, January 12, 2018.
[140] Rademaker, interview by author, January 12, 2018.
[141] *The Iraq Liberation Act of 1998* (October 31, 1998), section 8.
[142] Randy Scheunemann, interview by author, March 31, 2018.
[143] Benjamin Gilman, *Cong. Rec.*, 105th Cong., 2nd sess., October 5, 1998, 9586.
[144] Elizabeth Jones, phone interview by author, February 6, 2018.
[145] Jones, phone interview by author, February 6, 2018.

countries like France and Russia already believed the United States was acting too severely toward Iraq. The CIA and the Defense Department also objected to the ILA because they saw no feasible way of achieving regime change.[146] Clinton issued a statement upon signing the ILA that endorsed its general principles but stressed that it was a nonbinding resolution. He also distanced himself from regime change advocates' call for massive aid to the INC, saying: "US support must be attuned to what the opposition can effectively make use of as it develops over time."[147]

The conditionalist approach to containment also went through important changes during the late 1990s. Members of this school of thought had often criticized Bush and Clinton for the way that they pursued containment, but they agreed with the premises and structure of the policy. As the inevitable decline critics pushed for regime change in 1998, conditional thinkers increasingly became containment's defenders in the public square. Like Clinton, they highlighted the successes of inspections and sanctions in destroying the majority of Saddam's WMD and preventing Iraq's military recovery.[148] They believed that these tools would remain viable only if the United States kept the international community on board and avoided unilateral moves.[149] Furthermore, they saw the Iraqi opposition as divided, ineffective, and lacking in influence in Iraq, which made them too risky to seriously back against Saddam.[150] In addition, they argued that, in Richard Haass' terms, the removal of Saddam would not be the "panacea that many people suggest. The problems of Iraq go beyond Saddam Hussein."[151] Years of deprivation, trauma from decades

---

[146] Indyk, *Innocent Abroad*, 192; Walter Pincus, "Bill Tries to Shift U.S. Policy on Iraq," *Washington Post*, October 1, 1998, A30; Vernon Loeb, "Congress Stokes Visions of War to Oust Saddam," *Washington Post*, October 20, 1998, A28; Martin Kettle, "Pentagon Balks at 'Idiotic' Law Urging Bay of Pigs-Type Invasion of Iraq," *The Guardian*, October 21, 1998, 16.

[147] William Clinton, "Statement on Signing the Iraq Liberation Act of 1998," October 31, 1998, American Presidency Project, accessed February 27, 2018, www.presidency.ucs b.edu/ws/index.php?pid=55205&st=iraq&st1=.

[148] Michael Eisenstadt, House Committee on National Security, *United States Policy toward Iraq*, 105th Cong., 2nd sess., September 16, 1998, 45; Phebe Marr, "Why Saddam Craves a Crisis," *New York Times*, November 23, 1997, C19; Richard Murphy, "Calling Baghdad's Bluff," *Washington Post*, January 26, 1998, A23.

[149] Michael Mandelbaum and Richard Haass, *Building for Security and Peace in the Middle East: An American Agenda*, Report of the Presidential Study Group (Washington, DC: Washington Institute for Near East Policy Press, 1997), 17; Haass, House Committee on International Relations, *U.S. Options in Confronting Iraq*, February 25, 1998, 13.

[150] Anthony Cordesman, Subcommittee on Near Eastern and South Asian Affairs of the Senate Committee on Foreign Relations, *Iraq: Can Saddam Be Overthrown?* 105th. Cong., 2nd sess., March 2, 1998, 116; Haass, House Committee on International Relations, *U.S. Options in Confronting Iraq*, February 25, 1998, 14.

[151] Haass, House Committee on International Relations, *U.S. Options in Confronting Iraq*, February 25, 1998, 14.

of authoritarianism, crumbling infrastructure, and growing ethno-
sectarian conflict would persist, conditionalists argued, even if Saddam
was removed. They concluded that the risks of overthrowing Saddam and
inheriting these problems outweighed the considerable yet known costs of
containment.[152]

Members of the conditionalist school, of course, knew they had to
answer the charge that while Saddam may be somewhat restrained now,
inevitably containment would collapse and unleash him. Rather like the
Clinton administration, they retorted that the United States should moderate its expectations about what could be achieved vis-à-vis Iraq. The
United States needed a policy that could protect US interests and security
without requiring the risky and difficult task of toppling Saddam.
Containment, Haass argued, fit this bill: "If all this leads to a change in
Iraq's leadership, so much the better. But the advantage of containment
over the alternatives is that it protects our core interests even if Saddam
manages to hang on."[153]

Sticking with containment, however, meant that the United States
might have to accept Saddam having some WMD capability. "Even the
most unfettered and effective UNSCOM/IAEA effort cannot prevent
Iraq from conducting important covert efforts and from retaining and/
or developing some 'break out' capabilities," argued defense analyst
Anthony Cordesman.[154] Iraq's modern pharmaceutical and chemical
infrastructure could be shifted to weapons production relatively easily
and covertly, and the United Nations could not deny Iraq any capacity in
these areas. Saddam was aggressive and brutal but the historical record
showed, in policy scholar Michael O'Hanlon's terms: "Saddam is
unlikely to attack any country we are clearly committed to defend,"
which "probably means he can be deterred."[155] For the conditionalist
school, the best path was to accept some risk, restrain Iraq on more
serious technologies like nuclear weapons and long-range ballistic

---

[152] Senate Committee on Foreign Relations, *Iraq: Can Saddam Be Overthrown?* March 2,
1998, 115; Michael O'Hanlon, "The Butcher's Bill for Invading Iraq," *Washington Post*,
March 19, 1998, A20; Editorial, "Unseating Saddam Hussein," *New York Times*,
November 19, 1998, A34.

[153] Haass, Senate Committee on Foreign Relations, *Iraq: Can Saddam Be Overthrown?*
March 2, 1998, 38. See a similar statement on containment by General Anthony
Zinni in Senate Armed Services Committee, *U.S. Policy toward Iraq*, 106th. Cong.,
2nd sess., September 19, 2000, 64.

[154] Cordesman, Senate Committee on Foreign Relations, *Iraq: Can Saddam Be Overthrown?*
March 2, 1998, 120; Richard Haass, "Containing Iraq without War," *Washington Post*,
February 20, 1998, A23.

[155] Michael O'Hanlon, "Saddam Is Here to Stay," *Washington Times*, February 1,
1999, A19.

missiles, and take a clear deterrent stance against the deployment or use of WMD.

Defenders of containment offered a number of ways that the policy might be adjusted to new conditions rather than abandoned. Kenneth Pollack, a scholar of Middle Eastern politics who was hired by the NSC in 1999, argued that the very toughness of containment had sparked France, Russia, China, and many Arab states to oppose the policy. Pollack contended: "If we are going to keep containment this strong and this comprehensive, we will have to ... make very significant sacrifices on other issues to hold it together." The United States, Pollack argued, could shift to a policy of "narrow containment" that could get the coalition's cooperation on inspections and military sanctions while compromising on nonmilitary investment and trade and the flight bans on Iraqi citizens.[156] If the inspectors could verify full Iraqi compliance on WMD, the United States should permit unlimited oil exports while maintaining UN control over the funds generated by those sales.[157] Moreover, if the United States has to bomb Iraq, it should put no time limit on the campaign, forcing Iraqi generals, in Haass' words, "to calculate that he better take the risk of taking on his own regime."[158] Brent Scowcroft and Zbigniew Brzezinksi likewise suggested adjustments like easing of sanctions on nonmilitary goods, repairing relations with Iran to maintain Iraq's isolation, and greater humanitarian aid.[159]

In contrast to the inevitable declinists, conditionalist thinkers based their case on a view of the Cold War that stressed the role of containment's firmness, flexibility, and restraint in the US victory. If the United States could contain the massive, nuclear-armed Soviets for four decades, they could certainly do so with the vastly weaker Iraqis. Over time, they argued, containment exacerbated fissures and flaws within the Communist bloc that eventually sparked the system's collapse. Haass, for example, identified one lesson of the Cold War as: "Kennan's original formulation teaches us something else. A successful containment policy

---

[156] Kenneth Pollack, Joint Hearing of the Senate Committee on Foreign Relations and Senate Committee on Energy and Natural Resources, *Iraq: Are Sanctions Collapsing?* 105th Cong., 2nd sess., May 21, 1998, 41–43.

[157] Richard Haass, "Iraq: What Next? Containing Saddam Is the Most Likely U.S. Policy," *San Diego Union-Tribune*, March 1, 1998; Michael O'Hanlon, "Better than Air Strikes," *Washington Times*, November 16, 1998, A19.

[158] Frontline, Spying on Saddam, Richard Haass Interview, PBS, 1999, accessed March 23, 2018, www.pbs.org/wgbh/pages/frontline/shows/unscom/interviews/haass.html.

[159] Brent Scowcroft, Richard Murphy, and Zbigniew Brzezinski, *Differentiated Containment: U.S. Policy toward Iran and Iraq* (New York: Council on Foreign Relations Press, 1997), 7–8, 13, 23.

can set in motion forces that lead to the demise of the regime."[160] Brent
Scowcroft and James Baker recalled, moreover, that during the 1970s
neoconservatives, like contemporary Iraq hawks, fretted that the Soviet
Union would soon overtake the United States when it was actually
suffering crippling internal weaknesses.[161]

This point about the Cold War hints at a persistent problem facing the
conditionalists in the late 1990s: a stagnant theory of change.
Conditionalists had argued since shortly after the Gulf War that containment might lead Saddam to change his behavior or to the outright collapse
of his regime. However, the crushing of the internal opposition and
Saddam's increasingly effective campaign to stymie the inspectors and
break up the coalition raised the question of whether containment might
collapse or continue indefinitely in a weakened form. Conditionalist
thinkers in the late 1990s largely offered the same theory of change,
which was now less credible, even to themselves.[162] Most conditionalists
responded to this dilemma by lowering expectations for containment, but
many also shifted toward the regime change consensus view that the only
way out with Saddam in the long run was his removal from power. Henry
Kissinger, for example, had long promoted a tough containment policy,
but he concluded in November 1998: "The ultimate issue in the Persian
Gulf is not inspections but the government in Baghdad."[163] The best that
containment's defenders could do in the public discourse was argue that
containment was acceptable for the foreseeable future and that no responsible means of regime change existed for the moment.

One additional reason that the conditionalist approach to containment
garnered less support in the late 1990s was that one of its main tools,
sanctions, drew increasing criticism from the humanitarian school of
thought. This group had argued since the Gulf War that sanctions were
causing a health crisis in Iraq and that the United States should focus on
alleviating this disaster. In the late 1990s, this movement gained momentum, particularly when Denis Halliday and Hans von Sponeck, successive

---

[160] Haass, House Committee on International Relations, *U.S. Options in Confronting Iraq*,
February 25, 1998, 16. See also Michael O'Hanlon, "UN Struck a Good Deal for Peace
with Iraq," *Newsday*, February 25, 1998; James Baker, "Getting Ready for 'Next Time'
in Iraq," *New York Times*, February 27, 1998, A25.

[161] Baker, "Getting Ready," *New York Times*, February 27, 1998; Brent Scowcroft, "Taking
Exception: The Power of Containment," *Washington Post*, March 1, 1998, A22.

[162] Haass, House Committee on International Relations, *U.S. Options in Confronting Iraq*,
February 25, 1998, 16; Cordesman, Senate Committee on Foreign Relations, *Iraq: Can
Saddam Be Overthrown?* March 2, 1998, 120; Warren Strobel, "America's Plan to Get
Saddam," *U.S. News and World Report*, November 30, 1998, 34.

[163] Henry Kissinger, "Bring Saddam Down," *Washington Post*, November 29, 1998, C7.
See also Scowcroft, Murphy, and Brzezinski, *Differentiated Containment*, 7, 22; Editorial,
"A Necessary Response," *Washington Post*, December 17, 1998, A26.

UN Humanitarian Coordinators for Iraq, resigned in protest in 1998 and 2000. Halliday and von Sponeck objected to the Anglo-American blocking of important health- and infrastructure-related goods for import into Iraq because of potential dual-use goods.[164] Oil-for-food led to a significant economic recovery in Iraq, including the doubling of the GDP from 1997 to 2000, the stabilization of food prices, and significant increases in daily calorie intake for the average Iraqi.[165] These gains, however, were unequally distributed and the health crisis was not fully resolved.[166] UNICEF reported in 1999 that maternal and child mortality remained high, with an average rate of 131 deaths per 1,000 live births from 1994 to 1999.[167] Economic recovery remained a dream for the majority of Iraqis who suffered from high inflation, unemployment, and the collapse of government services.[168]

The Clinton administration received dozens of letters from Arab-American medical, religious, and charity groups calling for the lifting of sanctions.[169] Although many politicians avoided criticizing sanctions for fear of looking soft on Iraq, more liberal Democrats declared that the sanctions should be eased because they allowed Saddam "to exploit the suffering of his people to his political advantage."[170] They held numerous Congressional hearings in the late 1990s to give anti-sanctions activists a public platform. Some legislators from farm states, including Chuck Hagel (R-NE), also started to criticize the sanctions in the hope of reopening the Iraqi market.[171] Many critics pointed out that the sanctions were strengthening Saddam at home because he could use the rationing system to increase his control over civilian life and shift blame for

---

[164] Ewen MacAskill, "Second Official Quits UN Team," *The Guardian*, February 15, 2000, accessed May 5, 2018, www.theguardian.com/world/2000/feb/16/iraq.unitednations.

[165] Lisa Blaydes, *State of Repression: Iraq under Saddam Hussein* (Princeton, NJ: Princeton University Press, 2018), 120–123.

[166] Phebe Marr, *The Modern History of Iraq* (Boulder, CO: Westview Press, 2012), 283.

[167] "Iraq Surveys Show 'Humanitarian Emergency,'" August 12, 1999, unicef.org, www .unicef.org/newsline/99pr29.htm; Joy Gordon, *Invisible War: The United States and the Iraq Sanctions* (Cambridge, MA: Harvard University Press, 2010), 36–37.

[168] Human Rights Watch, "Explanatory Memorandum Regarding the Comprehensive Embargo on Iraq," January 14, 2000, hrw.org, accessed March 5, 2018, www.hrw.or g/print/226817; "When Sanctions Don't Work," *The Economist*, April 8, 2000, 25.

[169] Letters, Archdiocese of Boston to William Clinton, February 12, 1998; National Arab American Medical Association to William Clinton, February 17, 1998; Quakers General Conference to William Clinton, March 3, 1998; OA/ID 21687, White House Office of Records and Management, Crisis With Iraq, William Clinton Presidential Library.

[170] One letter to Clinton protesting the sanctions was signed by Nancy Pelosi, John Conyers, David Bonior, and Maxine Waters, among others. See Letter, John Conyers et al. to William Clinton, October 6, 1998, OA/ID 2070, National Security Council Records, William Clinton Presidential Library, 1–2.

[171] Gordon, *Invisible War*, 161–162.

domestic problems to outsiders.[172] They argued that oil-for-food was inadequate because even though it enabled some relief, the United States still blocked equipment and materials needed to restore Iraq's electric, sanitary, and medical infrastructures. They pressed for "de-linking," or the lifting of sanctions that hurt the civilian population while preserving military and WMD-related restrictions.[173]

The Clinton administration responded with a public relations campaign to defend sanctions and oil-for-food as crucial policy tools while pinning the blame for Iraq's health crisis on the Baathists. A State Department report made public in 1998 charged Iraq with inflating mortality statistics and showed that Saddam had constructed eight new palace complexes since 1991 at a cost of $2 billion. The Iraqi elite was also smuggling in luxury cars, yachts, and top-shelf liquor. In a country suffering from a potable water crisis, this report observed that one of Saddam's palaces had artificial lakes, moats, and a 15-foot-tall indoor waterfall.[174] The administration further noted that Iraq by 1999 was exporting oil at pre-Gulf War rates through oil-for-food but was not purchasing and distributing adequate resources to its people. In northern Iraq, where UN and Kurdish agencies facilitated distribution, mortality rates had plummeted while remaining high in the Baathist-controlled center and south.[175]

In addition, US officials cited UN reports that showed that Iraq had kept $200 million worth of much-needed medicine in warehouses and had tried to re-export food and medicine for the state's gain.[176] The administration concluded: "Ultimately, Baghdad's deliberate policy choices are responsible for any increase in mortality rates."[177] In general,

---

[172] Nimah Mazaheri, "Iraq and the Domestic Political Effects of Economic Sanctions," *Middle East Journal* 64, no. 2 (Spring, 2010): 253–259.

[173] Joy Gordon, "Sanctions as Siege Warfare," *The Nation*, March 22, 1999, 18–22; Hans von Sponeck, "Iraq: International Sanctions and What Next," *Middle East Policy* 7, no. 4 (October, 2000): 149–155; Meghan O'Sullivan, *Shrewd Sanctions: Statecraft and State Sponsors of Terrorism* (Washington, DC, Brookings Institution Press, 2003), 147–148.

[174] State Department Report, "Saddam Hussein's Iraq," September 1999, Digital National Security Agency, Targeting Iraq, Part 1 Collection, 6–7.

[175] For more on the highly contested issue of the causes and scope of the Iraqi health crisis in the 1990s, see Tim Dyson and Valeria Cetorelli, "Changing Views on Child Mortality and Economic Sanctions in Iraq: A History of Lies, Damned Lies, and Statistics," *British Medical Journal of Global Health* 2, no. 2 (July, 2017): 1–4; Amatzia Baram, "The Effect of Iraqi Sanctions: Statistical Pitfalls and Responsibility," *Middle East Journal* 54, no. 2 (Spring, 2000): 194–223; Mohamed M. Ali and Iqbal H. Shah, "Sanctions and Childhood Mortality in Iraq," *The Lancet* 355, no. 9218 (2000): 1851–1857.

[176] State Department Report, "Saddam Hussein's Iraq," September, 1999, 7; Sandy Berger, "Saddam Is the Root of All Iraq's Problems," *Financial Times*, May 4, 2000, A21.

[177] CIA/State Department Report, "Facts on Iraq's Humanitarian Situation," July 17, 1998, OA/ID 21687, White House Office of Records and Management, William Clinton Presidential Library, 2.

most figures in the inevitable decline and conditonalist camps agreed that the Iraq government was responsible for this crisis. Nevertheless, by the late 1990s the sanctions policy, like containment as a whole, was increasingly squeezed between inevitable decline critics who saw it as ineffective and humanitarian critics who saw it as immoral. The conditionalist approach was losing supporters to both of these groups, leaving few in the public square who still argued that containment could be successfully adapted to new circumstances.

The Rollback Alternative to Containment

Regime change supporters had suggested since the Gulf War that the United States should help Iraqi opposition groups foment an uprising against Saddam. This idea did not become a coherent strategy until the late 1990s when the INC and its neoconservative allies developed the rollback plan as a means of achieving regime change. Rollback became a central part of the campaign against containment because it provided an alternative strategy that promised, at low risk to the United States, Saddam's downfall and a democratic Iraq. It countered Clinton's argument that there was no intermediate strategy between containing Saddam and a complete invasion of the country. Critics of rollback, however, believed it would lead to a bloodbath in Iraq and the direct involvement of US military forces.

The concept of a rollback strategy comes from the early Cold War when the CIA sought to undermine communist control of Eastern Bloc countries by supporting "politico-psychological relations," sabotage, and the creation of cadres of resistance fighters in Eastern Europe.[178] This policy became popular among Republicans who wanted a tougher approach to the Cold War than containment. Future secretary of state John Foster Dulles endorsed the idea during the 1952 campaign as a strategy of "liberation" of the "captive peoples" of Eastern Europe.[179] Still, by the time Dwight Eisenhower took office in 1953, rollback had produced little more than the deaths of hundreds of exiles whom the CIA had smuggled into the Eastern Bloc. Eisenhower and Dulles quickly soured on this version of rollback and ceased operations by 1954.[180]

---

[178] Peter Grose, *Operation Rollback: America's Secret War behind the Iron Curtain* (Boston: Houghton Mifflin, 2000), 7–8; Laszlo Borhi, "Rollback, Liberation, Containment, or Inaction? U.S. Policy and Eastern Europe in the 1950s," *Journal of Cold War Studies* 1, no. 3 (Fall, 1999): 78–89.

[179] Christopher Tudda, "Reenacting the Story of Tantalus: Eisenhower, Dulles, and the Failed Rhetoric of Liberation," *Journal of Cold War Studies* 7, no. 4 (Fall, 2005): 9.

[180] Tudda, "Story of Tantalus," 16; Grose, *Operation Rollback*, 200–207, 216.

Rollback was revived in the 1980s under the Reagan Doctrine, which pledged support to anti-communist insurgencies in places like Afghanistan and Nicaragua to challenge and possibly reverse Soviet influence in the developing world.[181] In keeping with their narrative of the Cold War, inevitable decline critics of containment believed these insurgencies had contributed to Soviet retrenchment in the mid-late 1980s.[182] Congressman Dana Rohrabacher (R-CA), for instance, claimed: "The Communists, then, were defeated through our strong support of democracy, and by providing those willing to fight for their rights the means to win their freedom."[183] They wanted to reapply the concept to Iraq, and when the INC started working on rollback in the early 1990s, they drew on the help of former military and intelligence personnel who had been involved with the Reagan Doctrine.[184]

The rollback plan for Iraq would start with the United States recognizing the INC as the legitimate provisional government of Iraq. The next step was to create opposition bases in areas of northern and southern Iraq protected by the NFZs. The United States would lift sanctions in these areas and unfreeze Iraqi assets to help the opposition build support and military strength. The United States would then provide money, military training, supplies, and weaponry, including anti-air and anti-tank weapons. US military forces would defend these "safe havens" from Saddam as the opposition developed. The INC, in turn, would foster a broader resistance movement in Iraq, uniting the Kurdish parties of the north and Shia groups in the south who would provide most of the manpower for the fight against Saddam. The INC hoped to gather around 10,000 light infantry soldiers as the "nucleus" of this offensive as well as several elite units that would counter the Republican Guard.[185]

Once the opposition had gained enough strength, it would take the offensive against the Baathist regime. Under what it called the "Afghan approach," the INC envisioned insurgent attacks on military outposts and the steady expansion of enclaves of opposition control. This process, it

---

[181] Hal Brands, *Making the Unipolar Moment: U.S. Foreign Policy and the Rise of the post–Cold War Order* (Ithaca, NY: Cornell University Press, 2016), 102, 113; John Lewis Gaddis, *Strategies of Containment: A Critical Appraisal of American National Security Policy during the Cold War*, 2nd ed. (New York: Oxford University Press, 2005), 373.

[182] Zalmay Khalilzad, "It's Not Too Late to Topple Saddam," *Wall Street Journal*, February 25, 1998, A22; Joshua Muravchik, "Apply the Reagan Doctrine to Iraq," *Wall Street Journal*, November 4, 1999.

[183] Rohrabacher, House Committee on International Relations, *U.S. Options in Confronting Iraq*, February 25, 1998, 39.

[184] Roston, *Man Who Pushed*, 126–130.

[185] W. Patrick Lang, "Drinking the Kool-Aid," *Middle East Policy* 9, no. 2 (Summer, 2004): 43–44; Michael Gordon and Bernard Trainor, *Cobra II: The Inside Story of the Invasion and Occupation of Iraq* (New York: Pantheon Books, 2006), 514.

argued, would draw defectors, delegitimize the Iraqi government, and possibly spark a coup or urban rebellion against Saddam. At some point, rollback supporters claimed the regime would collapse, although the specific mechanism for this outcome was often unclear.[186] One key assumption underlying this strategy was that Saddam's regime held on to power through sheer terror alone and that morale in the army was abysmal. The plan also assumed that the Iraqi population's seething hatred for the Saddam needed only direction and protection to overthrow the regime.[187]

Rollback's most enthusiastic supporters in US politics were neoconservatives and Republican Congressmen. The 1998 CPSG letter to Clinton endorsed rollback, calling for safe havens inside Iraq, military aid to the opposition, "a systematic air campaign" against the Iraqi Republican Guard, and the positioning of US ground forces to be ready to "protect and assist the anti-Saddam forces" as a "last resort."[188] This letter was one of dozens of articles, speeches, and Congressional hearings in which regime change advocates pushed rollback as a viable alternative to containment.[189] The INC and many of its US supporters made grandiose promises about rollback. For example, Ahmed Chalabi told a Senate hearing in March 1998:

Give the Iraqi National Congress a base, protected from Saddam's tanks, give us the temporary support we need to feed and house and care for the liberated population, and we will give you a free Iraq, an Iraq free of weapons of mass destruction, and a free market Iraq. Best of all the INC will do all this for free. The U.S. commitment to the security of the gulf is sufficient. The maintenance of the no-fly-zones and the air interdiction of Saddam's armor by U.S. forces assumed in the INC plan is virtually in place.[190]

---

[186] For descriptions of the Afghan approach to rollback, see Daniel Byman and Patrick Clawson, ed., *Iraq Strategy Review: Options for U.S. Policy* (Washington, DC: Washington Institute for Near East Policy, 1999), 59–88; Editorial, "How to Attack Iraq," *The Weekly Standard*, November 17, 1998.

[187] Wolfowitz, Senate Committee on Foreign Relations, *Iraq: Can Saddam Be Overthrown?* March 2, 1998, 8–10; Wolfowitz, House Committee on International Relations, *U.S. Options in Confronting Iraq*, February 25, 1998, 9, 26; Max Singer, "Saddam Must Go," *The Weekly Standard*, February 16, 1998; Eliot Cohen, House Committee on International Relations, *U.S. Options in Confronting Iraq*, February 25, 1998, 20–23.

[188] Committee for Peace and Security in the Gulf, "Open Letter to the President," February 19, 1998; See also statement by Chalabi, Senate Committee on Foreign Relations, *Iraq: Can Saddam Be Overthrown?* March 2, 1998, 17.

[189] Paul Wolfowitz, House Committee on National Security, *United States Policy toward Iraq*, September 16, 1998, 75–76; Robert Kagan, "A Way to Oust Saddam," *The Weekly Standard*, September 28, 1998, 14; Joshua Muravchik, "What to Do about Saddam Hussein," *Commentary*, June 1, 1998; Trent Lott, *Cong. Rec.*, 105th Cong., 2nd sess., October 7, 1998, 11811.

[190] Chalabi, Senate Committee on Foreign Relations, *Iraq: Can Saddam Be Overthrown?* March 2, 1998, 8. See also Richard Perle, Subcommittee on Near Eastern and South Asian Affairs of the Senate Committee on Foreign Relations, *The Liberation of Iraq: A Progress Report*, 106th Cong., 1st sess., June 28, 2000, 10.

Chalabi added that this plan would take "only a matter of months" and that Iraqi oil wealth would pay for reconstruction.[191]

Despite these promises, rollback came under heavy criticism from supporters of the conditionalist approach to containment, especially among military experts. These critics identified massive military problems with the strategy, including the difficulties of providing permanent air cover for small, weak ground forces and providing close air support as opposition forces tried to seize cities. The flat, open desert of southern Iraq was terrible terrain for an insurgency, and it favored the movement of Saddam's tanks.[192] Rollback's detractors also feared that if the plan went poorly, the United States would have to choose between entering a wider war against Saddam and allowing the opposition to be crushed. US CENTCOM Commander Anthony Zinni called this scenario the "Bay of Goats," invoking an Iraqi version of the 1961 Bay of Pigs fiasco. He argued that rollback could lead to heavy US losses, ethnic civil war or fragmentation, and US occupation of parts or all of Iraq.[193] A classified war game commissioned by Zinni in 1999, entitled "Desert Crossing," concluded that even if Saddam was overthrown, the aftermath would probably be chaotic and bloody as various factions competed for power and carried out vendettas. The United States, this study stressed, would be better off distancing itself from this situation.[194] Finally, rollback's opponents conceded that the regular Iraqi army might be weak, but they viewed the Republican Guard and other elite units as competent and motivated to fight for Saddam.[195]

Critics also noted important political flaws in the rollback strategy. Richard Haass argued that the Sunni population, especially the elite, dreaded what might happen if Saddam fell to a mostly Shia and Kurdish rebellion. This segment of the population, he claimed, would probably rally to Saddam against an insurgency or at best stay on the sidelines like they did in the post–Desert Storm uprisings.[196] Kenneth Pollack, who coauthored an influential *Foreign Affairs* article in 1999

---

[191] Perle, Senate Committee on Foreign Relations, *The Liberation of Iraq: A Progress Report*, June 28, 2000, 17.

[192] Daniel Byman, Kenneth Pollack, and Gideon Rose, "The Rollback Fantasy", *Foreign Affairs* 78, no. 1 (January/February, 1999): 27–32. See also Daniel Byman and Matthew Waxman, *Confronting Iraq: U.S. Policy and the Use of Force since the Gulf War* (Arlington, VA: RAND Publishing, 2000), 62.

[193] Quote is from Lang, "Drinking the Kool-Aid," 24; see also Anthony Zinni, Senate Armed Services Committee, *U.S. Policy toward Iraq*, January 28, 1999, 28.

[194] Michael Gordon and Bernard Trainor, *The Endgame: The Inside Story of the Struggle for Iraq, from George W. Bush to Barack Obama* (New York: Pantheon Books, 2012), 7–8.

[195] Byman, Pollack, and Rose, "The Rollback Fantasy," 27.

[196] Senate Committee on Foreign Relations, *Iraq: Can Saddam Be Overthrown?* March 2, 1998, 32.

against rollback, predicted that this strategy would lead to a "bloodbath" and that "it would be criminal for the U.S. to go ahead and back these people."[197] Furthermore, critics noted that rollback would need the equivalent of a Pakistan for the Afghan insurgency: a compliant ally bordering the target that could funnel supplies and personnel to the opposition.[198] Rollback would need Turkey to play this role in the north, but Turkey would oppose any scheme that might strengthen Kurdish separatism. Moreover, key states like Saudi Arabia and the Gulf monarchies would probably oppose a strategy designed to establish a Shia-dominated government in Iraq that might align with Iran.[199] Finally, rollback's critics, especially the Clinton administration, believed that this strategy would seriously damage the international coalition behind containment.[200]

Numerous politicians and intellectuals, especially Democrats and liberals, who backed the ILA and the regime change consensus did not endorse rollback for many of these reasons. Legislators like Robert Kerrey, Charles Robb (D-VA), and Lee Hamilton (D-IN), for example, viewed rollback as unrealistic and risky.[201] In sum, while the US political world was ever more convinced that only Saddam's removal could end the threat from Iraq, the rollback debate showed the persistence of deep divisions on how to achieve that goal and how much to risk in the process. Rollback marked the outside edge of what regime change proponents could call for in strategic terms until 2001. Even the plan's most vehement supporters labored to show that it would be low risk and low cost to the United States. The idea of openly advocating the use of ground troops to achieve regime change was still a red line on both sides of the debate.[202]

---

[197] Kettle, "Pentagon Balks at 'Idiotic' Law Urging Bay of Pigs-Type Invasion of Iraq," *The Guardian*, October 21, 1998, 16.

[198] Byman, Pollack, and Rose, "The Rollback Fantasy," 30–32; Milt Berden, "Lessons for Afghanistan: Why Covert Action in Iraq Probably Wouldn't Work," *New York Times*, March 2, 1998, A17.

[199] US Central Command, *Desert Crossing Seminar: After Action Report*, June 28–30, National Security Archives, accessed January 30, 2016, http://nsarchive.gwu.edu/NSA EBB/NSAEBB207/, 6; Byman, Pollack, and Rose, "The Rollback Fantasy," 30–32.

[200] US Central Command, *Desert Crossing*, 21; Daniel Byman, "Proceed with Caution: U.S. Support for the Iraqi Opposition," *The Washington Quarterly* 22, no. 3 (Summer, 1999): 24; Clawson, *Iraq Strategy Review*, 97–98.

[201] Representative Lee Hamilton, US House, *Cong. Rec.*, 105th Cong., 2nd sess., October 5, 1998, 9489. Senator Robert Kerrey of Nebraska, US Senate, *Cong. Rec.*, 106th Cong., 1st sess., February 25, 1999, Vol. 145, pt. 30: 1994. Robb, Subcommittee on Near Eastern and South Asian Affairs of the Senate Committee on Foreign Relations, *Iraq: Can Saddam Be Overthrown?* March 2, 1998, 8.

[202] Commentators who did consider the use of ground troops to achieve regime change before 9/11 included Kristol and Kagan, "Bombing Iraq," *New York Times*, January 30, 1998; Kim Holmes and James Phillips, "The Anatomy of Clinton's Failure in Iraq," February 27, 1998, Heritage Foundation Backgrounder No. 1161, accessed

The Anticlimax: Iraq Policy after Desert Fox, 1999–2000

After reaching a fever pitch in 1998, the debate over Iraq policy entered an anticlimactic stage for Clinton's last two years in office. With the ejection of inspectors in December 1998, containment needed adjustments to remain viable. The Clinton administration considered shifting to a more active regime change position after the exhausting year of confrontations. Nevertheless, they found no reasonable, cost-effective way of reaching this goal. They ended up sticking with containment, calibrating it to new realities, and doing just enough for regime change to fend off domestic critics.

Before Desert Fox in late 1998, the administration concluded that they must break the cycle of confrontations with Saddam. The old approach was not "sustainable in the long run," Sandy Berger argued in December 1998, because "the longer the standoff continues, the harder it will be to maintain international support."[203] The administration therefore adopted the position that it would not push to get inspectors back into Iraq unless there was high assurance of Iraqi cooperation and robust international backing. For example, Clinton told Blair at the end of Desert Fox that the United States would only support readmission after "concrete, affirmative, and demonstrable action by Iraq showing that it will provide full cooperation."[204] Until a strong inspection regime could be reinstituted, the United States would pursue a policy based on three "red lines" that would trigger the use of force. The first line was threatening or attacking his neighbors. The second was attacking the Kurdish zone in northern Iraq. The third line would be triggered if the United States found clear evidence of Iraq reconstituting or deploying WMD.[205]

The year of showdowns with Iraq hardened the administration's belief in the necessity of Saddam's removal and motivated it to explore new ways of achieving regime change. Berger's NSC staff and Martin Indyk's Near East Office reviewed Iraq policy in early 1999 with the hope of finding better ways to pressure Iraq, but they found massive obstacles to

---

October 18, 2017, http://web.archive.org/web/20150814143442/http://www.iraq watch.org/perspectives/heritage-clinton-failure-2-27-98.htm.

[203] Chollet, *America between the Wars*, 202.

[204] Memorandum of Telephone Conversation, William Clinton and Tony Blair, December 19, 1998, Clinton Digital Library, Declassified Documents Concerning Tony Blair, accessed February 2, 2018, https://clinton.presidentiallibraries.us/items/show/48779.

[205] Erlanger, "U.S. Set to Give Up Arms Inspections," *New York Times*, November 8, 1998; Thomas Lippman, "Two Options for Iraq in U.S. Policy," *Washington Post*, December 24, 1998, A14; Alfred Prados and Kenneth Katzman, *Iraq–U.S. Confrontation*, November 17, 2000 (CRS Issue Brief) (Washington DC: Congressional Research Service, 2000), 3.

a tougher strategy. The CIA did not want to try bold operations in Iraq after the fiascoes of the mid-1990s, and the military viewed invasion as the only way to defeat Saddam. Moreover, no one trusted the Iraqi opposition enough to make them the centerpiece of their strategy.[206] When the Kosovo crisis erupted in March 1999, the administration turned its attention to this conflict, which culminated in a three-month bombing campaign against Serbia. By the time it returned to Iraq later in the year, the administration was not keen on another risky foreign policy adventure, especially as Clinton made the Middle East Peace Process (MEPP) the focus of his remaining months in office.[207] Furthermore, many in the government believed that the Iraqi threat was not serious enough to merit an effort at regime change. Intelligence reports stated that Iraqi conventional military strength had actually deteriorated since 1994. One report predicted that Iraq's military capabilities would continue "a slow and steady decline as long as both economic sanctions and the arms embargo are maintained." It added that "smuggling and other efforts to circumvent the embargo will be inadequate to halt the trend."[208]

As for WMD, the intelligence agencies assessed that Saddam's intention to build WMD had not changed, but he was still nearly a decade from having a nuclear weapon and a viable missile delivery system.[209] One 1999 report judged that with foreign assistance he could have an ICBM capacity within fifteen years, but this report also viewed China, North Korea, and Iran as more immediate ballistic missile threats.[210] Intelligence reports in the late 1990s did suggest that Iraq was "revitalizing its BW program" and maintaining a breakout capacity for chemical weapons, although the intelligence community could not assess whether it had actually produced these weapons.[211] In the administration's view,

---

[206] Pollack, *Threatening Storm*, 96; Indyk, *Innocent Abroad*, 202.

[207] Pollack, *Threatening Storm*, 98–99.

[208] National Intelligence Council, National Intelligence Estimate 94–19, "Iraqi Military Capabilities through 2003," April 1999, Digital National Security Agency, Targeting Iraq, Part 1 Collection, 1, 8–9; CIA Report, "Stability of the Iraq Regime: Significant Vulnerabilities Offset by Repression," April 2002, in Senate Select Committee on Intelligence, *Postwar Findings about Iraq's WMD Programs and Links to Terrorism and How They Compare with Prewar Assessments*, 109th Cong., 2nd sess., September 8, 2006, S. Report 109–331, 389

[209] CIA Report, "Iraq Prospects for Confrontation," July 17, 1998, in Senate Select Committee on Intelligence, *Postwar Findings about Iraq's WMD Programs*, September 8, 2006, 385.

[210] National Intelligence Council, "Foreign Missile Developments and the Ballistic Missile Threat to the United States through 2015," September 1999, dni.gov, accessed October 17, 2017, www.dni.gov/files/documents/missilethreat_2001.pdf, 1.

[211] Senate Select Committee on Intelligence, *Postwar Findings about Iraq's WMD Programs*, September 8, 2006, 82–83, 115–121.

Saddam's overall weakness left little reason to make regime change an urgent priority.[212]

Some Clinton officials described the post–Desert Fox strategy as "containment-plus," the plus being enhanced covert efforts to topple Saddam.[213] What actual policy changes emerged from this new label are hard to define, as many officials have admitted.[214] The administration continued to defend containment from 1999 to 2000 even as it offered rhetorical homages to regime change. Walter Slocombe, the Undersecretary of Defense for Policy, claimed in March 1999: "What we are working to do is to help create the political and military conditions that will permit a successful change of the regime."[215] While the administration played up the novelty of this approach for political reasons, the idea of establishing conditions that might lead to Saddam's ouster by Iraqi hands had been central to Bush's and Clinton's Iraq policies since the Gulf War. It mostly emphasized, as Albright did in early 2000, that containment was managing the problem well enough: "I think we have been successful in keeping him in his box in terms of the threat to the region."[216]

One significant escalation in US Iraq policy following Desert Fox was the intensification of the air war in the NFZs in northern and southern Iraq. In January 1999, Iraqi forces increased antiair attacks and other provocations against US and British planes in the NFZs. The United States and Great Britain responded by expanding the rules of engagement to allow planes to strike any air defense or related communications site, not just "the particular source of the violation or the source of the threat."[217] Coalition air forces also received wider latitude to respond aggressively to Iraqi provocations such as antiaircraft fire or radar lock-ons.[218] The deployments required to maintain this "forgotten war," as

---

[212] National Intelligence Estimate 94–19, "Iraqi Military Capabilities through 2003," April 1999, 24.

[213] Cable, US Embassy in Riyadh to Secretary of State, June 26, 1999, Digital National Security Agency, Targeting Iraq, Part 1 Collection, 1; Jane Perlez, "Albright Introduces a New Phrase to Promote Hussein's Ouster," *New York Times*, January 29, 1999, A3.

[214] Chollet, *America between the Wars*, 202; Lance Gay, "White House Has Second Thoughts on Toppling Saddam," *Pittsburgh Post-Gazette*, March 22, 1999, A4.

[215] Steven Lee Myers and Tim Weiner, "Weeks of Bombing Leave Iraq's Power Structure Unshaken," *New York Times*, March 7, 1999, A6. See also Romanowski Testimony in Hearing of House Committee on International Relations, *U.S. Policy toward Iraq*, 106th Cong., 2nd sess., March 23, 2000, 51–52.

[216] Meet the Press Excerpted Transcript, January 2, 2000, in Ehrenberg, McSherrey, Sanchez, and Sayej, *The Iraq Papers*, 38–39.

[217] Quotation is from Sandy Burger in Elizabeth Becker, "U.S. Pilots over Iraq Given Wider Leeway to Fight Back," *New York Times*, January 27, 1999, A2.

[218] John Tirpak, "Legacy of the Air Blockades," *Air Force*, February 2003, 52; Stephen Glain and Thomas Ricks, "Air Attacks against Iraq Are Inconclusive," *Wall Street Journal*, March 17, 1999, A23.

journalist Thomas Ricks called it, cost over $1 billion per year, involving 200 aircraft, 19 warships, and 22,000 military personnel.[219] The administration viewed this campaign as a way to keep Saddam weak and off-balance, but it adamantly disassociated it from regime change. As State Department spokesman Richard Boucher stated in 2000: "There is no relationship between enforcement of the no-fly-zones and the United States' regime change policy for Iraq."[220] One reason it did not want to further escalate the air war was the fear of a US pilot being shot down and captured by Iraq. Saddam was offering $14,000 per person to any unit that captured a US pilot, whom he would use to extort concessions from the United States.[221]

The Clinton administration also believed that rollback was an unrealistic and dangerous plan.[222] The sight of General Zinni criticizing rollback was widely interpreted as signaling the administration's negative view of the strategy.[223] As for the ILA, Pollack recalls that the administration "did comply with the letter of the Iraq Liberation Act, but in spirit we ignored it."[224] In keeping with the ILA's requirements, the State Department did designate nine opposition groups, including the INC, as eligible to receive US military aid. It also appointed diplomat Frank Ricciardone as an official liaison to the opposition.[225] Clinton officials argued that they might someday provide military aid to the opposition, but first they would focus on building the INC's capacity to effectively use aid and unify the fractious opposition.[226] The United States provided legal and managerial training, aid for the INC's work on Baathist crimes, and office and communications equipment.[227] The INC ultimately

[219] Quotation is from Thomas Ricks, "Containing Iraq: A Forgotten War," *Washington Post*, October 25, 2000, A1. See also Ricks, *Fiasco*, 15; Steven Lee Myers, "In Intense but Little Noticed Fight, Allies Have Bombed Iraq All Year," *New York Times*, August 13, 1999, A1.

[220] Richard Boucher, "Press Briefing," June 16, 2000, State Department, accessed October 18, 2017, http://web.archive.org/web/20150814142212/http://www.iraq watch.org/government/US/State/state-boucher-6-16-00.htm.

[221] Katzman and Prados, *Iraq–U.S. Confrontation*, 3.

[222] Bonin, *Arrows of the Night*, 145.

[223] Anthony Zinni, Senate Armed Services Committee, *U.S. Policy on Iraq*, January 28, 1999, 14, 28.

[224] Pollack, interview by author, November 6, 2017.

[225] Vernon Loeb, "Anti-Saddam Group Named for U.S. Aid," *Washington Post*, January 16, 1999, A8.

[226] See testimony of Martin Indyk, House Committee on International Relations, *Developments in the Middle East*, 106th Cong., 1st sess., June 8, 1999, 5–7.

[227] State Department Near Eastern Affairs Office, "Report on Support for Democratic Opposition of Iraq," 1999, OA/ID 2549, National Security Council Office of Multilateral and Humanitarian Affairs, William Clinton Presidential Library, 1–3.

received about $2 million worth of aid of this nature but no weapons or military equipment and minimal military training.[228]

The State Department and the CIA in particular were wary of offering money or military aid to the opposition. Elizabeth Jones, whose office at the State Department was responsible for handling INC funding requests, recalls that they staunchly refused to hand the INC cash and demanded of Chalabi: "If you can show us the soldiers you are training, we will pay them, not you." Jones had worked with the Afghan mujahedin in the 1980s, and she said that the INC never came up with a "muj equivalent" beyond about twenty-five men who showed up to be trained at a Polish base.[229] The INC held a conference for the disparate opposition groups in October 1999, but it collapsed in internecine squabbling. By 2000, the opposition was in disarray and the administration had lost interest in organizing the opposition.[230]

The continuing erosion of sanctions posed another persistent challenge for US policy following Desert Fox. Illicit trade between Iraq and its neighbors surged during and after 1999, including the opening of an oil pipeline between Iraq and Syria, which provided the Iraqi government with another $1–2 billion in 2000.[231] Iraq tried to widen the split in the coalition by selectively signing oil-for-food contracts with countries that called for the end of sanctions. France, Russia, and China, for instance, received a third of all oil-for-food contracts.[232] The State Department estimated that the Iraqi government took in at least $1 billion per year in revenue from smuggling, kickbacks, and other sources. However, it stressed that before sanctions were imposed in 1990, Iraq received an average of around $10 billion per year from the oil trade.[233]

In contrast to the inevitable decline critics' desire to scrap multilateral restraints and embrace regime change, the Clinton administration

---

[228] Bonin, *Arrows of the Night*, 168.

[229] Elizabeth Jones, phone interview by author, February 6, 2018. For more on the INC's misuse of US funding, see US Department of State, Office of Inspector General, "Review of Awards to Iraqi National Congress Support Foundation," September 2001, accessed May 6, 2020, www.stateoig.gov/system/files/7508.pdf.

[230] Barbara Crossette, "French Flight Tests Ban against Iraq," *New York Times*, September 23, 2000, A7.

[231] Pollack, *Threatening Storm*, 101, 214.

[232] Judith Miller, "CIA Is Said to Find Iraq Gives Contracts to Nations that Want to End Economic Sanctions," *New York Times*, September 7, 2000, A14. On the extent of the corruption of the Oil-for-Food Program, see Paul Volcker, Independent Inquiry into the United Nations Oil-for-Food Programme, Report on Program Manipulation, October 27, 2005, accessed October 17, 2017, http://web.archive.org/web/201508141 43613/http://www.iraqwatch.org/un/IIC/un_iic_final_report_27Oct2005.pdf, 1–9.

[233] Anthony Cordesman, *Iraq: Sanctions and Beyond* (Boulder, CO: Westview Press, 1997), 169; Colum Lynch, "U.S. Says Sanctions on Iraq Not Crumbling," *Washington Post*, September 30, 2000, A16.

continued to treat containment and regime change as compatible goals. Thus, keeping the international coalition on board with sanctions and the reinsertion of inspectors remained a crucial goal after Desert Fox. In contrast to its rhetoric in domestic politics, in international diplomacy, the administration conveyed flexibility on sanctions in an updated version of the Clinton fudge. Clinton told Blair, for instance, in October 1999: "Now I am prepared to say that if he meets his disarmament obligations and puts a system in place where he's complying, I would be prepared to suspend sanctions and liberalize the oil-for-food program." Clinton then said that in order to lift the oil export ban he would need a tough inspections and monitoring regime because "our guys here in Congress, even the Democrats, are attacking me because I haven't done enough to get rid of him. I think they will eat me alive if I agree to lift sanctions while he has his weapons program going on."[234] The administration also wanted to reduce import restrictions on Iraq for nonmilitary or dual-use items in order to, in Elizabeth Jones' words, "get rid of the argument that the U.S. was responsible for the deprivation in Iraq."[235]

The centerpiece of Clinton's post–Desert Fox diplomacy was the push to pass a Security Council resolution to create a new inspection agency and specify what Iraq had to do to earn sanctions relief. France, Russia, and China believed that Saddam had virtually no proscribed weapons left and proposed that the oil export ban be lifted once Iraq merely accepted inspectors into its territory. These nations also proposed an inspection regime with far less independence than UNSCOM.[236] The United States originally wanted to reinsert UNSCOM and demanded that sanctions only be eased if the inspectors verified full Iraqi compliance.[237] This impasse was broken in the spring of 1999 when Great Britain and the Netherlands proposed that UNSCOM be completely replaced by a new agency. They also proposed that instead of lifting sanctions, the Security Council should abolish the cap on oil-for-food sales, hopefully allowing Iraq to import more food and medicine.[238]

---

[234] Memorandum of Telephone Conversation, William Clinton and Tony Blair, October 13, 1999, Clinton Digital Library, Declassified Documents Concerning Tony Blair, accessed February 2, 2018, https://clinton.presidentiallibraries.us/items/show/48779, 22, 25.

[235] Elizabeth Jones, phone interview by author, February 6, 2018.

[236] Frederic Bozo, *A History of the Iraq Crisis: France, the United States, and Iraq, 1991–2003* (Washington, DC: Woodrow Wilson Center Press, 2016), 57; Craig Whitney, "Allies Are Cool to French Plan to Monitor Iraq," *New York Times*, January 10, 1999, A10.

[237] Paul Lewis, "Russia Proposes New System for Monitoring Iraqi Arms," *New York Times*, January 16, 1999, A6.

[238] Paul Lewis, "U.N. Is Asked to Enlarge Iraq Inquiry," *New York Times*, April 16, 1999, A3.

Further disputes at the United Nations delayed the passage of Security Council Resolution 1284 until December 17, 1999. This resolution removed the ceiling on oil-for-food sales and relaxed some import controls on medical, agricultural, and educational supplies. It also created the United Nations Monitoring, Verification, and Inspection Commission (UNMOVIC), a new inspections agency empowered to confirm Iraq compliance on WMD. If UNMOVIC verified compliance, the Security Council would then vote to suspend sanctions. This suspension would have to be renewed every 120 days, giving the United Nations a chance to punish Iraq if it reneged.[239] US hopes that this resolution would forge a new unity in the international coalition were dashed when France decided to abstain at the last minute after learning that Russia and China planned to abstain. France feared that voting for this resolution would put it at a disadvantage in making economic deals with Iraq.[240] The United States was further chagrined when France, Russia, and China vetoed Kofi Annan's appointment of former UNSCOM chief Rolf Ekeus to lead UNMOVIC because he had a reputation for being too tough.[241] Instead, Annan proposed IAEA director Hans Blix, whom the United States thought might be too lenient but voted for anyways to make sure UNMOVIC could function at all.[242]

The aftermath of Resolution 1284's passage was its own anticlimax because Iraq refused to accept the new inspection regime and the United States did little to compel its compliance. The result was policy drift and the continued atrophying of Iraq's constraints. France, Russia, and China did their best throughout 2000 to weaken UNMOVIC, mandating that all UNMOVIC members be UN employees, which barred a number of non-UN experts with extensive experience.[243] The United States continued to permit the loosening of restrictions on exports into Iraq, including $1.2 billion in oil industry equipment needed to revive Iraqi oil production.[244] In the fall of 2000, France, Russia, and several other countries permitted civilian flights into Iraq, claiming that the air

---

[239] United Nations Security Council Resolution 1284, December 17, 1999, un.org, accessed April 15, 2018, www.un.org/Depts/unscom/Keyresolutions/sres99-1284.htm.

[240] Pollack, *Threatening Storm*, 100–101.

[241] Barbara Crossette, "Annan Faces Growing Split Over Arms Inspector for Iraq," *New York Times*, January 19, 2000, A10. For more on the Russian–Iraqi relationship in the late 1990s, see Alexei Vassilev, "Russia and Iraq," *Middle East Policy* 7, no. 4 (October, 2000): 127–129.

[242] Barbara Crossette, "U.N. Names Ex-head of Atomic Energy Agency to Lead Monitoring," *New York Times*, January 27, 2000, A8.

[243] Barbara Crossette, "Security Council Approves New Arms Inspection Agency for Iraq," *New York Times*, April 14, 2000, A12.

[244] Barbara Crossette, "Security Council Votes to Let Iraq Buy Oil Gear," *New York Times*, April 1, 2000, A5.

embargo was not meant to apply to civilians. Iraq's economic reintegration continued, with one trade fair in November 2000 attracting twenty foreign economics ministers and over a thousand firms.[245] Although it did not control these revenues, licit Iraqi oil sales reached $16 billion in 2000, four times more than 1997.[246]

Boosters of regime change and rollback excoriated Clinton's post–Desert Fox policy as a failure to follow through on the ILA. Trent Lott, Robert Kerrey, Joseph Liebermann, and other prominent legislators wrote to Clinton repeatedly to protest the "continued drift" and "reduced priority" of Iraq policy since Desert Fox. Lott argued: "In providing authority for a military drawdown, it was our intention to train and equip a force dedicated to bringing democracy to Iraq."[247] Clinton had not taken concrete steps toward this goal, and regime change advocates mocked the provision of furniture, computers, and office supplies to the INC as evidence of an unserious policy.[248] These critics also disliked Security Council Resolution 1284, which they saw as rewarding Iraq and again demonstrating Clinton's caving to the lowest common denominator of the United Nations. They argued that the continual reforming of the sanctions simply watered them down and prevented them from imposing real punishment. Even though Clinton had escalated the air war in the NFZs, most inevitable declinists viewed this as further management of the Iraqi problem rather than a clear attempt to resolve it.[249] By the time the presidential election started to heat up in the summer of 2000, most critics of containment judged that Clinton, in Senator Sam Brownback's (R-KS) words, "had absolutely no intent of implementing the provisions" of the ILA.[250] They reserved their hopes for a concerted regime change strategy for the next president.

---

[245] Crossette, "French Flight," *New York Times*, September 23, 2000.

[246] "Saddam Chips His Way to Freedom," *The Economist*, November 25, 2000, 95.

[247] This letter was also signed by Jesse Helms, Richard Shelby, Sam Brownback, Benjamin Gilman, and Howard Berman. See Letter, Trent Lott et al. to William Clinton, August 11, 1999, National Security Council Records, Legislative Affairs, William Clinton Presidential Library, 1–2.

[248] Perle, "Saddam Unbound," 100.

[249] Jim Hoagland, "Wishing Iraq Away," *Washington Post*, January 13, 2000, A21; Editorial, "Iraq's Devoted Allies," *Washington Post*, January 20, 2000, A22; Editorial, "Outside the Box," *Wall Street Journal*, December 5, 2000, A26; Gordon, *Invisible War*, 158–160.

[250] Sam Brownback, Senate Committee on Foreign Relations, *The Liberation of Iraq: A Progress Report*, June 28, 2000, 1. For similar criticism, see Frank Murkowski, "Our Toothless Policy on Iraq," *Washington Post*, January 25, 1999, A21; Jim Hoagland, "Virtual Policy," *Washington Post*, March 7, 1999, B7; Richard Perle, Senate Armed Services Committee, *U.S. Policy toward Iraq*, September 19, 2000, 77–78; Kerrey, *Cong. Rec.*, March 2, 2000, 2053; Lawrence Kaplan, "Rollback," *New Republic*, October 30, 2000, 28–30.

Conclusion: Containment as of November 2000

With the loss of the inspectors and the erosion of sanctions by the decade's end, the United States faced a choice between modulating containment to fit new conditions or intensifying efforts for regime change. Clinton essentially chose to adapt containment while telling domestic audiences that no normalization with Iraq would occur while Saddam remained in power. Inevitable decline critics wanted to prioritize regime change, even at the expense of containment, which they saw as confining and ineffective. These critics failed to change the actual policy, but they made massive gains in the political debate as the inspections crises of 1997–1998 bolstered their case that containment was not working and could not work in terms of changing Saddam's behavior or regime.

Furthermore, inevitable declinists in this period succeeded in shifting the essential question on Iraq from Saddam's capabilities, which remained feeble, to his intentions as measured by his compliance. Following this logic, the most reasonable interpretation was that Saddam remained inalterably fixated on defying the United Nations and acquiring WMD. This principle laid important groundwork for the post-9/11 argument by the second Bush administration that Saddam had to be removed before his WMD production came to full fruition.

The regime change consensus became firmly entrenched in US politics in the late 1990s, putting defenders of containment at a disadvantage. Advocates of the conditionalist case had shifted to moderating goals, downplaying the threat, adjusting the tools, and hoping for something to happen to solve the Saddam problem. This argument depended on a political atmosphere in which the US people felt secure from foreign threats and hesitant to support massive foreign interventions. By 2000, containment's defenders were wedged between an increasingly powerful inevitable decline case and the humanitarian critics who wanted to undo sanctions. They had to defend what was, in Senator Joseph Biden's words, "a very unsatisfying policy at an emotional level" that "lacks finality" but was "the best of three bad options available to us," compared to an invasion or normalization.[251] For Richard Haass, these limits inhered in containment, which "is not meant to be a solution. It is a mechanism for management."[252]

---

[251] Joseph Biden, *Cong. Rec.,* 105th Cong., 1st sess., February 12, 1998, 708.
[252] Richard Haass, "U.S. Objectives in Iraq: Rollback vs. Containment," March 6, 1998, Washington Institute for Near East Policy Forum with Richard Haass and William Kristol, accessed March 2, 2018, www.washingtoninstitute.org/policy-analysis/view/u.s.-objectives-in-iraq-rollback-vs.-containment.

Despite the entrenchment of the regime change consensus, certain questions remained unresolved at the end of Clinton's presidency. How could Saddam be removed without an invasion? Was it worth it to risk lives, money, and prestige to pursue regime change? How vital was his removal to national security and interests? A tense exchange between ILA sponsor Chuck Robb and Ahmed Chalabi in 1998 revealed the lingering uncertainties on these questions. Robb had grilled Chalabi on rollback and ultimately found the strategy unfeasible. He concluded: "The Iraqi people would be far better off in a post-Saddam environment than they are today. I do not think anyone would question that. The means to accomplish that objective are disputed."[253] This anecdote shows how the terms of debate on Iraq had narrowed to the means and urgency of regime change, which by no means meant the United States was destined for war. What was settled, at least in the perception of the majority of the political establishment, was that containment could not handle the Iraqi menace.

---

[253] Charles Robb, Senate Foreign Relations Committee, *Iraq: Can Saddam Be Overthrown?* March 2, 1998, 18.

5   Not Whether, but How and When: The Iraq Debate from 9/11 to the Invasion

Introduction

The September 11 attacks transformed both the stagnant Iraq debate and the broader US perception of the international security environment. They created a deep sense of vulnerability to mass casualty and Islamist terrorism, intensified public fear and anger, and widened the range of acceptable actions for assuring security. Preventing another attack became an overwhelming priority for the George W. Bush administration. The imperative to "do something" to prevent another attack was immense for this administration, which held itself responsible for the security of a shaken nation.

That this "something" would become an invasion of Iraq, however, was by no means inevitable or obvious despite the preexisting regime change consensus on Iraq. US and allied intelligence agencies did not link Iraq to 9/11 or establish a sudden Iraqi effort to reconstitute its weapons of mass destruction (WMD). Nor was there significant outcry from the public, US allies, or the military for targeting Iraq. Despite these realities, Vice President Dick Cheney, Defense Secretary Donald Rumsfeld, Undersecretary of Defense Paul Wolfowitz, and other Iraq hawks in the executive branch reoriented the response to 9/11 away from the direct culprits and toward Iraq. 9/11 served as both opening and impetus for this group to finally discredit containment and press for an invasion.

The core of the administration's argument was that removing Saddam in the short term had become necessary for preserving US security and preventing future terrorist attacks. Intelligence about Iraq had to be reevaluated, it argued, in the light of US exposure to mass casualty terrorism. The administration claimed that Saddam might hand WMD to terrorist groups like al-Qaeda to use against the United States or its allies. Building on the inevitable decline argument from the 1990s, it claimed that containment inherently could not address this "nexus" threat because Saddam could strike the United States by proxy and mask his responsibility, thus avoiding retaliation. Thus, the Bush administration claimed a unilateral right to use preventive force against states like Iraq. The nexus concept was not the administration's sole reason for pursuing regime change, but it did serve as its primary argument against containment. This argument became known as the "Bush Doctrine." To make the nexus a credible plank of its case for war, the administration systematically manipulated the intelligence process in order to create the perception that Iraq had or was developing these weapons and would use them against the United States, possibly through a terrorist ally.

Thus far, this story will appear familiar to scholars of modern US foreign policy. Indeed, the literature on the causal road from 9/11 to the Iraq War focuses on the importance of 9/11 in creating an atmosphere of fear and emphasizes the role of neoconservatives in reorienting US policy and manipulating intelligence.[1] Still, after bringing about this reorientation, Iraq hawks still had to build a successful public case for invasion. This required not only persuading the political establishment and the international community that the nexus threat was real but also that the main alternative of containment could not guarantee US security.

Existing work on the causes of the US decision to invade Iraq rarely examines the broader political and intellectual structures of debate.[2] In 2002 and early 2003, the administration's hawks faced some pushback and skepticism on this case from sources like the Democrats, some Republicans, Middle East policy experts, liberal intellectuals, major allies like Great Britain, and former policy-makers from both parties. Colin Powell and other officials at State reflected this skepticism inside the administration. This broad group believed that the intelligence on Iraq's WMD and links to al-Qaeda was less clear than the hawks asserted and that the administration did not take the challenges of occupation seriously. Most of all, they believed that before rushing into war Bush needed to present the evidence against Saddam, earn Congressional

---

[1] George Packer, *The Assassins' Gate: America in Iraq* (New York: Farrar, Straus, and Giroux, 2005); Lloyd Gardner, *The Long Road to Baghdad: A History of U.S. Foreign Policy from the 1970s to the Present* (New York: New Press, 2008); James Bamford, *A Pretext for War: 9/11, Iraq, and the Abuse of America's Intelligence Agencies* (New York: Doubleday, 2004).

[2] Packer, *Assassins' Gate;* Bamford, *Pretext for War;* Craig Unger, *The Fall of the House of Bush* (New York: Simon & Schuster, 2008); Stephen Kinzer, *Overthrow: America's Century of Regime Change from Hawaii to Iraq* (New York: Times Books, 2006); Christian Alfonsi, *Circle in the Sand: Why We Went Back to Iraq* (New York: Doubleday, 2006).

approval, and pass a UN resolution that would build a broad coalition while exhausting peaceful means of disarmament.

However, a closer look at these partial skeptics demonstrates that they shared most of the hawks' major assumptions about Iraq. Reflecting the entrenchment of the regime change consensus, these assumptions were: Iraq would remain a threat until Saddam's removal; the ultimate cause of Iraq's aggression and brutality was the totalitarian Baathist regime; Saddam would never cease pursuing WMD; inspections and sanctions could not fully disarm him or change his intentions; and only democratization could definitively solve the Iraq problem. These perceived lessons of containment in the 1990s delimited the terms of the Iraq debate from 9/11 to March 2003 and primed a wide swathe of Americans to believe Bush's worst-case portrayal of the threat.

This chapter's central point is that because the post-9/11, prewar conversation about Iraq mostly operated within these assumptions rather than challenging them, these ostensible skeptics of the war failed to develop a robust alternative to Bush's position. Most skeptics followed what Congressman Brad Sherman (D-CA) called the Powell–Blair approach, which focused on influencing how and when the administration confronted Iraq but ceded the point that regime change was ultimately necessary, ethical, and prudent.[3] Members of this Powell–Blair approach and the camp of open Iraq hawks like Rumsfeld and Wolfowitz both operated within the regime change consensus.

It may seem odd to lump British Prime Minister Tony Blair, an interventionist liberal, with Colin Powell, a realist-minded skeptic of US interventionism. However, although Blair was more enthusiastic about removing Saddam, he, Powell, and many other members of the US political establishment did not support a return to containment even though they disagreed with Bush on how to pursue regime change. In contrast, the dwindling number of conditionalist supporters of containment as well as the anti-war left both operated outside of the regime change consensus in that they contested the fundamental necessity, morality, and wisdom of invading Iraq, although the left did not support a return to containment. The prewar spectrum of thought on Iraq can thus be condensed to two large camps: those operating within the regime change consensus and those operating outside of it.

Self-identified skeptics, especially Powell and Blair, slowed down the push to war in September 2002 by persuading Bush to seek a UN

---

[3] Brad Sherman, House Committee on International Relations, *Authorization for Use of Military Force against Iraq*, 107th Cong., 2nd sess., October 2–3, 2002, 44.

Security Council resolution that demanded the return of inspections to Iraq and threatened Iraq with war if it did not comply.[4] They won another tactical victory in compelling Bush to seek a new Congressional authorization for war in October 2002. These tactical victories, however, were not about rebuilding containment; they were about making sure Bush pursued regime change "the right way": multi-laterally, procedurally, responsibly. In achieving these tactical gains, however, they granted their support to an administration that saw peaceful means of disarming Iraq as futile and made half-hearted efforts to pursue those means.

The entrenchment of the regime change consensus in US thinking on Iraq was such that even these partial skeptics shared the core assumption that for the United States to achieve security and protect its interests vis-à-vis Iraq, Saddam must be removed. While lacking the hawks' enthusiasm for regime change, they too believed inspections would falter and that any renewal of containment would relapse into the stasis of the 1990s while failing to address the root of the problem: the regime. Former National Security Advisor Sandy Berger summarized the Powell–Blair approach in saying: "Saddam was, is, and continues to be a menace to his people, to the region, and to us. He cannot be accommodated. Our goal should be regime change. The question is not whether, but how and when."[5]

Bush's Case for War, Fall 2001–Fall 2002

Bush entered office with little experience or knowledge on foreign policy or Iraq in particular. During the campaign, he had argued that the United States should play an active role in the world but that it should avoid using the military in nation-building exercises. He pledged to refocus US foreign policy on great power challengers and prevent multi-lateral institutions like the United Nations from shackling US power. He promised to be tougher on Iraq than Clinton, but he did not recommend any major breaks from Clinton's policy. Cheney and Rumsfeld, however, entered office with more hawkish and defined views on Iraq and a deeper commitment to an assertive, unilateral foreign policy. They also filled their staffs with neoconservatives who had supported regime change throughout the 1990s, including Wolfowitz, Douglas Feith as

---

[4] "United Nations Security Council Resolution 1441," November 8, 2002, in *The Iraq Papers*, ed. John Ehrenberg, J. Patrice McSherrey, Jose Sanchez, and Caroleen Sayej (New York: Oxford University Press, 2010), 97.

[5] Sandy Berger, Senate Foreign Relations Committee, *What's Next in the War on Terrorism*, 107th Cong., 2nd sess., February 7, 2002, 9.

Undersecretary of Defense for Policy, and Scooter Libby as Cheney's Chief of Staff.[6]

In contrast to Cheney and Rumsfeld, Powell and his Deputy Secretary of State, Richard Armitage, prioritized alliances and institutions and showed more skepticism about the use of force.[7] Powell hired defenders of containment like Richard Haass, who became Director of Policy Planning at State. Powell and Haass viewed Saddam as a "mid-level threat," and they held that reviving sanctions and inspections would restrain him.[8] At his 2001 nomination hearing before the Senate, Powell described Iraq as "fundamentally a broken, weak country, one-third the military force it had some ten years ago."[9] National Security Advisor Condoleezza Rice likewise recommended a moderate approach, arguing in 2000 that Iraq could be deterred by the threat of "national obliteration" even if it built a WMD arsenal.[10]

Upon taking office, the Bush administration initially focused on reviving sanctions on Iraq.[11] The administration believed that the United Nations would not support a tough inspections regime, which left reviving sanctions as the main way to constrain Saddam.[12] Intelligence reports in early 2001 warned that cheating on the embargo was rampant and that Iraq was also expanding diplomatic ties.[13] Powell aimed to shore up this leaking system through his "smart sanctions" plan. He wanted to refocus sanctions on preventing the entry of military and possible dual-use goods and on maintaining UN control of Iraqi revenues from Oil-For-Food sales.[14] In turn, the United Nations would permit more normal travel

---

[6] Ivo Daalder and James Lindsay, *America Unbound: The Bush Revolution in Foreign Policy* (Hoboken, NJ: Wiley, 2005), 37–40; James Mann, *Rise of the Vulcans: The History of Bush's War Cabinet* (New York: Viking, 2004), 256–258.

[7] Daalder and Lindsay, *America Unbound*, 56.

[8] Quote is from Richard Haass, *War of Necessity, War of Choice: A Memoir of Two Iraq Wars* (New York: Simon & Schuster, 2009), 180.

[9] Colin Powell, Senate Foreign Relations Committee, *Nomination of Colin Powell to be Secretary of State*, 107th Cong., 1st sess., January 17, 2001, 63.

[10] Condoleezza Rice, "Promoting the National Interest," *Foreign Affairs* 79, no. 1 (January, 2000): 61.

[11] Eric Schmitt and Steven Lee Myers, "Bush Administration Warns Iraq on Weapons Programs," *New York Times*, January 23, 2001, A1; Nicholas Lemann, "How It Came to War," March 31, 2003, www.newyorker.com/magazine/2003/03/31/how-it-came-to-war.

[12] Haass, *War of Necessity*, 174–175.

[13] CIA Report, Office of Near Eastern and South Asian Analysis, "Iraq: Restoring Diplomatic Representation in Baghdad," February 6, 2001, Digital National Security Archive, Targeting Iraq Part 1, 3; Cable, Unknown Source to Colin Powell, "The Possibility and Implications of Iraq Breaking Out of International Sanctions," February 6, 2001, Digital National Security Archive, Targeting Iraq Part 1,1–3.

[14] Read Ahead Document, "NSC Principals Meeting-Iraq," February 20, 2001, Digital National Security Archive, Targeting Iraq Part 1, 1.

and commerce with Iraq. Powell reasoned that if sanctions could be tapered, containment would be strengthened and Saddam could no longer credibly blame the sanctions for the Iraqi health crisis.[15] Powell further hoped that this deal would discourage sanctions-busting by allowing foreign countries to trade with Iraq while preventing Saddam from importing military or WMD-related items and from accessing the proceeds of trade.[16]

To Powell's chagrin, smart sanctions failed to garner sufficient support at the United Nations. Russia and France posed the main obstacles because they received billions in oil-for-food trade with Iraq and wanted to suspend sanctions as soon as inspectors were merely readmitted into Iraq – a position the United States rejected.[17] Iraq's neighbors also benefitted from cheap, illicit Iraqi oil and feared the public reaction if they granted support to renewed sanctions.[18] Under the threat of a Russian veto, Powell abandoned the effort to reform sanctions, returning the coalition to a stalemate.[19]

The administration's hawks, meanwhile, did little to shift Iraq policy in these first nine months. Douglas Feith's office drafted "A Strategy to Liberate Iraq" in the spring, which called for a serious effort at rollback under INC leadership. Arguing that containment was doomed to "inevitably weaken over time," they called for US air power to protect an insurgency against Saddam.[20] As in the late 1990s, rollback represented the outer limits of what policy-makers could call for as a means of regime change. Wolfowitz also pushed for rollback and argued that Iraqi-sponsored terrorism was an immediate threat, but Powell and the CIA responded that covert action and/or an insurgency had virtually no chance of toppling Saddam.[21] Despite these disputes, there simply was not a tremendous level of urgency on Iraq in the first nine months of

---

[15] Jane Perlez, "Powell Proposes Easing Sanctions on Iraqi Civilians," *New York Times*, February 27, 2001; Thomas Ricks, *Fiasco: The American Military Adventure in Iraq* (New York: Penguin Press, 2006), 28.

[16] Karen DeYoung, *Soldier: The Life of Colin Powell* (New York: Knopf, 2006), 313–314.

[17] Meghan O'Sullivan, *Shrewd Sanctions: Statecraft and State Sponsors of Terrorism* (Washington, DC: Brookings Institution Press, 2003), 134–136; Jane Perlez, "Plan to Modify U.N. Sanctions against Iraq Bogs Down," *New York Times*, June 30, 2001, A3.

[18] Neil King, "New Iraq Sanctions Are Short on Support," *Wall Street Journal*, June 18, 2001, A15.

[19] Barbara Crossette, "Effort to Recast Iraq Oil Sanctions Is Halted for Now," *New York Times*, July 3, 2001, A1.

[20] Memorandum, Special Assistant to the Secretary for Policy to Office of Undersecretary of Defense, "Iraq Strategy Paper: A Strategy to Liberate Iraq," April 23, 2001, Digital National Security Archive, Targeting Iraq Part 1, 1–9.

[21] DeYoung, *Soldier*, 348; Bob Woodward, *Plan of Attack* (New York: Simon & Schuster, 2004), 22–23.

Bush's presidency.[22] Other crises and priorities held the administration's attention, including the Hainan Island incident, Rumsfeld's campaigns for military modernization, and domestic goals like tax cuts.[23] Regime change advocates in political circles lamented Bush's Iraq policy as a betrayal of the Iraq Liberation Act.[24] Bush ordered an interagency review of Iraq policy, which was ongoing on 9/11.[25] Rumsfeld fittingly summarized this policy drift in a note to Powell on September 5, 2001: "We simply must get a policy for Iraq settled fast."[26]

The September 11 terrorist attacks dramatically raised the nation's sense of vulnerability and created a massive impetus to retaliate against the perpetrators and prevent further attacks. An anguished sense of guilt and responsibility set in after the attacks, as Rice affirmed: "I could not have forgiven myself had there been another attack."[27] They felt that their jobs had suddenly transformed and that other responsibilities had melted away. As they watched civilians jumping from skyscrapers, they felt deep grief and anger, as did the rest of the country.[28] Bush reportedly told Rumsfeld on 9/11: "I don't care what the international lawyers say, we are going to kick some ass."[29] Bush adopted a morally unambiguous view of terrorism, calling al-Qaeda "flat evil. That's all they can think about, is evil."[30]

With the intelligence agencies now on high alert, the administration was bombarded with reports of possible follow-up attacks, including attempts to decapitate the government. As CIA Director George Tenet remembered: "It seemed inconceivable to us that Bin Laden had not

---

[22] Michael Mazarr, *Leap of Faith: Hubris, Negligence, and America's Greatest Foreign Policy Tragedy* (New York: Public Affairs, 2019), 82–85, 90–92.

[23] Fred Kaplan, *Daydream Believers: How a Few Grand Ideas Wrecked American Power* (Hoboken, NJ: Wiley & Sons, 2008), 98–111; Michael Gordon and Bernard Trainor, *Cobra II: The Inside Story of the Invasion and Occupation of Iraq* (New York: Pantheon Books, 2006), 8–9.

[24] Memorandum, Tom Donnelly of Project for a New American Century to Opinion Leaders, "Liberate Iraq," July 6, 2001, Digital National Security Archive, Targeting Iraq Part 1, 1; Reuel Marc Gerecht, May 14, 2001, 23; Ahmed Chalabi, "We Can Topple Saddam," *Wall Street Journal*, May 21, 2001, A22.

[25] Mazarr, *Leap of Faith*, 93.

[26] Memorandum, Donald Rumsfeld to Colin Powell, CC Richard Cheney and Condoleezza Rice, "Iraq," September 5, 2001, Digital National Security Archive, Targeting Iraq Part 1, 1.

[27] Condoleezza Rice, *No Higher Honor: A Memoir of My Years in Washington* (New York: Crown Publishers, 2011), 121.

[28] Melvyn Leffler, "The Foreign Policies of the George W. Bush Administration: Memoirs, History, Legacy," *Diplomatic History* 37, no. 2 (April, 2013): 194.

[29] Richard Clarke, *Against All Enemies: Inside America's War on Terror* (New York: Free Press, 2004), 24; Ron Suskind, *The One Percent Doctrine: Deep Inside America's Pursuit of Its Enemies since 9/11* (New York: Simon & Schuster, 2006), 15.

[30] Peter Baker, *Days of Fire: Bush and Cheney in the White House* (New York: Anchor Books, 2013), 158.

already positioned people to conduct second, and possibly third and fourth waves of attacks."[31] The Secret Service even rushed the president and Laura Bush from their beds to a bunker on the night of 9/11 because an F-16 fighter had activated the wrong transponder code, making it look like a hijacked plane.[32] Though 9/11 led to a surge of popular support for the president, the administration judged that a second massive attack would doom Bush in political terms.[33]

The administration initially held that the reaction to 9/11 should center on al-Qaeda and its main sponsor, the Taliban regime in Afghanistan. However, first-hand testimony and some documentary evidence show that Iraq hawks argued that Iraq may have been involved in 9/11 attacks and that it should be a major target in the US response. Some scholars have accused these hawks of using 9/11 as a pretext to reorient US policy toward their preexisting fixation on Iraq regardless of the evidence.[34] A more balanced view suggests that 9/11 added greater urgency for action against what they already viewed as a serious threat by lowering their willingness to tolerate this threat and changing their view of the entire international security environment.

Rumsfeld and Wolfowitz led the effort to immediately focus on Iraq in response to 9/11. Rumsfeld's notes from 9/11 read: "Best info fast. Judge whether good enough [to] hit SH [Saddam Hussein] at same time-not only UBL."[35] Wolfowitz wrote to Rumsfeld after the attacks: "If there is even a 10% chance that Saddam Hussein was behind Tuesday's horrors, a maximum priority has to be put on eliminating that threat."[36] On multiple occasions in the week after 9/11, they suggested to Bush and other members of the Cabinet that Saddam may have been involved in 9/11. Even if he was not, they claimed that toppling Saddam would deter other rogue states with WMD.[37] Hugh Shelton, the Chairman of the Joint

---

[31] Leffler, "Foreign Policies," 195.   [32] Baker, *Days of Fire*, 131.

[33] Leffler, "Foreign Policies," 194.

[34] For examples, see Paul Pillar, *Intelligence and U.S. Foreign Policy: Iraq, 9/11, and Misguided Reform* (New York: Columbia University Press, 2011), 15–17; Andrew Bacevich, *America's War for the Greater Middle East: A Military History* (New York: Random House, 2016), 225, 249; Bamford, *A Pretext for War*, 269; Stephen Kinzer, *Overthrow: America's Century of Regime Change from Hawaii to Iraq* (New York: Times Books, 2006), 290–293.

[35] Julian Borger, "Blogger Bares Rumsfeld's Post-9/11 Orders," February 26, 2006, theguardian.com, accessed October 18, 2018, https://www.theguardian.com/world/2006/f eb/24/freedomofinformation.september11.

[36] David Crist, *The Twilight War: The Secret History of America's Thirty-Year Conflict with Iran* (New York: Penguin Press, 2012), 425. See also Memorandum, Paul Wolfowitz to Donald Rumsfeld, "War on Terror-Coordination with Joint Staff," September 17, 2001, Digital National Security Archive, Targeting Iraq Part 1, 1.

[37] DeYoung, *Soldier*, 352; Ron Suskind, *The Price of Loyalty: George W. Bush, the White House, and the Education of Paul O'Neill* (New York: Simon & Schuster, 2004), 184–187;

Chiefs of Staff, recalled: "Rumsfeld and Wolfowitz started pushing really hard on September 12, '01 to attack Iraq." They even asked Shelton to raise Iraq as a possible target at the next Cabinet meeting.[38] Other neoconservatives in the administration, especially Douglas Feith and Scooter Libby, frequently advocated for striking Iraq immediately after 9/11.[39] Bush appears to have been somewhat persuaded by this early push, as he asked counterterrorism expert Richard Clarke on September 12 to "[s]ee if Saddam did this. See if he's linked in any way."[40] He also told Tony Blair on September 13: "There might be a connection between Saddam Hussein and Osama bin Laden."[41] Treasury Secretary Paul O'Neill recalled that just a few days after 9/11 "[g]etting Hussein was now the administration's focus, that much was already clear."[42]

While the early advocates of an attack on Iraq were a minority in the Bush administration, their views were echoed by powerful advocates of regime change in broader political discourse. On September 20, PNAC published an open letter to the president that read: "[E]ven if evidence does not link Iraq directly to the attack, any strategy aiming at the eradication of terrorism and its sponsors must include a determined effort to remove Saddam Hussein from power."[43] On December 6, Bush received a letter from nine prominent legislators, including Trent Lott, Joseph Liebermann, and John McCain. They similarly argued that "the nexus of terrorism and weapons of mass destruction makes the removal of Saddam key to success in the overall war on terrorism." They reassured

---

Douglas Feith, *War and Decision: Inside the Pentagon at the Dawn of the War on Terrorism* (New York: Harper Collins, 2008) 49–51; Mazarr, *Leap of Faith*, 158–162.

[38] Hugh Shelton, interview by Russell Riley, May 29, 2007, William J. Clinton Presidential History Project, Miller, Center, 94. See corroborating testimonies by Clarke, *Against All Enemies*, 30–33; Haass, *War of Necessity*, 192; Baker, *Days of Fire*, 140.

[39] Feith, *War and Decision*, 52; Crist, *Twilight War*, 425; Glenn Kessler, "U.S. Decision on Iraq Has Puzzling Past," *Washington Post*, January 12, 2003, A1.

[40] Clarke, *Against all Enemies*, 32.

[41] Douglas Little, *Us versus Them: The United States, Radical Islam, and the Rise of the Green Threat* (Chapel Hill: The University of North Carolina Press, 2016), 156.

[42] Suskind, *The Price of Loyalty*, 75.

[43] Letter, Project for a New American Century to George Bush, September 20, 2001, Digital National Security Archive, Targeting Iraq Part 1, 1–2. Signers included William Kristol, Robert Kagan, Eliot Cohen, Francis Fukuyama, Charles Krauthammer, Richard Perle, and Stephen Solarz. For others who called for an early focus on Iraq after 9/11, see Editorial, "War Aims," *Wall Street Journal*, September 20, 2001; William Safire, "The Ultimate Enemy," *New York Times*, September 24, 2001, A31; Elaine Sciolino and Patrick Tyler, "Some Pentagons Officials and Advisers Seek to Oust Iraq's Leader in War's Next Phase," *New York Times*, October 12, 2001, B6; R. James Woolsey, "The Iraq Connection," *New York Times*, October 18, 2001, A26; Kanan Makiya, "Help the Iraqis Take Their Country Back," *New York Times*, November 21, 2001, A19.

Bush that "there will be bipartisan political support for the president when he moves on to the next crucial phase of the war."[44] There was also broad public suspicion of Saddam even before the administration began its public push for war, demonstrated by one poll from January 2002 that found that 76 percent of respondents believed that Saddam supported al-Qaeda and 72 percent said it was very or somewhat likely that he was "personally involved in the September 11 attacks."[45] Still, most of the early post-9/11 calls for focusing on Iraq came from the usual suspects: long-standing and passionate advocates of regime change. No wave of public or international calls for Saddam's removal emerged after 9/11, making the neoconservatives' role in putting Iraq on the agenda essential for understanding the road to invasion.

This early push to focus on Iraq failed to convince the rest of the Cabinet. Powell and Shelton opposed this move, arguing that Iraq was not connected to these attacks and that any shift to Iraq would undermine the international coalition for the fight against al-Qaeda.[46] Cheney agreed and argued that any move against Iraq should be postponed.[47] Despite his query to Clarke, Bush saw al-Qaeda as the perpetrators and the proper first targets of the War on Terror. He asked Wolfowitz and Rumsfeld to wait on Iraq, although he told several people that he would soon return to Iraq.[48] In the fall of 2001, Bush launched a war against the Taliban and al-Qaeda in Afghanistan, which he conceived as the first phase of a broader War on Terror that would tackle the actors and structural forces that sustained global terrorism.[49]

In the months after 9/11 Bush and his administration formed a new conception of how to combat mass terrorism that set the groundwork for a revived focus on Iraq. More passive, long-term strategies of containment and deterrence appeared woefully inadequate against terrorists that hurtled themselves into buildings to achieve maximized devastation.[50]

---

[44] Memorandum, William Kristol to Opinion Leaders, December 6, 2001, IraqWatch.org, accessed March 6, 2018, http://web.archive.org/web/200312230955103/http://www.ne wamericancentury.org/congress-120601.htm.

[45] Baker, *Days of Fire*, 190.

[46] Miller Center Interview with Hugh Shelton, William J. Clinton Presidential History Project, May 29, 2007, Interview by Russell Riley, 94; Hugh Shelton, *Without Hesitation: The Odyssey of an American Warrior* (New York: St. Martin's Press, 2019), 444; Bamford, *A Pretext for War*, 268.

[47] Bob Woodward and Dan Balz, "At Camp David, Advise and Dissent," *Washington Post*, January 31, 2002, A1.

[48] National Commission on Terrorist Attacks upon the United States, *The 9/11 Commission Report* (New York: W. W. Norton, 2011), 335; Mazarr, *Leap of Faith*, 175–176; Baker, *Days of Fire*, 150.

[49] *9/11 Commission Report*, 334; Leffler, "Foreign Policies," 198.

[50] Richard Cheney, *In My Time: A Personal and Political Memoir* (New York: Threshold Editions, 2011), 388.

The administration, however, did not think that focusing on terrorist groups alone would eliminate the threat. Terrorists did not operate in a vacuum, they reasoned, but in the territories of state sponsors. To truly eradicate this menace, as Rumsfeld argued, the United States would have to "support the creation of an international political environment hostile to terrorism to dissuade individuals, non-state actors, and states from entering into or initiating support for terrorism."[51]

The only contingency that could make a follow-up attack worse, Bush officials reasoned, was if al-Qaeda gained access to WMD. The anthrax attacks in October enhanced the fear that a rogue actor like Iraq might give biological or other unconventional weapons to terrorists.[52] Thus, the second phase of the War on Terror must focus on state sponsors of terrorism.[53] While top officials disagreed about targeting Iraq early on, they concurred that tackling state sponsors was necessary for preventing future attacks.[54] In a press conference on September 13, Wolfowitz signaled this shift in saying that "it's not just simply a matter of capturing people and holding them accountable, but removing the sanctuaries, removing the support systems, ending states who sponsor terrorism."[55]

The state sponsor paradigm for the War on Terror served as the basis for the Bush administration's shift back toward Iraq in late 2001 and early 2002. The administration formulated a case for war with Iraq that hinged on what it called the "nexus" between rogue states, WMD, and terrorists. Rice illustrated this concept: "Terrorists allied with tyrants can acquire technologies allowing them to murder on an ever more massive scale. Each threat magnifies the danger of the other."[56] While al-Qaeda, the administration argued, would certainly use WMD on US targets, it

---

[51] Memorandum, Donald Rumsfeld to Joint Chiefs of Staff, Secretaries of the Military Departments, Combatants Commanders, Assistant Secretaries, "Strategic Guidance for the Campaign against Terrorism," October 3, 2001, US Intelligence in the Middle East Database, accessed April 13, 2018, http://primarysources.brillonline.com/reader/open?rotate=1&searchTerms=iraq&starEnabled=1&shareLink, 6.

[52] Kessler, "Puzzling Past," *Washington Post*, January 12, 2003; George W. Bush, *Decision Points* (New York: Crown Publishers, 2010), 229.

[53] Rice, *Higher Honor*, 148; For other early supporters of the state sponsor paradigm, see Jim Hoagland, "Hidden Hand of Horror," *Washington Post*, September 12, 2001, A31; Charles Krauthammer, "To War, Not to Court," *Washington Post*, September 12, 2001, A29; William Kristol and Robert Kagan, "The Right War," *The Weekly Standard*, October 1, 2001, 9.

[54] Bush, *Decision Points*, 137.

[55] Julian Borger, "Washington's Hawk Trains Sights on Iraq," September 25, 2001, theguardian.com, accessed January 26, 2019, www.theguardian.com/world/2001/sep/26/iraq.afghanistan.

[56] Condoleezza Rice, "Wriston Lecture," October 1, 2002, American Presidency Project, accessed July 23, 2018, www.presidency.ucsb.edu/ws/index.php?pid=79793&st=iraq&st1=; George Bush, "State of the Union Address," January 29, 2002, in Ehrenberg, McSherrey, Sanchez, and Sayej, *The Iraq Papers*, 60.

probably lacked the capacity to produce them. Moreover, rogue states by themselves could not strike the United States or their neighbors because of the certainty of massive retaliation.

However, if a rogue state handed WMD to terrorists, each side would offset the other's weaknesses and help the other achieve their goals. Terrorists would acquire the means to inflict mass casualties while rogue states could inflict damage on countries like the United States without leaving clear evidence of their culpability.[57] The administration argued that through this behavior rogue states forfeited their sovereignty, justifying military action to remove the threat.[58] Moreover, the administration argued that the margin of error with biological weapons was particularly low because a small, easily transportable vial of anthrax or smallpox could kill thousands. Even if the evidence was lacking that rogue states and terrorists were collaborating in these ways, key administration figures like Cheney believed that after 9/11 the United States had to assume that such contingencies were real rather than leave the country exposed to another massive attack.[59]

The Bush administration identified Iraq as the most dangerous state actor within this category of threat. Cheney later claimed: "When we looked around the world in those first months after 9/11, there was no place more likely to be a nexus between terrorism and WMD capability than Saddam's Iraq."[60] However, this shift rested on a deeper foundation of ideas and assumptions about Iraq held by key policy-makers before 9/11. Despite the more advanced nuclear programs of Iran and North Korea, there had been no equivalent for these states of the political movement that led to the Iraq Liberation Act, nor had United States recently fought a war with these states. Moreover, as Feith argued, the administration felt that all possible means of ending the Iraqi threat had been "tried comprehensively, and without success, for a decade," whereas the United States had not applied similar pressures to Iran and North Korea.[61]

Bush explained why Iraq in particular needed to be targeted in October 2002: "By its past and present actions, by its technological capabilities, by the merciless nature of its regime, Iraq is unique," citing its use of chemical weapons in the 1980s and its invasions of Iran and

---

[57] George W. Bush, "Graduation Speech at West Point," June 1, 2002, in Ehrenberg, McSherrey, Sanchez, and Sayej, *The Iraq Papers*, 66; Bush, *Decision Points*, 229.

[58] Feith, *War and Decision*, 296.

[59] Suskind, *The One Percent Doctrine*, 62; "Transcript: Confronting the Iraqi Threat 'Is Crucial to Winning War on Terror,'" *New York Times*, October 8, 2002, A12; "Transcript: President's State of the Union Message to Congress and the Nation," *New York Times*, January 29, 2003, A12.

[60] Cheney, *In My Time*, 369.   [61] Feith, *War and Decision*, 233.

Kuwait.[62] The assertion that Iraq posed a more advanced threat than Iran or North Korea ignored the greater progress of these nations on WMD and ballistic missiles. However, the "lessons" about containment had become entrenched in US thinking about Iraq in ways that had not occurred with these states, which had received far less political attention throughout the 1990s. Iraq came to be broadly seen as uniquely uncontainable because of its totalitarian ideology, its unalterable desire to acquire WMD, and the intransigent personality of its dictator. Key players in the pre-9/11 movement against containment, especially Rumsfeld and Wolfowitz, advanced these ideas within the administration and maintained a drumbeat against Iraq after 9/11.[63]

When exactly Iraq returned to the forefront of the Bush administration's focus is not entirely clear because of the limits on available sources and the apparent lack of an organized decision-making process in the administration.[64] In November 2001, Bush asked Rumsfeld to start developing war plans for Iraq, and in February he asked CENTCOM Commander Tommy Franks to start moving forces from Afghanistan to the Persian Gulf.[65] In public, Bush demanded that inspectors be allowed back into Iraq in November and then identified Iraq as part of the "Axis of Evil" in January 2002.[66] He also told an interviewer, "I've made up my mind that Saddam needs to go" in April 2002.[67] By June, when Richard Haass approached Rice to express his concerns about a possible war, Rice replied: "You can save your breath, Richard. The president has already made up his mind on Iraq."[68] Most accounts suggest that by the spring of 2002 the administration had determined to press for a confrontation with Iraq, and by the early summer of 2002, they were publicly arguing for regime change.

This case for war depended on the idea that most likely alternative policies, containment and deterrence, could not handle the nexus category of threat. Deterrence, they argued, relied on the enemy's rationality, desire to survive, and the certainty that any attack on the United States would prompt massive retaliation. The United States succeeded in

---

[62] Bush, "Confronting Iraq Threat," *New York Times*, October 8, 2002. See also George W. Bush, "Speech to the U.N. General Assembly," September 12, 2002, in *The Iraq War Reader: History, Documents, Opinions*, ed. Micah Sifry and Christopher Cerf (New York: Touchstone Books, 2003), 314; Feith, *War and Decision*, 181.

[63] Crist, *Twilight War*, 427; DeYoung, *Soldier*, 375.

[64] Pillar, *Intelligence and U.S. Foreign Policy*, 15.

[65] Woodward, *Plan of Attack*, 30; For more on war planning, see Gordon and Trainor, *Cobra II*, 75–118; Donald Rumsfeld, *Known and Unknown: A Memoir* (New York: Sentinel, 2011), 425.

[66] Daalder and Lindsay, *America Unbound*, 131.

[67] Kessler, "Puzzling Past," *Washington Post*, January 12, 2003; Suskind, *The One Percent Doctrine*, 70–75.

[68] Haass, *War of Necessity*, 214.

deterring Soviet use of WMD during the Cold War because the Soviets possessed these traits.[69] However, terrorist groups like al-Qaeda lacked both the desire to survive and territory or infrastructure to retaliate against. Bush officials also questioned Saddam's rationality; at the minimum, he was a reckless gambler cut off from reality, and at the maximum, he was irrational. As Wolfowitz argued, "the containment case assumes that we understand the way his mind works and that he will always avoid actions that would endanger his survival, even though there is an enormous body of evidence that we do not understand the way his mind works."[70] Bush officials believed, moreover, that terrorists and tyrants were provoked by weakness, and that the faltering US response to attacks since the 1980s had convinced al-Qaeda and Saddam that, in Scooter Libby's words, "[t]he Americans don't have the stomach to defend themselves. ... They are morally weak."[71] Containment would only reinforce that perception of docility and encourage more attacks. Containment and deterrence were far too passive for an administration whose risk tolerance had been drastically lowered by 9/11.[72]

In an address at West Point in June 2002, Bush spelled out his argument that containment was steadily collapsing, that it had failed to compel Saddam to comply with the United Nations, and that it could not prevent Saddam from building WMD or covertly handing them to terrorists. He claimed:

Deterrence – the promise of massive retaliation against nations – means nothing against shadowy terrorist networks with no nation or citizens to defend. Containment is not possible when unbalanced dictators with weapons of mass destruction can deliver those weapons on missiles or secretly provide them to terrorist allies.[73]

---

[69] Condoleezza Rice and George W. Bush, "The National Security Strategy of the United States of America," September 2002, in Ehrenberg, McSherrey, Sanchez, and Sayej, *The Iraq Papers*, 83; John Lewis Gaddis, *Surprise, Security, and the American Experience* (Cambridge, MA: Harvard University Press, 2004), 70.

[70] Paul Wolfowitz, "Remarks by Paul Wolfowitz," October 16, 2002, IraqWatch.org, accessed July 10, 2018, www.iraqwatch.org/government/US/Pentagon/dod-wolfowtiz-1 01602.htm. See also Lawrence Kaplan and William Kristol, *The War Over Iraq: Saddam's Tyranny and America's Mission* (San Francisco, CA: Encounter Books, 2003), 82–83.

[71] Nicholas Lemann, "The Next World Order," *The New Yorker*, April 1, 2002, 77. For arguments that parallel Libby's claim, see Reuel Marc Gerecht, "Crushing al-Qaeda Is Only a Start," *Wall Street Journal*, December 19, 2001, A18; Max Boot, "The End of Appeasement," *The Weekly Standard*, February 10, 2003, 21; Bernard Lewis, "Did You Say 'American Imperialism?'" *The National Review*, December 17, 2001, 27; Norman Podhoretz, "How to Win World War IV," *Commentary*, February 7, 2002, 20.

[72] Hal Brands, *What Good Is Grand Strategy: Power and Purpose in American Statecraft from Harry S. Truman to George W. Bush* (Ithaca, NY: Cornell University Press, 2014), 158–159.

[73] Bush, "Speech at West Point," June 1, 2002, 65–66. See also "In Cheney's Words: The Administration's Case for Removing Saddam Hussein," *New York Times*, August 27,

Even if Saddam did not hand WMD to terrorists, he could still use them to bully his neighbors and deter a US response.[74] Bush thus saw the containment of Iraq as both a broken policy and something that even if revived could not fulfill perceived US security needs following 9/11.

The administration also argued that the United States might need to launch "preemptive" attacks on WMD-armed state sponsors of terrorism. According to philosophical and legal tradition, preemption is justified when an enemy's attack is imminent, revealed by active preparation, likely to be destructive, and unstoppable by nonviolent means.[75] A preventive war, in contrast, seeks to destroy a possible threat and/or prevent a shift in the balance of power between two states.[76] While "imminence" is hard to prove, legitimate preemptive wars are generally accepted in international politics while preventive wars are considered unlawful aggression.

The Bush administration, however, argued that the nexus threat demanded a rethinking of the concept of imminence. In past cases of preemption like the 1967 Arab–Israeli War, the threatened state could see the enemy's conventional military preparations and hear their bellicose rhetoric. Terrorists, in contrast, planned secretly and used "weapons that can be easily concealed, delivered covertly, and used without warning."[77] Clear, "smoking gun" evidence of collusion between rogue states and terrorists might come only in the form of a "mushroom cloud" from an attack, as Bush officials often repeated.[78] The United States could not consistently preempt attacks it did not see coming, which means it had to stop state sponsors of terror from developing or possessing those weapons in the first place.[79] The Bush Doctrine endorsed preventive war based on the need to "adapt the concept of 'imminent threat' to contemporary realities" and the enormous consequences of

2002, A8; Bradley Graham, "Containment Has Not Eased the Iraqi Threat," *Washington Post*, August 10, 2002, A5.

[74] Rice and Bush, "National Security Strategy," September 2002, 82; Feith, *War and Decision*, 215; Woodward, *Plan of Attack*, 27.

[75] Michael Walzer, *Just and Unjust Wars: A Moral Argument with Historical Illustrations* (New York: Basic Books, 2006), 81–85; Karl Zemanek, "Armed Attack," October 2013, opil.ouplaw.com, accessed November 2, 2018, http://opil.ouplaw.com/view/10.1093/law:epil/9780199231690/law-9780199231690-e241.

[76] Walzer, *Just and Unjust Wars*, 76–77; Lawrence Freedman, "Prevention, Not Preemption," *The Washington Quarterly* 26, no. 2 (March, 2003): 106.

[77] Rice and Bush, "National Security Strategy," September 2002, 83. See also Rice, "Wriston Lecture," October 1, 2002; Bush, "President's State of the Union," *New York Times*, January 29, 2003.

[78] Todd Purdum, "Bush Officials Say the Time Has Come for Action on Iraq," *New York Times*, September 9, 2002, A1.

[79] G. John Ikenberry, "America's Imperial Ambition," *Foreign Affairs* 81, no. 5 (September–October, 2002): 52; Freedman, "Preemption," 108.

missing just one attack.[80] As Rumsfeld put it: "Any who insist on perfect evidence are back in the 20th century and still thinking in pre-September 11 terms."[81]

This reorientation toward Iraq also relied in large part on errors in the intelligence community's assessments of Iraq's WMD programs. The 2002 National Intelligence Estimate (NIE) assessed that Saddam possessed chemical and biological weapons as well as ballistic missiles beyond what the United Nations permitted.[82] The intelligence community also judged that Saddam was pursuing nuclear weapons, although he was five to seven years from possessing such a weapon.[83] Most independent analysts and US allies, including countries that were skeptical of the invasion, also thought that Iraq was developing WMD and ballistic missiles.[84] These assessments were shown to be almost entirely inaccurate after the war.[85] Several post-2003 Congressional reports have shown the flaws in the intelligence community's analysis, which included inadequately explaining ambiguities to policy-makers and relying too much on outdated or poorly vetted information. Furthermore, many analysts recalled that the United States had severely underestimated the scope of the Iraqi WMD program before the Gulf War, and they wanted to avoid that mistake in 2002–2003.[86]

[80] Quote is from Rice, *Higher Honor*, 154; see also Gaddis, *Surprise, Security*, 85–87.

[81] Donald Rumsfeld, Senate Armed Services Committee, *U.S. Policy on Iraq*, 107th Cong., 2nd sess., September 19, 2002, 22. For background, see Robert Jervis, "Understanding the Bush Doctrine," *Political Science Quarterly* 118, no. 3 (Fall, 2003): 365–388; James Steinberg, "Preventive Force in US National Security Strategy," *Survival* 47, no. 4 (Winter, 2005–2006): 55–72.

[82] National Intelligence Estimate, "Iraq's Continuing Programs for Weapons of Mass Destruction," October 2002, Digital National Security Archive, Targeting Iraq Part 1, 5–6.

[83] National Intelligence Council Report, "Iraq's Weapons of Mass Destruction Programs," July 2002, Digital National Security Archive, Targeting Iraq Part 1, 7.

[84] The Iraq Inquiry, also known as the Chilcott Report, extensively documents British mistakes regarding WMD-related intelligence on Iraq. See House of Commons, "Report of the Iraq Inquiry," July 6, 2016, Vol. 4, accessed September 25, 2018, http s://webarchive.nationalarchives.gov.uk/20171123122743/http://www.iraqinquiry.org.u k/the-report/. See also Robert Jervis, *Why Intelligence Fails: Lessons from the Iranian Revolution and the Iraq War* (Ithaca, NY: Cornell University Press, 2010), 130–132.

[85] The following report is known as the Duelfer Report: Department of Central Intelligence, Iraq Survey Group, *Key Findings*, September 30, 2004, cia.gov, accessed July 15, 2018, www.cia.gov/library/reports/general-reports-1/iraq_wmd_2004/, 1–5; See also Senate Select Committee on Intelligence, *Postwar Findings about Iraq's WMD Programs and Links to Terrorism and How They Compare with Prewar Assessments*, 109th Cong., 2nd sess., September 8, 2006, S. Report 109–331, 14–16.

[86] Senate Select Committee on Intelligence, *Report on the U.S. Intelligence Community's Prewar Intelligence Assessments on Iraq*, 108th Cong., 2nd sess., July 7, 2004, especially 16, 24; Report to the President, *The Commission on the Intelligence Capabilities of the United States Regarding Weapons of Mass Destruction*, March 31, 2005, fas.org, accessed July 17,

These postwar reports largely excused Bush officials from their manipulation and misrepresentation of intelligence about Iraq's WMD and terrorist ties.[87] This manipulation took several forms. For one, the administration created alternative channels of intelligence gathering and analysis outside the normal intelligence agencies, which Cheney, Rumsfeld, and Wolfowitz believed had systematically underestimated the Iraqi threat since the Gulf War. Douglas Feith's Policy Counterterrorism Evaluation Group (PCTEG) and the Office of Special Plans (OSP) were created to, among other things, amass intelligence that linked Iraq to al-Qaeda and disseminate it throughout the executive branch.[88]

PCTEG and the OSP were staffed by neoconservatives with little intelligence experience but a clear political agenda. One staffer, David Wurmser, had written a book in the late 1990s calling for regime change in Iraq.[89] These offices filtered poorly vetted information from exile groups like the INC into the upper echelons of the administration.[90] They also provided "red team" or "B-team" analyses that criticized the intelligence agencies for not drawing more strident conclusions about Iraq.[91] Furthermore, numerous analysts have reported significant if not blatant pressure from Cheney, Rumsfeld, and others. This included repeated requests to look into pieces of evidence that would corroborate the case for war, unprecedented visits from Cheney and other top officials

2018, https://fas.org/irp/offdocs/wmd_report.pdf, 157–191; Gordon and Trainor, *Cobra II*, 132–133.

[87] The Robb–Silberman Report, for instance, "found no indication that the Intelligence Community distorted evidence regarding Iraq's weapons of mass destruction." See Report to the President, *Commission on the Intelligence Capabilities of the United States*, March 31, 2005, 1. Bush officials also made this assertion. See Rumsfeld, *Known and Unknown*, 432; Feith, *War and Decision*, 269.

[88] Bryan Burrough, Evgenia Peretz, David Rose, and David Wise, "The Path to War," *Vanity Fair*, December 19, 2008, accessed September 25, 2018, www.vanityfair.com/news/2004/05/path-to-war200405; Jeffrey Goldberg, "A Little Learning," *The New Yorker*, May 9, 2005, 55. For an example of a misleading and exaggerated PCTEG briefing, see Briefing, Department of Defense, "Assessing the Relationship between Iraq and al-Qaeda," September 16, 2002, US Intelligence in the Middle East, accessed September 25, 2002.

[89] David Wurmser, *Tyranny's Ally: America's Failure to Defeat Saddam Hussein* (Washington, DC: AEI Press, 1999).

[90] See Richard Bonin, *Arrows of the Night: Ahmad Chalabi's Long Journey to Triumph in Iraq* (New York: Doubleday, 2011), 190–203; Seymour Hersh, "The Stovepipe," *The New Yorker*, October 27, 2003, 78–83; Jane Mayer, "The Manipulator," *The New Yorker*, June 7, 2004, 60–65.

[91] For a high-level request for a "red team" report, see Memorandum, Donald Rumsfeld to Douglas Feith, "Iraq's WMD," July 19, 2002, Digital National Security Archive, Targeting Iraq Part 1, 1. For a PCTEG memo that cast aspersions on the mainstream intelligence community's analysis, see Senate Select Committee on Intelligence, *U.S. Intelligence Community's Prewar Intelligence Assessments on Iraq*, July 7, 2004, 308.

to individual analysts, and the creation of a pressurized atmosphere in which analysts knew what the policy-makers wanted and feared contradicting them.[92]

In public, Bush officials frequently inflated the Iraqi threat beyond what the intelligence justified. They often presented a data point as unambiguous evidence of Iraq's production of WMD even though different intelligence agencies disagreed about that data. For example, the Department of Energy, the State Department's intelligence service, and the IAEA all argued that specialized aluminum tubes that Iraq had tried to import were probably designed for conventional rockets rather than nuclear weapons production.[93] The agencies that did believe the tubes were for nuclear enrichment worded their analysis in probabilistic terms.[94] Yet, Bush officials claimed to know with "absolute certainty," in Cheney's words, that the tubes were for a nuclear program.[95]

Moreover, administration statements about the Iraq–al-Qaeda link contrasted sharply with the intelligence community's highly parsed assessments. For example, the CIA judged that Iraq had "sporadic, wary contacts with al-Qaida since the mid-1990s" and possibly a sort of nonaggression pact rather than an operational relationship.[96] Bush, however, claimed in the 2003 State of the Union Address: "Saddam Hussein

---

[92] CIA Report, Kerr Group, *Intelligence and Analysis on Iraq: Issues for the Intelligence Community*, July 29, 2004, National Security Archive, accessed March 29, 2018, https://nsarchive2.gwu.edu//news/20051013/kerr_report.pdf, 1. This report is known as the Kerr Report. See also Pillar, *Intelligence and U.S. Foreign Policy*, 32, 155; Tyler Drumheller, *On the Brink: An Insider's Account of How the White House Compromised American Intelligence* (New York: Carroll & Graf Publishers, 2006), 43, 86; Mazarr, *Leap of Faith*, 245–247.

[93] Department of Energy Report, "Iraq: High Strength Aluminum Tube Procurement," April 11, 2001, Digital National Security Archive, Targeting Iraq Part 1, 1–2; Memorandum, Thomas Fingar and Robert Einhorn to Colin Powell, May 16, 2001, Digital National Security Archive, Targeting Iraq Part 1, 1; Memorandum, Carl Ford to Colin Powell, "Iraq's Quest for Aluminum Tubes," October 9, 2002, Digital National Security Archive, Targeting Iraq Part 1, 2, 7.

[94] Military Intelligence Digest Supplement, Department of Defense, "Iraq: Producing Possible Nuclear-Related Gas Centrifuge Equipment," November 30, 2001, Digital National Security Archive, Targeting Iraq Part 1, 1–2; CIA Report, Office Near Eastern and South Asian Analysis, "Iraq: Expanding WMD Capabilities Pose Growing Threat," August 1, 2002, Digital National Security Archive, Targeting Iraq Part 1, 12.

[95] Senate Select Committee on Intelligence, *Whether Public Statements Regarding Iraq by U.S. Government Officials Were Substantiated by Intelligence Information*, 110th Cong., 1st sess., June 5, 2008, 15. For other instances of Bush officials making unsubstantiated statements about Iraq's WMD program, see "In Cheney's Words," *New York Times*, August 27, 2002; Donald Rumsfeld, interview by Tom Clancy, October 24, 2002, IraqWatch.org, accessed July 9, 2018; Bush, "Speech to the U.N. General Assembly," September 12, 2002, 314.

[96] CIA Report, "Iraq and al-Qa'ida: Interpreting a Murky Relationship," June 21, 2002, US Intelligence in the Middle East Database, accessed September 25, 2002, 3; National Intelligence Estimate, "Iraq's Continuing Programs," October 2002, 67–68.

aids and protects terrorists, including members of al-Qaeda."[97] Rice was equally unequivocal in a February 2003 interview: "There is no question in my mind about the al-Qaeda connection."[98] This threat inflation reframed the prewar debate from how to deal with a future threat to how to stop an imminent threat, thereby raising the stakes of Iraq policy and lowering the threshold for military action.

Finally, Bush publicly promoted information in the public case for war that the intelligence agencies had flagged as false or unreliable. For example, they touted Iraq's attempt to acquire "yellowcake" uranium ore from Niger as evidence of a current nuclear weapons program. The CIA, however, had repeatedly judged that this did not happen, removed the reference from other public statements, and stated that Iraq already had yellowcake that was in sealed containers subject to IAEA inspection.[99] This manipulation of intelligence suggests that top Bush officials were so convinced that Saddam had major WMD programs and links to al-Qaeda that they made the policy decision to topple Saddam and then sought evidence to support that decision. Numerous observers have reported this dynamic, including an aide to Foreign Policy Adviser David Manning, who wrote in July 2002: "Bush wanted to remove Saddam, through military action, justified by the conjunction of terrorism and WMD. . . . But the intelligence and facts were being fixed around the policy."[100]

One major problem the administration faced in making the nexus-based argument was that the intelligence community generally did not believe that Saddam would give WMD to terrorists or that he played any role in 9/11. They judged that Saddam wanted WMD for deterrence and probably would not hand them to terrorists unless attacked by the United States.[101] The evidence for an operational relationship between Iraq and

---

[97] George W. Bush, "2003 State of the Union Address," January 28, 2003, C-Span.org, accessed October 29, 2018, www.c-span.org/video/?174799–2/2003-state-union-address.

[98] Mazarr, *Leap of Faith*, 385.

[99] Bush, "2003 State of the Union." For CIA's assessment of the veracity of the Niger story, see CIA Report, "Iraq-Niger," February 14, 2002, Digital National Security Archive, Targeting Iraq Part 1, 1; Bamford, *Pretext for War*, 302–307.

[100] Matthew Rycroft, "Iraq: Prime Minister's Meeting, 23 July," July 23, 2002, in *The Secret Way to War: The Downing Street Memo and the Iraq War's Buried History*, ed. Mark Danner (New York: New York Review of Books, 2006), 89. For similar views of the intelligence process from contemporaneous policy-makers, see Pillar, *Intelligence and U.S. Foreign Policy*; Clarke, *Against All Enemies*; Haass, *War of Necessity*; Drumheller, *On the Brink*.

[101] CIA Report, Office of Near Eastern and South Asian Analysis, "Iraq: Developing Biological Weapons as a Strategic Deterrent," August 10, 2001, Digital National Security Archive, Targeting Iraq Part 1, 1; Report, Defense Intelligence Agency, "Iraqi Chemical/Biological Support to al-Qaida Unlikely," February 28, 2002, Digital

al-Qaeda was sparse, relying on circumstantial and poorly sourced information.[102] Administration hawks, however, addressed this problem by appealing to the long-standing belief in US thinking about Iraq that Saddam was hell-bent, to the point of irrational obsession, on revenge against the United States. This focus on revenge was not a perfunctory assertion of Saddam's villainy but a specific claim rooted in the conspiratorial research of Laurie Mylroie, who worked as a fellow at AEI in the years before the Iraq War.

Through a web of tendentious connections, Mylroie argued that Saddam had sponsored several terrorist attacks on US targets, including the World Trade Center in 1993, Oklahoma City in 1995, the Khobar Towers in 1996, and the US Embassies in Kenya and Tanzania in 1998, as part of a campaign of vengeance for the Gulf War.[103] Immediately after 9/11, she and several of her adherents suggested that Saddam had a hand in the attacks, declaring it "merely another phase of the Gulf War."[104] She became a frequent media commentator and an advisor to the Iraqi National Congress (INC), promoting her theory and accusing the CIA of engaging in an "enormous cover-up" of Iraq's role in 9/11.[105]

While discounted by the intelligence agencies, Mylroie had gained significant influence in neoconservative and pro-regime change circles. Her book on Saddam's purported responsibility for these terrorist attacks, published in 2000 by AEI Press, received fulsome praise from former CIA Director R. James Woolsey, Richard Perle, Scooter Libby, and Paul Wolfowitz. She thanked Wolfowitz and the neoconservative intellectual John Bolton, then working as an Undersecretary of State, by name in the acknowledgments section for their help on the book.[106]

National Security Archive, Targeting Iraq Part 1, 1; Defense Intelligence Agency, Joint Intelligence Task Force on Combatting Terrorism, "Iraq's Inconclusive Ties to Al-Qaida," July 31, 2002, Digital National Security Archive, Targeting Iraq Part 1, 1–3.

[102] Chaim Kaufmann, "Threat Inflation and the Failure of the Marketplace of Ideas: The Selling of the Iraq War," *International Security* 29, no. 1 (Summer, 2004): 17; Defense Intelligence Agency, "Iraq's Inconclusive Ties to Al-Qaida," July 31, 2002, 3; CIA Report, "Interpreting a Murky Relationship," June 21, 2002, 1; James Risen, "Prague Discounts an Iraqi Meeting," *New York Times*, October 21, 2002, A1.

[103] Laurie Mylroie, *Study of Revenge: Saddam Hussein's Unfinished War against America* (Washington, DC: AEI Press, 2000).

[104] Laurie Mylroie, "The Iraqi Connection," *Wall Street Journal*, September 13, 2001, A20; Hoagland, "Hidden Hand," *Washington Post*, September 12, 2001. Editorial, "The Anthrax War," *Wall Street Journal*, October 18, 2001, A26; Woolsey, "Iraq Connection," *New York Times*, October 18, 2001.

[105] David Korn and Michael Isikoff, *Hubris: The Inside Story of Spin, Scandal, and the Selling of the Iraq War* (New York: Crown Publishers, 2006), 75, 83–84.

[106] Peter Bergen, "Armchair Provocateur: Laurie Mylroie: The Neocons' Favorite Conspiracy Theorist," *Washington Monthly* 35, no. 12 (December, 2003): 28.

Wolfowitz had defended her ideas throughout the 1990s, telling Congress in 1998: "There are all kinds of reasons to suspect connections between the Iraqis and this Osama bin Laden fellow."[107] Richard Clarke recalled that in a January 2001 NSC meeting, Wolfowitz said the United States needed to focus more on "Iraqi terrorism" and told Clarke that Bin Laden "could not do all these things like the 1993 attack on New York, not without a state sponsor. Just because the FBI and CIA have failed to find the linkages does not mean they don't exist."[108] Wolfowitz mentioned Saddam's ostensible responsibility for the 1993 attacks to Rumsfeld on September 17, 2001, and later in 2002, Wolfowitz described Saddam in a speech as having "an enormous thirst for revenge."[109] He pressed other officials on whether they had read Mylroie's book, and he sent Woolsey to Great Britain to find data that would bolster this claim.[110]

The revenge hypothesis bled into the administration's thinking about Iraq. One Defense Department briefing stated: "For Saddam, the Gulf War never ended."[111] In a major speech in October 2002, Bush stated that Iraq held "unrelenting hostility toward the United States" before explaining Iraq's links to al-Qaeda.[112] This hypothesis bolstered the plausibility of the administration's nexus case by appealing to the deeply embedded sense that Saddam was an irrational actor with a record of revenge-driven terrorist attacks. This belief legitimized the idea that he might strike again through his terrorist allies regardless of the risk of US retaliation, in contrast to the intelligence community's estimates.

The Bush administration's exaggerated presentation of intelligence fostered broad public and political consensus that Saddam was making significant progress on WMD and had meaningful links to al-Qaeda. A poll from March 2003 found that 80 percent of Americans believed Saddam had or was making nuclear weapons.[113] Another survey from February 2003 found that 72 percent of Americans believed eliminating Saddam's WMD was a "very convincing" or "fairly convincing" reason

---

[107] Paul Wolfowitz, House Committee on National Security, *United States Policy toward Iraq*, 105th Cong., 2nd sess., September 16, 1998, 49.

[108] Clarke, *Against All Enemies*, 232. For corroboration of Clarke's account, see Memorandum, British Foreign and Commonwealth Office, Christopher Meyer to David Manning, "Iraq and Afghanistan: Conversation with Wolfowitz," March 18, 2002, Digital National Security Archive, Targeting Iraq Part 1, 1.

[109] *9/11 Commission Report*, 337; Wolfowitz, "Remarks," October 16, 2002.

[110] Clarke, *Against All Enemies*, 95; Kaufmann, "Threat Inflation," 5–48.

[111] Briefing, Department of Defense, "Assessing the Relationship," September 16, 2002, 6.

[112] Bush, "Confronting Iraq Threat," *New York Times*, October 8, 2002; Barton Gellman, *Angler: The Cheney Vice Presidency* (New York: Penguin, 2007), 117–119.

[113] Harris Telephone Survey, March 6, 2003, Polling the Nations, accessed September 20, 2018.

for war.[114] Furthermore, by mid-March of 2003, 80 percent of Americans had come to believe that without military action "Saddam Hussein would be instrumental in helping al-Qaeda terrorists carry out future attacks."[115]

Bush's top foreign policy advisors unanimously viewed Iraq as a threat to national security, but many of them also saw Saddam's removal as an opportunity to spark broader reforms in the Middle East that would address the causes of terrorism. Donald Rumsfeld did not endorse this idea, but it seems to have been supported by Wolfowitz, Rice, numerous neoconservative advisors, and Bush himself.[116] For these actors and many supporters of regime change in the public discourse, after 9/11 spreading democracy in Iraq and the greater Middle East became not just an ideal but a strategic imperative. Regime change advocates like Wolfowitz, Ahmed Chalabi, and Fouad Ajami had long argued that democratizing Iraq was essential for uprooting the violent Baathist political culture and making Iraq an unthreatening country.[117] They interpreted the rise of terrorism in the Middle East as the product of deficits in democracy, development, and dignity.[118] Tyrannical governments and extremist ideologies bred anti-Western and anti-Israeli terrorism throughout the region.[119] Ajami, for instance, argued that 9/11 stemmed from the "deep structure" of Arab politics, referring to "its repressed young people, its mix of belligerence and self-pity, [and] the terrible anti-Americanism."

Drawing on these ideas and the democratic peace concept, Bush officials argued that democratization would grant Middle Eastern peoples a chance to participate in their own governance so they would not succumb to despair and extremism. As Bush claimed in a February 2003 speech: "The world has a clear interest in the spread of democratic values because stable and free nations do not breed the ideologies of murder." Regime change in Iraq could empower liberal forces, intimidate other

---

[114] Time/CNN Telephone Survey, February 21, 2003, Polling the Nations, accessed September 20, 2018.

[115] Newsweek Telephone Survey, March 15, 2003, Polling the Nations, accessed September 20, 2018.

[116] Daalder and Lindsay, *America Unbound*, 47.

[117] Fouad Ajami, "A Settling of Accounts Past Due," *U.S. News and World Report*, March 24, 2002, 34; Ahmed Chalabi, "Iraqi for the Iraqis," *Wall Street Journal*, February 19, 2003, A14.

[118] Bernard Lewis, *The Crisis of Islam: Holy War and Unholy Terror* (New York: Modern Library, 2003), 113–119, 162–163.

[119] Fouad Ajami, "Two Faces, One Terror," *Wall Street Journal*, November 11, 2002, A12; For more on the role of pro-Israeli sentiment in Bush administration's case for war with Iraq, see Gary Dorrien, *Imperial Designs: Neoconservatism and the New Pax Americana* (New York: Routledge, 2004), 182–221.

autocratic states like Iran, and possibly spark a broad democratic transformation that would inoculate the Middle East against terrorism.[120]

Bush officials adopted a universalistic rhetoric of human rights and
democracy that had become prominent in the US political establishment
after the Cold War to bolster the argument that democracy could flourish in
the Middle East. While Bush emphasized this idealist reasoning more once
the post-invasion search for Iraqi WMD proved fruitless, there is considerable evidence that democracy and human rights served as important
motives beforehand.[121] In the 2002 National Security Strategy, the administration declared that the great struggles of the twentieth century had ended
in a "decisive victory" for "a single sustainable model for national success:
freedom, democracy, and free enterprise."[122] In turn, it rejected, in Rice's
words, the "condescending view that freedom will not grow in the soil of the
Middle East or that Muslims somehow do not share in the desire to be
free."[123] This type of claim first developed shortly after the Persian Gulf
War, when regime change advocates excoriated the first Bush administration's realists for assuming that democracy was unlikely to take root in Iraq.
The second Bush administration argued that containment was a passive,
status quo-oriented policy that could not foment positive change. Only
a bold move premised on the assumption of universal human values could
put the region on a more peaceful and humane track.

In making the case that war was less risky than containment, the Bush
administration adopted an unrealistically optimistic view of the aftermath of
the conflict, especially the rebuilding of the Iraqi economy, society, and
government. Officials frequently cited Ajami and Kanan Makiya, who
argued that Iraqis would joyously welcome US soldiers and cooperate in
rebuilding Iraq.[124] Makiya, for one, wrote shortly after 9/11: "Iraq's

---

[120] Quote is from "In the President's Words: 'Free People Will Keep the Peace of the
World,'" *New York Times*, February 27, 2003, A10. See also "In Cheney's Words,"
New York Times, August 27, 2002; John McCain, "The Road to Baghdad," *Time*,
September 11, 2002, 107; Richard Perle, "The U.S. Must Strike at Saddam
Hussein," *New York Times*, December 28, 2001, A19; Editorial, "Arabs and
Democracy," *The Wall Street Journal*, April 3, 2002, A22; Thomas Friedman, "Iraq,
Upside Down," *New York Times*, September 18, 2002, A31; Tom Lantos, House
Committee on International Relations, *U.S. Policy toward Iraq: Administration Views*,
107th Cong., 2nd sess., September 19, 2002, 5; William Kristol, Senate Foreign
Relations Committee, *What's Next*, February 7, 2002, 22; Lawrence Kaplan, "Regime
Change," *The New Republic*, March 3, 2003, 21–23.
[121] Michael MacDonald, *Overreach: Delusions of Regime Change in Iraq* (Cambridge:
Harvard University Press, 2014), 4–5.
[122] Rice and Bush, "National Security Strategy," September 2002, 81.
[123] Rice, "Wriston Lecture," October 1, 2002; "In the President's Words," *New York Times*,
February 27, 2003.
[124] Cheney cites Ajami in "In Cheney's Words," *New York Times*, August 27, 2002.
Wolfowitz cites him in "Remarks," October 16, 2002.

infrastructure, its middle class, its secular intelligentsia, its high levels of education ... are all reason for thinking that a new kind of westward political order can, with help from the West, be set up in Iraq."[125] On January 10, 2003, he met with Bush and Cheney and told them that "[p]eople will greet the troops with sweets and flowers."[126] Ajami boldly prophesied: "We shall be mobbed when we go there by people who are eager for deliverance ... from the great big prison of Saddam Hussein."[127] Overlooking the devastation of a decade of sanctions, Wolfowitz likewise contended:

It is hard to believe that the liberation of the talented people of one of the most important Arab countries in the world from the grip of one of the world's worst tyrants will not be an opportunity for Americans and Arabs ... to begin to move forward in what the president had described as "building a just and peaceful world beyond the War on Terror."[128]

Ajami, Makiya, and the like-minded historian Bernard Lewis met repeatedly with Cheney, Wolfowitz, and others following 9/11.[129] The administration's egregious lack of planning for the aftermath of invasion, including Rumsfeld's tireless efforts to reduce troop numbers in spite of warnings from top generals, resulted not just from incompetence but also from ideological assumptions constructed in the previous decade. Particularly important were beliefs about the universality of democracy and the Iraqi people as middle class and pro-Western rather than divided on ethnic, sectarian, and tribal lines, impoverished, and resentful of the United States.[130]

The ideas that the United States would be "greeted as liberators," in Cheney's words, and that the war would benefit the region became additional reasons to embrace regime change.[131] This hope, however, contradicted the warnings of the intelligence agencies and other area

[125] Makiya, "Help the Iraqis," *New York Times*, November 21, 2001. See also Barham Salih, "Give Us a Chance to Build a Democratic Iraq," *New York Times*, February 5, 2003, A27; Kaplan and Kristol, *War Over Iraq*, 99; Fouad Ajami, "Iraq and the Arabs' Future," *Foreign Affairs* 82, no. 1 (January–February, 2003): 2–18.

[126] Baker, *Days of Fire*, 235.

[127] Fouad Ajami, Senate Foreign Relations Committee, *Hearings to Examine Threats, Responses, and Regional Considerations Surrounding Iraq*, 107th Cong., 2nd sess., July 31, 2002, 126.

[128] Paul Wolfowitz, "United on the Risks of a War with Iraq," *Washington Post*, December 23, 2002, A19. See also "In the President's Words," *New York Times*, =February 27, 2003; Rumsfeld, Senate Armed Services Committee, *U.S. Policy on Iraq*, September 19, 2002, 32.

[129] Bonin, *Arrows of the Night*, 192; Daalder and Lindsay, *America Unbound*, 130.

[130] James Fallows, *Blind into Baghdad: America's War in Iraq* (New York: Vintage Books, 2006); David Phillips, *Losing Iraq: Inside the Postwar Reconstruction Fiasco* (Boulder, CO: Westview Press, 2005); Gordon and Trainor, *Cobra II*, 95–105, 138–163.

[131] Transcript, Meet the Press, Interview of the Vice President, March 16, 2003, whitehouse.archives.gov, accessed November 9, 2018, https://georgewbush-whitehouse.arch ives.gov/news/releases/2006/09/20060910.html.

experts. Intelligence assessments of Iraqi political culture as backward and illiberal had persisted throughout the 1990s, including one 1993 CIA report that stated: "Many of the nationalistic, xenophobic, and Pan-Arab themes that pervade Saddam's policies and propaganda resonate with the Iraqi public and probably would be used by likely Arab Sunni successors."[132]

In 2002, Middle East experts at the CIA similarly judged that "[a] transformation of Iraq to a true democracy could require a U.S. role lasting a generation."[133] These analysts noted the "lack of ingrained democratic traditions, innate distrust of other groups, and the tendency to substitute tribal, ethnic, or sectarian loyalties" as obstacles to democracy and pluralism in Iraq.[134] They also doubted that over-throwing Saddam would foment regional political transformation, arguing that Arab societies still lacked "such important components of democracy as the concept of a loyal opposition, vibrant civil society institutions, respect for the rule of law, transparency, and a strong middle class."[135] CENTCOM planners throughout the 1990s had estimated that if the United States invaded Iraq, it could have soldiers there for up to ten years.[136]

Bush's case for war with Iraq rested on more than preventing another terrorist attack and defeating a rival. Iraq would serve as the cornerstone in a grand strategy of global primacy that matched both neoconservative and assertive nationalist views of US power.[137] The key tenets of this vision predated 9/11, but 9/11 served as both impetus and opening for the establishment of these ideas as the guiding principles of US foreign policy. Bush officials aimed to transform the international political order in

---

[132] CIA Report, National Intelligence Estimate 93–42, "Prospects for Iraq; Saddam and Beyond," December 1993, accessed April 10, 2018, http://primarysources.brillonline.com/reader/open?rotate=1&searchTerms=iraq&starEnabled=1&shareLink=, 1.

[133] CIA Report, Office of Near Eastern and South Asian Analysis, "The Postwar Occupation of Germany and Japan: Implications for Iraq," August 7, 2002, Digital National Security Archive, Targeting Iraq Part 1, 2. See also CIA Report, "The Perfect Storm: Planning for Negative Consequences of Invading Iraq," August 13, 2002, 1–3.

[134] Quote is from Assessment, National Intelligence Community, "Principal Challenges in Post-Saddam Iraq," January 2003, Digital National Security Archive, Targeting Iraq Part 1, 14; See also Pillar, *Intelligence in U.S. Foreign Policy*, 14; Phebe Marr, Senate Foreign Relations Committee, *Threats, Responses, and Regional Considerations*, July 31, 2002, 166; Fawaz Gerges, "Illusions of Iraqi Democracy," *Washington Post*, October 8, 2002, A25.

[135] Assessment, National Intelligence Council, "Regional Consequences of Regime Change," January 2003, Digital National Security Archive, Targeting Iraq Part 1, 30. See also Greg Miller, "Democracy Domino Theory 'Not Credible', a State Department Report Disputes Bush's Claim," *Los Angeles Times*, March 14, 2003, A1.

[136] Gordon and Trainor, *Cobra II*, 26–27.

[137] Daalder and Lindsey, *America Unbound*, 45–47.

a time of crisis.[138] The United States would guarantee the security and openness of an increasingly interconnected world by using overwhelming military power to deter great power challengers and defeat the nexus of rogue states and terrorists.[139] In contrast to the "realist" first Bush administration, US global primacy would ensure "a balance of power that favored freedom" and enable the flourishing of democracies that would respect human rights and eschew aggression.[140] In contrast to the anemic Clinton administration, the United States would possess the will to act unilaterally or with small coalitions, and it would not be restrained by international treaties and institutions.[141] Bush's case for war emerged from this global vision, their interpretation of the post-9/11 security environment, and more deeply rooted discrediting of containment as the main alternative to regime change.

"The Right Way to Change a Regime": The Public Debate on Iraq and the Powell–Blair Approach

Compared to Bush's case for war, the public debate on Iraq from 2002 to 2003 has been relatively underexamined. This debate had roughly four camps. Two of these camps dissented from the regime change consensus and opposed the war, albeit for radically different reasons: conditionalist supporters of containment and anti-war leftists. Operating within the regime change consensus were two larger, more powerful groups: open, enthusiastic hawks inside and outside of the administration as well as members of the Powell–Blair approach. Members of the Powell–Blair camp constituted the largest and most powerful camp of "skeptics." They consisted of politicians, intellectuals, and policy-makers who disagreed with many of Bush's claims about Iraq and criticized how it pursued regime change. They argued that Bush should build an international coalition to confront Iraq, attempt nonviolent means of disarmament first, and plan more realistically for the aftermath of invasion. Among those with intimate access to

---

[138] Condoleezza Rice, "Remarks by National Security Advisor on Terrorism and Foreign Policy," April 29, 2002, whitehouse.archives.gov, accessed October 2, 2018, https://ge orgewbush-whitehouse.archives.gov/news/releases/2002/04/20020429-9.html.

[139] Barry Posen and Andrew Ross, "Competing Visions for U.S. Grand Strategy," *International Security* 21, no. 3 (Winter, 1996–1997): 5–53; David Hastings Dunn, "Myths, Motivations, and 'Misunderestimations', the Bush Administration and Iraq," *International Affairs* 79, no. 2 (March, 2003): 279–297; Daalder and Lindsay, *America Unbound*, 116–128.

[140] Rice, "Remarks by National Security Advisor," April 29, 2002. For similar universalistic claims, see Transcript, "In the President's Words," *New York Times*, February 27, 2003.

[141] Stefan Halper and Jonathan Clarke, *America Alone: The Neoconservatives and the Global Order* (New York: Cambridge University Press), 121–131.

the president, Colin Powell and Tony Blair best represented this view-point. Other prominent persons spanned the ideological gamut, but they clustered in the leadership of major political parties and institu-tions, which gave them greater ability to shape the Iraq debate. They included leading Democrats like Joseph Biden, Al Gore, and John Kerry; former policy-makers like Zbigniew Brzezinski, Sandy Berger, Richard Holbrooke, and James Baker; as well as Republicans such as Chuck Hagel and Richard Lugar.

If any group could have slowed or hampered Bush's push for war, it was these members of the political and policy establishment. They had access to the ears of top policy-makers, influential media outlets, and Congressional hearings. They played an enormous role in shaping what ideas were heard by the broader public and which were margin-alized. Most importantly, the legislators in this camp could deny Congressional authorization for war or impose serious restraints on that power. They were the figures in political life best situated to raise serious questions not just about how regime change was pursued but also the fundamental wisdom, necessity, and morality of that choice.

Nonetheless, proponents of this approach did not dissent from the core assumptions of the official case for war and did not defend contain-ment as an alternative to war. They approached inspections, for example, mainly in procedural terms, a box to check to rally an inter-national coalition before pursuing regime change. Because of the rise of the regime change consensus in US thinking about Iraq in the previous decade, the central debate over Iraq encompassed a narrow range of perspectives and options. The mainstream Iraq debate was much more about "the right way to change a regime," in James Baker's phrasing, than whether the United States should seek regime change or restore containment.[142]

Blair and Powell shared similar concerns about the impending Iraq War even though they approached foreign policy from different perspectives. Blair passionately defended the "responsibility to protect" (R2P) doctrine and argued for intervention in the Balkans and Kosovo crises. He eventually came to support the Iraq War largely on the liberal grounds of humanitarian interventionism and democracy.[143] In contrast, Powell opposed the Balkan intervention as the JCS Chairman because he believed US forces should not be used for humanitarian crusades that did not serve the national

[142] James Baker, "The Right Way to Change a Regime," *New York Times*, August 25, 2002, C9.
[143] Tony Blair, "Speech before Chicago Economic Club," April 22, 1999, globalpolicy.org, accessed September 26, 2018, www.globalpolicy.org/component/content/article/154/2 6026.html.

interest.[144] Nevertheless, they both endorsed a multilateral foreign policy in which great powers should work with international institutions and eschew military force until peaceful strategies have been exhausted. These positions put Powell and Blair somewhat at odds with the administration's more unilateralist and aggressive neoconservatives and assertive nationalists, as did their more practical concerns about invading Iraq.

The Blair government became concerned in early 2002 that Bush had decided upon war without consulting US allies.[145] Cheney had even told several British officials that a coalition "would be nice" but was "not essential."[146] They also feared, in David Manning's words, that "[t]here is a real risk that the Administration underestimates the difficulties" of occupying Iraq.[147] While Blair did not see strong links between Iraq and al-Qaeda, he agreed with many of the assumptions of Bush's case for war: "Getting rid of Saddam is the right thing to do. He is a potential threat. He could be contained. But containment, as we found with al-Qaida, is always risky. His departure would free up the region."[148] Nevertheless, Blair believed that any move against Saddam needed to be complemented by a diplomatic push to counter regional proliferation and resolve the Israeli–Palestinian conflict, which he saw as the main driver of radicalism in the Middle East. Blair told Bush that the MEPP was "the huge undercurrent in this situation. It is the context in the Arab world."[149] Blair wanted to make Iraq "a problem for the international community as a whole, not just for the U.S." by focusing on Saddam's violation of UN resolutions rather than the controversial nexus and preemptive war concepts.[150]

---

[144] David Halberstam, *War in a Time of Peace: Bush, Clinton, and the Generals* (New York: Simon & Schuster, 2001), 34–42, 139–142; Colin Powell, *My American Journey* (New York: Random House, 1995), 543–544, 560–562; Mann, *Rise of the Vulcans*, 221.

[145] House of Commons, "Report of the Iraq Inquiry," July 6, 2016, Vol. 1, Section 3.1, 377, 395; United Kingdom Overseas and Defense Secretariat Cabinet Office, "Iraq: Options Paper," March 8, 2002, in Danner, *The Downing Street Memo*, 103.

[146] John Prados and Christopher Ames, "The Iraq War-Part II: Was There Even a Decision?" October 1, 2010, National Security Archive Electronic Briefing Book No. 328, accessed March 5, 2017, www2.gwu.edu/~nsarchiv/NSAEBB/NSAEBB328/index.htm.

[147] House of Commons, "Report of the Iraq Inquiry," July 6, 2016, Vol. 1, Section 3.1, 377, 455.

[148] Note, Tony Blair to George W. Bush, "Note on Iraq," July 28, 2002, Iraqinquiry.org.uk, accessed September 10, 2018, http://webarchive.nationalarchives.gov.uk/2017112312 2728/http://www.iraqinquiry.org.uk/media/243761/2002–07-28-note-blair-to-bush-no te-on-iraq.pdf, 1.

[149] Underlined in original. Letter, Tony Blair to George W. Bush, October 11, 2001, Iraqinquiry.org.uk, accessed September 9, 2018, http://webarchive.nationalarchives.g ov.uk/20171123122709/http://www.iraqinquiry.org.uk/media/243721/2001–10-11-let ter-blair-to-bush-untitled.pdf, 2.

[150] Peter Ricketts, "Iraq: Advice for the Prime Minister," March 22, 2002, in Danner, *The Downing Street Memo*, 141.

The British started pressing US officials on these points in the early spring of 2002. In talks with Bush, however, Blair said he supported Saddam's removal and he did not defend containment as a viable strategy. At a meeting in Crawford, Texas, in April 2002, Blair assured Bush that Britain would support military action against Iraq once certain conditions had been satisfied. A British Cabinet Office Memo detailed these terms:

When the Prime Minister discussed Iraq with President Bush at Crawford in April he said that the UK would support military action to bring about regime change, provided that certain conditions were met: efforts had been made to construct a coalition/shape public opinion, the Israel-Palestine Crisis was quiescent, and the options for action to eliminate Iraq's WMD through the UN weapons inspectors had been exhausted.[151]

Christopher Meyer, the British ambassador to the United States, claimed in February 2002 that the British objective was "to persuade the U.S. .... that they must show that they are serious about implementing the resolutions-even if only to prepare the ground properly in the international community for action if Saddam fails to comply."[152] The Blair government decided to use its status as the United States' closest ally to shape how the United States confronted Iraq, acknowledging that force would be an option if other means failed.[153]

Colin Powell was on a similar wavelength to Blair in the summer of 2002 in terms of his concerns about how Bush was developing a regime change strategy. As Richard Armitage later confirmed: "Powell and I did not object to the prospect of taking out Saddam Hussein, but we had real questions about timing."[154] Powell had watched with concern as Cheney and Rumsfeld pressed Bush to shift focus to Iraq throughout early 2002.[155] Powell held that Saddam could be disarmed if the United States rallied a large coalition and threatened him with force if he failed to comply.[156] In a meeting on August 5, he conveyed to Bush the possible consequences of invading Iraq without a large coalition, including regional chaos, rising oil prices, and alienated allies.[157] Without a coalition, the United States would face the massive challenges of rebuilding Iraq virtually by itself.[158]

---

[151] United Kingdom, Cabinet Office Options Paper, "Iraq: Conditions for Military Action (A Note by Officials)," July 21, 2002, National Security Archives, accessed March 5, 2017, www2.gwu.edu/~nsarchiv/NSAEBB/NSAEBB328/index.htm.

[152] House of Commons, "Report of the Iraq Inquiry," July 6, 2016, Vol. 1, Section 3.1, 395.

[153] House of Commons, "Report of the Iraq Inquiry," July 6, 2016, Vol. 1, Section 3.2, 526.

[154] Gordon and Trainor, *Cobra II*, 85.

[155] Alan Sipress and Peter Slevin, "Powell Wary of Iraq Move," *Washington Post*, December 21, 2001, A1.

[156] Haass, *War of Necessity*, 221–224; Bamford, *A Pretext for War*, 268.

[157] Feith, *War and Decision*, 246.   [158] DeYoung, *Soldier*, 401; Baker, *Days of Fire*, 218.

Blair likewise intervened with Bush in August 2002 by warning that without the exhaustion of alternatives and a UN mandate, he would not be able to rally public support in Britain, which was evenly split on war with Iraq.[159] In a September 7 NSC meeting, Bush decided to follow Blair's and Powell's advice, despite Cheney's and Rumsfeld's pleas that Saddam already had enough chances and that the United States should give Iraq thirty to sixty days to comply and then invade.[160] Rice says that Bush stated: "Either he will come clean about his weapons, or there will be war."[161] Before the UN General Assembly on September 12, Bush called for a resolution that would readmit inspectors to Iraq and authorize the use of force if Iraq failed to comply.[162]

Blair and Powell envisioned that going the "UN route" might lead to the peaceful disarmament of Iraq. Powell, for instance, reportedly told Bush on August 5: "If you take it to the U.N., you've got to recognize that they might be able to solve it. In which case there's no war."[163] In exchange, Bush pressed Blair and Powell to promise that if diplomacy failed, they would support the use of force.[164] They made these pledges despite signals that the hawks were fixated on war and would not make a good-faith effort to back inspections and build multilateral support. Ambassador Meyer, for instance, warned Blair in September that Bush's instincts were "with the hawks," that the hawks believed the destruction of Iraq's WMD to be "inseparable from the elimination of Saddam himself," that "inspections were a discredited instrument," and that the United Nations was "not to be trusted."[165] Nonetheless, both Blair and Powell believed, although for different reasons, Saddam's removal was an important objective that justified military action after other methods were attempted. While Powell had some reservations, he and Blair did not represent an anti-war faction nor defend alternative approaches like containment within Bush's inner circle.[166]

In the public discourse, adherents of the Powell–Blair approach constituted the largest and most influential body of critics of the Bush

---

[159] Pew Research Global Attitudes Project, "What the World Thinks in 2002," December 4, 2002, accessed September 24, 2014, www.pewglobal.org/2002/12/04/what-the-world-thinks-in-2002.

[160] Rice, *Higher Honor*, 180; Karen DeYoung, "For Powell, a Long Path to Victory," *Washington Post*, November 10, 2002, A1.

[161] Rice, *Higher Honor*, 181.

[162] Bush, "Speech to the U.N. General Assembly," September 12, 2002, 314.

[163] Woodward, *Plan of Attack*, 178; House of Commons, "Report of the Iraq Inquiry," July 6, 2016, Vol. 2, Section 3.4, 165.

[164] Woodward, *Plan of Attack*, 178. See also Note, Blair to Bush, "Note on Iraq," July 28, 2002, 1.

[165] House of Commons, "Report of the Iraq Inquiry," July 6, 2016, Vol. 2, Section 3.4, 153.

[166] Mazarr, *Leap of Faith*, 122–123, 269.

administration and other hawks. They created the sense of a wider debate without fundamentally contesting the goal of regime change in Iraq. They particularly disliked Bush's unilateralism, arguing that the legitimacy of US global power depended on working through partners and rules-based institutions. Bush needed to slow down and build a coalition just as his father had done during the Gulf War, which required a Security Council resolution demanding the return of inspectors.[167] Gore noted, for instance, that George H. W. Bush had patiently rallied "every Arab nation except Jordan" and our European and Asian allies "without exception" for a more limited undertaking, in stark contrast to the second Bush's cavalier ambivalence toward his allies.[168] These steps would, in Berger words, help with "isolating Saddam and gaining broader international support for what may be necessary if we fail."[169]

Backers of the Powell–Blair approach pledged to not support war until Bush had taken these steps.[170] They wanted to focus the case against Saddam on his repeated defiance of the United Nations, making war an "enforcement of a binding international legal commitment," as Biden put it.[171] They preferred this justification to the doctrine of preventive war, which they believed alienated allies and corroded international norms against the use of force.[172] Brzezinksi captured this perspective: "If it is to be war, it should be conducted in a manner that legitimizes U.S. global hegemony and, at the same time, contributes to a more responsible system of international security."[173]

---

[167] Albert Gore, "Speech at the Commonwealth Club of California against a Doctrine of Pre-Emptive War," September 23, 2002, in Sifry and Cerf, *Iraq War Reader*, 328; Sandy Berger, "Building Blocks to Iraq," *Washington Post*, August 1, 2002, A27.

[168] Gore, "Speech at Commonwealth Club," 329.

[169] Sandy Berger, Senate Armed Services Committee, *U.S. Policy on Iraq*, September 19, 2002, 178; Sandy Berger, "We Can Outmaneuver Saddam Hussein," *Washington Post*, October 3, 2002, A19; Wesley Clark, "Let's Wait to Attack," *Time*, October 14, 2002, 36; Fareed Zakaria, "Invade Iraq, But Bring Friends," *Newsweek*, August 5, 2002, 37.

[170] Baker, "Right Way," *New York Times*, August 25, 2002; Editorial, "A Time for Candor on Iraq," *New York Times*, A14.

[171] Joseph Biden, Senate Foreign Relations Committee, *UNMOVIC and IAEA Reports to the U.N. Security Council on Inspections in Iraq*, 108th Cong., 1st sess., January 30, 2003, 7.

[172] Gore, "Speech at the Commonwealth Club," 330; Sandy Berger, Senate Armed Services Committee, *U.S. Policy on Iraq*, September 19, 2002, 205; Gary Ackerman, House Committee on International Relations, *Authorization for Use of Military Force against Iraq*, October 2–3, 2002, 8; Editorial, "The Iraq Debate Continues," *Washington Post*, August 18, 2002, B6.

[173] Zbigniew Brzezinski, "If We Must Fight," *Washington Post*, August 18, 2002, B7; John Kerry, "We Still Have a Choice on Iraq," *New York Times*, September 6, 2002, A23; Madeleine Albright, "Where Iraq Fits in the War on Terror," *New York Times*, September 13, 2002, A27; William Cohen, "The Real Case Against Iraq," *Wall Street Journal*, February 5, 2003, A18; Gore, "Speech at the Commonwealth Club," 328.

One of the main reasons that members of the Powell–Blair school supported a more multilateral approach was that they believed that war with Iraq would be much harder than the Bush administration promised. As Hagel argued: "I can think of no historical case where the United States succeeded in an enterprise of such gravity and complexity as regime change in Iraq without the support of a regional and international coalition."[174] They anticipated a costly invasion and occupation as well the risk of a wider regional war if countries like Iran tried to gain influence in a weakened Iraq. If the United States hoped to create a stable, democratic Iraq, it would need a multilateral, multiyear effort.[175]

Iraq was only part of a broader post-9/11 struggle for adherents of the Powell–Blair approach, and the United States should not jeopardize the coalition it needed to fight terrorism by rushing into Iraq.[176] Gore, for one, claimed that Bush's narrow obsession with Iraq had "disposed of the sympathy, good will, and solidarity compiled by America and transformed it into a sense of deep misgiving and even hostility."[177] They also recommended, like Blair and Powell, more concerted action on the MEPP as a means of countering extremism.[178] Brzezinski, for instance, argued that Bush viewed terrorists too simplistically, describing them as simple "evildoers" who emerged from an "historical void." Rather, to counter extremism the United States needed to address the complex "political antecedent[s]" that fueled it, including colonial legacies, the treatment of Palestinians, and US-backed dictators.[179]

While members of the Powell–Blair approach criticized Bush's case on many points and viewed themselves as skeptics, they nonetheless agreed with the underlying tenets of the regime change consensus. Chuck Hagel, for instance, stated: "I support regime change and a democratic transition in Iraq. That's easy. ... [T]he tough questions are when, how, with whom, and at what cost."[180] Al Gore, for instance, criticized almost

[174] Chuck Hagel, *Cong. Rec.*, 71st Cong., 2nd sess., August 1, 2002, 7863.

[175] Baker, "Right Way," *New York Times*, August 25, 2002; Kerry, "Choice on Iraq," *New York Times*, September 6, 2002; Richard Cohen, "The Dangers of an Unexplained War," *Washington Post*, July 25, 2002, A21.

[176] Gore, "Speech at the Commonwealth Club," 329; Berger, "Building Blocks," *Washington Post*, August 1, 2002.

[177] Gore, "Speech at the Commonwealth Club," 330.

[178] Editorial, "A Coalition for Iraq," *Washington Post*, March 24, 2002, B6; Brzezinski, "Must Fight," *Washington Post*, August 18, 2002; Berger, "Building Blocks," *Washington Post*, August 1, 2002.

[179] Zbigniew Brzezinski, "Confronting Anti-American Grievances," *New York Times*, September 1, 2002, C9; Editorial, "Double Talk on Democracy," *New York Times*, October 6, 2002, A12.

[180] Charles Hagel, Senate Foreign Relations Committee, *Threats, Responses, and Regional Considerations*, July 31, 2002, 45.

every aspect of Bush's foreign policy but still supported a multilateral military effort at regime change on the grounds of enforcing international law.[181] For proponents of the Powell–Blair approach, the question was how to do regime change correctly and in balance with other foreign policy priorities, not whether to pursue it. If inspections failed, most of these skeptics conceded that war would be necessary and justified. James Baker, for example, argued about Iraqi obstruction of inspectors: "The first time he resorts to those tactics, we should apply whatever means are necessary to change the regime."[182] In contrast to the conditionalist approach, they usually agreed with Bush that containment had already collapsed and that shifting back to this policy would only lead to more obstruction of inspections while Saddam built additional WMD.

A sampling of public opinion before the Iraq War shows that the Powell–Blair approach mirrored public views more closely than any other perspective. A Brookings Institution study aptly described US public opinion as "permissive: it was willing to follow the White House to war but not demanding war." According to their summary of polls, about 30 percent of Americans strongly believed the war was just and necessary, while another 30 percent opposed war under almost any circumstance. The other 40 percent wavered depending on a number of factors.[183] For instance, in one August 2002 poll, backing for invasion dropped from 57 percent to 36 percent when respondents were asked if they would support a war that caused "significant" US casualties.[184] Americans were more equivocal about invasion if Saddam had only the potential to produce WMD compared to the possession of actual weapons, with support dropping from 76 percent to 46 percent in these scenarios.[185] Moreover, Americans consistently wanted Bush to build a broader coalition, attempt inspections, and gain UN and Congressional authorization for the use of force.[186] However, in keeping

---

[181] Gore, "Speech at the Commonwealth Club," 326.

[182] Baker, "Right Way," *New York Times*, August 25, 2002; Cohen, "Without Evidence" *Washington Post*, September 10, 2002; Dianne Feinstein, *Cong. Rec.*, 107th Cong., 2nd sess., September 5, 2002: 16162.

[183] James Lindsay and Caroline Smith, "Rally Round the Flag: Opinion in the United States before and after the Iraq War," *Brookings Review* 21, no. 3 (Summer, 2003): 21–22.

[184] Richard Morin and Claudia Deane, "Poll: Americans Cautiously Favored War in Iraq," *Washington Post*, August 13, 2002, A10.

[185] Pew Telephone Survey, January 16, 2003, Polling the Nations, accessed September 20, 2018.

[186] See ABC News/Washington Post Telephone Survey, February 24, 2003, Polling the Nations, accessed September 20, 2018; CBS News Telephone Survey, September 7, 2002, Polling the Nations, accessed September 20, 2018; Gallup Telephone Survey, September 18, 2002, Polling the Nations, accessed September 20, 2018.

with the regime change consensus, a December 2002 Gallup poll found that 81 percent of respondents believed that Iraq could only be disarmed if Saddam was overthrown.[187]

One subgroup of political and intellectual actors who operated within the regime change consensus but offered a significantly different case for war were the liberal hawks. They included figures like the scholar Michael Ignatieff, *New Yorker* writer George Packer, *New York Times* columnist Thomas Friedman, and former senator Robert Kerrey who embraced both security-based and liberal idealist arguments for war.[188] Liberals often argued that Bush was exaggerating Iraq's WMD programs and objected to the Bush Doctrine as harmful to international law.[189] Nonetheless, they believed that removing Saddam's regime with the blessing of the United Nations would reinforce the authority of international law and the doctrine of humanitarian interventionism. Columnist Jonathan Chait argued, for example: "War with Iraq does not require trashing international law. Just the opposite: sustaining international law is central to its very rationale."[190]

Saddam did not pose an imminent threat, most liberal hawks argued, but the totalitarian nature of the regime meant that it would continue to pursue WMD and abuse its people "the way junkies seek a fix," as Richard Cohen put it.[191] Prowar liberals took this danger seriously, but the moral importance of liberating the Iraqi people from this "morally outrageous regime" motivated them at least as much.[192] Prowar liberals consistently referred to Baathist Iraq as a "penitentiary" or "concentration camp," evoking a liberal narrative of an ongoing struggle against totalitarianism dating to the early

---

[187] Gallup Telephone Survey, December 12, 2002, Polling the Nations, accessed September 20, 2018; Gallup Telephone Survey, January 27, 2003, Polling the Nations, accessed September 20, 2018.

[188] MacDonald, *Overreach*, 64–65, 155–158.

[189] Bill Keller, "The I-Can't-Believe-I'm-a-Hawk Club," *New York Times*, February 8, 2003, A17; Jonathan Chait, "False Alarm: Why Liberals Should Support the War," *The New Republic*, October 21, 2002, 18–21; Michael Tomasky, "Between Cheney and Chomsky: Making a Domestic Case for a New Liberal Foreign Policy," in *The Fight Is for Democracy: Winning the War of Ideas in America and the World*, ed. George Packer (New York: Harper Collins, 2003), 41.

[190] Chait, "Liberals Should Support the War," 20.

[191] Richard Cohen, "Ready for War," *Washington Post*, October 10, 2002, A33; Robert Kerrey, "Finish the War, Liberate Iraq," *Wall Street Journal*, September 12, 2002, A14.

[192] Quote is from interview with Makiya. See also Salman Rushdie, "A Liberal Argument for Regime Change," *Washington Post*, November 1, 2002, A35; Thomas Friedman, "Tell the Truth," *New York Times*, February 19, 2003, A25; Leon Wieseltier, "Against Innocence," *The New Republic*, March 3, 2003, 26–28; Thomas Cushman, "Introduction: The Liberal-Humanitarian Case for War in Iraq," in *A Matter of Principle: Humanitarian Arguments for War in Iraq* (Berkeley: University of California Press, 2005), 22–23.

Cold War.[193] Former Democratic Senator Robert Kerrey, for instance, told Congress: "We want to have the same experience we had when Kim Dae June, Nelson Mandela, Vaclev Havel, and Lech Walesa came to a joint session of Congress and said 'thank you for liberating us'."[194] These liberals wanted to position themselves "between Cheney and Chomsky," in writer Michael Tomasky's memorable phrasing.[195] This meant that liberals should challenge both Cheney's narrow, unilateral nationalism and the leftist scholar Noam Chomsky's evocation of moral equivalence between the United States and its enemies. They promoted a "vibrant, hard-headed" liberalism that was more cautious and self-critical than the imperialistic neoconservatives but still defended liberal values against the new totalitarians of al-Qaeda and the Baathists.[196]

Containment, for many liberals, had not only failed to disarm Saddam, it tolerated an oppressive status quo in the Middle East that bred terrorism and permitted massive human suffering.[197] Liberals like the sociologist Thomas Cushman linked their support for the war to the R2P doctrine: "Coming to the rescue and aid of a people who had been subjected to decades of brutality and crimes against humanity is entirely consistent with the basic liberal principle of solidarity with the oppressed and the fundamental humanitarian principle of rescue."[198] They also wanted regime change in Iraq to be part of a nation-wide "transforming moment" in which the United States developed alternative energy

---

[193] Natan Sharansky, "AEI World Forum Speech," June 20, 2002, AEI.org, accessed September 22, 2018, www.aei.org/publication/democracy-for-peace/print/; Thomas Cushman, "Anti-totalitarianism as a Vocation: An Interview with Adam Michnik," in *A Matter of Principle*, 271–281; Garry Kasparov, "The War Is Not Yet Won," *Wall Street Journal*, August 5, 2002, A10; Kanan Makiya, phone interview by author, November 1, 2017.

[194] Robert Kerrey, Subcommittee on Near Eastern and South Asian Affairs of the Senate Foreign Relations Committee, *United States Policy toward Iraq*, 107th Cong., 1st sess., March 1, 2001, 34.

[195] Tomasky, "Cheney and Chomsky," 21–48. This argument is echoed in Cushman, "Liberal-Humanitarian Case," 10–13.

[196] Quote is from George Packer, "Introduction: Living Up to It," in *The Fight Is for Democracy*, 17. In the same volume, see also Tomasky, "Cheney and Chomsky," 44–45; Paul Berman, "Thirteen Observations on a Very Unlucky Predicament," in *The Fight is for Democracy: Winning the War of Ideas in America and the World*, ed. George Packer (New York: Harper Collins, 2003), 279–288.

[197] Bill Keller, "The Selective Conscience," *New York Times*, December 14, 2002, A29; David Ignatius, "Wilsonian Course for War," *Washington Post*, August 30, 2002, A23; Paul Berman, *Terror and Liberalism* (New York: W. W. Norton, 2003), 197.

[198] Cushman, "The Liberal-Humanitarian Case," 2. See also Michael Ignatieff, "Intervention and State Failure," *Dissent* 49, no. 1 (Winter, 2002): 118–122. For a liberal dissent from the idea of the Iraq War as a legitimate humanitarian intervention, see Michael Walzer, "Inspections Yes, War No," *The New Republic*, September 30, 2002, 21–22.

sources to reduce dependence on foreign oil, pressured its allies for democratic change, and pursued progressive reforms at home.[199]

In the Middle East, liberal hawks urged the United States to promote better governance, open economies, women's empowerment, and a free press, even if that meant embracing a semi-imperial role.[200] The writer Paul Berman, for instance, said that the real goal of the Iraq War should be "to begin a rollback of the several ... political movements that add up to Muslim totalitarianism" and "foment a liberal revolution in the Middle East."[201] Without these larger changes, simply overthrowing Saddam would not defeat radicalism in the region.[202] The liberal case for war demonstrated that the perceived bankruptcy of containment had spread beyond neoconservative circles, as did the belief that politically transforming the Middle East was both ethical and vital to US security.

In contrast to the Powell–Blair approach and the liberal hawks, there were two primary groupings that opposed the war and dissented from the regime change consensus: conditionalist supporters of containment and anti-war leftists. By the early 2000s, conditionalist defenders of containment had been severely reduced in numbers and influence, but they still held significant influence in the political and policy establishment. Key supporters of this position included policy scholars like Carnegie Endowment President Jessica Mathews and political scientists John Mearsheimer and Stephen Walt, Democrats like Senators Edward Kennedy and Robert Byrd, and some notable policy-makers, including Brent Scowcroft and Richard Haass. Haass was one of the few high-ranking members of the Bush administration to argue for containment while in office.[203]

The remaining conditionalists proposed that containment was a superior alternative to war, especially if it could be strengthened and adjusted to changing conditions, and denied that war with Iraq was necessary in the absence of open Iraqi aggression. They also attacked the foundational assumptions of the regime change consensus. Conditionalists believed that the Iraqi threat should be measured not by

---

[199] Quote is from Thomas Friedman, "Bush, Iraq, and Sister Souljah," *New York Times*, December 8, 2002. See also Packer, "Introduction," 19.

[200] Michael Ignatieff, "The Burden," *The New York Times*, January 5, 2003, www.nytimes .com/2003/01/05/magazine/the-american-empire-the-burden.html (accessed May 1, 2019).

[201] Berman quoted in "Roll Call: Who's for War, Who's against It, and Why," February 19, 2003, Slate.com, accessed September 28, 2018, www.slate.com/articles/news_and_po litics/politics/2003/02/roll_call.html. For more on the concept of Islamic and Baathist totalitarianism, see Berman, *Terror and Liberalism*, 54–58.

[202] Thomas Friedman, "Thinking about Iraq," *New York Times*, January 22, 2003, A21; Keller, "Hawk Club," *New York Times*, February 8, 2003; Zakaria, "Invade Iraq," 37.

[203] Haass, *War of Necessity*, 222–223, 233.

the seemingly fixed intentions of its regime but by its capability to do harm, which could be limited by US actions. They wanted to use the urgency of the post-9/11 political moment to revive containment by tightening sanctions, reinserting even tougher inspections, and diplomatically isolating Saddam.[204]

Conditionalists offered a fundamentally different interpretation of Saddam's behavior and psychology in an attack on a key plank of the regime change consensus. In contrast to the hawkish portrayal of Saddam as irrational and revenge-driven, the defenders of containment claimed instead that Saddam mainly desired power and survival and that containment had kept him preoccupied with domestic security rather than external aggression.[205] Moreover, they argued that Saddam's major acts of aggression were not signs of the uselessness of deterrence because the United States had not offered a clear deterrent threat in cases like Iran or Kuwait. John Mearsheimer and Stephen Walt noted that Saddam's invasion of Iran sought limited goals and responded in part to Iranian subversion.[206] The United States actually supported Saddam during this war, even when he used chemical weapons on the Kurds. This crime, however heinous, did not demonstrate that Saddam would use WMD on Americans because the Kurds, unlike the Americans, could not respond in kind. In 1990, the United States also failed to signal to Saddam that he should not invade Kuwait. Mearsheimer and Walt claimed: "Deterrence did not fail in this case; it was never tried."[207]

Under containment, in contrast, Saddam had avoided open aggression and quickly withdrawn his own threats when the United States threatened him, as in the 1994 Kuwaiti border crisis. The lesson here for Mearsheimer and other defenders of containment was that "Iraq has never gone to war in the face of a clear deterrent threat." There was no reason to think 9/11 had changed this fact, especially when Saddam's

---

[204] Haass, *War of Necessity*, 211; Michael O'Hanlon, House Committee on Armed Services, *United States Policy toward Iraq*, 107th Cong., 2nd sess., October 2, 2002, 349–352; Morton Halperin, "A Case for Containment," *Washington Post*, February 11, 2003, A21; Michael Walzer, "The Right Way," *New York Times Book Review*, March 13, 2003, 34.

[205] Jessica Matthews, "The Wrong Target," *Washington Post*, March 4, 2002, A19; Michael O'Hanlon and Philip Gordon, "Is Fighting Iraq Worth the Risks?" *New York Times*, July 25, 2002, A17; Thomas Ricks, "Ex-Commander Opposes Iraq Invasion," *Washington Post*, October 11, 2002, A7; Patrick Leahy, *Cong. Rec.*, 107th Cong., 2nd sess., September 26, 2002: 18180; Morton Halperin, Senate Foreign Relations Committee, *Threats, Responses, and Regional Considerations*, July 31, 2002, 82.

[206] John Mearsheimer and Stephen M. Walt, "An Unnecessary War," *Foreign Policy* 134 (January–February, 2003): 52–53.

[207] Mearsheimer and Walt, "Unnecessary War," 53.

military still had not recovered from the Gulf War and sanctions.[208] Even if inspections did not fully succeed and Saddam developed some WMD, the threat of massive US retaliation would still deter him. Thus, Mearsheimer and other defenders of containment contested the crucial idea, shared by the Bush administration and the Powell–Blair approach, that if inspections failed, then war would become necessary.[209]

The pro-containment school also dissented from the widely held idea that 9/11 should change the way Americans viewed Iraq. They argued that 9/11 changed Americans' psychology and worldview, while the Iraqi threat remained the same.[210] The core of the nexus concept, Iraqi hand-off of WMD to terrorists, was as unrealistic after 9/11 as it was beforehand. Scowcroft argued, for instance, that there was "scant evidence to tie Saddam to terrorist organizations," that Iraq and al-Qaeda held disparate goals and ideals, and that Saddam was "unlikely to risk his investment in weapons of mass destruction, much less his country, by handing such weapons to terrorists who would use them for their own purposes."[211] Saddam mainly wanted these weapons to "deter us from intervening to block his aggressive designs" and to protect himself from domestic and regional challengers.[212] The 98-year-old George Kennan echoed this assessment, calling the administration's attempts to link Iraq and al-Qaeda "pathetically unsupportive and unreliable," adding that the invasion "seems to me well out of proportion to the dangers involved."[213]

Defenders of containment further argued that a global consensus had arisen around stopping al-Qaeda, and the United States should keep its focus there rather than take on a divisive and costly war with Iraq.[214] They

---

[208] Quote is from Mearsheimer and Walt, "Unnecessary War," 54. See also O'Hanlon, House Committee on Armed Services, *United States Policy toward Iraq*, October 2, 2002, 353; William Delahunt, House Committee on International Relations, *Authorization for Use of Military Force against Iraq*, October 2–3, 2002, 116; Richard Betts, "Suicide from Fear of Death?" *Foreign Affairs* 38, no. 5 (January, 2003): 38; Philip Gordon and Michael O'Hanlon, "Should the War on Terrorism Target Iraq?" Brookings Institute, Policy Brief No. 93, January 1, 2002, 5–7.

[209] Mearsheimer and Walt, "Unnecessary War," 57; Nicholas Kristof, "War and Wisdom," *New York Times*, February 7, 2003, A25.

[210] Bartholomew Sparrow, *The Strategist: Brent Scowcroft and the Call of National Security* (New York: Public Affairs, 2015), 516.

[211] Brent Scowcroft, "Don't Attack Saddam," *Wall Street Journal*, August 15, 2002, A12. For similar arguments, see Daniel Benjamin, "Saddam Hussein and Al Qaeda Are Not Allies," *New York Times*, September 30, 2002, A25; Paul Krugman, "Still Living Dangerously," *New York Times*, October 15, 2002, A27; Mearsheimer and Walt, "Unnecessary War," 57–58.

[212] Scowcroft, "Don't Attack," *Wall Street Journal*, August 15, 2002.

[213] Alfonsi, *Circle in the Sand*, 398.

[214] Haass, *War of Necessity*, 200–201; Joseph Nye, "Attacking Iraq Now Would Harm War on Terror," *Wall Street Journal*, March 12, 2002, A26; Scowcroft, "Don't Attack," *Wall Street Journal*, August 15, 2002, A12.

maintained that Iraq was not the most dangerous rogue state, often pointing to North Korea. North Korea possessed an active uranium enrichment program and announced in October 2002 that it was restarting several reactors and withdrawing from the Nuclear Nonproliferation Treaty.[215] While these actions far exceeded Saddam's suspected activities, Bush claimed that this was a "diplomatic showdown" and that the United States had "no intention of invading" North Korea.[216] Senator Russ Feingold (D-WI) noted that the discrepancy between US policies toward Iraq and North Korea suggested a clear lesson for any rogue state: "Acquire weapons and then be free from the threat of military action, or do not acquire weapons and then perhaps be subject to invasion." Thus, conditionalist defenders of containment held that preventive war in Iraq would incentivize WMD proliferation rather than curb it.[217]

Many pro-containment figures also challenged the morality and legality of Bush's case for war. Bush had not shown that Saddam could strike the United States or that he had imminent plans to do so, making the war preventive rather than preemptive.[218] The doctrine of preventive war could not become "an acceptable norm of international behavior," in Jessica Mathews words, lest any state cite the mere possibility of being struck as justification for striking first.[219] Preventive war would lower the bar for violence from imminence and self-defense to suspicion and fear, possibly even excusing thinly veiled aggression.[220] Other countries, as Senator Robert Byrd (D-WV) argued, saw the United States as asserting "the right to turn its firepower on any corner of the globe which might be suspect in the war on terrorism. We assert that right without the sanction of any international body."[221] Humanitarian intervention, moreover, did

---

[215] Robert Litwak, *Regime Change: U.S. Strategy through the Prism of 9/11* (Washington, DC: Woodrow Wilson Center Press, 2007), 267.

[216] Litwak, *Regime Change*, 269; David Sanger, "President Makes Case that North Korea Is No Iraq," *New York Times*, January 1, 2003, A1; Mann, *Rise of the Vulcans*, 346.

[217] Russell Feingold, Senate Foreign Relations Committee, *UNMOVIC and IAEA Reports*, January 30, 2003, 39; Matthews, "Wrong Target," *Washington Post*, March 4, 2002; John Mearsheimer and Stephen Walt, "Keeping Saddam Hussein in a Box," *New York Time*, February 2, 2003, A15.

[218] William Galston, "Perils of Preemptive War," *The American Prospect*, September 23, 2002, 15; Walzer, "Right Way," *New York Times Book Review*, March 13, 2003, 34.

[219] Matthews, "Wrong Target," *Washington Post*, March 4, 2002. See also Editorial, "Saying No to War," *New York Times*, March 9, 2003, A1; Sherrod Brown, Barbara Lee, and William Delahunt in House Committee on International Relations, *Authorization for Use of Military Force against Iraq*, October 2–3, 2002, 17, 34, 116.

[220] Edward Kennedy, *Cong. Rec.*, 107th Cong., 2nd sess., October 7, 2002, 10001; Robert Byrd, *Cong. Rec.*, 107th Cong., 2nd sess., October 7, 2002, 10007.

[221] Robert Byrd, "Speech in the Senate," March 19, 2003, salon.com, accessed September 25, 2018, www.salon.com/2008/03/19/byrd/.

not justify an invasion because Saddam's worst crimes occurred over a decade ago, and the regime was horrible but not uniquely immoral.[222]

Finally, like Middle East experts in the US government, defenders of containment cast doubt on the idea that the war would be easy and the Iraqi people would welcome Americans as liberators. *New York Times* columnist Nicholas Kristof, for instance, had traveled to Iraq and encountered great hostility for the United States, which Iraqis saw as a new colonial power that had caused immense suffering under sanctions. One university president waved a pencil in Kristof's face and said angrily: "You see this? It took 15 months just to import pencils for our students."[223] Democratic transformation was a neoconservative fantasy, these critics argued, as Iraq lacked the preconditions for democracy or liberalism.[224] They also excoriated the administration for inadequate preparation for occupying and rebuilding an economically devastated and socially divided country. The more probable outcome of invasion was retribution and civil war along ethnic lines, interference from regional actors, and terrorist groups finding haven and recruits in the chaos.[225]

While the pro-containment position occupied a thin slice on the US spectrum of thought on Iraq, it was a mainstream viewpoint in countries like France and Germany. French President Jacques Chirac and German Chancellor Gerhard Schroeder did not believe that Saddam represented a severe enough threat to justify war. They disputed the Americans' dire assessment of Iraq's WMD programs and claimed that the MEPP was the key to deflating radicalism in the region.[226] Chirac warned Bush in February 2003 that "war will have catastrophic consequences, including on terrorism throughout the entire world."[227] Chirac, Schroeder, and

---

[222] Michael Walzer, "No Strikes: Inspectors Yes, War No," *The New Republic*, September 30, 2002, 19–20.

[223] Nicholas Kristof, "The Stones of Baghdad," *New York Times*, October 4, 2002, A27.

[224] Adam Garfinkle, "The Impossible Imperative? Conjuring Arab Democracy," *The National Interest* 69 (Fall, 2002): 156–167. Tony Judt, "The Wrong War at the Wrong Time," *New York Times*, October 20, 2002, C11.

[225] Sparrow, *The Strategist*, 522; Michael O'Hanlon, "The Price of Stability," *New York Times*, October 22, 2002, A31; Anthony Cordesman, "Security and WMD Issues in a Post-Saddam Iraq," February 11, 2003, csis.org, accessed January 26, 2019, https://csis-prod.s3.amazonaws.com/s3fs-public/legacy_files/files/attachments/ts030211_cordesman.pdf, 2–4.

[226] Frederic Bozo, *A History of the Iraq Crisis: France, the United States, and Iraq, 1991–2003* (Washington, DC: Woodrow Wilson Center Press, 2016), 111. David Malone, *The International Struggle Over Iraq: Politics in the U.N. Security Council, 1980–2005* (New York: Oxford University, 2005), 192.

[227] Frederic Bozo, "'We Don't Need You': France, the United States, and Iraq, 1991–2003," *Diplomatic History* 41, no. 1 (January, 2017): 200; Joschka Fischer, "Address before the United Nations Security Council," March 19, 2003, in Ehrenberg, McSherrey, Sanchez, and Sayej, *The Iraq Papers*, 154–157.

other leaders feared that Bush was driving US foreign policy in a unilateral and unethical direction, including violations of international law like indefinite detention and "enhanced" interrogation techniques.[228] For France, Germany, China, and Russia, containment through inspections would control Saddam's WMD programs and limit his menace to the region. Schroeder ruled out German participation in a war completely, with or without a UN mandate, and France refused to consider the question until inspections had a chance to disarm Iraq peacefully.[229]

The other significant group that dissented from the regime change consensus and opposed the Iraq War was the political and intellectual left. The anti-war left evolved from the humanitarian critics of sanctions in 1990s, who had argued that the US priority vis-à-vis Iraq must be lifting sanctions and alleviating the health crisis in Iraq. Unlike the pro-containment school, the left argued that both containment and war were immoral and unnecessary. A key underlying premise of the leftist approach was that the United States had little moral high ground in the struggle against extremism in the Middle East. As anti-sanctions activists like Phyllis Bennis argued, the United States had bombed and starved the Iraqi people, supported dictators, and backed Israeli aggression.[230] For the left, 9/11 was an unjustifiable but predictable manifestation of a justified subaltern rage at US crimes and hypocrisy. As Noam Chomsky put it: "We can think of the United States as an 'innocent victim' only if we adopt the convenient path of ignoring the record of its actions and those of its allies."[231] Leftists like historian Howard Zinn said that now that Americans had a taste of the suffering of "the victims of American military action – in Vietnam, in Latin America, in Iraq," they should rethink their capitalistic and hegemonic foreign policy.[232] From this vantage point, another US war in the Middle East would only exacerbate terrorism and extremism.

---

[228] James Rubin, "Stumbling into War," *Foreign Affairs* 82, no. 5 (September–October, 2003): 59; Steven Erlanger, "Russian Aide Warns U.S. Not to Extend War to Iraq," *New York Times*, February 4, 2002, A10.

[229] Rubin, "Stumbling into War," 52; Fischer, "Address before the United Nations Security Council," March 19, 2003, in Ehrenberg, McSherrey, Sanchez, and Sayej, *The Iraq Papers*, 154–157; Malone, *International Struggle*, 192.

[230] Phyllis Bennis, "The Failure of U.S. Policy toward Iraq and Proposed Alternatives," *Middle East Policy* 8, no. 3 (September, 2001): 104–107.

[231] Noam Chomsky, *9-11* (New York: Seven Stories, 2001), 35; Susan Sontag, "Reflections on September 11th," in Sifry and Cerf, *Iraq War Reader*, 215.

[232] Howard Zinn quoted in *Christopher Hitchens and His Critics: Terror, Iraq, and the Left*, ed. Simon Cottee and Thomas Cushman (New York: New York University Press, 2008), 12. See also Noam Chomsky, "Drain the Swamp and There Will Be No More Mosquitoes," in Sifry and Cerf, *Iraq War Reader*, 302.

The anti-war left also argued that human rights, democracy, and the nexus threat were all pretexts for an aggressive, illegal war in the name of oil interests and a vision of "absolute military hegemony over the earth."[233] Containment was hardly better, given its dependence on immoral sanctions and a large US military presence in the Middle East. Left-wing Democrats like Dennis Kucinich (D-OH) argued that the United States should support inspections but lift economic sanctions and end the no-fly zones.[234] They hoped that this strategy would enable a middle class to reemerge in Iraq and possibly moderate the regime.[235] Even the anti-war left did not support containment, which shows how narrow a slice of the political and intellectual spectrum the defenders of containment occupied.

The leftist and pro-containment viewpoints failed to gain broad support because they did not appeal to the standard "lessons" embedded in the now-dominant regime change consensus nor the mood of fear and vulnerability in post-9/11 America. While they organized several of the largest anti-war rallies, the leftists possessed little institutional power, and their rhetoric made them easy to tar as anti-American in an era of patriotic sentiment.[236] Defenders of containment had greater institutional influence, but they ran into the familiar problem of a hazy theory of change for containment. They could proffer containment as a short-term management strategy, but they could only elucidate the end point of this policy in vague terms. Conditionalists wanted to avoid putting a time limit on a policy they said was basically working.[237] However, this approach appeared to many in the political establishment and the public to require a seemingly indefinite toleration of a rogue actor like Saddam. This had been a flaw in containment's political viability in the 1990s, and it fit especially poorly with the post-9/11 climate, which lowered risk-tolerance and created a bias toward action against threats like Iraq.

---

[233] Quote is from Jonathan Schell, "The Case against the War," *The Nation*, March 3, 2003, 17. See also Editorial, "The War on Iraq Is Wrong," *The Nation*, July 8, 2002, 3–5; Arundathi Roy, "Wars Are Never Fought for Altruistic Reasons," in Sifry and Cerf, *Iraq War Reader*, 341–342.

[234] Dennis Kucinich, *Cong. Rec.*, 107th Cong., 2nd sess., September 18, 2002, 17010. See also Editorial, "War on Iraq Is Wrong," *The Nation*, July 8, 2002, 5; Phyllis Bennis, "The UN, the US, and Iraq," *The Nation*, November 11, 2002, 9.

[235] Editorial, "War on Iraq Is Wrong," *The Nation*, July 8, 2002, 4.

[236] Tony Judt, "Bush's Useful Idiots," *London Review of Books*, September 16, 2006, www.lrb.co.uk/v28/n18/tony-judt/bushs-useful-idiots (accessed May 3, 2019).

[237] Morton Halperin, Senate Foreign Relations Committee, *Threats, Responses, and Regional Considerations*, July 31, 2002, 82. Halperin was the State Department's Director of Policy Planning from 1998–2001.

Congress, Inspections, and the Coming of the Iraq War, October 2002–March 2003

In the months before the war began on March 20, 2003, skeptics of Bush's case for war had two major chances to impede the rush to war or find alternative means for disarming Iraq. The first was the Congressional debate in the fall of 2002 over authorizing the use of force. The second was the process of inspections itself, which restarted in November 2002. Nevertheless, followers of the Powell–Blair approach continued to argue in procedural terms without challenging the Bush administration's fundamental assumptions about the Iraqi threat, which they shared to a large degree. Congress, which was shaped by this line of thought, put no meaningful restrictions on Bush's authority to use force against Iraq, focusing instead on ensuring that he put a real effort into diplomacy and inspections. The Congressional debates on Iraq and the broader public conversation about inspections in late 2002 and early 2003 reveal just how narrow and ineffective the Powell–Blair criticism of Bush's Iraq policy was and how its shortcomings facilitated the coming of war.

Members of the Powell–Blair approach conceded to Bush the crucial point that the success of inspections would be measured by Saddam's level of compliance rather than the degree to which inspections constrained his WMD programs or whether or not inspectors found anything substantial. Like the hawks, they believed in what might be called "inspections entropy," a perceived lesson of the 1990s. Eventually, within this logic, the world would abandon tough inspections, Iraq would obstruct, and the process would collapse, letting Saddam off the hook again.[238] The Powell–Blair school's arguments for proper Congressional authorization and a last chance for inspections were mostly procedural, designed for pursuing regime change "the right way" rather than exploring alternatives.

Congressional debate started when Bush sent a draft authorization to Congress on September 13, 2002. Many Democrats and some Republicans objected to this draft, which carved out war powers that could be read as extending beyond Iraq.[239] Joseph Biden and Richard Lugar, both partial skeptics of the Bush case, drafted a bill that required Bush to receive Security Council authorization for the use of force after inspections had failed. Alternatively, under this version Bush could issue a presidential determination that the threat to the United States was "so

---

[238] Editorial, "Iraq's False Response," *Washington Post*, November 17, 2002, B6; Editorial, "Decisive Days for Iraq," *New York Times*, December 6, 2002, A34.

[239] Chuck Hagel, interview by Wil Hylton, January 21, 2007, GQ.com, accessed October 20, 2018, www.gq.com/story/republican-senator-chuck-hagel-war.

grave" that he needed to strike without UN support.[240] Whereas the White House resolution authorized the president to enforce all Security Council resolutions relevant to Iraq, the Biden–Lugar version authorized force only for UN resolutions relating to WMD disarmament.[241]

Bush announced a deal with House Minority Leader Richard Gephardt on October 2 that sidelined the Biden–Lugar bill and added a few more conditions in exchange for broader Democratic support.[242] The final resolution, House Joint Resolution 114 (H. J. Res. 114), required the president to issue a determination to Congress within 48 hours of launching any military action regarding why diplomatic measures could not protect national security or enforce the Security Council's resolutions. This resolution limited Bush's authority specifically to Iraq, whereas the original White House resolution expansively authorized Bush to use force to "restore international peace and security in the region."[243] Nonetheless, this resolution featured essentially the same authorization of force as the White House draft, empowering Bush to "defend the national security of the United States against the continuing threat posed by Iraq" and to "enforce all relevant United Nations Security Council resolutions regarding Iraq."[244]

On October 10, 2002, the House voted 296–133 for H. J. Res. 114, and the next day the Senate passed the same resolution by a vote of 77–23. Democrats voted against this bill 126–82 in the House and 29–21 in favor in the Senate.[245] Republicans voted overwhelmingly in favor of H. J. Res 114. The Senate was equally divided and the Republicans had a slim majority in the House, making Democratic votes vital for creating these large margins. In contrast to this vote, 179 out of 265 Democrats in the House and 45 of 55 in the Senate voted against the January 1991 authorization for the Gulf War.[246]

Democrats and skeptical Republicans who supported the authorization argued that a united domestic front was the best way to convince the

[240] Miles Pomper, "Evolution of the Resolutions," *Congressional Quarterly*, October 5, 2002, 2607.

[241] Elizabeth Bumiller, "Bush Strikes Deal for House Backing on Action in Iraq," *New York Times*, October 3, 2002, A1.

[242] Packer, *Assassins' Gate*, 388; Woodward, *Plan of Attack*, 200.

[243] S. J. Res. 45, September 26, 2002, govtrack.us, accessed November 2, 2018, www.go vtrack.us/congress/bills/107/sjres45/summary.

[244] H. J. Res. 114-Authorization for Use of Military Force against Iraq Resolution of 2002, Congress.gov, October 10, 2002, www.congress.gov/bill/107th-congress/house-joint-r esolution/114.

[245] H. J. Res. 114-Authorization for Use of Military Force against Iraq Resolution of 2002, October 10, 2002.

[246] Carroll Dohery and Pat Towell, "Democrats Try to Bury Image of Foreign Policy Weakness," *Congressional Quarterly*, March 23, 1991, 752–759.

United Nations to support a tough resolution against Saddam, which was ultimately the best way to resolve the crisis without war.[247] They also appeared to believe that Bush would thoroughly pursue the UN route. Chuck Hagel, for example, recalled: "I was told by the president – we all were – that he would exhaust every diplomatic effort."[248] Every prospective candidate for the Democratic nomination for president in 2004, including Kerry, Gephardt, Edwards, Biden, and Liebermann, voted for the resolution and mostly echoed Bush's arguments.[249] They were also influenced by the post-9/11 mood, as one Congressman said that Democrats "have changed in the same way the American people have changed. We are acutely aware of how vulnerable the country is."[250]

The desire to look tough on foreign policy before the 2002 midterm elections also influenced Democrats, many of whom were still trying to shed the post-Vietnam impression of weakness on foreign affairs. Bush still held high approval ratings, and he carried great political momentum from his superficial successes in Afghanistan. Indeed, many Republicans used Iraq and the War on Terror to assail Democrats' patriotism. Bush himself argued on September 13 that Democrats could not "wait for the United Nations to make a decision" before they voted. He added: "If I were running for office, I'm not sure how I would explain to the American people ... you know 'Vote for me, and oh, by the way, on a matter of national security, I think I'm going to wait for somebody else to act.'"[251] Democrats like Gephardt regretted that they had voted against the successful Persian Gulf War, and they feared further political fallout for not endorsing this war.[252] The Republicans nevertheless picked up eight seats in the House and regained control of the Senate in the midterms in November, using several Democrats' votes against the Iraq resolution to great effect.[253]

---

[247] See Statements of Howard Berman, Gary Ackerman, and Robert Wexler in House Committee on International Relations, *Authorization for Use of Military Force against Iraq*, October 2–3, 2002, 5, 7, 21.

[248] Hagel, interview by Wil Hylton, January 21, 2007, GQ.com.

[249] Dan Balz, "Democratic Hopefuls Back Bush on Iraq," *Washington Post*, September 14, 2002, A4.

[250] Jim VandeHei and Julie Eilperin, "9/11 Changed Equation for Democrats," *Washington Post*, October 6, 2002, A1.

[251] Miles Pomper, "Lawmakers Pushing Back from Quick Vote on Iraq," *Congressional Quarterly*, September 14, 2002, 2352–2357; Alison Mitchell, "Republicans Wielding Iraq as an Issue in Senate Races in Conservative States," *New York Times*, September 18, 2002, A28.

[252] VandeHei and Eilperin, "Changed Equation," *Washington Post*, October 6, 2002; Ricks, *Fiasco*, 61–64; Julian Zelizer, *Arsenal of Democracy: The Politics of National Security from World War II to the War on Terrorism* (New York: Basic Books, 2010), 460–461.

[253] Zelizer, *Arsenal of Democracy*, 464.

Democrats who voted against the resolution saw it as a vast and unjustified grant of authority, in advance of diplomacy, to declare war against an exaggerated threat.[254] Prominent Democrats who voted "no" included Carl Levin, Robert Byrd, and Edward Kennedy. Nevertheless, attempts by more skeptical Democrats to more substantially restrain the president's authority were both limited in scope and unsuccessful. Levin introduced a resolution that authorized Bush to use force only if he received a UN mandate. Nonetheless, upon presenting his resolution, Levin said: "I don't differ much from Bush in his detailing of the threat posed by Saddam." Levin mainly sought to prevent the United States from taking unilateral action against Iraq and to bind Bush more tightly to diplomacy.[255]

Furthermore, in the markup of H. J. Res. 114 in the House International Relations Committee, a group of Democrats proposed twelve alternative resolutions. Brad Sherman (D-CA) introduced a resolution that struck every justification for the use of force from H. J. Res 114 except those relating to WMD. This resolution treated WMD as the sole legitimate reason for invading Iraq, given other countries' dismal human rights practices.[256] His draft authorized force only if the president certified that Iraq had refused to readmit or cooperate with inspectors.[257] Most resolutions from skeptical Congressmen like Sherman still authorized Bush to use force, merely requiring him to offer more elaborate assurances to Congress that other means had failed. Sherman framed his amendment, for example, as authorizing Bush to take the "Powell–Blair approach," justifying war once inspections had been tried and encouraging but not requiring a UN mandate. Under his resolution, if the United States does go to war, Sherman argued: "We do so with considerably more international support and considerably more domestic support than we would have otherwise."[258]

Congresswoman Barbara Lee (D-CA) introduced a more restrictive amendment that noted the success of inspections in the 1990s in dismantling most of Iraq's WMD program. Her draft struck the entire war

[254] Barbara Lee, House Committee on International Relations, *Authorization for Use of Military Force against Iraq*, October 2–3, 2002, 35; Leahy, *Cong. Rec.*, September 26, 2002, 18178; Russell Feingold, *Cong. Rec.*, 107th Cong., 2nd sess., September 26, 2002, 18234.

[255] Carl Levin, *Cong. Rec.*, 107th Cong., 2nd sess., October 9, 2002, 10191–10192.

[256] Jo Ann Davis, House Committee on International Relations, *Authorization for the Use of Military Force against Iraq*, October 2–3, 2002, 145.

[257] Brad Sherman, House Committee on International Relations, *Authorization for Use of Military Force against Iraq*, October 2–3, 2002, 75–77.

[258] Sherman, House Committee on International Relations, *Authorization for Use of Military Force against Iraq*, October 2–3, 2002, 80, 86.

powers clause from H. J. 114 and called for the United States to pursue only diplomatic means at this time. Lee called for "an enhanced containment system," tough military sanctions and long-term inspections as an alternative to regime change.[259] Her resolution was rare in mandating a second Congressional vote after diplomacy had been attempted and for arguing that containment had managed the Iraqi threat well. None of these resolutions, however, gained much steam. Levin's amendment failed in the Senate 24–75, and Lee's failed in the House 72–355. Sherman's amendment failed 31–15 in committee, with most Democrats voting "no" in large part to avoid upsetting Gephardt's deal with the president.[260]

Robert Byrd was the only Senate Democrat who did not support the opening of debate on Iraq, and he eventually voted against the authorization.[261] On October 10, he upbraided his peers for granting vast war powers and failing to challenge a president who was "changing the conventional understanding of the term 'self-defense'" and using the upcoming midterm election to silence dissent. In his eyes, Congress had abdicated its responsibility to conduct a substantive debate about the war. His words capture the narrow terms of the Congressional debate on Iraq:

The debate that began in the Senate last week is centered not on the fundamental and monumental questions of whether and why the United States should go to war with Iraq, but rather on the mechanics of how to best wordsmith the president's use of force resolution in order to give him virtually unchecked authority to commit the nation's military to an unprovoked attack on a sovereign nation.[262]

Most Democrats who voted for the authorization continued to criticize Bush's Iraq policy, but in October 2002, they gave away their main opportunity to restrain the Bush administration in large part because they did not concur with the core tenets of the regime change consensus.

Following the passage of H. J. Res. 114, members of the Powell–Blair approach saw inspections and coercive diplomacy as the best opportunity to resolve the Iraq confrontation peacefully. Throughout the fall of 2002, Powell worked at the Security Council to draft such a resolution, which passed as Resolution 1441 on November 8. It declared that Iraq "remains in

---

[259] Barbara Lee, *Cong. Rec.*, 107th Cong., 2nd sess., October 10, 2002, H7740.

[260] House Committee on International Relations, *Authorization for Use of Military Force against Iraq*, October 2–3, 2002, 97. For the Lee amendment, see H. Amdt. 608, October 10, 2002, accessed November 12, 2018, http://clerk.house.gov/evs/2002/rol 1452.xml; for the Levin Amendment, see S. Amdt. 4862, October 10, 2002, accessed November 12, 2018, www.c-span.org/congress/bills/bill/?107/samdt4862.

[261] Alison Mitchell, "Lawmakers Begin Push to Give Bush Authority on Iraq," *New York Times*, October 4, 2002, A1.

[262] Robert Byrd, "Congress Must Resist the Rush to War," *New York Times*, October 10, 2002, A39.

material breach" of its obligation to disarm and afforded Iraq "a final opportunity to comply" with new inspections. The inspections would be conducted by the IAEA under Mohammed el-Baradei, which would handle nuclear weapons, and UNMOVIC under Hans Blix, which would focus on chemical and biological weapons as well as ballistic missiles. Resolution 1441 mandated that Iraq provide these teams "immediate, unimpeded, unconditional, and unrestricted access" to any site, equipment, or person, including the so-called presidential sites that had caused tension in 1998.[263] Ideally, the inspectors would destroy all of Iraq's remaining WMD programs and verify disarmament. If Iraq did not cooperate, Resolution 1441 warned that "it will face serious consequences."[264] Iraq accepted this resolution and readmitted inspectors at the end of November.

This resolution, however, papered over serious disagreements between the United States and Great Britain on one side and France, Russia, and China on the other. The United States believed that the phrase "serious consequences" authorized force without further Security Council approval. In the parlance of the United Nations, the phrase "all necessary means" is generally accepted as authorizing the use of force, whereas "serious consequences" is not. France, Russia, and China countered that before the Security Council authorized the use of force, the inspectors must report that Iraq was not complying and the Security Council must vote again on an explicit authorization.[265] In contrast to the United States, Tony Blair supported this idea of a "second resolution" in order to augment international support for the war and to legitimize it to a doubtful audience at home.[266] Resolution 1441 did not define how frequent or severe Iraqi noncompliance had to be to trigger the use of force, nor did it specify how long inspections should be allowed to continue. These ambiguities were necessary for passing Resolution 1441 given France, Russia, and China's deep skepticism about war, but these disagreements would reemerge as inspections proceeded in the winter of 2002–2003.[267]

The Bush administration and other hawks could hardly mask their distrust in inspections, which they had held since the 1990s. In early October, Christopher Meyer observed that within the Cabinet, "[t]he points of disagreement were relatively narrow: no one doubts that inspections will fail, the argument is how hard to try for international support for

---

[263] "Resolution 1441," 97.   [264] "Resolution 1441," 98.

[265] "In the Diplomats' Own Words," *New York Times*, November 9, 2002, A10; Philip H. Gordon and Jeremy Shapiro, *Allies at War: America, Europe, and the Crisis over Iraq* (New York: McGraw-Hill, 2004), 108–114.

[266] House of Commons, "Report of the Iraq Inquiry," July 6, 2016, Vol. 2, Section 3.5, 215, 242.

[267] Malone, *International Struggle*, 194–195; Gordon and Shapiro, *Allies at War*, 114.

the war."[268] Rumsfeld and Cheney feared that the United States would again become mired in Saddam's inspections games, undermining the momentum toward war and dividing the Security Council. Cheney openly disparaged inspections, claiming that in the 1990s they had "consistently underestimated or missed what it was Saddam Hussein was doing."[269] He added: "A return of the inspectors would provide no assurance whatsoever of his compliance. ... On the contrary, there is a great danger that it would provide false comfort that Saddam was somehow back in his box."[270] As inspections dragged on, as Rumsfeld warned: "Saddam's preparations to use weapons of mass destruction can be expected to advance daily."[271]

Bush officials contended that the standard of evidence for inspections should be simple: Was Saddam fully complying and turning over all relevant materials or not? This standard emerged from the lessons the hawks derived from the 1990s. Rumsfeld wrote to Bush that UNMOVIC's bureaucrats and scientists would be unable to "catch Saddam Hussein, as it were, with his pants down. The long history of weapons inspections in Iraq tells us that this is highly unlikely."[272] Without such a "flagrant obstruction" by the Iraqis, the process would inevitably stall in "a protracted period of inconclusive inspections" that offered Saddam his "best hope of inflicting a strategic defeat on the U.S."[273] They contended that past inspections owed most of their success to defections from Iraqi personnel.[274] As Rumsfeld argued, even tough inspections had been insufficient: "Even intrusive inspections over several years missed significant parts of the Iraq program and failed to detect an ongoing buildup."[275] Bush officials claimed that "inspections only work in

---

[268] House of Commons, "Report of the Iraq Inquiry," July 6, 2016, Vol. 2, Section 3.5, 252.

[269] Kaufmann, "Threat Inflation," 42.

[270] "Cheney's Words" *New York Times*, August 27, 2002. See also Christopher Marquis, "Cheney Doubts Weapons Inspectors Can End Baghdad's Threat," *New York Times*, August 8, 2002, A4.

[271] Memorandum, Donald Rumsfeld to George W. Bush, "UN Inspections of Iraq," October 14, 2002, Digital National Security Archive, Targeting Iraq Part 1, 1. See also Rumsfeld testimony in Senate Armed Services Committee, *U.S. Policy on Iraq*, September 19, 2002, 69.

[272] Memorandum, Rumsfeld to Bush, October 14, 2002, 1.

[273] "Flagrant obstruction" and "best hope" are from Memorandum, Rumsfeld to Bush, October 14, 2002, 1. "Protracted period" is from Memorandum, Donald Rumsfeld to Richard Cheney, Colin Powell, and Condoleezza Rice, "Iraqi Inspections/UN Strategy," October 14, 2002, Digital National Security Archive, Targeting Iraq Part 1, 2.

[274] Walter Pincus, "Rumsfeld Disputes Value of Iraq Arms Inspections," *Washington Post*, April 16, 2002, A13; Donald Rumsfeld, Senate Armed Services Committee, *U.S. Policy on Iraq*, September 19, 2002, 30; Richard Perle, House Committee on Armed Services, *United States Policy toward Iraq*, October 2, 2002, 287.

[275] Memorandum, Rumsfeld to Cheney, Powell, and Rice, October 14, 2002, 1.

a country that wants to cooperate with them," pointing to the example of South Africa's voluntary dismantling of its nuclear program in the early 1990s.[276] If Iraq decided to hide its programs, as Powell argued, "they can inspect for 12 years and not get anywhere."[277] Several former inspectors, including David Kay, Richard Spertzel, and Charles Duelfer, supported this standard of evidence and predicted that inspections would fail.[278]

The hawks concluded that inspectors should not be detectives but more verifiers of Iraqi compliance. They envisioned inspections as a test, in Rumsfeld's words, of "whether the Iraqi leadership has had a change of heart and is actually willing to give up the weapons."[279] If Iraq would "answer questions without being asked" and disclose programs "fully and voluntarily," it could demonstrate this change of heart.[280] Rumsfeld even suggested that only one or two inspectors were needed to verify Iraq's decision.[281] Iraq was too large and the government too "skilled at hiding and cheating" for inspections to do anything besides measure changed strategic intentions "at the highest political level."[282] If Iraq issued a false declaration of its WMD, Rumsfeld argued in October of 2002: "The U.N. should not proceed with inspections, for it would be clear then that there is lacking the good faith and cooperative attitude necessary to make the inspections work."[283] The experience of repeated inspections crises in 1990s showed that if, as Bush claimed, "Iraq's leaders stall inspections and impede their progress, it means they have something to hide."[284] This was a crucial claim: Even if the inspectors did not find illicit weapons programs, mere Iraqi obstruction or delay would demonstrate that these activities persisted. This standard freed the

---

[276] Rumsfeld, interview by Clancy, October 24, 2002.

[277] Transcript, Face the Nation Interview with Colin Powell by Bob Schieffer, November 10, 2002, Anthony Lewis Papers, Part II, Box 489, Folder 3, Iraq (1 of 4), Library of Congress, 3.

[278] Charles Duelfer, "Inspections in Iraq? Be Careful What You Ask For," *Washington Post*, January 9, 2002, A19; Richard Spertzel, "Iraq's Faux Capitulation," *Wall Street Journal*, September 24, 2002, A18; David Kay, "It Was Never about a Smoking Gun," *Washington Post*, January 19, 2003, B3; Charles Duelfer, *Hide and Seek: The Search for Truth in Iraq* (New York: Public Affairs, 2009), 215

[279] Memorandum, Rumsfeld to Bush, October 14, 2002, 1.

[280] State Department, Report, "What Does Disarmament Look Like?" January 23, 2003, State.gov, accessed July 11, 2018, https://2001–2009.state.gov/t/isn/rls/other/16820.htm, 2.

[281] Hans Blix, *Disarming Iraq* (New York: Pantheon Books, 2004), 216.

[282] State Department, "What Does Disarmament Look Like?" 1.

[283] Memorandum, Rumsfeld to Bush, October 14, 2002, 1; George Bush, "Remarks on the Passage of a United Nations Security Council Resolution on Iraq," November 8, 2002, American Presidency Project, accessed July 23, 2018, www.presidency.ucsb.edu/ws/index.php?pid=73175&st=iraq&st1=.

[284] "Transcript of Bush's Remarks on the Security Council's Iraq Resolution," *New York Times*, November 9, 2002, A12.

administration to invade Iraq even if the inspectors did not find major WMD programs.

In a sort of intellectual cul-de-sac, the Bush administration and other hawks maintained that because of the nature of Saddam and his regime, there was almost no chance that he would meet this standard of compliance. When asked if the inspections might disarm Iraq and leave Saddam in power, Rumsfeld replied, "[b]oy, that is a reach," even though going the UN route was predicated on the idea that if inspections succeeded war could be avoided.[285] Cheney, for example, said in an August 2002 speech: "Intelligence is an uncertain business, even in the best of circumstances. This is especially the case when you are dealing with a totalitarian regime that has made a science out of deceiving the international community."[286] When the inspectors failed to find an active nuclear program in Iraq by early 2003, Rice deployed a similar response: "We need to be careful about drawing these conclusions, particularly in a totalitarian state like Iraq."[287] Thus, the totalitarian Baathists' mastery in subterfuge and fabrication would trump the inspectors, leaving regime change as the only option.

The Bush administration's skepticism of the inspections process reflected its suspicion of the United Nations as a restraint on US power and a hive of dictatorial and anti-American states. Many hawks distrusted officials like Hans Blix, whom they believed were so "eager to avoid a war" that they might prevaricate on Iraqi behavior or "declare Iraq in compliance when it is not."[288] Cheney even confronted Blix, telling him that if his conclusions differed from the administration's views, "we will not hesitate to discredit you."[289] France, Russia, and China, moreover, could be expected to undermine tough inspections and make sure their Iraqi trading partner remained in power.[290] Conservative and neoconservative writers

---

[285] Donald Rumsfeld, House Committee on Armed Services, *United States Policy toward Iraq*, October 2, 2002, 110. See also Feith, *War and Decision*, 306.

[286] Richard Cheney, "Remarks Honoring Veterans of the Korean War," August 29, 2002, American Presidency Project, accessed July 23, 2018, www.presidency.ucsb.edu/ws/index.php?pid=79749&st=iraq&st1=.

[287] Quote is from Blix, *Disarming Iraq*, 235. For similar statements, see Richard Spertzel, House Committee on International Relations, *Russia, Iraq, and Other Potential Sources of Anthrax, Smallpox, and Other Bioterrorist Weapons*, 107th Cong., 1st sess., December 5, 2001, 40; David Brooks, "Saddam's Brain," *The Weekly Standard*, December 5, 2001, 40; Mortimer Zuckerman, "No More Cat and Mouse," *U.S. News and World Report*, October 28, 2002, 72.

[288] Quote is from Rumsfeld, Memorandum, Rumsfeld to Bush, October 14, 2002, 2. See also Memorandum, William Luti to Donald Rumsfeld, "Read Ahead for Principles Meeting on Diplomacy re Iraq," January 26, 2003, Memorandum, Rumsfeld to Bush, October 14, 2002, 1.

[289] Burrough, Peretz, Rose, and Wise, "The Path to War," *Vanity Fair*, December 19, 2008.

[290] Rumsfeld, *Known and Unknown*, 440–441; Kristol and Kaplan, *War Over Iraq*, 92.

openly mocked the United Nations, calling its leaders "timid" and its inspections a "farce" and a "trap."[291] If the United States put too much faith in this institution, entropy would once again take effect, isolating the United States and allowing Saddam to slip the noose.

Defenders of containment contested the administration's portrayal of the history of inspections and the proper standard of evidence. They argued that many of the major breakthroughs of the 1990s inspections came not just through defections but through a range of methods: environmental and chemical sampling, radiation detectors, ground-penetrating radar inventories, physical surveys, computer searches, aerial and satellite surveillance, and interviews.[292] Hawks often touted the Hussein Kamel episode as evidence of the flaws in inspections. Former UNSCOM chief Rolf Ekeus retorted that shortly before Kamel's defection, the inspectors had compelled Iraq to acknowledge the existence of a biological weapons program and discovered key information about its anthrax, botulism, and aflatoxin research. They did this largely by questioning a foreign firm that exported an agricultural spray drying system to Iraq. The firm said that the Iraqis wanted a machine that would suspend particles in the atmosphere, which was more suited to the inhalation of biological agents than civilian agriculture. The inspectors had also pressed Iraq to explain why it had imported industrial quantities of biological growth media before the Gulf War, far more than was necessary for civilian uses.[293] By looking into these inconsistencies and searching hospitals, research labs, and health centers, UNSCOM pieced together an undeclared biological weapons program. Kamel then revealed the full extent of this program.[294]

Defenders of inspections further contended that full Iraqi cooperation was unnecessary for restraining Iraq's programs because, as Blix argued,

---

[291] Editorial "The Inspections Trap," *Wall Street Journal*, March 8, 2002, A10; Martin Indyk and Kenneth Pollack, "How Bush Can Avoid the Inspections Trap," *New York Times*, January 27, 2003, A25; William Kristol and Robert Kagan, "The U.N. Trap," *The Weekly Standard*, November 18, 2002, 9 ; Editorial, "An Ominous Drift," *The National Review*, February 10, 2003, 11; Lawrence Kaplan, "End Game," *The New Republic*, February 10, 2003, 16–18; Garry Milhollin, "Hans the Timid," *Wall Street Journal*, November 26, 2002, A24.

[292] Blix, *Disarming Iraq*, 152; Jessica Mathews, "Iraq: A New Approach," Carnegie Endowment for International Peace, September 5, 2002, carnegieendowment.org, accessed September 28, 2018, https://carnegieendowment.org/2002/09/05/iraq-new-a pproach-pub-1164, 2–5. Mohamed El Baradei, "Let Us Inspect," *Wall Street Journal*, March 7, 2003, A10.

[293] United Nations Special Commission, "Final Compendium: Report 1: Disarmament," January 29, 1999, iraqwatch.org, accessed March 16, 2018, http://web.archive.org/web/20051124075332/http://www.iraqwatch.org:80/un/UNSCOM/disarmament.htm.

[294] Rolf Ekeus, "Yes, Let's Go into Iraq, with an Army of Inspectors," *Washington Post*, September 15, 2002, B1.

inspections and monitoring worked as "a form of containment" by inhibiting weapons development and providing early warnings of illicit activities.[295] El Baradei likewise claimed that the "presence of international inspectors in Iraq today continues to serve as an effective deterrent to and insurance against resumption of programs."[296] Advocates of inspections argued that they constrained Iraqi capabilities and, along with sanctions and the threat of force, made the resumption of significant WMD activities highly improbable. Furthermore, nuclear weapons infrastructure could be detected because, as Michael O'Hanlon noted, it was "expensive, sophisticated, hard to hide, and even harder to move."[297] As containment advocates had long held, el Baradei and others argued that the world had to accept "some degree of risk" on Iraq's WMD but that this risk must be weighed against the costs of invasion.[298]

Many defenders of containment argued for a more militarized form of inspections that would enable the United States to quickly destroy any WMD program. Jessica Mathews composed a plan for "coercive inspections" that many advocates of containment supported.[299] She sought to expand US surveillance and destroy from the air any site being sanitized or blocked or if suspected materials were being moved on the ground. She also advocated a multinational military force to protect inspectors and to immediately destroy suspected sites.[300] Matthews argued that this plan could "reduce Iraq's WMD threat, if not to zero, to a negligible

[295] Hans Blix, "United Nations Security Council Briefing-UNMOVIC," December 19, 2002, IraqWatch.org, accessed August 1, 2018, https://web.archive.org/web/20051 124080415/http://www.iraqwatch.org/un/unmovic/unmovic-blix-notes-121902.htm; Blix, *Disarming Iraq*, 114.

[296] Mohammed el Baradei, "The Status of Nuclear Inspections in Iraq-IAEA," January 27, 2003, IraqWatch.org, accessed August 10, 2018, https://web.archive.org/web/200509 04174554/http://www.iraqwatch.org/un/IAEA/iaea-elbaradei-012703.htm. See also Jessica Mathews, "War Is Not Yet Necessary," *New York Times*, January 28, 2003, A21; Kristof, "War and Wisdom," *New York Times*, February 7, 2003, A25; Walzer, "Right Way," *New York Times Book Review*, March 13, 2003, 35.

[297] Michael O'Hanlon, "The Weapons Inspectors Can Succeed," November 15, 2002, brookings.edu, accessed September 22, 2018, www.brookings.edu/opinions/the-weap ons-inspectors-can-succeed/.

[298] Quote is from El Baradei, "Let Us Inspect," *Wall Street Journal*, March 7, 2003; Mearsheimer and Walt, "In a Box," *New York Times*, February 2, 2003; Hans Blix, Lecture, "The UNMOVIC Mission," October 7, 2002, IraqWatch.org, accessed August 12, 2018, https://web.archive.org/web/20050218014433/http://www.iraq watch.org/un/unmovic/unmovic-training-100702.htm.

[299] For supporters of coercive inspections, see Editorial, "No to War," *New York Times*, March 9, 2003; Nicholas Kristof, "Iraq War: The First Question," *New York Times*, January 28, 2003, A21; Halperin, "Case for Containment," *Washington Post*, February 11, 2003; Ekeus, "Army of Inspectors," *Washington Post*, September 15, 2002; Leahy, *Cong. Rec.*, September 26, 2018, 18178.

[300] Jessica Matthews, "Is There a Better Way to Go?" *Washington Post*, February 9, 2003, B1.

level."[301] The Bush administration, however, rejected this idea because if the United States had to use coercion to back inspections, it meant that Iraq was still obstructing, which meant that Saddam had not decided to disarm.[302] For this reason, Powell, Rumsfeld, and Rice stymied a Franco-German attempt to triple the number of inspectors and possibly insert UN peacekeepers into Iraq in a version of coercive inspections.[303]

The inspections' first step was for Iraq to submit a complete declaration of its existing WMD programs, equipment, stockpiles, and related personnel. This declaration would provide a baseline for the inspectors, who would verify that Iraq had closed or destroyed all materials and programs.[304] Iraq provided this declaration in a 12,000-page report on December 7, 2002. The United States and the inspectors judged it as inadequate because it did not clarify the status of unaccounted-for weapons, featured recycled material from previous declarations, and included no further evidence that Iraq had abandoned its nuclear weapons program.[305]

Inspectors returned to Iraq in late November 2002 and steadily intensified their activities in the winter. Their reports to the Security Council, issued every two weeks, painted an ambiguous portrait of Iraq's compliance and weapons programs that offered evidence to supporters and detractors of inspections. On the positive side, Blix and El Baradei reported that Iraqi cooperation was "prompt," "expeditious," and "without conditions," in stark contrast to the 1990s. Iraq even allowed inspectors into the presidential sites that had caused so much consternation in 1998.[306]

Most importantly, the inspectors found few weapons or other evidence of ongoing WMD production. In December, UNMOVIC found around twelve artillery shells filled with mustard gas, which they destroyed. In

---

[301] Mathews, "A New Approach," September 5, 2002, 8.

[302] Colin Powell, House Committee on International Relations, *Administration Views*, September 19, 2002, 15.

[303] Cable, Christopher Meyer to Foreign and Commonwealth Office, February 11, 2003, Iraqinquiry.org.uk, accessed September 16, 2018, http://webarchive.nationalarchives .gov.uk/20171123123954/http://www.iraqinquiry.org.uk/media/232980/2003–02–11-t elegram-189-washington-to-fco-london-iraq-defence-secretarys-visit-to-washingto n-11–12-feb-ruary.pdf, 2; Blix, *Disarming Iraq*, 82.

[304] "Resolution 1441," 98.

[305] Blix, *Disarming Iraq*, 107–108; David Sanger, "Iraq Arms Report Has Big Omissions, U.S. Officials Say," *New York Times*, December 13, 2002, A1.

[306] Blix, "Security Council Briefing," December 19, 2002, 1; Mohammed El Baradei, "United Nations Security Council Briefing-IAEA," January 9, 2003, IraqWatch.org, accessed August 11, 2018, https://web.archive.org/web/20060102122815/http://www .iraqwatch.org/un/IAEA/iaea-elbaradei-unscbriefing-010903.htm.

February, they found and destroyed missile casting chambers and seventy illegal ballistic missiles.[307] Not only did the inspectors find few actual weapons, they also observed that Iraq's industrial infrastructure had decayed considerably since the Gulf War, undercutting its ability to produce WMD.[308] For Bush's claims about Iraq's nuclear program, however, the inspectors found no evidence. The IAEA assessed on February 14: "We have to date found no evidence of ongoing prohibited nuclear or nuclear related activities in Iraq," although el-Baradei noted several outstanding issues.[309] The IAEA also judged that the US claims about aluminum tubes and the importing of uranium from Niger were "unfounded."[310]

On the other hand, Iraq failed to clear up questions about its WMD in several areas, offering the hawks some evidence of inspections' flaws. Blix and el Baradei noted that Iraq still offered only "passive support, that is, responding as needed to inspectors' requests," rather than fulfilling Resolution 1441's demand for "proactive support, that is, voluntarily assisting inspectors by providing documentation, people, and other evidence."[311] Interviewing Iraqi personnel remained a sticking point, as the Iraqis insisted on having minders in the room. The inspectors believed Iraqi officials were still coaching and coercing their personnel to dissemble.[312] The Iraqis also resisted the use of U-2 spy planes for surveillance of suspected sites, even though Resolution 1441 specifically authorized these flights.[313] Furthermore, inspectors found 3,000 pages of documents related to uranium enrichment in the home of an Iraqi scientist in January, making them suspect that Iraq was hiding other information. These problems led Blix to conclude in late January: "Iraq appears not to have come to a genuine acceptance ... of the disarmament which was

---

[307] Hans Blix, "Briefing to the Security Council-UNMOVIC," February 14, 2003, IraqWatch.org, accessed August 11, 2018, https://web.archive.org/web/200502180 14156/http://www.iraqwatch.org/un/unmovic/unmovic-blix-briefing-021403.html; Malone, *International Struggle*, 197.

[308] Hans Blix, "Briefing to the United Nations Security Council-UNMOVIC," March 7, 2003, IraqWatch.org, accessed August 11, 2018, https://web.archive.org/web/200502 18014304/http://www.iraqwatch.org/un/unmovic/unmovic-blix-030703.htm.

[309] Mohammed el Baradei, "The Status of Nuclear Inspections in Iraq-IAEA," February 14, 2003, IraqWatch.org, accessed August 11, 2018, https://web.archive .org/web/20050426183325/http://www.iraqwatch.org/un/IAEA/iaea-elbaradei-021403 .htm.

[310] Mohammed el Baradei, "United Nations Weapons Inspectors Report to the UN Security Council on Progress in Disarmament of Iraq-IAEA," March 7, 2003, IraqWatch.org, accessed August 11, 2018, https://web.archive.org/web/20050426182 924/http://www.iraqwatch.org/un/IAEA/iaea-elbaradei-030703.htm.

[311] El Baradei, "The Status of Nuclear Inspections," January 27, 2003.

[312] El Baradei, "Security Council Briefing," January 9, 2003.

[313] Blix, *Disarming Iraq*, 120–121.

demanded of it."[314] In early March, Blix judged that Iraq still needed to provide evidence of the location or destruction of materials such as VX gas, anthrax, bacterial growth media, and chemical bombs.[315]

In January 2003, slightly over a month into inspections, Bush and other top US officials privately determined that inspections would fail.[316] Bush believed that "time is not on our side here" and that "the United States can't stay in this position while Saddam plays games with the inspectors."[317] Cheney told the Saudi ambassador on January 10 that Bush had already decided on invasion.[318] On January 15, Bush told Powell, "I think I have to do this. I want you with me," and Powell pledged his support.[319] In late January, US officials started to publicly declare that Saddam would not comply.[320] The administration opposed time extensions for inspections, arguing that offering more time "plays into the hands" of Saddam by enabling him to split the coalition.[321]

Although they wanted Bush to give inspections a genuine chance, adherents of the Powell–Blair approach did not contest Bush's standard of evidence, which virtually preordained the "failure" of inspections. This concession led them either to weakly defend inspections or to support abandoning them. Tom Daschle, Chuck Hagel, Christopher Dodd, and others faulted Bush for "rushing to war" without giving inspections and diplomacy more time, but they never proposed an alternative course beyond a few more months for these measures.[322] Joseph Biden argued that while "Saddam Hussein has to go," the United States should continue to pursue a second resolution to provide political cover to allies like Blair, broaden the coalition, and "share the burden" of reconstruction.[323] James Baker, who had called for restraint in the summer of 2002, declared

[314] Hans Blix, "UN Security Council Update on Inspections-UNMOVIC," January 27, 2003, IraqWatch.org, accessed August 10, 2018, https://web.archive.org/web/200512 24044516/http://www.iraqwatch.org/un/unmovic/unmovic-blix-012703.htm.

[315] Blix, "Briefing to Security Council, March 7, 2003.

[316] Bozo, "'We Don't Need You,'"197; House of Commons, "Report of the Iraq Inquiry," July 6, 2016, Vol. 3, Section 3.6, 2–3.

[317] Woodward, *Plan of Attack*, 254.   [318] Baker, *Days of Fire*, 233.

[319] Baker, *Days of Fire*, 234; Woodward, *Plan of Attack*, 271.

[320] James Dao and Richard Stevenson, "Bush Says Iraqis Are Still Resisting Demand to Disarm," *New York Times*, January 22, 2003; Gordon and Shapiro, *Allies at War*, 128.

[321] Karen DeYoung, "Rice Calls Security Council Actions Appeasement," *Washington Post*, February 17, 2003, A26.

[322] Quote is from Carl Hulse, "Top Democrats Say a War against Iraq is Premature," *New York Times*, March 7, 2003, A15. See also Jim Vandehei, "Hill Pressures Bush on Iraq," *Washington Post*, January 25, 2003, A16; Zbigniew Brzezinksi, "Why Unity Is Essential," *Washington Post*, February 19, 2003; Friedman, "Fire, Ready," *New York Times*, March 9, 2003; Christopher Dodd, *Cong. Rec.*, 108th Cong., 1st sess., March 7, 2003, 3356.

[323] Joseph Biden, "Why We Need a Second U.N. Resolution," *Washington Post*, March 10, 2003, A21.

in February that containment had failed and the only reason the United States should not strike Iraq immediately was to build more international support.[324]

The American public's views on inspections mirrored those of the Powell–Blair approach. Acolytes of this approach had supported continued efforts at inspections and diplomacy through the winter of 2002–2003.[325] However, this support plummeted in March as diplomacy started to collapse. One March poll showed that 67 percent of respondents believed Bush had "tried hard at diplomacy."[326] A Pew survey from March showed 60 percent saying that the inspections have proven that Saddam "will not cooperate," while another poll showed 75 percent saying that war was inevitable even if inspectors received more time.[327] Public support for war surged in March, with polls showing approval ratings well into the 70 percent range for the pending war.[328]

Blair and Powell also did not defend inspections once they were under way even though they had pushed for Bush to support them earlier in 2002. Blair wrote to Bush on January 24: "If we delay, we risk Saddam messing us about, sucking us back into a game of hide and seek with the inspectors where … the thing drags on forever until we give up or get distracted."[329] Blair called for more time for inspections mainly to see if they would provide a clearer *casus belli* that might convince the Security Council to authorize force.[330] Powell labored to preserve the coalition, but he soon turned on inspections, declaring in late January: "The question isn't how much longer do you need for inspections to work.

---

[324] James Baker, "The Case for Military Action," *Wall Street Journal*, February 3, 2003, A22; this argument was echoed by William Cohen, "The Real Case against Iraq," *Wall Street Journal*, February 5, 2003, A18.

[325] CBS News Telephone Survey, January 28, 2003, Polling the Nations, accessed September 20, 2018.

[326] CBS News Telephone Survey, March 18, 2003, Polling the Nations, accessed September 20, 2018; Washington Post/ABC News Telephone Survey, March 18, 2003, Polling the Nations, accessed September 20, 2018.

[327] For "will not cooperate," see Pew Telephone Survey, March 18, 2003, Polling the Nations, accessed September 20, 2018. For "inevitable," see CBS News Telephone Survey, March 17, 2003, Polling the Nations, accessed September 20, 2018.

[328] Richard Morin and Claudia Deane, "71% of Americans Support War, Poll Shows," *Washington Post*, March 19, 2003, A14; Pew Research Center, "Public Attitudes toward the War in Iraq: 2003–2008," March 19, 2008, pewresearch.org, accessed September 21, 2018, www.pewresearch.org/2008/03/19/public-attitudes-toward-the-war-in-iraq-20032008/.

[329] Note, Tony Blair to George W. Bush, January 24, 2003, Iraqinquiry.org.uk, accessed September 16, 2018, http://webarchive.nationalarchives.gov.uk/20171123122510/http://www.iraqinquiry.org.uk/media/244006/2003-01-24-note-blair-to-bush-undated-note.pdf, 1.

[330] Woodward, *Plan of Attack*, 296–297; Gordon and Shapiro, *Allies at War*, 117.

Inspections will not work."[331] Blair and other members of this approach did not, however, endorse Blix's argument that the inspections themselves acted as a form of containment. They also did not take seriously the fact that the inspectors had turned up little evidence of continuing WMD programs. Their arguments remained tactical and procedural, focusing on ensuring that the inspections box had been checked and as large a coalition as possible assembled before the war began.

In late February and early March, Blix and el Baradei pleaded for more time, claiming that they were still inserting teams and setting up bases. Blix noted that since mid-February Iraq had increased cooperation and accepted the inspectors' demands for private interviews with Iraqi personnel and aerial surveillance.[332] With this new "pro-active attitude" and the continued threat of war, Blix predicted that resolving outstanding issues "would not take years, nor weeks, but months."[333] France, Germany, China, and Russia all supported the inspectors' appeals and devised plans to strengthen inspections.[334] The United States and Great Britain, however, introduced a Security Council resolution on February 24 stating that "Iraq has failed to take the final opportunity afforded it in Resolution 1441."[335] They accused Saddam of not cooperating and hiding weapons and information. Reflecting the Bush administration's binary standard of evidence on Iraqi WMD, Powell declared a few weeks later: "Nothing we have seen since the passage of 1441 indicates that Saddam Hussein has taken a strategic and political decision to disarm."[336]

The United States delayed the start of war in March 2003 only to let Tony Blair try to pass a second resolution authorizing the use of force, which Blair wanted before Parliament voted on the war.[337] This was a futile task because France, Russia, China, and Germany all believed inspections were making progress, and they pledged to veto any resolution that endorsed war.[338] Rather than worsen a diplomatic break with

[331] Glenn Kessler, "Moderate Powell Turns Hawkish on War with Iraq," *Washington Post*, January 24, 2003, A1.

[332] El Baradei, "Report to the UN Security Council," March 7, 2003; El Baradei, "Let Us Inspect," *Wall Street Journal*, March 7, 2003; Blix, *Disarming Iraq*, 177–178, 188–189.

[333] Blix, "Briefing to the Security Council," March 7, 2003.

[334] Blix, *Disarming Iraq*, 180–181.

[335] "U.S.-British Draft Resolution Stating Position on Iraq," *New York Times*, February 25, 2003, A14.

[336] Colin Powell, "Remarks at the Center for Strategic and International Studies," March 5, 2003, State.gov, accessed September 30, 2018, https://2001–2009.state.gov/secretary/former/powell/remarks/2003/18307.htm.

[337] Woodward, *Plan of Attack*, 341, 365.

[338] "In Delegates' Words: Hawks and Doves Debate at the Security Council," *New York Times*, March 8, 2003, A9; Bozo, *Iraq Crisis*, 197–199.

key allies, the United States and Great Britain decided to withdraw their resolution.[339] On March 17, President Bush announced a 48-hour ultimatum for Saddam and his sons to leave Iraq or face war. On March 20, coalition forces launched the opening air strikes of Operation Iraqi Freedom.

Conclusion: The Path to the Iraq War

The United States invaded Iraq because the Bush administration believed the threat of Saddam's WMD programs and links to terrorist groups to be intolerable after 9/11. The decision to invade was shaped by manipulated intelligence, visions of democratic transformation, and the belief that the war would be quick and easy. For regime change advocates, containment had collapsed, but even if it could be restored to its earlier strength, it still could not address the nexus threat. This assessment rested on a bedrock of ideas about Iraq that developed in the 1990s, especially the perceived lesson of containment: no combination of incentives and pressures could either topple Saddam or force him to change his behavior given his psychology and the totalitarian nature of his regime.

The neoconservatives and other Iraq hawks in the Bush administration played an indispensable role in bringing about the Iraq War. They put Iraq on the agenda after 9/11, ensured that it became the centerpiece of US foreign policy, and articulated a case for war. It seems doubtful that members of the Powell–Blair approach, including the US public, would have otherwise recommended an invasion of Iraq, as their instincts directed them toward the struggle with al-Qaeda and the MEPP. Nevertheless, once Bush put Iraq "on the table," he found he was pushing on a half-open door with respect to the political establishment and the public.

Many proponents of the Powell–Blair approach tried to shape how Bush confronted Iraq, making sure he built a coalition and exhausted nonviolent measures before going to war. Once Bush had checked these boxes, however perfunctorily, they offered little significant opposition to the war because of their underlying concurrence with the regime change consensus. They too believed that containment was discredited and regime change a necessity. This combination of a passionate, highly placed minority and a supportive if hardly enthusiastic majority created a narrow prewar debate that marginalized alternatives to war.

---

[339] Stephen Weisman, "A Long, Winding Road to a Diplomatic Dead End," *New York Times*, March 17, 2003, A7.

Conclusion
Containment, Liberalism, and the Regime

"It's the regime, stupid." R. James Woolsey, March 11, 1999.[1]

By the time R. James Woolsey addressed the House Armed Services Committee with this cheeky line in 1999, Americans had been debating for almost a decade whether Saddam Hussein's Iraq could be contained. Woolsey had been the Director of the CIA from 1993 to 1994, but he had little influence with Clinton and resigned in frustration.[2] He then joined an ascendant chorus of policy-makers, politicians, and intellectuals who over the course of the 1990s built a consensus in US politics that Saddam could not be contained. By 1999, such a statement had become unremarkable, a form of common sense about the nature Saddam's Iraq. Woolsey and the political movement he participated in established a dominant public interpretation of the Iraqi regime as totalitarian, fanatical, fixated on WMD and regional dominance, and obsessed with revenge against the United States.

Herein lies the double significance of the term "regime change consensus": It suggests a widely shared belief that the Iraqi regime, or its system of government and official ideology, was both the heart of the problem and the core of the solution. By defining the regime as the ultimate source of Iraq's threatening behavior, supporters of the regime change consensus primed a wide range of Americans to believe that even a resuscitated containment could not prevent Saddam from acquiring WMD. This belief became an important precondition for two key aspects of the Iraq debate from 2001 to 2003. First, it helps explain why Bush's argument for regime change, rooted in the idea that containment could not handle the "nexus" threat, successfully created political momentum for war. Second, it helps explain the actions and ideas of members of the Powell–Blair approach,

---

[1] R. James Woolsey, House Armed Services Committee, *United States Policy toward Iraq*, 106th Cong., 1st sess., March 10, 1999, 4.

[2] David Halberstam, *War in a Time of Peace: Bush, Clinton, and the Generals* (New York: Scribner, 2001), 191–192, 233–234.

who tried to influence how Bush pursued regime change but largely accepted that doing so was both necessary and prudent.

Comparing Cold War and Iraqi Containment

The main reference point for debates about containing Iraq was the Cold War policy of containing the Soviet Union. Many skeptics of the Iraq War have questioned, both before and after the invasion, why the United States could contain the Soviet Union, a massive, nuclear-armed superpower, but not Iraq, a vastly weaker regional power. In short, what made the containment of Iraq different? This book has already explored some answers: the apparent opportunities created by the unipolarity of the post–Cold War system, optimism regarding human rights and democracy in the 1990s, and the fact that the relative weakness of Iraq made it appear as a resolvable problem in contrast to the Soviet Union.

These factors all mattered, but this book delves deeper into this question by interrogating containment strategies as theories of social and political change. When policy-makers and theorists describe a policy as containment, they usually mean that the United States will try to limit the power and ideological influence of a rival state. However, containment rarely means the United States will simply box in the target indefinitely. Because containment strategies do not directly seek the overthrow of the target, they must create an atmosphere conducive to the target changing its behavior or its ruling regime.[3] Embedded within any containment strategy, therefore, is what I call a theory of change about that society.

The theory of change is a prediction of how the pressures, constraints, and incentives of containment will cause the target state to change its behavior or political system, either through reform or collapse. The theory of change addresses the question: What is the nature of this leader, political system, and society, and how can the United States change them, within certain limits of action, to further its foreign policy goals? A convincing answer to this question is crucial not just for coherent foreign policy but also for protecting the political flanks of containment strategies. A robust theory of change explains to the public, politicians, and foreign allies how containment will not go on forever and how, even though it is a more indirect, long-term strategy, it will ultimately resolve a given problem.

One of the primary differences between the Cold War and Iraqi containment strategies was that the former had a robust and flexible theory of change and the latter did not. The basic theory of change developed by

---

[3] Robert Litwak, *Rogue States and U.S. Foreign Policy: Containment after the Cold War* (Washington, DC: Woodrow Wilson Center Press, 2000), 101–110.

foundational Cold War strategists like George Kennan and Paul Nitze was that the United States needed to limit Soviet expansion, isolate it economically, maintain the health of its own political system and economy, and strengthen key allies. These steps would aggravate preexisting problems in the Soviet system, eventually bringing about its implosion or compelling its accommodation to the US-led international order.[4] As the historian John Lewis Gaddis argues, Kennan viewed the goal of containment as "behavior modification" that required countering Soviet aggression while seeking space for negotiation.[5]

Crucially, these diagnoses of the Soviet threat did not make war an inevitability. Kennan portrayed the Soviet government as driven by Russian xenophobia, an ideological conviction that there could be no legitimate opposition to its utopian project, and the need for "explaining away the maintenance of dictatorship at home" by conjuring foreign threats.[6] This outlook precluded "permanent peaceful coexistence" or compromise with the United States and drove the Soviets to destabilize US global power and its way of life.[7] However, because of the Soviet leadership's belief that the course of history remained in its favor, Kennan claimed it had no fixed plan for effecting capitalism's demise.[8] Where the Soviet Union met "unassailable barriers in its path," it usually retreated. This meant that over time containment could engender either a sudden "break-up" or a "gradual mellowing" of Soviet behavior as its internal weaknesses intensified.[9]

Kennan, Nitze, and other Cold War strategists identified these specific weaknesses in the Soviet system and predicted how containment would

---

[4] George Kennan, "The Sources of Soviet Conduct," in *American Diplomacy*, 2nd ed. (Chicago: University of Chicago Press, 1984), 127. See also John Lewis Gaddis, *Strategies of Containment: A Critical Appraisal of American National Security during the Cold War*, 2nd ed. (New York: Oxford University Press, 2005), 35–40; Walter LaFeber, *America, Russia, and the Cold War*, 5th ed. (New York: Knopf, 1985), 58–65; Glenn Anthony May, "Introduction: NSC-68: The Theory and Politics of Strategy," in *American Cold War Strategy: Interpreting NSC-68* (Boston: Bedford Books of St. Martin's Press, 1993), 5–7; Melvyn Leffler, *A Preponderance of Power: National Security, the Truman Administration, and the Cold War* (Stanford, CA: Stanford University Press, 1992), 108–109, 179–181.

[5] Gaddis, *Strategies of Containment*, 71; Paul Nitze, "NSC-68," in May, *American Cold War Strategy*, 41, 60–65.

[6] Quote is from Kennan, "Sources of Soviet Conduct," 112–113. See also George Kennan, "The Long Telegram," February 22, 1946, National Security Archives, accessed January 22, 2019, https://nsarchive2.gwu.edu//coldwar/documents/episode-1/kennan .htm, 9–10; George Kennan, "America and the Russian Future," in *American Diplomacy*, 2nd ed., 138–139; Gaddis, *Strategies of Containment*, 32–33:

[7] Kennan, "Long Telegram," 1, 10; Nitze, "NSC-68," 28–29.

[8] Kennan, "Long Telegram," 10; Kennan, "Sources of Soviet Conduct," 116–118.

[9] Quote is from Kennan, "Sources of Soviet Conduct," 118. See also Kennan, "Long Telegram," 10; Nitze, "NSC-68," 36, 79.

exacerbate them. These "seeds of its own decay," in Kennan's phrasing, included the people's exhaustion and disillusionment with brutal Soviet rule, the greater health, freedom, and productivity of the US system, and the desire of nations in the Eastern Bloc to escape the communist yoke.[10] Nitze wrote, for instance, that "developing the moral and material strength of the free world" and blocking Soviet efforts at expansion would "hasten the decay of the Soviet system" by convincing them of the futility of global revolution and demonstrating the superiority of the US way of life.[11]

Moreover, the creation of a *modus vivendi* with the Soviet Union did not require remaking the foe in the US image, in contrast to the post–Cold War discourse on Iraq. Kennan believed it was useless to aim for a liberal and democratic Russia, as these concepts were foreign to its historical experience. Hinging US security on other nations adopting US values and institutions defined US interests too broadly and exceeded its resources. On internal matters, Kennan instead prescribed: "Let them be Russians."[12] The United States simply had to compel the Soviets to abandon certain goals and perspectives, including "imperialist expansion," the destruction of competing types of government, and "paranoiac suspiciousness" of other states. This aim of "resocializing" the Soviets, to borrow a term from political scientist Alexander George, into basic norms of international relations fit with Kennan's "particularized" approach to world politics.[13] Within this philosophy, international order was based on consensus and coexistence among multiple states that share key interests even though they have different political systems and values.[14] The Soviet government did not have to be overthrown or democratized to make a *modus vivendi* possible, although important aspects of its behavior and ideology had to change.

In contrast, the George H. W. Bush and Clinton administrations struggled to develop a robust theory of change for Iraq that explained how

---

[10] For explorations of these weaknesses in the Soviet system, see Kennan, "Sources of Soviet Conduct," 121–124, 127–128; Kennan, "Long Telegram," 3, 10; Kennan "Russian Future," 131, 135; Nitze, "NSC-68," 35.

[11] Nitze, "NSC 68," 30–32.

[12] Kennan, "Russian Future," 131, 135; Kennan, "Long Telegram," 4. Gaddis, *Strategies of Containment*, 26–27; John Lewis Gaddis, *George F. Kennan: A Life* (New York: Penguin Press, 2011), 298–299. Robert Frazier, "Kennan, 'Universalism', and the Truman Doctrine," *Journal of Cold War Studies* 11, no. 2 (Spring, 2009): 3–34.

[13] Kennan, "Russian Future," 132–143. For more theoretical treatments of the concept of "resocialization" in international politics, see Alexander George, *Bridging the Gap: Theory and Practice in Foreign Policy* (Washington, DC: United States Institute of Peace Press, 1993), 49.

[14] Gaddis, *Strategies of Containment*, 26–27, 46–47; Frazier, "Kennan, 'Universalism,'" 5. Kennan, "Sources of Soviet Conduct," 110–112; Nitze, "NSC-68," 41, 60–65.

containment would bring about either the regime's downfall or behavioral change. The basic theory of change for Iraqi containment was that sanctions, covert operations, and military strikes would either compel the Iraqi elite to remove Saddam or force him to cooperate with inspections. Designers of the original strategy, such as Richard Haass, envisioned it as a way to limit the regional influence of a troublesome but minor power even if Saddam did not comply with inspectors. However, both administrations failed to adapt containment's theoretical underpinnings to changes on the ground in the 1990s, including Saddam's crushing of the internal opposition and escalating resistance to the inspectors. Moreover, unlike Kennan and Nitze, theorists of Iraqi containment rarely considered the role the Iraqi people might play in fomenting pressure on the regime besides their suffering from sanctions. This approach backfired by making Iraqis more dependent on the regime while Saddam insulated himself from the effects of sanctions.

At the same time, US policy-makers defined the end goals of Iraqi containment in rigid, absolutist terms, undermining Haass' more limited original vision. All three relevant presidencies declared that no normalization with the current regime was possible even if Iraq complied with the inspectors. This stance alienated allies, and the ensuing stalemate made containment more vulnerable to political criticism because success was now expansively defined as regime change. By 1998, the Clinton administration had no plausible way of explaining how containment would change Saddam's intentions (presumed to be immutable) or cause the downfall of his regime (presumed to be impossible).

The Iraqi case suggests that containment strategies may have a fundamental disadvantage in democratic political systems. Kennan himself feared the influence of democratic politics on foreign policy and warned that containment should have "nothing to do with outward histrionics: with threats or blustering or superfluous gestures of outward 'toughness'."[15] Kennan envisioned a "cool and collected" policy that avoided putting Soviet prestige on the line, responded flexibly to Soviet signals, distinguished between peripheral and essential regions, and largely ignored public opinion, which he described as a realm of "emotionalism and subjectivity."[16]

To Kennan's chagrin, threat exaggeration and tough-guy blustering are often crucial for mobilizing public opinion behind foreign policy

---

[15] Kennan, "Sources of Soviet Conduct," 119.

[16] First quote is from Kennan, "Sources of Soviet Conduct," 119; second quote is from George Kennan, "Diplomacy in the Modern World," in *American Diplomacy*, 2nd ed., 93. For more on Kennan's desire to isolate foreign policy from democratic pressures, see Anders Stephanson, *Kennan and the Art of Foreign Policy* (Cambridge, MA: Harvard University Press, 1989), 113, 178–180.

endeavors. Democratic politics rarely permit fine distinctions of the national interest when politicians can declare, for example, that if a distant nation like Vietnam falls to communism, more important alliances will be undermined and the rest of Southeast Asia will collapse like dominoes. Kennan, in another instance, criticized the Truman Doctrine's strident ideological tone and blanket promise of protection to countries facing communist subversion, but Truman believed these elements were necessary to convince the Senate and the American people to back his policy.[17]

Even though containment retained bipartisan support throughout the Cold War, domestic politics tended to inflate US interests, homogenize diverse communist movements as part of a Soviet-led conspiracy, and encourage armed intervention in peripheral areas.[18] For reasons of conviction and political gain, many politicians criticized containment for its ostensible passivity and amorality and even sought to replace the policy. In the 1950s, many Republicans embraced a rollback strategy that recommended covert operations in the Eastern Bloc to foment rebellions that would sever these states from Soviet control.[19] Although Eisenhower did little to execute rollback, the 1952 Republican platform condemned containment as "negative, futile, and immoral" for "abandoning countless human beings to despotism and godless terrorism."[20]

Barry Goldwater, the Republican presidential candidate in 1964, sought to replace containment with a nebulous strategy of "victory" that he described as "primarily offensive in character." He supported offensive action against communist regimes like Cuba and the withdrawal of diplomatic recognition from the Soviet Union, which he called an "outlaw" regime that was "neither legitimate nor permanent."[21] Kennan's containment implied competitive coexistence with the Soviets, but for Goldwater coexistence with an evil regime that aimed "to conquer the United States and enslave the world" was unethical and dangerous.[22]

[17] LaFeber, *America, Russia, and the Cold War*, 53–54.

[18] Hal Brands, *Making the Unipolar Moment: U.S. Foreign Policy and the Rise of the Post-Cold War Order* (Ithaca, NY: Cornell University Press, 2016), 85–87; Gaddis, *Strategies of Containment*, 388.

[19] Peter Grose, *Operation Rollback: America's Secret War Behind the Iron Curtain* (New York: Mariner, 2001), 206–208, 214–218; LaFeber, *America, Russia, and the Cold War*, 149–150.

[20] "Republican Party Platform of 1952," July 7, 1952, The American Presidency Project, accessed June 12, 2020, www.presidency.ucsb.edu/documents/republican-party-platform-1952.

[21] Colin Dueck, *Hard Line: The Republican Party and U.S. Foreign Policy since World War II* (Princeton, NJ: Princeton University Press, 2010), 119–122.

[22] Barry Goldwater, *Why Not Victory: A Fresh Look at Foreign Policy* (New York: McGraw Hill, 1962), 149.

The containment of Iraq suffered from similar difficulties related to domestic politics. Haass and other early designers of containment wanted the United States to mix punishments and incentives to compel Iraqi compliance, but this approach proved politically unsustainable. Shock and outrage at the invasion of Kuwait in 1990 caused the US political establishment to overlearn the lesson that negotiation and incentives were futile for compelling Saddam to comply with international mandates. The incomplete victory in Desert Storm and the conflict's messy, tragic aftermath created a powerful political bias for tougher measures against Saddam. The 1998 Iraq Liberation Act culminated this process by declaring the Iraqi regime to be illegitimate, something the United States never formally asserted about the Soviet Union.

Foreign policy is one of the least democratic areas of political life in a democracy given the power of the executive to make and direct policy, the expert status of the foreign policy bureaucracy, and the public's general lack of knowledge about global affairs. Still, Kennan's quasi-aristocratic dream of isolating foreign policy from democratic pressures remains impossible and probably undesirable given the risk of policies that are unaccountable to and disconnected from popular consent. Balancing consistency, vision, and restraint in foreign policy with the vicissitudes of democracy will remain a challenging but unavoidable task of politicians and strategists in a free society.

The Problem of the Regime in American Foreign Relations

Besides the pressures of democratic politics, there were deeper forces in the history of American political thought that undermined the containment of Iraq and bolstered the regime change consensus. In particular, this book speaks to the importance of ideas about regime type in US foreign relations. This concept needs to be differentiated from the idea of democracy promotion. Historians have long been skeptical of the idea that the United States has consistently sought to spread democracy, pointing to interventions to destabilize elected leaders and alliances with friendly autocrats.[23]

---

[23] Mahmood Mamdani, *Good Muslim, Bad Muslim: America, the Cold War, and the Roots of Terror* (New York: Pantheon Books, 2004); Andrew Bacevich, *American Empire: The Realities and Consequences of U.S. Diplomacy* (Cambridge, MA: Harvard University Press, 2002); Fred Anderson and Andrew Cayton, *The Dominion of War: Empire and Liberty in North America* (New York: Viking, 2005); Chalmers Johnson, *Blowback: The Costs and Consequences of American Empire* (New York: Henry Holt, 2001); Michael Hunt, *The American Ascendancy: How the United States Gained and Wielded Global Dominance* (Chapel Hill, NC: University of North Carolina Press, 2007).

As valid as these observations are, the history of ideas about regime type relates more to the view that a state's ideologies, internal power dynamics, and social and economic structures can shape its foreign policy as much as external forces like the balance of power. As Kennan put it regarding the Soviets: "The Soviet party line is not based on any objective analysis of the situation beyond Russia's borders; that it has indeed little to do with conditions outside of Russia; that it arises mainly from basic inner-Russian necessities."[24]

As this quotation implies, states' foreign policies are almost always part of an attempt to preserve an internal arrangement of power, resources, and ideas. US leaders have frequently understood the external behavior of states as stemming in large part from these internal traits and imperatives, or from the nature of different regimes. Within this tradition of what might be called "regime-thinking," democratic regimes are seen as peaceful, cooperative, respecting of human rights, preferring trade over costly conflict, and featuring norms and institutions that constrain aggression. Authoritarian and totalitarian states, in turn, are seen as aggressive, militaristic, liable to abuse human rights, and lacking in restraining institutions and norms.[25]

This tradition holds that states that are evil at home will be evil abroad. Regime-thinking unites liberals like Robert Kerrey with neoconservatives like Paul Wolfowitz under a broad understanding of liberalism. Despite disagreeing on many domestic political issues, their thinking about world politics is liberal in that they believe in universalist conceptions of human rights and democracy, the beneficial effects of free trade, the idea that a state's internal makeup inevitably shapes its external behavior, and the US responsibility for defending an international system based on these principles.[26]

Regime-thinking has played a foundational role in liberal and neoconservative conceptions of international order. Liberal internationalists like Woodrow Wilson, Harry Truman, and Bill Clinton sought to replace anarchic competition between states with international law, multilateral, rules-based institutions and free trade agreements, and norms of human rights and democracy.[27] Neoconservative conceptions of global order, such

---

[24] Kennan, "Long Telegram," 3. For a discussion of this aspect of Kennan's thought, see Stephanson, *Kennan*, 66–67.

[25] Tony Smith, *Why Wilson Matters: The Origin of American Liberal Internationalism and Its Crisis Today* (Princeton, NJ: Princeton University Press, 2017), 10–11.

[26] Michael Freeden and Marc Stears, "Liberalism," in *The Oxford Handbook of Political Ideologies* (Oxford, UK: Oxford University Press, 2013), 329; Stephen Walt, *The Hell of Good Intentions: America's Foreign Policy Elite and the Decline of U.S. Primacy* (New York: Farrar, Straus, and Giroux, 2018), 13; Michael MacDonald, *Overreach: Delusions of Regime Change in Iraq* (Cambridge, MA: Harvard University Press, 2014), 131, 145.

[27] G. John Ikenberry, *Liberal Leviathan: The Origins, Crisis, and Transformation of the American World Order* (Princeton, NJ: Princeton University Press, 2011), 67–78. Smith, *Why Wilson Matters*, xi, 11; John Mearsheimer, *The Great Delusion: Liberal*

as that of the second Bush administration, disdain multilateral institutions and hinge international peace on US hegemony and democratization. However, both liberals and neoconservatives have long imagined that if more countries embraced democracy and liberal values they would be more willing to support either a rules-based international order or a US-dominated one.[28] Realist conceptions of world order, by contrast, are based not in the internal traits of states but in preserving a balance of power and ironclad respect for national sovereignty.[29]

This connection between the building of a liberal international order and regime-thinking has the potential to drive liberal democracies like the United States toward destabilizing, universalistic conceptions of world politics. Liberal thinkers from Immanuel Kant to John Rawls have argued that international peace and the survival of liberalism itself can only be achieved if the majority of states are liberalized.[30] Kant held that representative and republican regimes act cooperatively rather than aggressively and eventually build a lawful international system among themselves. Authoritarian states, in contrast, remain in a state of aggression with their own people as well as the community of peace-loving democracies, forcing the democracies to adopt militaristic methods to combat the authoritarians.[31] Rawls, furthermore, argued that all states have a responsibility "to leave the state of nature and to submit themselves along with others to the rule of a reasonable and just law."[32] In addition, liberals as well as neoconservatives tend to universalize their core ideals

Dreams and International Realities (New Haven, CT: Yale University Press, 2018), 3–5; Barry Posen and Andrew Ross, "Competing Visions for U.S. Grand Strategy," *International Security* 21, no. 3 (Winter, 1996/1997): 23–24.

[28] On differences and similarities in liberal and neoconservative conceptions of global order, see Robert Jervis, "Understanding the Bush Doctrine," *Political Science Quarterly* 118, no. 3 (Fall, 2003): 365; Posen and Ross, "Competing Visions," 32; Michael Desch, "America's Liberal Illiberalism: The Ideological Origins of Overreaction in U.S. Foreign Policy," *International Security* 32, no. 3 (December, 2007): 20–21.

[29] Christopher Layne, "Kant or Cant: The Myth of the Democratic Peace," *International Security* 19, no. 2 (Fall, 1994): 46; Walt, *Hell of Good Intentions*, 261–265; John Mearsheimer, *The Tragedy of Great Power Politics* (New York: W. W. Norton & Company, 2001), 17–22.

[30] Desch, "America's Liberal Illiberalism," 14–15. For more on liberalism's historical influence on US foreign policy, see Immanuel Kant, *Perpetual Peace and Other Essays on Politics, History, and Morals* (Indianapolis: Hackett, 1983), 113–115; John Rawls, *The Law of Peoples* (Cambridge, MA: Harvard University Press, 1999); Michael Doyle, "Kant, Liberal Legacies, and Foreign Affairs," *Philosophy and Public Affairs* 12, no. 3 (July, 1983): 205–235.

[31] Eric A. Heinze, "The New Utopianism: Liberalism, American Foreign Policy, and the War in Iraq," *Journal of International Political Theory* 4, no. 1 (April, 2008): 109; Michael Doyle, "Liberalism and World Politics," *The American Political Science Review* 80, no. 4 (December, 1986): 1151; MacDonald, *Overreach*, 152–155.

[32] Desch, "Liberal Illiberalism," 15.

and expect other societies to adhere to certain basic standards.[33] The support of John Stuart Mill and other nineteenth-century British liberals for imperialism exemplifies this potential.[34]

Following this logic, states that abuse their own people and undermine international peace forfeit their sovereignty and may be subjected to regime change so that they may be absorbed into the peaceful community of democracies.[35] Kant called such states the "unjust enemy," or combatants who are outside the international community (or, in an earlier iteration, the civilized world). These ideas can create what one political theorist calls a "liberal illiberalism" in foreign affairs: the inability or unwillingness of liberal states to tolerate illiberal or nondemocratic states.[36] For instance, Woodrow Wilson, in his 1917 "Safe for Democracy" speech, argued that global democratization was ultimately the only way to preserve peace, claiming: "A steadfast concert for peace can never be maintained except by a partnership of democratic nations. No autocratic government could be trusted to keep faith within it or observe its covenants."[37]

The pro-regime change argument on Iraq reflects both the enduring importance of regime-thinking in US foreign policy and the potential of powerful liberal states to view the spread of their ideals, even by force, as the only way to ensure their security and world peace. Regime change advocates rarely said that Iraq had to replicate US values and institutions, but most of them adamantly believed that Iraq would continue to menace the region and the US homeland until it became open and democratic. Iraq's "resocialization," they imagined, had to include far more internal change than Kennan envisaged for the Soviet Union. The Baathists would have to be rooted out and a national identity, capitalist economy, and multiparty democracy forged. The universalist assumption that these concepts could easily be applied to Iraq fueled the sense that war and nation-building would be ethical and feasible.

Kennan critically described much of liberal thought as "universalistic" or "legalistic-moralistic" thinking: the naïve hope that geopolitical competition would subside if "all countries could be induced to subscribe to

---

[33] MacDonald, *Overreach*, 131, 147; Gary Dorrien, *Imperial Designs: Neoconservatism and the New Pax Americana* (New York: Routledge, 2004), 80; Mearsheimer, *Great Delusion*, 7–9.

[34] Uday Mehta, *Liberalism and Empire: A Study in Nineteenth-Century British Liberal Thought* (Chicago: University of Chicago Press, 1999); Duncan Bell, *Reordering the World: Essays on Liberalism and Empire* (Princeton, NJ: Princeton University Press, 2016), 211–236.

[35] Heinze, "New Utopianism," 106, 116; Doyle, "Liberalism and World Politics," 1160–1161.

[36] Desch, "Liberal Illiberalism," 25.

[37] Woodrow Wilson, "A World 'Safe for Democracy' Speech," 1917, in *Voices of Freedom: A Documentary History*, 5th ed., ed. Eric Foner (New York: W. W. Norton & Company, 2017), 107.

certain rules of behavior" that would reduce international affairs to "parliamentary procedures and majority decision."[38] Realists like Kennan have seen these ideas as dangerously utopian and likely to drag the United States into unnecessary conflicts to democratize the world.[39] He held that these ideas manifested in the US tendency to demand "complete submissiveness" and "unconditional surrender" from its foes. Kennan believed this led the United States to fight total wars that were "more enduring, more terrible, and more destructive to political stability" than limited wars for the national interest.[40]

The anti-universalist notion of "Let Iraqis be Iraqis," to paraphrase Kennan, was far more likely to be a pro-containment sentiment. Figures like Haass and John Mearsheimer contended that the United States could not remake Iraqi society, and did not even have to in order to achieve its goals. With his preference for a particularized approach to foreign policy, it is unsurprising that Kennan, at 98 years old, objected to the Iraq War. He decried the Bush Doctrine as a "great mistake in principle," declared that inspections had greatly reduced Saddam's WMD and that he was deterrable regardless, and warned of the unforeseen consequences of invasion.[41]

This book suggests a trend in US diplomatic history in which a broadly defined liberalism and democratic politics cultivate a desire for total victories and the transformation of recalcitrant, illiberal states into liberal democracies, especially when there is no superpower rival to moderate US ambitions. Historians should ask whether these uncompromising potentials in liberal democracy systematically disadvantage containment strategies in US thought and politics because this type of strategy seeks to shape the structural conditions in which rivals operate rather than targeting their regimes for transformation.[42] Instead of accepting containment strategies premised on living with threats and evil, at least for a time, this

---

[38] Gaddis, *Strategies of Containment*, 26–27; Kennan, "Diplomacy in the Modern World," 95–101.

[39] Prominent texts in the realist school of international relations include: E. H. Carr, *The Twenty Years' Crisis, 1919–1939: An Introduction to the Study of International Relations* (London: Macmillan, 1940); Hans Morgenthau, *Politics among Nations: The Struggle for Power and Peace* (New York: Knopf, 1948); Kenneth Waltz, *Theory of International Politics* (Reading, MA: Addison Wesley, 1979); Mearsheimer, *Tragedy of Great Power Politics*. Influential defenses of liberal international order include Robert Keohane, *After Hegemony: Cooperation and Discord in the World Political Economy* (Princeton, NJ: Princeton University Press, 1984); G. John Ikenberry, *After Victory: Institutions, Strategic Restraint, and the Rebuilding of Order after Major Wars* (Princeton, NJ: Princeton University Press, 2001).

[40] Kennan, "Diplomacy in the Modern World," 101–102.

[41] Albert Eisele, "George Kennan Speaks Out About Iraq," *History News Network*, September 26, 2002, accessed April 18, 2020, https://historynewsnetwork.org/article/997.

[42] Ikenberry, *Liberal Leviathan*, 67, 78.

mindset can drive the United States toward trying to definitively "solve" problems like Iraq by changing the perceived root cause of their behavior: their illiberal regimes.[43]

It is tempting to conclude this study with a call for humility in US foreign policy. If anything suggests the need for such humility, it is that the containment of Iraq was viewed as an excessively humble policy in the 1990s. The containment of Iraq was humbler than the regime change alternative, but in reality, it was a tremendously ambitious project. It involved the permanent stationing of US troops in an inhospitable climate and culture, the patrolling of air space and waterways, and the ramping up and down of military power to respond to Saddam's actions. It demanded weapons inspections of unprecedented thoroughness in the face of constant Iraqi obstruction. It required a global diplomatic effort to corral dozens of nations to sever trade with a major oil provider. The fact that this all could be considered a modest exercise of power suggests just how radically expansive Americans' notions of security became after the Cold War.

A deep, driving assumption behind the regime change consensus was that problems like Iraq could be solved rather than managed. To regime change advocates, it was not safe, ethical, or necessary for a "benevolent hegemon" to tolerate the existence of an odious tyrant and his totalitarian regime. The deeper historical tendency of Americans to universalize their ideals and explain the actions of states by the nature of their regimes encouraged this perspective. To correct these tendencies, we can borrow the insights of theologian Reinhold Niebuhr, who wrote in 1944: "Democracy is a method of finding proximate solutions for insoluble problems."[44]

If "foreign policy" is inserted here instead of democracy, we have philosophical grounding for a more realistic view of the US global role. This would not mean that the United States should abandon a prominent role that aims to shape the global environment in ways that foster peace, prosperity, democracy, and human rights. Rather, this view would recognize that all "solutions" to the enduring dilemmas of international politics are temporary and that all remedies generate their own problems, especially when we imagine those remedies to be final.

---

[43] Desch, "Liberal Illiberalism," 25–26; Mearsheimer, *Great Delusion*, 153–160.
[44] Reinhold Niebuhr, *The Children of Light and the Children of Darkness*, 2nd ed. (New York: Scribner, 1960), 118.

Bibliography

Archives

George H. W. Bush Presidential Library, College Station, TX.
George W. Bush Presidential Library, Dallas, TX.
James A. Baker III Papers at the Seeley G. Mudd Library, Princeton, NJ.
The Library of Congress, Anthony Lewis Papers, Washington, DC.
The National Archives, Records of the U.S. Senate, Foreign Relations Committee, Washington, DC.
William Jefferson Clinton Presidential Library, Little Rock, AR.

Interviews by Author

Hamid Bayati	November 18, 2017
William Delahunt	August 27, 2018
Edward Djerejian	October 20, 2017
Richard Haass	October 4, 2017
Elizabeth Jones	February 6, 2018
	September 24, 2018
Robert Kerrey	February 7, 2018
Robert Kimmitt	September 19, 2017
Kanan Makiya	November 1, 2017
Joshua Muravchik	April 9, 2018
Ronald Neumann	November 20, 2017
Kenneth Pollack	November 6, 2017
Stephen Rademaker	January 12, 2019
Randy Scheunemann	March 31, 2018
Christopher Straub	January 30, 2018

US Government Publications and Databases

Reports

Central Intelligence Agency. "Comprehensive Report of the Special Advisor to the DCI on Iraq's WMD." cia.gov. September 30, 2004. Last modified

April 5, 2013. www.cia.gov/library/reports/general-reports-1/iraq_wm
d_2004/index.html.

Cohen, Eliot. *Gulf War Air Power Survey.* Washington, DC: US Government
Printing Office, 1993.

Commission on the Intelligence Capabilities of the United States Regarding
Weapons of Mass Destruction. *Report to the President.* Washington, DC:
Commission on the Intelligence Capabilities of the United States,
March 31, 2005.

Congressional Research Service. *Iraq-U.S. Confrontation.* Washington, DC: US
Government Printing Office, November 17, 2000.

Library of Congress. *American Public Opinion on the Iraq-Kuwait Crisis until
January 15.* Washington, DC: US Government Printing Office, 1991.

National Commission on Terrorist Attacks upon the United States. *The 9/11
Commission Report,* 2nd edition. New York: W. W. Norton, 2011.

Rayburn, Joel and Frank Sobchack. *The U.S. Army in the Iraq War, Volume 2:
Surge and Withdrawal, 2007–2011.* Carlisle Barracks, PA: United States
Army War College Press, 2017.

Senate Committee on Foreign Relations. Staff Report. "Civil War in Iraq."
102nd Cong., 1st Sess. Washington, DC: US Government Printing Office,
1991.

Senate Select Committee on Intelligence. *Whether Public Statements Regarding Iraq
by U.S. Government Officials Were Substantiated by Intelligence Information.*
Washington, DC: US Government Printing House, June 5, 2008.

*Postwar Findings about Iraq's WMD Programs and Links to Terrorism and How
They Compare with Prewar Assessments.* Washington, DC: US Government
Printing Office, September 8, 2006.

Report on the U.S. Intelligence Community's Prewar Intelligence Assessments on Iraq.
Washington, DC: US Government Printing House, July 7, 2004.

US Department of Defense. "Operation Iraqi Freedom, U.S. Casualty Status."
Last modified February 5, 2019. https://dod.defense.gov/News/Casualty-
Status/.

"Defense Casualty Analysis System Report." Office of the Secretary of
Defense. Last modified August 7, 1991. www.dmdc.osd.mil/dcas/pages/rep
ort_gulf_sum.xhtml.

Government Websites and Databases

Association for Diplomatic Studies and Training Foreign Affairs Oral History
Project, https://adst.org/oral-history/.

The Congressional Record, Daily Edition, accessed through Proquest
Congressional. Freedom of Information Act Electronic Reading Room,
Central Intelligence Agency, www.cia.gov/library/readingroom/home.

Freedom of Information Act Virtual Reading Room, Department of State, https://
foia.state.gov/Default.aspx.

George H. W. Bush Presidential Library and Museum Public Papers, https://bu
sh41library.tamu.edu/archives/public-papers/.

National Archives Declassified Records, https://catalog.archives.gov.

The British National Archives, Records of the Prime Minister's Office, https://d
    iscovery.nationalarchives.gov.uk/browse/r/h/C1228.
US Department of State Online Archive, 2001–2009, https://2001-2009
    .state.gov/t/isn/rls/other/16820.htm.
William Jefferson Clinton Digital Library, Declassified Documents, https://clin
    ton.presidentiallibraries.us/items/browse?collection=36&sort_field=Dublin
    +Core%2CDate&sort_dir=a Whitehouse.archives.gov.

Nongovernmental Reports, Databases, and Websites

Think Tank Archives and Publications

American Enterprise Institute Digital Archives. www.aei.org/policy/foreign-and-
    defense- policy/?s=iraq&fq=| |categories:%22foreign+and+defense+policy
    %5E%5E%22.
Alaaldin, Ranj. "Sectarianism, Governance, and Iraq's Future." Last modified
    November 26, 2018, www.brookings.edu/research/sectarianism-governance
    -and-iraqs-future/.
Byman, Daniel and Patrick Clawson, eds. *Iraq Strategy Review: Options for U.S.
    Policy.* Washington, DC: Washington Institute for Near East Policy Press, 1999.
Byman, Daniel and Matthew Waxman. *Confronting Iraq: U.S. Policy and the Use of
    Force since the Gulf War.* Arlington, VA: RAND Publishing, 2000.
Center for Security Policy Digital Archives. www.centerforsecuritypolicy.org/?
    s=iraq.
Cordesman, Anthony. "Security and WMD Issues in a Post-Saddam Iraq." Last
    modified February 11, 2003, https://csis-prod.s3.amazonaws.com/s3fs-
    public/legacy_files/files/attachments/ts030211_cordesman.pdf.
"The Military Effectiveness of Desert Fox." Last modified December 26, 1998,
    www.csis.org/analysis/military-effectiveness-desert-fox- warning-about-
    limits-revolution-military-affairs-and.
The Heritage Foundation, Reports and Backgrounders Archive. www
    .heritage.org/middle-east?f%5B0%5D=keywords%3A222.
Mandelbaum, Michael and Richard Haass. *Building for Security and Peace in the
    Middle East: An American Agenda, Report of the Presidential Study Group.*
    Washington, DC: Washington Institute for Near East Policy Press, 1997.
Mathews, Jessica. "Iraq: A New Approach." Carnegie Endowment for
    International Peace. Last modified September 5, 2002, https://carnegieen
    dowment.org/2002/09/05/iraq-new-approach-pub-1164.
The Washington Institute for Near East Policy, Policy Watch Papers, www
    .washingtoninstitute.org/policy-analysis/all.

Foreign Government Reports

Great Britain House of Commons. "The Iraq Inquiry." The National Archives.
    July 6, 2016. Last modified November 23, 2017. https://webarchive
    .nationalarchives.gov.uk/20171123123237/http://www.iraqinquiry.org.uk/.

Non-Governmental Publications and Databases

The American Presidency Project. University of California at Santa Barbara. w
 ww.presidency.ucsb.edu.
Digital National Security Archive Collections. George Washington University.
 "Targeting Iraq, Part 1: Planning, Invasion, and Occupation, 1997–2004."
 http://proquest.libguides.com/dnsa/iraq97.
 "Iraqgate: Saddam Hussein, U.S. Policy, and the Prelude to the Persian Gulf
 War, 1980-1994." https://proquest.libguides.com/dnsa/iraqgate.
Human Rights Watch. "Explanatory Memorandum Regarding the
 Comprehensive Embargo on Iraq." Last modified January 14, 2000. www
 .hrw.org/print/226817.
Iraq Body Count. "Iraqi Deaths from Violence, 2003–2011." Last modified
 January 2, 2012. www.iraqbodycount.org/analysis/numbers/2011/.
Iraq Watch. Wisconsin Project on Nuclear Arms Control, www.wisconsinproject.org
 /category/countries/iraq/.
National Security Archive. Electronic Briefing Booklets, Iraq, https://nsarchive
 .gwu.edu/project/iraq-project.
Presidential Oral Histories. Miller Center at the University of Virginia, https://
 millercenter.org/the-presidency/presidential-oral-histories,
The United Nations Internet Archives, un.org.
U.S. Intelligence on the Middle East. Brill Online, https://primarysources
 .brillonline.com/browse/us-intelligence-on-the-middle-east.

Public Polling Databases and Resources

Pew Global Forum
Gallup
Polling the Nations

Newspapers, Periodicals, and Media Sources

Air Force Magazine
The Air and Space Power Journal
The American Prospect
The Atlantic Monthly
CNN.com
Commentary Magazine
Congressional Quarterly Weekly
The Defense Democrat: A Newsletter on Foreign Affairs and National Defense
Dissent
The Economist
Financial Times
Foreign Affairs
Foreign Policy
Frontline

Gentleman's Quarterly
Harper's Magazine
The Guardian
The Hill
The Los Angeles Times
Middle East Policy
The Middle East Quarterly
Middle East Report
The Nation
The National Interest
The National Review
The New Republic
The New Yorker
Newsday
Newsweek
The New York Times
The New York Times Book Review
PBS News Hour
Pittsburgh Post-Gazette
The Progressive
Salon
San Diego Union-Tribune
Slate
Time Magazine
U.S. News and World Report
Vanity Fair
The Wall Street Journal
The Washington Monthly
The Washington Quarterly
The Washington Post
The Washington Times
The Weekly Standard
ZNet Communications

Dissertations and Theses

Herr, W. Eric. "Operation Vigilant Warrior: Conventional Deterrence Theory, Doctrine, Practice." MA Thesis, School of Advanced Air Power Studies, 1996. https://apps.dtic.mil/dtic/tr/fulltext/u2/a360732.pdf.

Index

Afghanistan, 196, 198, 201
Ajami, Fouad, 49–50, 210–212
Al-Qaeda, 134, 151, 155, 190, 195–197,
    206–210, 216, 226
Albright, Madeleine, 118, 145, 181
aluminum tubes, 206
American Enterprise Institute, 160
Annan, Kofi, 149, 185
anthrax, 122
Armitage, Richard, 193, 217
Aspin, Les, 35, 92
assertive nationalism, 7, 213
Axis of Evil, 201
Aziz, Tariq, 37, 82, 145–146, 147

Baath Party, 43, 165, 166, 222
    crimes, 68, 118, 164
    ideology, 210
Baer, Robert, 125
Baker, James, 14, 19–21, 23, 30, 37, 65, 69,
    84, 87, 90, 215, 221, 244
ballistic missile defense, 162, 180
Baradei, Mohammed el, 241, 242–243, 246
Barzani, Massoud, 127
Basra, 65
Bazoft, Farzad, 18
Bennis, Phyllis, 229
Berger, Sandy, 140, 152, 179, 192
Biden, Joseph, 34, 187, 231, 244
bin Laden, Osama, 195–196
Blair, Tony, 4, 150, 153, 191–192,
    215–218, 236, 245, 246
    Crawford meeting, 217
Blix, Hans, 82, 185, 239, 242–244, 246
Bolton, John, 208
Brownback, Sam, 186
Brzezinski, Zbigniew, 219–220
Bush Doctrine, 190, 201–203, 222
Bush, George H.W., 21–24, 25, 31, 37,
    44–45, 53, 55–56, 58–61, 63–72, 83,
    101, 251
    general foreign policy, 195

Iraqi assassination plot against, 114
Bush, George W., 189–193, 195–205, 233,
    244, 247
    general foreign policy, 192, 213–214
Butler, Richard, 144–147, 150, 154
Byrd, Robert, 227

CENTCOM, 58, 155, 177, 213
Central Intelligence Agency, 28, 42, 71, 88,
    123, 168, 180, 207
    assessments of Iraqi politics, 112, 124,
    143, 213
    support for Iraqi opposition, 71, 89,
    123–125
Chalabi, Ahmed, 75, 88–90, 124–127, 158,
    165, 176, 188, 210
Cheney, Richard, 6, 22, 84, 159, 192,
    205–206, 216, 237, 239, 244
China, 115–116, 149, 155, 183, 185, 195
Chirac, Jacques, 129, 148, 228
Chomsky, Noam, 223, 229
Christopher, Warren, 103, 123, 127
Clarke, Richard, 38–39, 197, 209
Clinton, Bill, 3, 98–114, 118–120,
    127–129, 138–139, 142–143,
    146–154, 167, 179–187, 192, 251
    Clinton fudge, 99, 110–112, 184
    general foreign policy, 102, 107, 114
Cohen, William, 148
Cold War, 11–12, 163–164, 170, 174, 202,
    223, 249–251
Committee for Peace and Security in the
    Gulf, 36, 161, 176
Congress, 18–20, 30, 34, 36, 37, 79–80, 92,
    136, 141–142, 158–159, 166–168,
    186, 231–235
    2003 Iraq War authorization, 231–235
    war powers, 34, 232, 234
conservatism, 45, 76, 239
containment, Iraq, 2–11, 24–28, 37–40, 45,
    49, 51, 55–56, 57–58, 62, 64, 65,
    81–90, 96–97, 98–101, 107–112,

114–123, 126–130, 142, 152, 161,
    163, 179–187, 192, 198, 201–203,
    215, 223, 247, 248–249, 258–259
  conditionalist view of, 5, 91–92, 96,
    130–132, 137, 142, 168–171, 174,
    177, 187, 221, 224–228, 230
  humanitarian view of, 94–95,
    171–173, 229
  inevitable decline view of, 93–94, 96–97,
    132–137, 139, 141–142, 174, 175,
    187, 189
  military strikes to enforce, 103–104
  theory of change, 138, 168–171, 230,
    249–252
  US military strikes to enforce, 84, 85–86,
    114–115, 128–129, 148, 153–155
containment, Soviet Union, 33, 138, 163,
    170, 174, 249–251
Cordesman, Anthony, 92, 130, 137, 169
coup d'etat, 16, 44, 70, 73, 88, 100,
    124, 181

D'Amato, Alphonse, 20, 51
democracy, 254, 259
  and containment strategies, 252
  in Middle East, 42, 51, 73–74, 76, 166,
    210–213
  in US foreign policy, 77–78, 102,
    105–107, 159, 163, 165, 210–212,
    224, 254
Democratic Leadership Council, 35, 104
Democratic Party, 15, 36, 73, 78–81, 91,
    130, 164, 231–234
  image of weakness on foreign policy,
    36, 233
democratic peace theory, 105, 210, 255
Desert Fox, 154–156
Desert Shield, 14, 22, 29
Desert Storm, 37, 57–60
détente, 163
deterrence, 161, 170, 198, 201, 225–226
  conventional, 119
Djerejian, Edward, 112
Dole, Robert, 135, 136, 137
domestic politics, 15, 28, 32–37, 76, 78–81,
    96, 99, 110, 130–137, 141–142, 155,
    156–174, 218–222, 233, 252–254
dual containment, 107, 112–114

Eagleburger, Lawrence, 103
Eisenhower, Dwight D., 174, 253
Ekeus, Rolf, 83, 85, 115, 118, 122, 143, 240
election
  1992, 80, 101–103
  1996, 137

2000, 192
engagement policy, 14, 16–21, 79
enlargement, strategy of, 105–106

Feith, Douglas, 161, 194, 200
foreign policy establishment, 3–5, 190–192,
    215, 230, 247, 254
France, 115–117, 129, 183, 185, 194, 228
Franks, Tommy, 201

Galbraith, Peter, 74
Gates, Robert, 28
Gejdenson, Sam, 79
Gephardt, Richard, 232
Germany, 64, 228
Gilman, Benjamin, 161
Gingrich, Newt, 162
Glaspie, April, 19, 21, 78
globalization, 105–107
Goldwater, Barry, 253
Gonzalez, Henry, 95
Gorbachev, Mikhail, 23
Gore, Al, 73, 91, 101, 123, 125, 219
Great Britain, 128, 148, 153, 216–217,
    246–247
Gulf War, 12, 14–16, 37–38, 53, 55–56
  critics of Bush's handling of end phases,
    57–58, 60, 72–73, 75
  supporters of Bush's handling of end
    phases, 75

Haass, Richard, 17, 19, 24–26, 32, 38–39,
    41, 43, 62–63, 71, 84, 88, 90, 131, 168,
    170, 177, 193, 201, 224, 252
Hagel, Chuck, 172, 220, 233
Halliday, Denis, 171
health crisis, Iraq, 87, 120–121, 171
Helms, Jesse, 18
Hoagland, Jim, 18
human rights, 116, 165–166, 211
humanitarian intervention, 69–70, 164,
    215, 222–224, 227
Hussein, Saddam, 16, 18, 27, 40, 70,
    81, 252
  control of Iraq, 44–45, 66, 68, 100, 111,
    127, 172, 176
  evading of sanctions, 87, 172, 183
  strategic intentions, 71, 143, 155, 238
  strategy to undermine containment, 81
Hussein, Uday, 122

IAEA, 63, 82, 145, 151, 206
Ignatieff, Michael, 164, 222
Indyk, Martin, 42, 107–108, 113, 118, 137,
    152, 179

inspections, weapons, 10, 85, 115,
    121–123, 142–154, 179, 184–186,
    192, 215, 231, 235–246
  coercive, 241
  criticism of, 94, 135, 149, 237–239
  Iraqi obstruction of, 82–85, 104, 123,
    144–147, 152–154, 237, 243
  sensitive sites, 145–147, 149
  verification and monitoring, 115,
    118, 152
Iran, 1, 17, 41, 67, 107, 109, 200, 225
  US perceptions of, 112–113
Iran–Iraq War, 16–17
Iraq
  economy, 19, 120, 186
  ethnicities, 1, 11, 41–42, 65–68, 177,
    213, 228
  history, 166
  internal revolts, 54, 65–69, 74–75,
    124–126, 136, 177
  invasion of Kuwait, 22
  politics, 176, 228, 257
  territorial integrity, 41, 68, 109, 177
  threat to region, 15, 24, 25, 31, 151
Iraq Liberation Act, 3, 141–142, 159,
    166–168, 182, 186, 254
Iraq War, 1, 178, 247
Iraqgate
  scandal, 102
Iraqgate scandal, 79–80
Iraqi military, 60, 67, 68, 71, 109, 180
  Republican Guard, 37, 45, 59, 123, 177
Iraqi National Accord, 71, 88, 123–124
Iraqi National Congress, 49, 88–90,
    123–127, 158, 165, 174, 175–176, 205
  US skepticism of, 89, 124, 126, 167, 183
Israel, 18, 31, 36, 46

Jones, Elizabeth, 167, 183
Jordan, 121, 124

Kagan, Robert, 6, 159
Kamel, Hussein, 121–123, 135, 240
Kant, Immanuel, 256
Kay, David, 82, 136
Kelly, John, 19, 21, 69
Kennan, George, 138, 170, 226, 249–255,
    257–258
Kennedy, Edward, 73, 74, 224
Kerrey, Robert, 73, 136, 159, 164, 165, 223
Kerry, John, 233
Kimmitt, Robert, 62
Kirkpatrick, Jeane, 48
Kissinger, Henry, 163, 171
Kosovo, 180

Krauthammer, Charles, 51, 53, 75, 77,
    93, 133
Kristof, Nicholas, 228
Kristol, William, 6, 159
Kucinich, Dennis, 230
Kurdish Democratic Party, 89
Kurdistan Democratic Party, 125, 127
Kurds, 127, 178
  refugee crisis, 68–70
Kuwait, 15, 17, 20–25, 37, 58, 114,
    118–119

Lake, Anthony, 105–107, 108, 112
Lantos, Tom, 78
Lee, Barbara, 234
left, political, 223, 229–230
  anti-war activism, 229
Levin, Carl, 234
Lewis, Bernard, 161, 212
Libby, Scooter, 159, 202
liberalism, 49, 76–78, 164–165, 222–224,
    255–258
Liebermann, Joseph, 73, 91, 164, 186,
    197, 233
Lott, Trent, 155, 158, 186, 197
Lugar, Richard, 136, 231

Makiya, Kanan, 49–50, 89, 211
Manning, David, 207, 216
Marr, Phebe, 43, 76, 132
Mathews, Jessica, 224, 227, 241
McCain, John, 136, 158, 197
McGovern, George, 163
Mearsheimer, John, 224–226
Meyer, Christopher, 217, 236
Middle East
  international relations, 41–42, 127,
    149
  politics, 13, 31, 50, 165, 210
  US presence in, 38
Middle East Peace Process, 107, 112, 119,
    180, 216, 220, 228
multilateralism, 23, 34, 40, 76, 106,
    132, 137, 149, 168, 192, 193, 216,
    219–220
Muravchik, Joshua, 77, 163
Mylroie, Laurie, 50, 134–135, 208–209
  criticism of, 134

National Intelligence Estimate, 204
National Security Council, 118, 170, 179
nation-building, 40, 192
neoconservatism, 5–7, 45, 49, 73, 77–78,
    93, 135, 159–161, 163, 171, 176, 189,
    192, 198, 213, 239, 247, 255–256

nexus threat, 7, 150, 151, 190, 197,
    199–200, 201–204, 209, 226
Niebuhr, Reinhold, 47, 259
Nitze, Paul, 249–251
no-drive zone, 118, 133
no-fly zone, 10, 70, 85–86, 103, 128, 181
North Korea, 200, 227
Nunn, Sam, 28, 32

occupation
    of Iraq, 40, 67
    US expectations for, 211–212, 228
    US skeptics of, 213
Office of Special Plans, 205
O'Hanlon, Michael, 169, 241
oil, 177, 224, 230
    embargo on Iraq, 115–118, 170, 184, 193
oil-for-food, 121
oil-for-food plan, 87, 172–173, 183,
    185, 193
O'Neill, Paul, 197
Operation Provide Comfort, 68–70, 72
Operation Vigilant Warrior, 118–120

Parris, Mark, 111, 123
Patriotic Union of Kurdistan, 89, 125, 127
Pell, Claiborne, 18, 32
Pelletreau, Robert, 121, 129
Perle, Richard, 36, 52, 140, 158, 161
Perry, William, 118
Pletka, Danielle, 159
Policy Counterterrorism Evaluation
    Group, 205
Pollack, Kenneth, 110, 170, 177, 182
post–Cold War era, 12, 14, 26, 135
    fear of US power, 116
    international order, 22–24, 76, 105–106
Powell, Colin, 4, 27, 29–30, 32, 43, 58–59,
    67, 72, 84, 95, 190–194, 198,
    215–218, 244, 245
Powell–Blair approach, 4–5, 190–192,
    214–221, 231, 244–246, 247
preemptive war, 219, 227
Primakov, Yevgeny, 147
Project for a New American Century,
    159–160, 162, 197
public opinion, 54, 75, 110, 115,
    119, 128, 132, 151, 156, 198, 209,
    221, 245
    Iraq, 32, 52

Rademaker, Stephen, 167
Reagan, Ronald, 163
    Reagan Doctrine, 167, 175
realism, 25, 53, 76, 91, 256, 258

regime change, 11, 15–16, 25–28, 38,
    40–45, 53, 55–56, 99–100, 109–112,
    114, 127, 129, 139, 171, 179–181,
    187, 189–192, 215, 218–221, 247,
    248–249, 257
    Iran, 113
    US advocates of, 45–47, 51–53, 72–74,
        132–135, 136, 156–167, 175–177,
        186, 197, 222–223, 248–249, 259
regime, concept of, 47–51, 52, 53, 73–74,
    93–94, 96, 136, 165, 239, 248, 259
Republican Party, 15, 80–81, 133, 135,
    166, 176, 232–233, 253
responsibility to protect, 164, 215, 223
Ricciardone, Frank, 182
Rice, Condoleezza, 193, 199, 201, 207,
    211, 218, 239
Riedel, Bruce, 126, 127
Robb, Charles, 35, 188
rogue states
    concept of, 106–107, 112, 162, 200
rollback, 174–178, 188, 194, 253
    critics of, 177–178, 182
Rosenthal, A.M., 73
Rumsfeld, Donald, 6, 9, 159, 162, 192,
    196–197, 201, 237–239
Russia, 115–116, 128, 147, 149, 155, 183,
    185, 194

Safire, William, 18, 46, 51
Safwan agreement, 60–61, 75
sanctions, 28–29, 30–31, 33
    anti-sanctions activism, 94–95, 171–173
    Iran, 113
    Iraq, 19, 38–39, 55, 63–65, 86–88,
        99–100, 120–121, 143, 183, 228
    smart sanctions, 193–194
    US defense of, 173–174
sanctions, Iraq, 145
Saudi Arabia, 22, 149, 178
Scheunemann, Randy, 159, 167
Schlesinger Jr., Arthur, 42, 47
Schroeder, Gerhard, 229
Schwarzkopf, Norman, 58–61
Scowcroft, Brent, 19, 84, 86, 90, 96, 130,
    132, 170, 226
September 11th, 8–9, 12–13, 189–191,
    195–200, 226
    post-September 11 policy reorientation
        toward Iraq, 196–198
Shelton, Hugh, 196
Sherman, Brad, 191, 234–235
Slocombe, Walter, 181
Solarz, Stephen, 35–36, 158
Somalia, 140

sovereignty, 11, 25, 76, 86, 149, 164, 200, 256
Soviet Union, 23, 162, 249–251, 253
Sponeck, Hans von, 171
State Department, 19, 183, 206
Syria, 1

Tenet, George, 195
terrorism, 150–151, 189–191, 195–197, 201–204
  state sponsorship, 199–200
totalitarianism, 2, 3, 47–48, 111, 133, 222–223, 239, 255
Truman, Harry S., 253
Turkey, 64, 116, 127, 178

United Nations, 22–24, 165, 219, 222, 233, 239
  disagreement on sanctions, 86–87, 115–118, 120
  international coalition, 55, 64–65, 86, 98–100, 110–111, 119–120, 121, 128, 143, 146–147, 148, 154, 155, 178, 184–186, 193–194, 217, 236, 246
  Security Council resolutions, 14, 21–22, 29, 37, 55, 63, 70, 87, 99, 115–116, 117, 120–121, 131, 184–186, 235–236, 246
United States
  imperialism, 229
  interests in Middle East, 22, 128
  invasion of Iraq, 189–190, 247
  views of Middle Eastern politics, 42–44, 50–51, 75
universalism
  moral, 73, 164, 222, 259

political, 11, 105, 211, 255–257
  skeptics of, 251, 257
UNMOVIC, 185, 237, 242
UNSCOM, 63, 82–85, 115, 122–123, 142–154, 156, 184, 240

Vietnam War, 1, 29, 33, 40, 67, 253

Walt, Stephen, 3, 224–226
War on Terror, 198–200, 220
weapons of mass destruction, 2
  Iraqi declarations on, 84, 242
  Iraqi programs, 18, 31–32, 82–85, 122, 143, 156, 169, 180, 187, 205–208
  Iraqi use of, 17
  manipulation of intelligence by Bush administration, 8, 190, 205–208
  proliferation, 227
  threat to United States, 151, 201–203
  US intelligence on, 31, 34–35, 180, 204–207
Wilson, Woodrow, 257
Wolfowitz, Paul, 6, 60, 136, 140, 157, 159, 161, 163, 194, 196–197, 202, 208, 212
Woolsey, R. James, 208, 248
World Trade Center terrorist attack, 134, 209
World War II, 31, 36, 47
Wurmser, David, 157, 165, 205

yellowcake uranium, 207
Yeltsin, Boris, 155
Yugoslavia, 77, 109

Zinn, Howard, 229
Zinni, Anthony, 177, 182

For EU product safety concerns, contact us at Calle de José Abascal, 56–1°, 28003 Madrid, Spain or eugpsr@cambridge.org.

www.ingramcontent.com/pod-product-compliance
Ingram Content Group UK Ltd.
Pitfield, Milton Keynes, MK11 3LW, UK
UKHW040620240426
470322UK00011B/238